Overturning *Dr. Faustus*

Studies in German Literature, Linguistics, and Culture

Overturning *Dr. Faustus*

Rereading Thomas Mann's Novel in Light of *Observations of a Non-Political Man*

Frances Lee

CAMDEN HOUSE

First published 2007
by Camden House

Camden House is an imprint of Boydell & Brewer Inc.
668 Mt. Hope Avenue, Rochester, NY 14620, USA
www.camden-house.com
and of Boydell & Brewer Limited
PO Box 9, Woodbridge, Suffolk IP12 3DF, UK
www.boydellandbrewer.com

ISBN-13: 978–1–57113–356–4
ISBN-10: 1–57113–356–9

Library of Congress Cataloging-in-Publication Data

Lee, Frances, 1939–
    Overturning Dr. Faustus: rereading Thomas Mann's novel in light of
observations of a non-political man / Frances Lee.
    p. cm. — (Studies in German literature, linguistics, and culture)
Includes bibliographical references and index.
ISBN-13: 978–1–57113–356–4 (hardcover; alk. paper)
ISBN-10: 1–57113–356–9 (hardcover; alk. paper)
    1. Mann, Thomas, 1875–1955. Doktor Faustus.   2. Mann, Thomas,
1875–1955. Betrachtungen eines Unpolitischen.   3. Mann, Thomas,
1875–1955 — Political and social views.   I. Title.

PT2625.A44D69417 2007
833'.912—dc22

                                                              2006030539

A catalogue record for this title is available from the British Library.

This publication is printed on acid-free paper.
Printed in the United States of America.

Contents

Acknowledgments

I WOULD LIKE particularly to recognize Dr. Alan D. Latta at the University of Toronto, for his infinite patience and his acute and rigorous guidance throughout the preparation of the original doctoral dissertation on which this book is based. I was further encouraged and supported by Dr. Michael Minden at Jesus College, Cambridge. I also owe a great deal to my husband, Terence Lee, who put up with the considerable time invested in my studies and listened endlessly and critically to my arguments. I benefited greatly from the practical support and assistance of my daughters, Mary and Elizabeth Johnson. Jim Walker at Camden House guided me gently through the complications and frustrations of turning a dissertation into a book. And I must not forget Karin Wilckens Oberpauer, who taught me to appreciate the subtleties of the German language.

Thank you.

F. L.
October 2006

Abbreviations

The following abbreviations are used in the text.

BeU   Thomas Mann, *Betrachtungen eines Unpolitischen*, in
         Gesammelte Werke in zwölf Bänden, 12:7–589.

DF   Thomas Mann, *Doktor Faustus*, vol. 6 of *Gesammelte*
         Werke in zwölf Bänden.

GW   Thomas Mann, *Gesammelte Werke in zwölf Bänden*
         (Oldenburg: Fischer, 1960).

TMUB Paul Egon Hübinger, *Thomas Mann, die Universität Bonn und*
         die Zeitgeschichte (Munich: Oldenbourg, 1974).

VDR   Thomas Mann, "Von Deutscher Republik," in *Gesammelte*
         Werke in zwölf Bänden, 11:809–52.

Introduction

IN THIS BOOK I ATTEMPT TO PROVIDE a clear explanation of what I think Mann had in mind in writing *Doktor Faustus*.[1] The following study is the result of having, so to speak, tipped the kaleidoscope in looking at the novel. I have disregarded the accepted assumptions of what the novel is about, on the grounds that they do not lead to an intelligible interpretation of the text, and posited new assumptions. The book originated in a suspicion, which soon developed into the conviction, that *Doktor Faustus* is an autobiographical novel. In their readings of the novel most critics have largely misunderstood or ignored the material underlying *Doktor Faustus*: the historical setting, Mann's theory of the intellectual position underlying the development of fascism, and the events surrounding Mann's personal life at the time the story is set. As a result they have developed elaborate analyses that, quite simply, fail to explain the novel. Of course, history and political theory are just as controversial as literary interpretation, and historical events are equally open to a variety of interpretations. However, the particular historical and political interpretation presented in the novel concerning the rise of intellectual fascism — as distinct from applied fascism — reflects, as I understand it, the same interpretation of the rise of totalitarianism found elsewhere in Mann's work, particularly in *Die Betrachtungen eines Unpolitischen*, a series of essays on politics, published in 1918.[2] The theory presented there has a large following and, as such, it is not new or peculiar to Mann.[3] The basic notion underlying this theory is that modern totalitarianism is based essentially on a return to the application of medieval Roman Catholic values to social organization, most specifically on the subordination of the individual to the community in the service of a collective goal. When the novel is read within the historical and political context suggested by this theory and with a focus on Mann's own experience, a new and somewhat radical understanding of what is going on in the novel becomes apparent, one that is at odds with the generally accepted reading of the novel. If the novel is, as I argue, based on Mann's experience of fascism, and if this experience is not taken into account in reading the novel, the reader will not easily recognize the confusions and distortions introduced by the perspective of the narrator, who introduces himself as a Roman Catholic humanist. Discussing the difference in worldview between Catholicism and Protestantism tends today to elicit little if any response, yet historically this difference has been central to European politics. One does not come across many references to this question in the literature on *Doktor Faustus*. Ignoring the significance to Mann of this difference is, in my opinion, to miss the fundamental underlying argument of the novel. Most existing interpretation is, in effect, nothing more than a reworded repetition of what the narrator says. This leads to interpretations of the novel that simply do not make sense, either in the context of the novel itself or in the broader context of Mann's life and work. Peter de Mendelssohn's comment on the literature in his *Von Deutscher Repräsentanz* (1972) amply supports the premise on which this study is based:

> Diese riesige Sekundärliteratur ist für den Biographen weitgehend irrelevant, weil sie nahezu ausschließlich aus analytischen und kritischen Einzeluntersuchungen der Werke besteht und jeden nur vorstellbaren Aspekt dieses Werkes — den literarischen, historischen, künstlerischen, philosophischen, politischen, medizinischen, musikalischen und hundert andre mehr — in jedem nur denkbaren Zusammenhang durchforscht und auf jeder nur möglichen Ebene interpretiert — außer in Bezug auf das Leben Thomas Manns; und wo sie es tut, geschieht es nur am Rande und setzt entweder eine sehr ins einzelne gehende Kenntnis der Ereignisse seines Lebens voraus oder verrät, nicht selten, eine unzureichende Kenntnis dieser Lebensgeschehnisse.[4]

Equally, if the novel is, as I argue, based on the events of Mann's life, and if critics do not take these events into account in their readings of the novel, they are not likely to recognize the confusions and distortions introduced by the perspective of the narrator.

* * *

Die Betrachtungen eines Unpolitischen, Mann's major philosophical work, was published in 1918. It is a very definite and outspoken presentation of Mann's understanding of the underlying values influencing politics, and these same values — humanism, music, and Protestantism, as opposed to humanism, classical studies, and Catholicism — are the primary substance of the novel. It is, therefore, an invaluable backdrop to *Doktor Faustus*. All Mann's later writings are elaborations and extensions of these original arguments and it seems, in fact, that the only serious contradiction to these arguments in Mann's works is found in the narrator's position in *Doktor Faustus*. In his 1949 article in *Merkur*, "Die Welt ohne Transzendenz: Eine Studie zu Manns *Doktor Faustus* und seinen Nebenschriften," when the novel was first published, Hans Egon Holthusen noted that the narrator's account is in direct opposition to Mann's position on the relevant points as he expressed them in *Die Betrachtungen eines Unpolitischen*.[5]

Surprisingly, although one frequently comes across references to specific arguments taken out of context from the book, very few critics of

Doktor Faustus take *Die Betrachtungen eines Unpolitischen* seriously in their discussions of Mann's views. Where they do, there is a clear correlation between the opinions they express about *Die Betrachtungen eines Unpolitischen* and about *Doktor Faustus*. As will be discussed below, the question of the reliability of the narrator and of his identity with Mann is a central issue in the interpretation of *Doktor Faustus*. Those critics who insist on the narrator's reliability and identity with Mann and who have also commented on *Die Betrachtungen eines Unpolitischen* dismiss the latter as irrelevant, or as nonsense. Unfortunately, such a cavalier dismissal is both transparently self-serving and an inadequate response to the earlier work. The argument is tautological: the views expressed in *Die Betrachtungen eines Unpolitischen* cannot be used to point out that the narrator is not expressing Mann's views, because the narrator's views do not reflect these views. It is true that the book is difficult to understand, but it is far from nonsense, whether one agrees with it or not. The following brief survey of the attitude taken towards the book by critics of *Doktor Faustus* shows the extent of this rejection.

In *Thomas Mann: Das Leben als Kunstwerk* (1999), Hermann Kurzke essentially ignores it. He describes *Die Betrachtungen eines Unpolitischen* as an insignificant piece of rhetorical polemic against Heinrich Mann, Mann's brother.[6]

In *Der schwierige Deutsche* (1988) Helmut Koopmann dismisses *Die Betrachtungen eines Unpolitischen*, as well as most of Mann's political essays, as trivial, unsystematic, rhetorical, and illogical.[7] He objects to the eclectic character of the text of *Die Betrachtungen eines Unpolitischen* and to Mann's technique of presenting the material simultaneously from two different points of view. Therefore, he says, *Die Betrachtungen eines Unpolitischen* cannot be used as a source of Mann's views for an interpretation of his novels. In his interpretations of *Doktor Faustus* he ignores the use of these same techniques. Koopmann is concerned to show that Mann's views of Germany in *Die Betrachtungen eines Unpolitischen* are wrong. *Doktor Faustus*, he says, is Mann's recognition and acknowledgement of his previous erroneous thinking. In other words, he interprets *Doktor Faustus* as a negation of Mann's expressed views, because he himself does not agree with them.

Helmut Wiegand, in *Thomas Manns* Doktor Faustus *als zeitgeschichtlicher Roman* (1982) also dismisses *Die Betrachtungen eines Unpolitischen* as a source on the grounds that Mann's position in his novels does not correspond to his position in his essays.[8]

In *Serenus Zeitblom. Der Erzähler als Romanfigur in Thomas Manns* Doktor Faustus, Hans Hilgers does consider *Die Betrachtungen eines Unpolitischen* as a source for *Doktor Faustus*, but in a strange way. He argues that the narrator represents Mann's views, on the grounds that his Apocalypse, his comments about the Second World War, are the same as Mann's comments made in *Die Betrachtungen eines Unpolitischen* about the

First World War.[9] Apart from the fact that these comments on the Second World War only superficially and partially reflect Mann's comments on the First World War, Hilgers ignores the not very subtle distinction that Mann was lamenting the collapse of traditional nineteenth-century German culture, while the narrator's lament is for the collapse of fascist Germany. Hilgers asserts, moreover, that *Die Betrachtungen eines Unpolitischen* is irrational and that this irrationality is transferred to the narrator, which explains away the problems indicating unreliability (129). In his view, the narrator cannot represent fascism, because Catholic humanism is in contradiction to fascism. Thus, even having presumably read *Die Betrachtungen eines Unpolitischen*, he is reversing Mann's main point, that the tendency of Catholic humanism is to totalitarianism, and using this reversal to explain Mann's novel.

Lieselotte Voss comments frequently on the close affinity between the subject matter of *Die Betrachtungen eines Unpolitischen* and *Doktor Faustus* in *Die Entstehung von Thomas Manns Roman* Doktor Faustus: *Dargestellt anhand von unveröffentlichten Vorarbeiten* (1975). However, when the narrator says something different from what Mann says in *Die Betrachtungen eines Unpolitischen*, she just assumes that Mann has changed his mind in his old age.[10] She stops at the similarity in subject matter and does not seem to notice the difference in point of view that Mann has introduced in the narrator's arguments, simply taking for granted that Mann is writing a story about Nietzsche and Luther as Faust, and that he has fused this with the *Faustsaga* (44). She makes no comment on any philosophical significance such a combination implies. She notes that Mann attempted also to include fascism (180), but by and large she ignores, or does not recognize, the fascist element in the story. The inconsistencies that result in the novel, she claims, are inevitable, given the complicated nature of the plan (19).

In his 1984 article in *Michigan Germanic Studies*, "The Luther-Erasmus Constellation in Thomas Mann's *Doktor Faustus*," Herbert Lehnert recognizes that *Die Betrachtungen eines Unpolitischen* is against totalitarianism[11] and then claims that *Doktor Faustus* represents a reversal of the values expressed there in that the artist represents fascism (148–49). He does not like this, and he criticizes the use of Protestantism as the basis of an antidemocratic myth. He claims that *Die Betrachtungen eines Unpolitischen* is fiction written as essays and that *Doktor Faustus* is reality written as fiction.[12] Mann's arguments are again being turned on their heads.

Unfortunately, critics who take *Die Betrachtungen eines Unpolitischen* seriously have made few comments on *Doktor Faustus*, except for the important observation that *Doktor Faustus* is clearly based on the ideas expressed in *Die Betrachtungen eines Unpolitischen*. Kurt Sontheimer, who offers an excellent study of Mann's political views in his *Thomas Mann und die Deutschen* (1961), says he is not going to discuss *Doktor Faustus*, which is based on *Die Betrachtungen eines Unpolitischen*, because Mann himself has clarified it.[13] One can understand that he did not want to take on the task of analyzing *Doktor Faustus*, but his reason is extraordinary. In his analysis of *Die Betrachtungen eines Unpolitischen*, he makes it clear that the book is largely autobiographical, that the basic subject is the opposition between the Catholic humanist and the Protestant artist (31), and that the book provides the basis of all Mann's ideas (19).

Paul Egon Hübinger, whose book *Thomas Mann, die Universität Bonn und die Zeitgeschichte* (1974), a study of the reception of *Die Betrachtungen eines Unpolitischen*, reveals remarkable parallels with the story of *Doktor Faustus*, also sees the direct relationship of *Die Betrachtungen eines Unpolitischen* to the novel, but again he does not analyze it. He says that Mann's sympathy with Germany, but not National Socialism, is expressed in *Doktor Faustus*, but not recognized or understood by critics (58). Sontheimer's assessment of the reception of *Die Betrachtungen eines Unpolitischen* and of the attacks on Mann, documented in detail by Hübinger, stresses the indelible impression of these traumatic events on Mann's mind (122). He makes it clear that Mann was supporting democracy and that the book was sloppily read and completely misinterpreted (47).

Gert Sautermeister is an exception in that he has studied *Doktor Faustus* in the context of Mann's political views. In his article "Zwischen Aufklärung und Mystifizierung: Der unbewältigte Widerspruch in Thomas Manns *Doktor Faustus*" he shows, through an analysis of the *strenger Satz*, the basic statement of the artist's political theory: that he does not represent fascism, as is virtually universally asserted, but is arguing for democracy. He has, however, not followed up the implications of this to further elucidate the story of *Doktor Faustus*, but has simply defined it as a contradiction in the novel.[14] It is a devastating contradiction of virtually all interpretations, but not necessarily a contradiction in the novel. This argument will be elaborated below in the textual analysis.

Thus we see that, in the case of *Doktor Faustus* and *Die Betrachtungen eines Unpolitischen*, there is a radical difference of opinion between the literary critics and the historians. It is to be noted that Joachim Fest, in the chapter on intellectuals in his *Das Gesicht des Dritten Reich*, although he is not talking about either *Doktor Faustus* or *Die Betrachtungen eines Unpolitischen*, refers repeatedly to Mann as an authority on the nature of the enthusiasm for fascism on the part of the intellectual community, which is, ultimately, the environment of the novel.[15] The argument presented here tests the applicability of the thesis that the views expressed in *Die Betrachtungen eines Unpolitischen* can be used as a guideline for unraveling the plot of *Doktor Faustus*. Whether or not they represent Mann's views at the time of writing, they reflect Mann's views at the time portrayed in the novel.

* * *

The generally accepted view of what the novel is about is not based on firm ground. A virtually uncontested and fundamental notion about the novel is that it is the story of a questionable artist who sells his soul to the Devil by way of contracting a syphilitic infection in return for artistic inspiration. The narrator is Dr. Serenus Zeitblom and the subject of his narration is the life and opinions of Adrian Leverkühn. On the surface, it seems that Zeitblom is indeed telling the story in which Adrian deliberately contracts syphilis as a young man and goes progressively mad until finally he collapses in May 1930 and has to be held under constraint and treated with drugs. It is virtually universally assumed that Leverkühn suffers this fate because he has entered into a pact with the Devil in return for artistic inspiration, but Zeitblom himself does not say this. Neither Adrian's conversation with the Devil in chapter 25 nor his final speech in chapter 47, the evidence for this dubious conclusion, is reported by the narrator. These passages are in the cryptic words of Adrian himself. The syphilitic infection is accepted as a simple statement of undisputed fact and has, to my knowledge, very rarely been subjected to serious scrutiny. Although there have been various speculations about what it means, it has never been shown, step by step, how, or even if, the syphilis is revealed in the text and why it has been included. Such treatment is wholly inadequate, given that it is an essential part of the general view of what the book is about. Zeitblom himself makes remarks that cast doubt on this assumption.

The assumption that Adrian in fact has syphilis is combined with other fixed assumptions that stem from the first reviewers of the novel, who reacted emotionally to its content and simply did not read it carefully. Sensitivity to comments on Germany by outsiders was very high in the few years after the war and Mann was considered not only an outsider but even something of a traitor. The first readers of *Doktor Faustus* were, in this sense, expecting to find something to take issue with. The interpretations of the novel carelessly established by these early critics have rarely been questioned and have dominated interpretation ever since.

All of these early interpretations identify the artist as representing National Socialism. The arguments have been refined, extended, and modified, but not refuted, and new arguments are implicitly based on these few original basic statements about the novel. The argument that the artist represents the German catastrophe, which crops up again and again in the literature, was introduced in 1948 by Gotthard Montesi in his article "Thomas Mann, der Teufel und die Deutschen," in *Wort und Wahrheit* (1948)[16] and taken up again in 1949 by Georg Lukács in "Auf der Suche nach dem Bürger: Die Tragödie der modernen Kunst," in *Aufbau.*[17] The idea that Mann associates the Devil and everything evil with Luther and with music stems from Hans Egon Holthusen's 1949 article. This strange notion, which Holthusen himself points out (42) is in contradiction to the views Mann expressed in *Die Betrachtungen eines Unpolitischen*, has developed into a whole school of criticism. In 1948 Hubert Becher described the same theology as demonology in "Thomas Mann und sein Faustbuch," in *Stimmen der Zeit*.[18] Both Holthusen and Becher, however, comment favorably on the discussions of music. The association of fascism with *Innerlichkeit* and the hero's isolation was first made by Lukács (167). When all three of these basic interpretations are combined and developed, as, for example, by Helmut Jendreieck in his *Thomas Mann: Der demokratische Roman* (1977), a formidable theory of Mann's explanation of the rise of fascism in Germany is created:

> Die leitende Idee des Romans ist die Darstellung und kritische Analyse der deutschen Katastrophe und ihrer Verursachung durch politisch verantwortungslosen Ästhetizismus als eine historisch objektivierte Form deutscher Innerlichkeit. Symbolgestalten dieses Ästhetizismus sind in der Perspektive des Romans Luther und Nietzsche: Beide werden als die Pole und Repräsentanten einer kulturgeschichtlichen Epoche betrachtet, die zum Faschismus führt und mit dem Faschismus in die Katastrophe treibt.[19]

The idea that Mann ever supported fascism or thought that the whole of German culture since the Reformation led to fascism is simply wrong. The whole of Mann's writings shows clearly that he never supported fascism, but was consistently and vehemently against it. He said clearly that the whole idea of fascism was alien to German culture.

I cannot see that this simplistic and somewhat muddled understanding of the novel is supported by the text, which I read as saying virtually the opposite. Further, this interpretation is as directly opposed as possible to what I consider to be Mann's understanding of the rise of fascism in Germany. Ultimately, however, and much the most important point, such an interpretation of the novel simply does not accommodate in any intelligible way the entire dénouement, the development of the story from chapter 34 to the end, that is from the confusing years 1918 to 1930. It is also in direct contradiction to the specific definition of fascism given by Mann in chapter 34 (*Fortsetzung*). It is, in effect, incompatible with the text of the novel and cannot be accepted. As I read the text, the novel does not describe traditional German cultural values as the cause of fascism, but rather it describes their rejection as the cause of fascism, particularly the rejection of individualism as the basis of German cultural and ethical values.

On the other hand, the significance of the rise of fascism as an element in the novel has been ignored or minimized by a substantial number of respected critics, such as Gerhard vom Hofe in his article "Das unbehagliche Bewußtsein des modernen Musikers," in *Geist und Zeichen: Festschrift für Arthur Henkel zu seinem sechzigsten Geburtstag dargebracht von Freunden und Schülern* (1977);[20] Hans Heinrich Borcherdt in "Das Faust-Problem bei Thomas Mann," in *Jahrbuch des Wiener Goethe-Vereins*

(1961);[21] Eitel Timm in *Ketzer und Dichter: Lessing, Goethe, Thomas Mann und die Postmoderne in der Tradition des Häresiegedankens* (1989),[22] Hermann Kurzke in *Thomas Mann: Epoche — Werk — Wirkung* (1991),[23] Lieselotte Voss in *Die Entstehung von Thomas Manns Roman* Doktor Faustus*: Dargestellt anhand von unveröffentlichten Vorarbeiten* (1979), C. A. M. Noble in *Krankheit, Verbrechen und künstlerisches Schaffen bei Thomas Mann* (1970),[24] and Hans Rudolf Vaget in "Mann, Joyce, Wagner: the Question of Modernism in *Doctor Faustus*," in *Thomas Mann*, edited by Michael Minden, among many others.[25] Vaget has in fact written an assessment of the hero as representative of Germany and fascism based on the usual fundamental assumptions, although he makes it clear that he thinks the argument is only marginally about politics. He resolves the basic problem, that this argument is simply not supported by the text, by introducing the idea of a displacement in time. According to this thesis, the hero demonstrates all the characteristics of German political history, but at a different point in time, specifically, much earlier:[26]

Indeed, fascism is not openly discussed in the novel, except in oblique or isolated comments that can be overlooked, or dismissed, by the reader who prefers to read the novel as a discussion of art, or of theology. Apart from the conversation with the Devil in chapter 25, chapter 34 (*Fortsetzung*), the discussion of the deliberations of the Kridwiß *Kreis*, is the only chapter that clearly and openly analyzes the philosophy of fascism. This chapter can not be ignored if the novel is to be understood. *Doktor Faustus* is the novel of Mann's era, and the shadow of fascism was the distinguishing feature of that era. Fascism is ever present in the novel implicitly. To understand and identify the indications of fascism it is necessary to know something about what was going on in the real world in the setting of the events of the novel. The narrator does not, perhaps, always make this clear enough for today's reader. It could be said that the narrator takes fascism so much for granted that he finds it redundant to actually mention it. *Doktor Faustus* does not take place in an isolated sanatorium, as does *Der Zauberberg*, in biblical times, as do the Joseph novels, or in a historical time, as does *Lotte in Weimar*. It takes place primarily in the 1920s in Munich, the place where Mann lived and participated in German society at the time portrayed in the novel. The novel is about art and theology, but I believe that these aspects must be subordinated to the central theme of fascism if the novel is to be understood.

In my view, all discussions in the novel point to Mann's definition of the intellectual environment in which German fascism developed as a political philosophy, whether or not they are specifically about politics. Music, art, philosophy, theology, and politics are so intertwined that it is often not clear which exactly is being discussed. This ambivalence or instability does not, in my opinion, represent an inability on Mann's part to keep the lines clear, but rather indicates that they are not meant to be kept clear. *Doktor*

Faustus is made up of a convoluted interweaving of abstract ideas expressed in words that mean different things in different contexts. One important example of this is the use of the word *Erlösung* in the novel. In theology *Erlösung* means salvation or redemption. In the politics of the time of the events in the novel *Erlösung* was commonly used to indicate political "salvation." In the discussions of music, Adrian uses the term *Erlösung* with reference to that particular combination of tones by which we recognize that a piece of music has come to the end of a thought, either tentatively or conclusively: "Erlösung . . . , ein romantisches Wort; und ein Harmoniker-Wort, das Handlungswort für die Kadenz-Seligkeit der harmonischen Musik" (*DF*, 428). Its literal meaning, therefore, does not indicate the context in which *Erlösung* is used, and in *Doktor Faustus* this context is not always clear. A single paragraph can appear to begin as a discussion of music, or of theology, and to end as a discussion of politics. What all of these meanings have in common is the idea of an absolute goal to be striven towards that will determine the choice of steps taken to reach it, or, put another way, that the end determines the means. As is implicit in the idea of twelve-tone music, the solution offered by Adrian is the elimination of the need for this goal. This particular aspect of the novel is one that seems not to be taken into account, or even recognized. Arguments such as the above-quoted interpretation by Helmut Jendreieck consider only passages where it is clear that the question under discussion is politics, thus ignoring essential aspects of the argument presented in musical or theological terms that modify, indeed change, what is being said. Arguments about politics in the novel that do not include the political implications of the long discussions of music or theology are necessarily partial. What these three areas — religion, music, and politics — have in common, so that talking about one shifts naturally to talking about another, is elaborated extensively by Mann in *Die Betrachtungen eines Unpolitischen*. The overwhelming significance of *Die Betrachtungen eines Unpolitischen* to *Doktor Faustus* is discussed below in chapters 2 and 3 and elaborated in the textual analysis that follows.

This ambivalence of the subject matter of the novel is further complicated by the complexity of the material treated. It is, for example, the exception rather than the norm today for an educated person to have an extensive knowledge and understanding of either theology or music, let alone both. Judgments, therefore, tend not to be informed but to be based on prior assumptions and generalities. Such ignorance means that readers cannot appreciate the significance of the subtleties discussed in the novel. As for politics, a major problem in the interpretation of *Doktor Faustus* lies in the emotional charge associated with the historical problem of fascism. The very word triggers an automatic rejection and hostility in most readers and a refusal to give the subject objective consideration. However, this was not always the case, and specifically not the case at the time the novel is portraying, the period when intellectual fascist movements developed all over Europe as a theoretical alternative solution to the social problems resulting from massive industrialization and urbanization. The modern idea that no intelligent, respectable, or "good" person could be associated in any way with fascism dominates the interpretation of *Doktor Faustus* and has led to the most remarkable distortions of both the events and the arguments of the protagonists. Fascism, in its origin and goals, is a utopian political philosophy. It is not to be confused with Hitler's National Socialist government. The novel ends abruptly at the specific point in history when fascism stopped being theory and became practice in Germany. This study is not meant to be an analysis of the intricacies of fascism. It is essential to understanding the novel, however, to appreciate that, as with communism, those who accept the utopian arguments such philosophies offer tend to take an ideological stand and either close their eyes to any accompanying atrocities or stoically accept them as unfortunately necessary to the achievement of the greater good. The transition in the novel from a vague theoretical fascist position to a specifically National Socialist position occurs in the dénouement, the part of the text that is not generally taken into account.

Another question that has not been adequately addressed is the dialectical nature of the text. It is largely constructed through the use of oppositions. The opposition between the narrator's humanism and what the narrator describes as the hero's inhumanity has been discussed to death, but always on the assumption that everyone knows what the word "humanism" means and that it is a "good thing." "Humanism," like "democracy," is one of those emotive labels attached to the most contradictory ideas for the purpose of predisposing the hearer to understand the particular version being discussed as "good," or "moral." However, there are important differences between *bürgerlicher Humanismus,* or nineteenth-century Lutheran humanism, and Catholic humanism, differences that are not recognized in the literature on the novel. Other oppositions directing the arguments in the novel are: "the word" and "the music"; Protestantism and Catholicism; fascism and democracy; harmony and polyphony; cold and heat; good and bad; God and the Devil; intellect and emotion; sexual license and chastity; sickness and health. The meanings of these are never absolute, but depend, in the case of *Doktor Faustus*, on the particular definitions given by Mann in his various essays. Not checking them out in the context of Mann's thought leads to extrapolating unwarranted inferences from what is said. At the same time, the shifts in the meanings of these words from speaker to speaker are what turn the discussions into dialectic. Ignoring these shifts is to ignore the dialectic character of the discussions.

It occurs frequently that the hero makes a statement of his intentions, then the narrator says he does not believe him and offers some ulterior motive to explain these intentions. There is a marked tendency in the

critical literature to accept the narrator's psychological analyses in preference to the hero's clear statements without questioning these analyses and
in effect to replace the hero's statements with these, as though the hero
had not spoken. Disregarding the hero's expressed views is to ignore the
dialectic in the conversations. The dialectic in the conversation with the
Devil is also ignored by simply subsuming the Devil into the hero and
reading the Devil's arguments as though they were his. It is difficult to
accept that Mann constructed a novel on the basis of dialogue with the
intention that the reader should read it as monologue and give no consideration whatsoever to the intellectual interplay between the characters.

Further, Zeitblom is very free about giving his opinion on everything
under the sun. These are his opinions, not Adrian's, and should be understood as such.

Certainly there will always be disagreement on interpretation, as there
always is where philosophical questions are being discussed. In *Doktor
Faustus*, Mann is talking about very controversial abstract ideas, and discussion of abstract ideas can easily degenerate into a muddle of contradictions. Indeed, this is one of the most important points the novel makes, in
my view: arguments often seem to end up being interpreted as the opposite of what the speaker intended.

* * *

This leads to the problem of the narrator. The reliability of the narrator as
spokesman for Mann has largely been taken for granted. He has been studied at length, but virtually always on the assumption that his views and
opinions are Mann's. Indeed, the views the narrator expresses in *Doktor
Faustus* have even been used to determine Mann's personal views. This
approach further compounds the effect of dismissing the views of the hero,
which are nearly always in opposition to the views of the narrator. Various
not very convincing explanations have been offered in the past of why the
narrator is there at all, if his views simply reflect Mann's. For example, in
his *Thomas Mann: Werk und Entwicklung* (1950) Hans Mayer's explanation of the role of narrator is that it is to tie together historical periods,[27]
while Robert Faesi, in *Thomas Mann: Ein Meister der Erzählkunst* (also
1950), says it is to keep the novel from being boring.[28] Hans M. Wolff, in
Thomas Mann: Werk und Bekenntnis (1957), expresses the view that the
narrator is a humanist, a good man, and the embodiment of the mature
Mann, who has overcome his hero's problems.[29] This view is repeated by
Schäfermeyer in his *Thomas Mann: Die Biographie des Adrian Leverkühn
und der Roman* Doktor Faustus (1983).[30] Ilse Metzler, in her *Dämonie
und Humanismus: Funktion und Bedeutung der Zeitblomgestalt in Thomas
Manns* Doktor Faustus (1960), says that the use of the narrator makes an

improbable life believable (13). The very fact that this question is asked
shows how completely the assumption that the narrator represents Mann's
views has been subsumed into the critical approach. None of these explanations considers the possibility that he is there precisely because his views
do not reflect Mann's. The overwhelming assessment of the narrator is
that he is a normal, well-educated *Bürger*, who loves and admires the hero,
in spite of the fact that the latter is in some way not acceptable. Critics disagree on details of the interpretation of the relationship between the two
but, almost without exception, assume that the interpretation of the hero
given by the narrator reflects Mann's own interpretation of his character
and opinions and that it is Mann who is showing that there is something
wrong with the hero. However, the narrator in *Doktor Faustus* is a participating narrator. As Mann said in 1923, in his essay "Adolf von Hatzfeld,"
such a narrator can never be identical with the author:

> Erzählen [ist] etwas vollständig anderes als Schreiben; und zwar unter-
> scheidet sich jenes von diesem durch eine Indirektheit, die sogar am fein-
> sten und verschlagensten sein kann, wenn die innere Objektivität des
> Werkes durch eine humoristisch-scheinbare Direktheit verschleiert wird,
> wenn also dennoch ein monsieur sich meldet und peroriert, der aber
> keineswegs identisch mit dem epischen Autor, sondern ein fingierter und
> schattenhafter Beobachter ist.[31]

* * *

Those few critics who, in the face of established opinion, question
Zeitblom's account and claim that Mann has deliberately made him "unreliable" have shown that believing what he says about Adrian can only be
based on a very superficial reading of the novel. Close reading of the text
reveals many questionable aspects of Zeitblom's account of Adrian's life,
which put his position as Mann's spokesman in question, as well as the
story he is telling. This "unreliable" Zeitblom suggests a much more interesting character than he is usually considered to be. Unfortunately,
although these critics have provided clear evidence from the text that it is
indeed the case that Mann has Zeitblom distort his account of Adrian, they
have stopped at that, and no one has sufficiently studied the implications
of these conclusions for the plot of the novel. Again, if Mann has presented
his story through a narrator whom he has deliberately shown to be distorting his tale, not only the roles of both Adrian and Zeitblom as protagonists in the story have to be entirely reconsidered, but the whole story
itself. In this case, Mann is not telling the story his narrator claims to be
telling. He is telling the story of the narrator's interpretation of his subject.
If this is so, there must be sufficient information in the novel about Adrian
for the reader to question the legitimacy of Zeitblom's interpretation. The

prejudices and distortions in Zeitblom's account are, therefore, an aspect of the novel that calls out for further investigation.

Among the happy few critics who recognize Zeitblom's unreliability, James Campbell, in his 1999 article "Thomas Mann's *Doctor Faustus*: Weighing the Testimony of Serenus Zeitblom," approaches the novel using his training and experience as a lawyer in assessing impartially the validity of evidence.[32] He seriously questions Zeitblom's account of Adrian's life. He claims, for example, that Zeitblom's own account is seen "massively to contradict his view of Leverkühn as isolated, unfeeling, and self-centered (31)." Campbell notes that Zeitblom insists, "against the evidence that he himself reports, that the artistic genius is necessarily inhuman, isolated, and entirely separated from the rest of mankind by the demonic powers upon which art depends (35)." (Mann, incidentally, attributes this view of the artist as a combination of Lucifer and a clown to priests and liars.[33]) Campbell also points out that a large part of Zeitblom's evidence for this view is based on subjective opinion, not on fact. Campbell's judgments are based on a methodical interpretation of the evidence of the text, and his primary concern is to rescue the real image of Adrian from Zeitblom's distortion. The important thing about his assessment is that it clearly shows, first, that there is substantial evidence in the text itself that Zeitblom is deliberately portrayed as not telling the truth and, second, that the truth about Adrian can in fact be determined. Zeitblom the narrator is telling us one thing and showing us something quite different. Campbell points out this distortion, but does not further analyze the novel.

In his 1969 thesis, "Prädestination des Dämonischen: Zur Frage des bürgerlichen Humanismus in Thomas Manns *Doktor Faustus*," Hubert Orlowski systematically challenges the authority of the narrator.[34] This thesis has been remarkably little heeded, although it is a sound and serious academic work, carefully documented and supported with evidence from the text. Even when cited, Orlowski is then usually dismissed, although never refuted. Orlowski studies the structure of the novel, not the content, and establishes a framework within which the novel can be analyzed with some coherence. His thesis provides a firm basis, a point of reference for rational, rather than emotional and arbitrary, study of the text. It destroys any notion that Zeitblom's story can be taken at face value.

Orlowski points out that Zeitblom frequently breaks the conventions of the first-person narrator by relating events at which he was not present and about which nobody could have told him. He does not present such accounts as speculations but as fact (96), assuming the role of omniscient narrator (81–82). He often accompanies these occasions with statements that he is not an omniscient narrator. He also points out that Zeitblom's views into Adrian's inner life surpass the limits of the first-person narrator (100). On the one hand he is fastidiously correct, but on the other he is astoundingly arrogant. By overstepping the limitations of the first-person narrator Zeitblom shows his contempt for the truth and breeds mistrust in the reader — or should do so. Orlowski goes on to say that Zeitblom is giving us his own view of Adrian's life and is deforming it by telling us what he wants to tell us instead of just what he can tell us with authority (105–6). Most of Zeitblom's statements are not judgments, but descriptions of his feelings. Orlowski comments that Zeitblom also sets a murky, spooky, ambiguous atmosphere around Adrian, the effect of which is to criticize his person and his work, giving them the air of a demonic curse. This atmosphere influences the reader in his understanding of everything in the novel (84–96).

He goes on to show that Mann's seeming confusion of the first-person narrator with the omniscient narrator is not at all inconsistent. He concludes that Mann has not conceived of Zeitblom as a conventional first-person or omniscient narrator, but as a specific combination of the two that is recognized in literary theory: the hagiographer. Hagiography is a case of first-person narrative that allows the specific kind of liberties Zeitblom takes. This approach allows the use of theological and demonic elements (118). As Orlowski explains, medieval hagiography is in the antique tradition of rhetoric and is based on the use of specific literary techniques, all of which are specifically used by Zeitblom in *Doktor Faustus*. They are simply formulae and do not reflect reality, mere writing tools that the classical scholar has learned for the purpose of influencing the reader (121–23). Orlowski convincingly makes the case that Zeitblom's biography of Adrian follows the scheme too closely to be accidental (155).

Orlowski cites Nietzsche's argument that it is commonly and superstitiously thought that men of genius, or of outstanding intellect, have some magic ability that enables them to acquire knowledge through supernatural channels (167). He then goes on to quote Hellmut Rosenfeld's article "Legende" in the *Reallexikon der deutschen Literaturgeschichte*, 1959, as saying that hagiographies can no longer be written, because this kind of belief is not found today (157). Nevertheless, Mann has shown that he thinks Nietzsche was right, that he thinks a person like Zeitblom, a Catholic humanist, could have written such a work during the Second World War in Germany. In *Doktor Faustus* Mann is showing that this kind of belief was prevalent. Indeed, Zeitblom starts his account with a statement to this effect (*DF*, 11).

Orlowski asks the question whether Mann has presented Zeitblom as technically capable of writing such a hagiography, and concludes that he has. His argument is that Zeitblom has the necessary knowledge to use this form, because he is a classical scholar and must know about medieval rhetoric. He is familiar with the *Gesta Romanorum* and the Gregorius story and states that he has been influenced by his Catholicism (164). In my view, Orlowski has made far too weak a case for supporting this point. He neglects the very important point that Zeitblom teaches not only Latin but also history at the Catholic School of Theology. Catholic scholars do not learn Latin only to study the classics but also to study the Middle Ages. Zeitblom is a classicist, but, professionally, he is also a medievalist, a specialist in hagiography.

Orlowski concludes that Mann is saying, through his creation of Zeitblom, that a large part of the German middle class failed with respect to National Socialism and lied to itself about its responsibility for its rise to power. He argues that the reason they allowed it to happen was that they considered that the course of history is predetermined. If events are predetermined then, by definition, there is nothing the individual can do to prevent their becoming fact. Such a worldview releases the individual from all moral responsibility for what happened in Germany. One is outraged about the protagonists, but one's own hands are clean. The only thing to do is fold your hands and ask for mercy. Zeitblom feels no guilt. He is a Pharisee and his freedom from guilt is only possible because he believes in the predestination model (176–77). Orlowski argues that Zeitblom reverses traditional middle-class values and opts for emotion and irrationality because of the charismatic appeal of Adrian's personality. This conclusion is based exclusively on his analysis of Zeitblom's narrative approach and shows clearly that Zeitblom supports fascism (161). Zeitblom, therefore, cannot represent Mann's views.

Orlowski's analysis is convincing, but his conclusions are superficial. There is a jump between his argument and this conclusion, as is reflected in his title, "zur Frage des bürgerlichen Humanismus." His evidence shows clearly that Zeitblom's view of the world is medieval Roman Catholic and not nineteenth-century. His thesis does not deal at all with the question of nineteenth-century German humanism. What his study shows is that Zeitblom rejects this humanism in favor of a medieval Catholic worldview. It is also clear in his analysis that the Adrian Zeitblom sanctifies is not the Adrian he portrays but an invention based on wishful thinking. His assessment of Zeitblom in his study is accurate, but he just assumes without question, in keeping with the tradition, that Zeitblom represents nineteenth-century humanism, missing the point entirely that his views are medieval Catholic.

Orlowski's thesis says nothing about what actually happens in the novel. It also says nothing about Adrian other than that Zeitblom saw him as demonic and predestined to a terrible end, but worshipped him anyway. It does not show why. Nor does it deal with the other characters, or the events, or even seek to evaluate Adrian as a hero or an anti-hero. Having established that Zeitblom supports fascism, Orlowski reverts to the standard view that Adrian represents fascism. He does not follow up the substance of his thesis, his own evidence that Zeitblom is misrepresenting Adrian, nor does he study the implications for the story of the fact that Zeitblom is not telling the truth. In spite of his conclusions, what Orlowski's study shows beyond any doubt are two important points. Zeitblom is not telling the truth, and his reason for this is that he has returned to the medieval Roman Catholic practice of twisting the evidence in support of a cause.

There has been some reaction to Orlowski's argument. Dietrich Assmann, in his 1987 article, " 'Herzpochendes Mitteilungsbedürfnis und tiefe Scheu vor dem Unzukömmlichen': Thomas Manns Erzähler im *Doktor Faustus*," sees the implications of its substance and points out important problems in accepting Zeitblom's account, implying that Mann's message may be something else.[35] He particularly questions the Preßburg episode, the conversation between Rudi and Adrian, and the conversation between Rudi and Marie (92). These are the episodes that constitute the "plot" of Zeitblom's story. If, as Assman suggests, there is no Preßburg incident, there is no syphilis; if the conversation between Rudi and Adrian is an invention, then why is it there, unless to deliberately mislead the reader? What are Zeitblom's intentions? If the conversation between Rudi and Marie does not take place, then Adrian is not planning to marry Marie and does not send Rudi to his death, as Zeitblom says he does. In other words, if these accounts are deliberate fictions, then Zeitblom's account and the usual assumptions of what the story is about collapse. *Doktor Faustus* does not seem to be the story of an artist who, in the form of a pact with the Devil, deliberately contracts syphilis in exchange for inspiration. Assmann claims that the reader is not given an alternative explanation of events (93), but as Campbell has shown, this is not necessarily the case.

In 1996, in his article "Gegen-Lesen: Widerstände gegen die Rezeptionslenkung durch Erzähler, Hauptfigur und Autor bei der Lektüre von Thomas Manns Roman *Doktor Faustus*," Jürgen Petersen makes these same points, without reference to Orlowski.[36] He is quite devastating in his attack on the standard views. He questions the reliability of the narrator on the grounds that he portrays his intuitions rather than facts. He points out that Adrian did not sign a contract with the Devil — the Devil simply declares that they have a contract — and that Zeitblom associates all genius with the Devil. Petersen also questions whether contracting syphilis or writing twelve-tone music can be regarded as sins. He points out that Zeitblom is obsessed with the Devil and finds everything demonic with one exception — an exception that contradicts everything he has said: he denies the reality of the Devil with whom Adrian has a conversation about the pact. Petersen concludes, however, not that this throws some doubt on the standard interpretation, but that Mann did not succeed in getting across the message he intended, which, he says, following the usual assumption, was to make Adrian's fate parallel with Germany's fate. He, like Assmann, says that there is no way that textual analysis can show what the novel is attempting to say.

The critics discussed here have found serious discrepancies in the text, and some have concluded that the story told by Zeitblom is not the story told by Mann and have provided sound evidence from the text of the novel to support their contentions that this is the case. They have done this with virtually no reference to Mann's overall views on society, human nature, and politics and with no reference either to his own experience of fascism or to the historical background of the novel. Their conclusions have been drawn from the text of *Doktor Faustus* alone, but they have made no attempt to establish what is actually going on in the novel and what are the purpose and the implications of Zeitblom's deliberate distortion of the facts of Adrian's life.

Since the appearance of Orlowski's challenge, assertions that the narrator represents Mann's views have become much more vehement, but reference is rarely made to Orlowski's study. A few critics not only take this identification for granted but openly defend this position. Hermann Weigand says in his 1977 article, "Zu Thomas Manns Anteil an Serenus Zeitbloms Biographie von Adrian Leverkühn," that the narrator is absolutely trustworthy, almost a saint. Any errors or inconsistencies in his account are Thomas Mann's errors.[37] Helmut Koopmann claims in *Der schwierige Deutsche* that any observed differences between the narrator's views and Mann's are superficial (99), as does Margrit Henning in *Die Ich-Form und ihre Funktion in Thomas Manns* Doktor Faustus *und in der deutschen Literatur der Gegenwart* (1966, 142), while Hermann Kurzke says that the narrator is just a mask behind which Mann can distance himself from the hero, whatever that means. He insists in *Thomas Mann: Das Leben als Kunstwerk* (1999) that the opinions the narrator expresses are Mann's (512). One remains with the impression, from the tone of many of these statements, that the point at issue is a question of dogma, something that cannot be questioned. Indeed, the vehemence of these assertions is rather puzzling, since one so rarely comes across attempts to disagree with them. John Fetzer concludes from his 1996 historical study of interpretations of *Doktor Faustus, Changing Perceptions of Thomas Mann's Doctor Faustus: Criticism 1947–1992* (1996), that it is a foregone conclusion on the part of the literary community that the narrator is the alter ego of Thomas Mann.[38] Of course, since all the usual fundamental assumptions are based not only on trusting the narrator but also on unquestionably accepting his values as valid, questioning the narrator would invalidate or seriously modify interpretations based on these assumptions. In this sense, defending the narrator is a kind of self-defense.

In 2001 Gerhard Kaiser reviewed the evidence of Zeitblom's unreliability at length in "*. . . und sogar eine alberne Ordnung ist immer noch besser als gar keine*": *Erzählstratagien in Thomas Manns* Doktor Faustus.[39] However, rather than discuss the implications of this evidence for the interpretation of the novel, he dismisses its significance with the argument that

Mann gradually and deliberately changes his narrative position to that of all-knowing author. Kaiser does this on the grounds, as he says, that the views expressed by the narrator reflect increasingly Mann's own views, and that by making the narrator appear to be unreliable Mann removes himself from full responsibility for these views. This complicated effort to uphold Zeitblom's reliability in the face of the overwhelming evidence against it is quite remarkable. Kaiser's argument is not convincing, but rather a futile attempt to rescue an untenable position.

Kaiser's denial of Zeitblom's unreliability does not prevent him from finding other serious defects in the novel. He finds that the parallel the novel presents between Adrian's music and the development of fascism is highly questionable (48). He also finds the character of Adrian inconsistent with a Faust character, and questions whether the pact in fact exists. He makes the point already made by Hermann Kurzke, who is also very insistent that Zeitblom reflects Mann's views, that Mann has in fact presented Adrian's work in a way that shows that the pact with the Devil is redundant. In his *Thomas Mann: Epoche — Werk — Wirkung,* Kurzke extends this redundancy to include the syphilitic infection.[40] Neither takes these criticisms to be an indication that perhaps the original interpretations of *Doktor Faustus* do not reflect Mann's intentions, but simply see them as illustrations of the weakness of the novel, in that it is not tightly written enough to express these assumed intentions. Critics prefer to think that Mann himself did not understand what the novel is about and, as a result, made structural and logical errors.

Basically, the situation is that there are two sets of critics: those who offer an interpretation of the novel and do so by ignoring fundamental contradictions in the text to those interpretations, and those who point out the contradictions, but do not offer a new interpretation because they refuse to question the generally accepted, overall underlying assumptions, preferring to describe the contradictions as errors. These underlying assumptions appear to be understood by all as sacred, whereas all the evidence is that they are quite arbitrary.

* * *

This study will offer a new reading of *Doktor Faustus,* starting from a discussion of Mann's theory of how music, theology, and politics are interwoven and of the relationship of Catholic humanism to these spheres, as found in *Die Betrachtungen eines Unpolitischen,* followed by an account of Mann's personal experience of the rise of fascism, particularly the influence on his life of the reception of *Die Betrachtungen eines Unpolitischen* in its interpretation as a fascist document. Finally, a textual analysis of the main events of the novel will be offered, showing the implications of this background material for an understanding of what is actually going on in the story. Such an approach provides a radically new basis for subsequent interpretation of the message of the novel.

Reading the text of *Doktor Faustus* with Mann's other writings and with biographical references to Mann's life, particularly his life during the 1920s, does provide a plausible alternative view of the story, an alternative that does not throw up stumbling blocks but incorporates the so-called "contradictions" as building blocks. It is my argument that the story of *Doktor Faustus* is told simultaneously from two opposing points of view, that of the narrator of the biography and that of his subject. Parallel to Zeitblom's account, Adrian's point of view can always be perceived, and his interpretation of events is very different. The inconsistencies and ambiguity the above-mentioned critics find in Zeitblom's narration result primarily from not questioning his values. I suggest, however, that a much more serious problem results from the failure to recognize the existence of these two points of view. The periodic dominance of Adrian's own account of his intentions and opinions has been understood only in the context of Zeitblom's account, rather than as in opposition to it, as it is actually meant to be, thus distorting the interpretation of these parts of the novel. Not recognizing that these accounts are independent of one another has led to confusing the two perspectives and fusing them together to come up with an improbable, confused, and ambiguous tale. Margrit Henning pointed out in *Die Ich-Form und ihre Funktion in Thomas Manns* Doktor Faustus *und in der deutschen Literatur der Gegenwart* (1966) that there are two independent accounts, but it is her view that the reader is supposed to tie them together.[41] This unwarranted assumption contributes substantially to the ultimate confusion and irrationality of much of the literature on *Doktor Faustus*. In the novel, it is the narrator who insists on blurring the independence of these accounts, and he ties them together by negating the account of his opponent and by providing "alternative" motivations to those shown in the novel, for the purpose of discrediting the hero. However, even when the narrator makes it clear that it is not his account but Adrian's, critics do not distinguish the different points of view. The story resulting from this fusion of the two accounts will never be resolved, not because the novel's two interpretations of the rise of fascism in Germany contradict one another on points of fact, but because the difference between the two positions lies in their contradictory value judgments. The story of *Doktor Faustus* is the story of the interplay of these contradictory interpretations of events. The two positions are kept separate throughout the novel by the simple expedient of being expressed by two separate individuals, and it is up to the reader to stand apart and take a critical view. In effect, Mann has the narrator consistently showing the reader one thing and telling him another.

* * *

The extraordinary disregard for the facts of the novel, described by critics as contradictions and weaknesses, as well as of the facts of history, not to mention Mann's own expressed opinions, seems not to be based on any deliberate theoretical argument that such mundane considerations are irrelevant to an interpretation of the novel. It appears far more to be a question of a paralysis induced by the burden of traditional views. Why are all observations that there are aspects of the novel that do not support these traditional interpretations explained as compositional errors on Mann's part? The discussion of the relationship of *Doktor Faustus* to the times it is describing, which is, after all, what Mann claimed the novel was about, has been so colored by prejudice and lack of objectivity that, improbable as it may seem, it can truly be said that the only exception to date dealing in depth with the position of the narrator on fascism is still that written over thirty years ago by Orlowski. In the novel Zeitblom comments, at the beginning of chapter 5, that Adrian's work would not be properly understood by his eventual audience, because it would not appear at a time in history when its arguments were relevant and, furthermore, that his account of Adrian's life is not intended for persons who know nothing of Adrian (*DF*, 44–46). I understand the implication of these remarks to be that one has to have knowledge of the background against which the novel is written in order to understand it correctly.

Notes

[1] Thomas Mann, *Doktor Faustus: Das Leben des deutschen Tonsetzers Adrian Leverkühn erzählt von einem Freunde*, vol. 6 of *Gesammelte Werke in zwölf Bänden* (Oldenburg: Fischer, 1960).

[2] Thomas Mann, *Die Betrachtungen eines Unpolitischen*, in *GW*, 12:7–589.

[3] Two classic works, Karl Popper's *The Open Society and Its Enemies*, and Friedrich Hayek's *The Road to Serfdom*, starting from different points of view, present fundamentally the same explanation of the rise of totalitarianism as that by Mann in *Die Betrachtungen eines Unpolitischen*.

[4] Peter de Mendelssohn, *Von Deutscher Repräsentanz* (Munich: Prestel, 1972), 71–72.

[5] Hans Egon Holthusen, "Die Welt ohne Transzendenz: Eine Studie zu Mann's *Doktor Faustus* und seinen Nebenschriften," *Merkur* 3 (1949): 38–58, 161–80; here, 42.

[6] Hermann Kurzke, *Thomas Mann: Das Leben als Kunstwerk* (Munich: Beck, 1999), 249–50.

[7] Helmut Koopmann, *Der schwierige Deutsche* (Tübingen: Niemeyer, 1988), 22.

[8] Helmut Wiegand, *Thomas Manns* Doktor Faustus *als zeitgeschichtlicher Roman: Eine Studie über die historischen Dimensionen in Thomas Manns Spätwerk* (Frankfurt am Main: Fischer, 1982), 205.

[9] Hans Hilgers, *Serenus Zeitblom: Der Erzähler als Romanfigur in Thomas Manns Doktor Faustus* (Frankfurt am Main: Peter Lang, 1995), 114.

[10] Lieselotte Voss, *Die Entstehung von Thomas Manns Roman Doktor Faustus: Dargestellt anhand von unveröffentlichten Vorarbeiten* (Tübingen: Niemeyer, 1975), 155.

[11] Herbert Lehnert, "The Luther-Erasmus Constellation in Thomas Mann's *Doktor Faustus*," *Michigan Germanic Studies* 10 (1984): 142–58; here, 142.

[12] Herbert Lehnert, "Zur Theologie in Thomas Manns Doktor Faustus," *Deutsche Vierteljahrsschrift für Literaturwissenschaft und Geistesgeschichte* 40 (1966): 248–56.

[13] Kurt Sontheimer, *Thomas Mann und die Deutschen* (Munich: Nymphenburger, 1961), 15.

[14] Gert Sautermeister, "Zwischen Aufklärung und Mystifizierung: Der unbewältigte Widerspruch in Thomas Manns *Doktor Faustus*," in *Antifaschistische Literatur*, ed. Lutz Winkler (Königstein: Scriptor, 1979), 77–125.

[15] Joachim Fest, *Das Gesicht des Dritten Reiches* (1963; rpt., Munich: Piper, 1993), 338–55.

[16] Gotthard Montesi, "Thomas Mann, der Teufel und die Deutschen," *Wort und Wahrheit* 3 (July 1948): 495–510.

[17] Georg Lukács, "Auf der Suche nach dem Bürger: Die Tragödie der modernen Kunst," *Aufbau* 5, 1 (1949): 59–79, 154–69.

[18] Hubert Becher, S. J., "Thomas Mann und sein Faustbuch," *Stimmen der Zeit* 3 (1948): 213–22; here, 221.

[19] Helmut Jendreiek, *Thomas Mann: Der demokratische Roman* (Düsseldorf: Bagel, 1977), 434.

[20] Gerhard vom Hofe, "Das unbehagliche Bewußtsein des modernen Musikers," in *Geist und Zeichen: Festschrift für Arthur Henkel zu seinem sechzigsten Geburtstag dargebracht von Freunden und Schülern*, ed. Herbert Anton, Bernard Gajek, and Peter Pfaff (Heidelberg: Winter, 1977), 144–56.

[21] Hans Heinrich Borcherdt, "Das Faust-Problem bei Thomas Mann," *Jahrbuch des Wiener Goethe-Vereins* 65 (1961): 5–12.

[22] Eitel Timm, *Ketzer und Dichter: Lessing, Goethe, Thomas Mann und die Postmoderne in der Tradition des Häresiegedankens* (Heidelberg: Winter, 1989).

[23] Hermann Kurzke, *Thomas Mann: Epoche — Werk — Wirkung* (Munich: Beck, 1991).

[24] C. A. M. Noble, *Krankheit, Verbrechen und künstlerisches Schaffen bei Thomas Mann* (Bern: Lang, 1970).

[25] Hans Rudolf Vaget, "Mann, Joyce, Wagner: the Question of Modernism in *Doctor Faustus*," in *Thomas Mann*, ed. Michael Minden (New York: Longman, 1995), 217–36.

[26] Hans Rudolf Vaget, "Kaisersaschern als geistige Lebensform: Zur Konzeption der deutschen Geschichte in Thomas Manns *Doktor Faustus*," in *Der deutsche Roman und seine historischen und politischen Bedingungen*, ed. Wolfgang Paulsen (Berne: Francke, 1977), 200–35.

[27] Hans Mayer, *Thomas Mann: Werk und Entwicklung* (Berlin: Volk und Welt, 1950), 378–79.

[28] Robert Faesi, *Thomas Mann: Ein Meister der Erzählkunst* (Zurich: Atlantis, 1955), 144–45.

[29] Hans M. Wolff, *Thomas Mann: Werk und Bekenntnis* (Bern: n.p., 1957), 122.

[30] Michael Schäfermeyer, *Thomas Mann: Die Biographie des Adrian Leverkühn und der Roman* Doktor Faustus (Frankfurt am Main: Lang, 1983), 132.

[31] Thomas Mann, "Adolf von Hatzfeld," in *GW*, 10:631–32.

[32] James Campbell, "Thomas Mann's *Doctor Faustus*: Weighing the Testimony of Serenus Zeitblom," in *Doctor Faustus: Archetypal Subtext at the Millennium*, ed. Armand E. Singer and Jürgen Schlunk (Morgantown: West Virginia UP, 1999), 25–42.

[33] Thomas Mann, "Der alte Fontane," in *GW*, 9:9–34; here, 18.

[34] Hubert Orlowski, "Prädestination des Dämonischen: Zur Frage des bürgerlichen Humanismus in Thomas Manns *Doktor Faustus*" (diss., University of Posen, Poland, 1969).

[35] Dietrich Assmann, " 'Herzpochendes Mitteilungsbedürfnis und tiefe Scheu vor dem Unzukömmlichen': Thomas Manns Erzähler im *Doktor Faustus*," *Hefte der Thomas Mann Gesellschaft* 6–7 (1987): 87–97.

[36] Jürgen H. Petersen, "Gegen-Lesen: Widerstände gegen die Rezeptionslenkung durch Erzähler, Hauptfigur und Autor bei der Lektüre von Thomas Manns Roman *Doktor Faustus*," in *Erzähler — Erzählen — Erzähltes: Festschrift für Rudolf Freudenberg*, ed. Wolfgang Brandt (Stuttgart: Franz Steiner, 1996), 1–12.

[37] For details of these errors and inconsistencies, see Hermann J. Weigand, "Zu Thomas Manns Anteil an Serenus Zeitbloms Biographie von Adrian Leverkühn," *Deutsche Vierteljahrsschrift für Literaturwissenschaft und Geistesgeschichte* 51 (1977): 476–501.

[38] John F. Fetzer, *Changing Perceptions of Thomas Mann's Doctor Faustus: Criticism 1947–1992* (Columbia, SC: Camden House, 1996), 127.

[39] Gerhard Kaiser, *". . . und sogar eine alberne Ordnung ist immer noch besser als gar keine": Erzählstratagien in Thomas Manns* Doktor Faustus (Stuttgart: Metzler, 2001), 92–115.

[40] Kurzke, *Thomas Mann: Epoche — Werk — Wirkung*, 277.

[41] Margrit Henning, *Die Ich-Form und ihre Funktion in Thomas Manns* Doktor Faustus *und in der deutschen Literatur der Gegenwart* (Tübingen: Niemeyer, 1966), 125.

Background

1: *Die Betrachtungen eines Unpolitischen*

*D*IE BETRACHTUNGEN EINES UNPOLITISCHEN goes much beyond being simply an argument against Mann's brother Heinrich's political position, which is what Mann started out to write. It is a sophisticated and sound discussion of political philosophy, although it is presented in rather unorthodox fashion. Published in 1918, the book is a collection of complementary essays written during the First World War, all revolving around the problem of the imminent political upheaval in Germany. Since it is inevitable that Germany will soon be a democratic country, no matter who wins the war, it is necessary, Mann argues, to face the problem and to develop some criteria for directing this change. Those who are actively advocating the introduction of democracy are, like Heinrich, advocating democracy based on Rousseau's Social Contract or its logical extension, Communism. Mann argues that this kind of democracy is French, based on Roman Catholic views of social organization, and is opposed to the nature of German society, to traditional German Protestant values, and would, therefore, lead to the destruction of this liberal humanism and Germany's cultural achievement. He develops an alternative approach: a democracy based on the preservation and fostering of these values. The kind of democracy he advocates in *Die Betrachtungen eines Unpolitischen* is based on the concept of the open society, fundamentally the democracy practiced in the English-speaking countries. Since he very much fears that his views will not prevail, the book is partly a lament about the impending destruction of German Protestant values — something of an Apocalypse.

The importance of these essays to the interpreter of *Doktor Faustus* lies in the nature of the underlying discussion Mann develops to explain why the kind of democratic government that developed in France did not develop in Germany and should not be accepted by Germany. He does not develop this argument as a historian would, but through an analysis of fundamental underlying cultural values. The basic argument of *Die Betrachtungen eines Unpolitischen* is that the Roman Catholic and Protestant cultures are radically opposed, based on two radically opposed understandings of the word "humanism." All other differences in ways of looking at society and at oneself stem from this fundamental dichotomy in the view of humanity: the concept of freedom; the significance of solitude, or of individualism; the concept of morality, or the understanding of good and evil; the nature of responsibility, or guilt; and, of course, the best way to organize society, or politics. Put another way, the difference explains the significance of the Reformation in the formation of German culture. It is

Mann's argument that the German break from the Roman Church was a break from the classical Roman ideal, derived from the Roman Empire, of the desirability of uniformity as expressed in Roman Catholic Church organization and its underlying assumptions (43–44). The basic polarity in Mann's political thought is, then, Roman Catholic versus Protestant humanism. French ideas of democracy are the application to politics of Catholic humanism, the secularization of the medieval social order based on the principles of the Roman Church. The goal is the complete control of all aspects of life to achieve uniformity and conformity in the pursuit of the abstract ideal of "mankind." German culture is Protestant and must organize society in such a way as not to apply but to protect Protestant humanism. The purpose of government is to provide the order necessary to accommodate diversity and dissent and to allow each individual to get on with the task of making life better.

What Mann says, in effect, is that modern political totalitarianism is based on the same view of social control as was medieval Catholicism. In this view, an intellectual elite decides what it is necessary to think and to believe, and dissent from this dogma is considered dangerous to public order. For this reason it is deemed necessary in such a system to root out dissent and to eliminate it. To question the dogma that provides the basis of the social order is to threaten its destruction. All members of the community are presumed to have the same goal and are expected to submit to the interpretation of the ultimate authority on how to achieve it and to perform their prescribed roles to this end. The individual is defined by the community. The idea that to question the official interpretation of dogma is to threaten the social order is the concept of heresy, and the social history of the Middle Ages is the story of holy crusades against heretics. Mann was concerned, not about external crusades against the infidel, but about the crusades at home against internal dissenters. This means of social control, held to be in the public interest, culminated in the Inquisition. The difference between the Inquisition and previous control of heresy was that the accused was no longer simply eliminated, but was given the opportunity to repent in order to save his own soul. This is a concession to individual responsibility, an expression of Catholic humanism. The pressure to conform, through torture, was expressed as in the interest of the victim, in the service of the overall goal of the salvation of mankind. The effect of the Reformation was to destroy this concept of social control through the collapse of the idea that an intellectual elite, a dogma, and a central, universal, and communal goal are necessary for society to function. All that is necessary are rules of social behavior for the purpose of preventing one individual from exercising his right to do and think as he deems in his best interests by infringing on the equal right of others to do the same. The concept of heresy has become meaningless and the community is defined by the individual. This is defining the general through the specific.

Mann defines the political arguments based on Rousseau's Social Contract as "enlightenment." "Enlightenment" is the application of secularized Catholic humanism to politics. He disagrees vehemently, both conceptually and in practice, with such an approach to government, which he considers foreign to Germany, a reflection of the values of the eighteenth century in France. Its infiltration into Germany is threatening to destroy German culture, which is nineteenth-century in character. This new "enlightenment" is a return to seeing life as an idyll, the ideal as pastoral, and a rejection of all doubt and relativity (which are essential to the true German way). It rejects particularly the nineteenth century's lack of belief and demands belief, based on a quite unjustifiable optimism that takes no account of what we know about human nature, in order to force mankind to fit the mould of its Utopia. This eighteenth-century-style enthusiasm for mankind is not pessimistic, skeptical, or cynical; it is based on wishful thinking (*BeU*, 26). Mann finds this modern version of Roman Catholic humanism intolerable in its intolerance and its rejection of all doubt (402).

In his view, those advocating government-imposed equality inevitably end up leveling downwards and persecuting personal eccentricities, which is potentially totalitarian, whereas a German democracy would lead to a leveling upwards and would respect individualism. The pursuit of equality as a goal in itself would end in the annihilation of art and culture, since a culture is defined by its eccentricities. There is a tendency to forget, although it is perfectly obvious, that ultimately, in practice, equality means uniformity and that, logically, there can be no other way to measure equality except by uniformity. Indeed Rousseau did mean uniformity. Mann quotes him advocating the wiping out of national differences: "Heute . . . gibt es keine Franzosen, Deutschen, Spanier, Engländer mehr, was man darüber denke; es gibt nur noch Europäer, die alle denselben Geschmack, dieselben Leidenschaften, dieselben Sitten haben, weil keiner durch besondere Institutionen ein nationales Gepräge erhielt" (263). This is in the international context, but the same arguments apply with reference to the individual's relationship with the State.

Mann's argument is that anyone who likes the truth and is a respectable pessimist would recognize the impossibility of the compatibility of freedom and equality and reject this political "enlightenment" (*BeU*, 255–56). He considers such political "enlightenment" to be oily magnanimity and self-satisfied religious faith and finds it repulsive. Any clear-thinking person also knows, Mann claims, that the happiness promised by this "enlightenment" is not only impossible but undesirable, unworthy of mankind, and contrary to intelligence and culture. It is also a complacent rehashing of old material from the eighteenth century and has no soul. In Mann's view it is nonsense to raise social life to religious status (256). "Enlightenment" individualism, the liberal individualism of France, is contrary to the basic principles of social organization. It is a kind of anti-individualism, because it denies the enlightenment of the individual. Its advocates call for subordinating the individual to the State, which is State absolutism and absolutism of the organization is inhuman (280). It does not matter whether it is based on freedom or on the sword: this utilitarian "enlightenment" leads to a vicious circle of anarchy and despotism (257).

Everybody would be in favor of a more representative and genuine form of government, Mann argues, but not of the change in the German mind that these "enlightenment" politicians find desirable (272). By this change in mental approach, Mann means coming to see every aspect of life as requiring a political decision and as the responsibility of the State, rather than seeing the State as functional, as a public service. The "enlightenment" politicians want this kind of democracy for its own sake, not because it is necessary. They see it as an absolute good, as synonymous with progress, and want a leveling out to conformity (283). This, says Mann, has nothing to do with society and mankind, has no reference to reality and the needs of the moment, but is pure service to an ideal, to an abstract concept (283). The solution to the problem of mankind can only be found through *Innerlichkeit*, only in the soul — that is, by the individual consulting his conscience.

Mann argues that the democracy the liberal German wants is not a doctrine or an eighteenth-century, rhetorical philosophy of virtue. What he wants is a technical state, socially free-reined, and a means for selecting its leaders, that is, the management of national affairs by persons competent to do it, or by a meritocracy, not by demagogues. This kind of democracy would lead to an ever-expanding opening up of life rather than a narrowing. Such a democracy is not an object of enthusiasm, not hallelujah-type religious "enlightenment" based on belief in dogma, but something to be accepted with understanding. Neither intellect nor virtue has anything to do with this kind of government. By intellect Mann means figuring out theories of government that appear logical on paper and are based on abstract principles, and then imposing them on society with no regard to reality. By virtue he means the literal, dogmatic application of moral truisms, or right opinions, such as "human rights." Political opinions are by their very nature expressions of wishes, Mann argues, and right answers do not result from the application of theories and dogmas, but from arriving at a consensus on the particular question at hand in the circumstances in which it is raised. What is the right thing to do today could be wrong tomorrow (*BeU*, 260). Mann argues that it is necessary to put social questions back into the realm of the moral and the human. Society depends on attitudes, not institutions (259). Culture is a question of experience, common sense, practicality; it is a question of manners, of social organization, not a question of morality. It is utopian to think that improving the social order so as to make society more responsible can eliminate suffering, since changes in social conditions just introduce new evils. Every scheme for a perfect social order, technical or moral, leads to the absurd. This is because there are differences of opinion about what the desirable is and because the parties hate one another to the death (400–401): "Demokratie [left-wing radicalism] als stehende Einrichtung würde jedes individuellen Verdienstes ermangeln, und soziale Versöhnung ist nicht eine Frucht der Politik, sondern der Sympathie und der Besserung des einzelnen" (447).

Mann considered that, in the practical sense of self-administration, there was as much democracy in German society before the First World War as there was anywhere else. Small differences in the constitutional form of states do not mean that societies are not democratic. States are drawn to democratic procedures by the very fact that they exist in a utilitarian society, that is, a society dedicated to the principle of usefulness, where the driving force is increasing well-being and the dominating measure of everything is money (*BeU*, 240–41). Mann contends that Bismarck established the basis for democracy in Germany and that this would inevitably develop organically and practically into a specifically German type of democracy. The idea of democracy was already established when the war broke out. This was democracy in the sense of the establishment of institutions for the administration of the State, with the people as subject as well as object, or, as the Americans would say, government for the people by the people. The war confirmed the fact that the people and the State were one and the same (244–46):

> Ein Riese [Bismarck] setzte Deutschland in den Sattel: nun muß es reiten, denn herunterfallen darf es nicht. Dieser Satz scheint mir die gelassene, präzise und alle Wünschbarkeit oder Nicht-Wünschbarkeit außen lassende Umschreibung dessen zu sein, was ich das Notwendige der Entwicklung nenne. Diejenigen, die heute ein demokratisches Deutschland fordern, erheben diese Forderung, deren Erfüllung der Reichskanzler verspricht, nicht aus doktrinären, theoretischen, sondern aus durchaus praktischen Gründen: damit Deutschland erstens leben und damit es zweitens stark und herrenhaft leben könne. (244)

Mann argued not only for democracy but also for socialism in *Die Betrachtungen eines Unpolitischen*. However, it was for a particular kind of socialism. Mann was not against Bismarck's social legislation, but he was against giving it undue importance to the exclusion of consideration of other aspects of life. The correct German socialism is ethical, State socialism on the Bismarckian model, not Marxism: "Es bleibt die Eigenart des deutschen Individualismus, daß er sich mit ethischem Sozialismus, den man Staatssozialismus nennt und der etwas anderes ist als der menschenrechtlerisch-marxistische, sehr wohl verträgt" (279–80).

It is difficult to interpret these remarks taken from *Die Betrachtungen eines Unpolitischen* as arguments against democracy. They are in favor of democracy and opposed to totalitarianism. The central argument is the need for developing a democracy that is based on the maximum preservation of the freedom of the individual to think and act according to his own view of what is in his best interests and that at the same time provides the order necessary for his being able to do this. Order is necessary to prevent one individual from infringing on the freedom of another. The argument was directed primarily against extreme left-wing radical theories of politics, which Mann saw as the main threat at the time. However, it applies equally to fascism, to radical reaction, as Mann pointed out. Unfortunately, this important parallel in his argument was completely ignored by his readers at the time.

* * *

In *Die Betrachtungen eines Unpolitischen* Mann stresses his opposition to Roman Catholic humanism again and again. The problem with Roman Catholic humanism is that it separates the intellect from the elementary, attributing the intellect to God and the elementary to the Devil, whereas, in Mann's view, humanity is defined as a synthesis of intellect and nature. Roman Catholic humanism is an expression of contempt for human nature, since it disregards the uniqueness of the individual. The intellect is an abstraction, whereas the human is concrete, expressed through the individual. The Catholic humanist is an enthusiastic lover of mankind in the abstract and in its homogeneity. This is what he means by humanism. He sees himself as superior to the common people, teaching them in the name of mankind (296). However, the modern Catholic humanist excepts sex from the realm of the Devil, thus reducing his definition of human to an expression of eroticism, or to finding a sexual motivation for all human behavior:

> Und nur *eine* Erscheinungsform des Elementaren ist es, die er bejaht und in der er merkwürdigerweise kein Hindernis der literarischen Heiligung erblickt; es ist das Geschlecht. Hier ist seine Ehrerbietung, seine Liberalität und Duldsamkeit durchaus ohne Grenzen, man muß das anerkennen. Geschlechtsliebe und politische Philanthropie, das heißt Demokratie, hängen ihm eng zusammen; diese ist ihm nur die Sublimierung der anderen; und in striktem Gegensatz zur christlichen Kirche und zu Schopenhauer, welche im "Weibe" ein *instrumentum diaboli* erblickten, adoriert er in ihm die begeisternde Führerin auf dem Weg des politischen Fortschritts, will sagen: der Tugend. (464–65)

In traditional theology, sex is the primary source of all evil, the preferred tool of the Devil. It is the one area of the elementary where freedom to behave as one likes is proscribed.

Mann repeated the same arguments about the relationship of humanism to politics in 1938 in "Vom kommenden Sieg der Demokratie"[1] and again in 1939 in "Das Problem der Freiheit."[2] The difference between these arguments and the arguments in *Die Betrachtungen eines Unpolitischen* is that in these articles Mann explicitly discusses the same points in their political context.

In "Vom kommenden Sieg der Demokratie," Mann argues that democracy is inspired by the feeling and awareness of the worth of the individual human being. The relationship between mind and nature is that nature is innocent and comes to an awareness of itself in mankind in that man puts intellect into nature. This awareness is expressed as having a conscience, of being aware of one's fallibility. This, Mann says, is original sin, but not a fall. It is an elevation, since having a conscience is superior to innocence. The concept of intellect cannot be understood as one-sided, isolated and arrogantly hostile to life, but as tied to life, directed to achievement and to life itself. Humanity, like democracy, honors this interplay of intellect and nature. The danger of conceptually separating the intellect from the world of nature and feelings in politics is that, if the intellect is deemed to have failed in achieving the desired improvements, the Catholic humanist is liable to abandon intellect and fall back on feelings, on irrationality, and the result is fascism.

In "Das Problem der Freiheit," Mann elaborates again on the relationship between democracy and Christian humanism, specifically Protestant Christian humanism in its secularized version, as compared with the secularized Catholic humanism he is talking about in *Die Betrachtungen eines Unpolitischen*. Heathen societies only consider the physical aspects of the human being, and ascetic Christianity, that is Catholicism, sees only the intellectual side. Real humanity is using the intellect for the betterment of nature and this is socialism. He uses the examples of Goethe's *Faust II* and his pedagogical province in *Wilhelm Meisters Wanderjahre* to show that democracy is by its very nature socialism. It is surprising to find Mann suddenly associating Goethe with democracy, since in *Die Betrachtungen eines Unpolitischen* he uses Goethe to support his arguments against democracy. It is not, however, a contradiction, but a repetition and elaboration of the arguments presented in *Die Betrachtungen eines Unpolitischen* in favor of a specifically German democracy, based on the nineteenth-century Protestant German tradition.

In 1944, in "Schicksal und Aufgabe,"[3] Mann defined again what he meant by democracy. The form of expression is quite different, but there is no change in the philosophical content:

Ich verstehe Demokratie nicht hauptsächlich als einen Anspruch und ein Sichgleichstellen von *unten*, sondern als Güte, Gerechtigkeit und Sympathie von *oben*. Ich finde es nicht demokratisch, wenn Mr. Smith oder Little Mr. Johnson Beethoven auf die Schulter schlägt und ruft: "How are you, old man!" Das ist nicht Demokratie, sondern Taktlosigkeit und Mangel an Sinn für Distanz. Wenn aber Beethoven singt: "Seid umschlungen,

Millionen, diesen Kuß der ganzen Welt!," *das* ist Demokratie. Denn er könnte sagen: "Ich bin ein großer Genius und etwas ganz Besonderes, die Menschen aber sind mob; ich bin viel zu heikel, sie zu umarmen." Statt dessen nennt er sie alle Brüder und Kinder eines Vaters im Himmel, der auch der seine ist. Das ist Demokratie in ihrer höchsten Form, die fern ist von Demagogie und schmeichlerischer Umwerbung der Massen. Von jeher habe ich es mit dieser Art von Demokratie gehalten; gerade darum aber empfinde ich tief, daß es nichts Abscheulicheres gibt als Massenbetrug und Verrat an den Völkern. (*GW*, 12:933)

The Catholic humanist bases his politics on his theology in Mann's argument. His politics are simply a secularization of his theology, and his political views can be understood by listening to him talk about his theology. His definition of human nature as being either god-like — pure intellect, or demonic — pure emotion is central to his theology. It is also central to Mann's theory of why the Catholic humanist rejects democracy in favor of totalitarian utopian political philosophies. This is not true of the German Protestant humanist, who does not recognize this opposition. His theology precludes totalitarianism, since he sees the unique expression of the fusion of intellect and emotion in each autonomous individual.

Another characteristic that distinguishes the Catholic humanist from the German is his facility with words and his trust in words. He thinks that beautiful writing is the source of all good action. Mann claims that French literature, rather than just depicting society, as does German literature, is always directed to advocating social improvement. It is a surreptitious form of political activism. The German, however, does not express himself with words easily, but depends on his will, on inarticulate opposition to the word. The Catholic humanist sees such inarticulateness as a form of barbarism and associates it with music, which he sees as fundamentally suspicious and unreliable and not a suitable vehicle for educating the young (*BeU*, 50–51). This is tantamount to a distrust of the whole German Protestant tradition as represented by Luther and Goethe, who made music the basis of their philosophies of education. This is German, says Mann, not a progressive attitude, and makes it difficult to communicate with the Catholic humanist, who understands music as a tenor solo with a brass underlay, in the Italian taste, and hates music as a national soporific and tool of Quietism. Music has a history of four hundred years and is closely tied to Protestantism, continues Mann. Luther started educating the Germans in music. He was theologian, pedagogue, and musician in one — a typical German combination. Luther thought music was a beautiful, glorious gift of God and close to theology. He introduced congregational singing, which supplanted Gregorian Chant. The Roman Catholic Church made fun of such singing. Since Luther, German music has been the expression of the Protestant ethic and, with its powerful, many-toned weaving in and out of self-will and order, the image and artistic and spiritual mirroring of German life. By this analogy, music is the expression of Protestant humanism. Speaking of one is speaking of the other. Thus, just as the Catholic humanist expresses his political views in theological concepts, by means of "the word," the German Protestant humanist expresses his political views through "the music." In *Die Betrachtungen eines Unpolitischen* Mann sees this difference as fundamental. He asks: How can a musician understand the message of the Catholic humanist, the *Zivilisationsliterat*? (320) He should have asked himself how the Catholic humanist could ever understand his own argument.

Mann has here identified music with Protestantism, with God, and with the values of nineteenth-century humanism. The Catholic humanist identifies music with barbarism, or Protestantism, or with the Devil. However, his understanding of music is different. Whereas Mann describes music as a complex proceeding of many voices expressing their will, controlled by a system of order, the Italian view of music is that it is a solo voice accompanied by a brass band that provides a simplistic background function. Mann's kind of music is participatory and creative, whereas the Catholic humanist understands music as a kind of opium for the masses.

* * *

Mann was a novelist. His way of presenting arguments is to illustrate them by creating characters to represent the opposing ideas and to let them argue it out. He describes the general through the specific. In *Die Betrachtungen eines Unpolitischen* there are two major personifications. Critics have paid little attention to this personification of political types, even though they are prototypes of many of the characters in his novels and, in particular, in *Doktor Faustus*.[4] It seems to be time to examine the two main protagonists of *Die Betrachtungen eines Unpolitischen* a little more seriously.

These are the Catholic humanist, whom Mann calls the *Zivilisationsliterat*, and the Protestant artist. Mann clearly identifies himself with the latter, sometimes discussing him in the third person, but more often just assuming his role and directly expressing his own opinion of the *Zivilisationsliterat*, which is, to say it mildly, negative. In his rage, Mann has created quite a delightful character in the *Zivilisationsliterat*, a very comic personality. He identifies not just his views but also his attitudes and behavior in social situations. In the reader's mind the *Zivilisationsliterat* takes on the form of someone he knows. The differences in the approaches to life of the Protestant artist and the *Zivilisationsliterat* are many, but these really only become significant when applied to politics. This is because the application to politics of the values of the *Zivilisationsliterat* leads logically and inevitably to totalitarianism and to the annihilation of the liberal Protestant artist. Politically, they are deadly opponents.

Mann actually says that the annihilation of music is the theme of *Die Betrachtungen eines Unpolitischen*:

> Richard Wagner erklärte einmal, vor der *Musik* vergehe die *Zivilisation* wie Nebel vor der Sonne. Daß eines Tages die Musik, sie ihrerseits, vor der Zivilisation, der Demokratie [Rousseau], wie Nebel vor der Sonne vergehen könnte, hat er sich nicht träumen lassen. . . . Dies Buch läßt sich davon träumen, — verworren und schwer und undeutlich, aber dies und nichts anderes ist der Inhalt seiner Ängste. (39)

Mann is talking about music in the sense of composition, of the creation of new music, not about the interpretation of existing music. He is certainly not talking about listening to music. He is also talking about music as synonymous with Protestant culture.

* * *

Der Zivilisationsliterat ist ein Humanist. (*BeU*, 402)

As a Roman Catholic, the *Zivilisationsliterat* believes in ideals and abstract absolutes, which Mann calls virtues, and the suppression of all deviations from the norm, or of individualism. This is his humanism, his conviction that he knows what is best for mankind (*BeU*, 59). He is virtuous and idealistic, then, and an expert on human nature. The trouble with Catholic humanism is that it is in itself an abstraction, or an ideal, because it is not based on humanity or on an understanding of human nature (536). Mann considers such humanism inhuman (510). He has often used this basic humanist character in his novels. He is, for instance, the model for Settembrini in *Der Zauberberg* and for Madame Houpflé in *Felix Krull* as well as for Girolamo, the theocratic demagogue, in *Fiorenza*. In those works, Mann shows these personages as caricatures of a foreign type. They are not German.

The *Zivilisationsliterat* assumes that there is only one kind of intellectuality, "enlightenment," which means that he thinks there is only one right opinion, and he puts an abyss between his kind — the activists, demonstrators, those with principles, politicians — and the others — the aesthetes, the self-seeking, the egocentrics, the bad citizens. He is not interested in humanity but in right opinion. He makes clear distinctions for the sake of the cause, so he is very exclusive and keeps the company of those who do not contradict him, because he needs to be right. The result is that his conscience, his sense of truth and justice, is dulled and he becomes a bigot. His intellectual freedom is the freedom to conform. His humanism is the humanity of the stiff and cold Pharisee (320–24).

Mann considers that the morality of the *Zivilisationsliterat* is not morality in the Protestant sense, because he is more interested in his pride than his conscience. The Protestant approach to morality is primarily directed to self-denial:

> Es kommt vor im Geistesleben, daß man die Begriffe "moralisch" und "politisch" als Gegensätze behandelt findet, wie zum Beispiel an jener wichtigen Stelle, wo Taine den Revolutionsfranzosen mit seinem englischen Gegenstück, dem Puritaner, in Vergleich bringt, von dem er sagt, daß seine Tätigkeit vor allem nach innen gerichtet sei, zunächst die Selbstverleugnung bezwecke: sie sei moralisch, bevor sie politisch werde. Der französische Typ zeige das entgegengesetzte Bild. Dieser bekümmere sich in erster Linie um die politische, nicht um die moralische Seite der Dinge; er lege auf seine Rechte viel mehr Gewicht als auf seine Pflichten; und statt ein Sporn für das Gewissen zu sein, schmeichele seine Lehre dem Stolz. — Das ist, wie gesagt, äußerst wichtig und interessant. Es ist ein psychologischer Gegensatz, den, unabhängig voneinander, große Schriftsteller mehrfach behandelt haben. (*BeU*, 291)

The *Zivilisationsliterat* is a contemptible person in Mann's eyes, in that he has no ideas of his own but simply follows the latest fashion and considers this virtue:

> Am wenigsten aber liebe und achte ich jene Kleinen, Nichtigen, Spürnäsigen, die davon leben, daß sie Bescheid wissen und Fährte haben, jenes Bedienten- und Läufergeschmeiß der Zeit, das unter unaufhörlichen Kundgebungen der Geringschätzung für alle weniger Mobilen und Behenden dem Neuen zur Seite trabt; oder auch die Stutzer und Zeitkorrekten, jene geistigen Swells und Elegants, welche die letzten Ideen und Worte tragen, wie sie ihr Monokel tragen. . . . Sie sind nichts, wie ich im Texte sagte, und also sind sie ganz frei, zu meinen und zu urteilen, und zwar immer nach neuestem Schnitt und à la mode. Ich verachte sie redlich. (*BeU*, 21)

The *Zivilisationsliterat* always accuses his opponent of having base motives. This is because he is a psychologist. To Mann, psychology is the cheapest and most vulgar thing there is. There is nothing on earth that cannot be exposed and dirtied by psychology, no act or opinion, sentiment or passion. Psychology has never done anything useful in the world, not for art or for life or for human dignity. It is only useful for feeding hatred and compromising things and is the most superfluous development of recent times. However, when you ask a *Zivilisationsliterat* to question his own motives, he has no shame; he is not even slightly embarrassed at declaring himself pure, virtuous, and disinterested. He considers himself the embodiment of righteousness and truth and, with recklessness, arrogance, and complete lack of conscience, never doubts his absolute virtue (*BeU*, 199–200). Psychology is also destructive of art:

> Muß ich noch sagen, welches ihre stärkste Waffe, ihr wirksamstes Zersetzungsmittel ist? Aber es ist die *Psychologie*! — die Psychologie, die

mir immer als die Wissenschaft an sich, als die Erkenntnis selbst erschienen ist. Die Psychologie entmutigt jede Dummheit und Leidenschaft, sie entmutigt Leben und Kunst — durch Wissen. Denn die Kunst wird unmöglich, der Künstler wird unmöglich, wenn sie durchschaut sind. Die Psychologie wirkt also nichts weniger als kulturbildend, sondern im höchsten Grade fortschrittlich zersetzend, im höchsten Grade zivilisatorisch. (*BeU*, 171)

The *Zivilisationsliterat* is a Pharisee, doctrinaire, impatient, and self-righteous:

> Kümmerliche Verbissenheit nebst sentimentalem Schmiß, doktrinäre Verhärtung, Überheblichkeit, starr-kalte Unduldsamkeit, das pharisäisch hinopfernde Pathos des "Mögt ihr verkommen, *ich wohne im Licht*" — all das ergibt kein herrliches Menschentum, und tausendmal schlimmer als "Weltgerechtigkeit," welche aus Sympathie, aus Liebe kommen mag, — tausendmal schlimmer ist *Selbstgerechtigkeit*: sie ist die Sünde, die nicht vergeben wird. (*BeU*, 477–78)

Literaten are the most virtuous people in the world, know-alls about mankind. They are respectable to the point of absurdity. They are estranged from the artist because they think the artist is not respectable by his very nature and temperament, which, says Mann, is not the case (*BeU*, 100).

What is to be respected is the uprightness of the *Zivilisationsliterat*, says Mann, summing up. The *Zivilisationsliterat* finds no criticism of himself, feels no doubt. Virtue for him no longer means humility and awe in the new rational age, but overcoming nineteenth-century liberal doubt. Virtue is reason, with no doubt and no humility (*BeU*, 388–89). The *Zivilisationsliterat* is a pedant. He has principles. He goes his narrow way of virtue and doctrine, looking neither left nor right, and is terrified of dialectic:

> Denn der Politiker widersteht dem Bösen — und ob er ihm widersteht! Müssen wir versichern, daß er schlechterdings kein Zigeuner und Abenteurer ist, vielmehr das Gegenteil davon, ein Pedant, ein Prinzipieller, ein Gefestigter, ein Tugendhafter, ein Mann der geborgenen Seele, der jeder geistigen Vagabondage Valet gesagt hat, der nicht nach rechts noch links blickt, sondern unverwandt den Weg, den schmalen Weg der Tugend und des Fortschritts im Auge behält, den man nur an der Hand der Doktrin zu wandeln vermag? Was die Dialektik betrifft, so hat er selbstverständlich eine Höllenangst vor ihr, und hastig nennt er jeden Einwand gegen die "Lehre" ein Sophisma, — ungeachtet man mit demselben Recht jeden seiner eigenen Heilssätze sophistisch nennen könnte. (*BeU*, 403)

* * *

The Protestant artist is everything that the *Zivilisationsliterat* is not. As well as this he has further distinguishing characteristics that the *Zivilisationsliterat* finds suspect. Representing the Protestant tradition is emphatically the most important single characteristic of the German artist, as Mann describes him in *Die Betrachtungen eines Unpolitischen*. All his other characteristics result from this. Mann, however, has a very personal idea of what Protestantism is. For him it has nothing to do with the church and organized religion or even with belief in God, but is an approach to life, a moral position. It is synonymous with the artist, with nineteenth-century values, and with Mann's views, which he says are based on Wagner, Nietzsche, Schopenhauer, Kant, and Goethe. Protestantism is essentially musical. It embodies the whole German Protestant culture that the *Zivilisationsliterat* wants to wipe out:

> Ob er nun "Glaube" sagt oder "Freiheit," — der Politiker ist abscheulich. Wenn ich aber sage: Nicht Politik, sondern Religion, so brüste ich mich nicht, Religion zu besitzen. Das sei ferne von mir. Nein, ich besitze keine. Darf man aber unter Religiosität jene Freiheit verstehen, welche ein Weg ist, kein Ziel; welche Offenheit, Weichheit, Lebensbereitwilligkeit, Demut bedeutet; ein Suchen, Versuchen, Zweifeln und Irren; ein Weg, wie gesagt, zu Gott oder meinetwegen auch zum Teufel — aber doch um Gottes willen nicht die verhärtete Sicherheit und Philisterei des Glaubensbesitzes. (*BeU*, 536)

This differs from Roman Catholicism in the sense that it rejects the idea of a central authority that defines belief as dogma and requires of the members of the community the belief in and adoration of an abstract ideal, as expressed in this dogma.

Protestantism is living one's life as an imitation of Jesus: the Protestant artist is a Christ-figure, personally responsible directly to God for his actions. It is precisely this characteristic that lends art its power to influence society: "Als ob nicht die Kunst, wie sehr sie immer eine Sache der einsamen Seele, des Gewissens, des Protestantismus und der Gottesunmittelbarkeit sei, — als ob sie nicht an und für sich und allewege eine soziale Macht wäre, welche immer 'die Menschen eng zusammenhielt'!" (*BeU*, 314).

The artist insists on his individuality, solitude, and freedom:

> Der Künstler und Dichter wenigstens wird seiner tiefsten Natur nach immer ein unveräußerliches Recht auf individualistisches Ethos haben, er ist der notwendige und geborene Protestant, der einzelne mit seinem Gott. Es kann und darf um seine Einsamkeit, seine "evangelische Freiheit" auch in Zeiten straffster sozialer Gebundenheit nicht geschehen sein. (*BeU*, 491)

Mann describes both Nietzsche and Wagner as Christ figures (*BeU*, 146–47). C. F. Meyer is also a Christian of this type:

> Er war Christ, indem er sich nicht verwechselte mit dem, was darzustellen er sich sehnte: dem ruchlos-schönen Leben; er wahrte Treue dem Leiden

und dem Gewissen. Christlichkeit, Bürgerlichkeit, Deutschheit, das sind, trotz aller romanisierenden Neigung im Artistischen, wenn nicht die Bestandteile, so doch Grundeigenschaften seines Künstlertums, und das Merkmal von allen dreien ist Gewissenhaftigkeit, dies Gegenteil der Leidenschaft. (*BeU*, 542)

The artist is concerned primarily with form. Music is the moral art, because in music morality becomes form (*BeU*, 317): "Dieser Spielart des Tätigen ist der Sinn für Können und Meisterschaft, der Abscheu vor der Stümperei am tiefsten eingeboren: souveräne Beherrschung der Materie scheint ihm Voraussetzung aller Kunst, denn diese bedeutet ihm Vertilgung des Stoffs durch die Form" (301). Beauty has nothing to do with German Protestant art: ethics prevails over aesthetics. Ethics is ugliness, sickness, and decline. The German artist is a moralist: "Man wird nicht zum Ästheten erzogen in Schopenhauerisch-Wagner'scher Schule, man atmet ethisch-pessimistische Luft dort, deutsch-bürgerliche Luft: denn das Deutsche und das Bürgerliche, das ist eins" (107).

According to Mann, the model for the real German Protestant culture and the German national type is Dürer's work, which is the origin of the synonyms *Bürgerlichkeit* and *Intellectualismus*, *Bürgerlichkeit* and *Kunstmeistertum*.

Es ist kein Zufall, daß mir, indem ich nach dem Bilde bürgerlicher Geistigkeit, des bürgerlich-kulturellen Typus trachte, ein mittelalterlich-nürnbergisch Gesicht erscheint. Man forscht in den Büchern, man forscht in der Not der Zeit nach den fernsten Ursprüngen, den legitimen Grundlagen, den ältesten seelischen Überlieferungen des bedrängten Ich, man forscht nach Rechtfertigung. (*BeU*, 114)

All of these characteristics are variations on the theme of melancholy, or *Innerlichkeit*. The archetypal model for this most German characteristic is, of course, Hamlet.

* * *

Having made it clear that the difference between the *Zivilisationsliterat* and the Protestant artist is that the *Zivilisationsliterat* represents "enlightenment" and therefore expresses himself with words, and that the Protestant artist is a musician and not comfortable with words, Mann modifies this absolute opposition. The German artist, since Goethe and particularly Nietzsche, has taken increasing interest in words, he says. This development is synonymous with "enlightenment" and with democracy. The contamination of the German artist with "enlightenment" is acceptable so long as it is kept under control. It is a question of degree and, above all, of approach. Modifying the relationship of "the word" to "the music" is the theme of

Wagner's *Die Meistersinger*.[5] In the argument of *Die Meistersinger*, the purpose of giving more attention to "the word" is specifically to prevent the dominance of French influence and is associated with democracy.

"Enlightenment" is the intellectual, or literary, means of social progress. It is a principle, while conservatism, on the other hand, is an attitude. Such an attitude can be described as sickly, but in the individualistic, cultural sense, sickness is not an argument against it:

> *Krankhaft* möge man diese Stimmung immerhin nennen, ohne auf viel Widerspruch zu stoßen; denn in einem gewissen Sinn, nennen wir ihn aushilfsweise den individualistisch-kulturellen, ist Krankheit ja kein Gegenargument. Sie hat kostbarste Werte gezeitigt. Und im übrigen ist der Begriff der Krankheit und Depression viel zu unsicher, als daß nicht Vorsicht in seiner Handhabung geboten wäre. (*BeU*, 401)

In *Die Betrachtungen eines Unpolitischen* Mann is trying to establish a synthesis of "the music" and "the word," or of democracy and German Protestant culture. He has acquired a degree of "enlightenment" and this has resulted in his taking an interest in politics and advocating democracy.

* * *

Mann frequently refers to fascism in *Die Betrachtungen eines Unpolitischen*, a movement he considered to be specifically French, as illustrated by authors such as Maurras, Barrès, and Sorel, and essentially foreign to German thought. Such political philosophies he described as nationalistic, belligerent, and radically reactionary, essentially a rejection of the French Revolution and a protest against the break with the Middle Ages (401). Only a real Roman Catholic intellectual could develop or support this reactionary version of totalitarianism, in Mann's view in 1918. This alternative, reactionary totalitarianism could not take hold in Germany, because Germany is Protestant (210). Fascism is based on the Catholic trust in the cult of tradition rather than on the Protestant sense of moral responsibility (201). Mann interpreted fascism as a logical extension of the mentality of the "enlightenment" politician when he found that his "democracy" was ineffective. It is equally a product of the mind of the *Zivilisationsliterat*, an alternative to utopian democracy. Fascism, like Rousseau's democracy, is eighteenth-century, idyllic, idealistic, rhetorical, revolutionary, a philosophy where doubt means heresy (392). The specific application of metaphysics to politics that Mann attributed to this movement was not Christianity but Nietzsche's glorification of life, the sacrifice of truth to the glory of the State, something that no German would do (210). Mann argues that the use by the *Zivilisationsliterat* of the late mad Nietzsche for political agitation was not madness but irresponsibility, simple literary artistic pleasure in making gestures (347–48). He is essentially a Philistine, not operating just with his head, but with his heart, reflecting the Jacobean tendency to anarchy, despotism, sentimentality, terrorism, and fanaticism (384–86). The most important characteristic of the *Zivilisationsliterat*, however, is his compulsion to always join the latest fashionable movement (490). Whereas "enlightenment" politics are based on the intellect, fascism is based on the erotic. Mann did not see fascism as a threat in Germany at the time he was writing, but he was clearly aware of its nature and undesirability.

Fundamentally, fascism is the same as radical democracy, the only difference being that the radical content, "mankind," is replaced with the equally abstract notion of "the nation" (*BeU*, 549). Nationalism is an essential part of French revolutionary democracy, but is not characteristic of Germany. This is apparent three years into the war, after the initial surge of patriotism has died down, says Mann. Germans are simply concerned to maintain the physical integrity of the national borders. In Mann's opinion, the only thing that could lead to the development of nationalism in Germany would be extreme national humiliation (206), and the important thing about the introduction of democracy in Germany is that it must not be seen as imposed (272). It is interesting that Mann did not anticipate Germany's dreadful humiliation by France at the end of the war. It is entirely in line with his basic thesis that there is no limit to the hostility of France against Germany. He did anticipate that the conservative movements in Germany that were trying to hinder the coming of democracy would lead to irrationality and a new kind of reaction (347–48).

Die Betrachtungen eines Unpolitischen is apocalyptic in the sense that it expresses a real fear that the *Zivilisationsliterat* would predominate after the war and that that would mean the end of German culture: "Dies ist seine Stunde, die Stunde des Zivilisationsliteraten; sie ist da" (304). The reason Mann is worried that it could look as if Germany were being forced to become a formal democracy from outside is because he sees danger in the possibility that the people could confuse such a democracy with democracy in the Rousseau sense and that it could be argued that democracy could not exist in any other form. Mann's arguments against Rousseau's democracy are very eloquent and thorough. However, it must be remembered that, confusingly, he calls it simply "democracy." However, he is not arguing against democracy. He is consistently advocating democracy — just not Rousseau's type of democracy.

Die Betrachtungen eines Unpolitischen is a discussion of opposites: Protestantism and Catholicism; humanism and humanity; democracy and totalitarianism; God and the Devil; intellect and nature; "the word" and "the music." However, what these words mean and the way in which they are opposites wavers. It depends on who is talking, and the basic definition of the difference between the two speakers is Catholic humanist versus

Protestant artist. Theology is another word for politics and music is another word for politics, also depending on who is speaking. Thus theology is another word for music. However, the nature of the relationship of music to theology also depends on who is speaking: music is either a gift of God or in the province of the Devil. In *Die Betrachtungen eines Unpolitischen* Mann argues that the correct road to a true German democracy is the continuation of the traditional adaptation of "the music" to "the word," of German culture to democracy. The origin of this interest in democracy is "enlightenment." Mann's idea is to develop a synthesis that is both democratic and German, based on Protestant, not Catholic, humanism and centered on the protection of individual freedom. He puts forward the idea of this synthesis, but does not elaborate on it. It does not need elaboration, because it is a process, a means, not a goal in itself. Government does not have a predetermined goal, but is a system of organization. By its very nature, such a democracy would evolve in Germany as the result of the attitude of German Protestant participants cooperating in a democratic situation in accordance with nineteenth-century liberal values.

Notes

[1] Thomas Mann, "Vom kommenden Sieg der Demokratie," in *GW*, 11:910–41.

[2] Thomas Mann, "Das Problem der Freiheit," in GW, 11:952–72.

[3] Thomas Mann, "Schicksal und Aufgabe," in GW, 12:918–39.

[4] I am not aware of a single reference to these characters in the literature on *Doktor Faustus*. This is not surprising, given that nothing more than cursory attention is given to *Die Betrachtungen eines Unpolitischen*.

[5] Richard Wagner, *Die Meistersinger von Nürnberg* (Reinbek bei Hamburg: Rowohlt, 1981).

2: The Reception of *Die Betrachtungen eines Unpolitischen*

SOME CRITICS REJECT *DOKTOR FAUSTUS* on the grounds that it does not reflect the realities they themselves see as underlying the rise of National Socialism in Germany. But what if the novel was never intended to reflect such realities? It seems more reasonable to expect to find, not a broad historical account, but a specific, more personal account. Paul Egon Hübinger's historical study of the events surrounding the granting in 1919 and subsequent withdrawal in 1936 of Mann's honorary doctorate, *Thomas Mann, die Universität Bonn und die Zeitgeschichte* (1974),[1] looks specifically at Mann's relationship with the academic community in Munich during the 1920s. Since Adrian's relationship with this very group is the setting of the plot of *Doktor Faustus*, it seems advisable to explore the incident in some depth.

The Bonn Literary Society was founded in 1905. From its inception this group studied Thomas Mann's works more than those of any other author (*TMUB*, 26). It was unusual at the time to study living authors; moreover, Mann was still quite young, only thirty, really just beginning his career as a writer, when he became the center of attention of this society. The result was a close relationship between Mann and this circle (28). In 1919 the Society proposed Mann as candidate for an honorary degree (32) at the instigation of Ernst Bertram, Mann's very close friend at the time (51). Recognizing Mann in this way was quite extraordinary, because only once before, in 1856, had the University of Bonn given an honorary doctorate to a writer (35–36). Thus Mann was singled out by this group in two senses: not only were writers, in general, not considered for such honors, but living writers were not even considered worthy of academic interest. The diploma said that Mann was "[ein] Dichter von großen Gaben, der in strenger Selbstzucht und beseelt von einem starken Verantwortungsgefühl aus innerstem Erleben das Bild unserer Zeit für Mit- und Nachwelt zum Kunstwerk gestaltet hat" (34). There is no doubt that Mann was granted the degree for *Die Betrachtungen eines Unpolitischen*, although this was concealed for political reasons and the university said that it was given for *Buddenbrooks* (68), thus associating the two books.

As we have seen, in *Die Betrachtungen eines Unpolitischen* Mann waxes eloquent and venomous against France and French-style democracy and provides extensive arguments to justify his position. At this time Bonn was under French occupation and there was considerable trouble between the troops and the students. The university was under threat of closure, and it was thought that admitting that the degree was given for *Die Betrachtungen eines Unpolitischen* would certainly have brought this about. Even awarding the degree was seen as a demonstration against Versailles and Weimar.

Shortly after Mann received the honorary doctorate, Ernst Bertram published a study of *Die Betrachtungen eines Unpolitischen* in the 1920 edition of the society's journal.[2] In this article, he selectively interprets Mann's arguments as relevant to the political situation of the moment. If Bertram had not done this, the book would probably have gone unnoticed, since its relevance was not obvious to the current times, nor can *Die Betrachtungen eines Unpolitischen* be considered as directed to the general public. In his interpretation of the work, Bertram insinuated a subtle twist that adapts the arguments to a political mandate to reject democracy and adaptation to Europe, and to return instead to a mythical Romantic musical metaphysics. He did this by ignoring entirely Mann's central argument about the significance of individualism to German culture and the way in which this will influence the nature of German democracy. He argued first that, although, like *Buddenbrooks, Tonio Kröger,* and *Tod in Venedig,* it was written subjectively as a personal exploration of himself, it is simultaneously a biography of the German character in general, thus removing the subjectivity from the individual and applying it to the collectivity (99–100). Then he politicizes Mann's argument that Germany is the country of "the great man," once again meant by Mann to be an aspect of individualism that requires Germany to develop a functional democracy that does not define a goal. Bertram implies that the logical implication of the German admiration of "the great man" must now be applied to politics:

> Der Große Mensch — das ist die letzte Zitadelle seines Romantizismus.
> Und auch ihre Verteidigung ist eine Verteidigung fast ohne Hoffnung . . . , wo die geistige Herrscherlosigkeit des Volkes zum ersten Male nicht nur Tatsache geworden, sondern auch zur Parteiforderung gemacht wird. (115)

He argues that *Die Betrachtungen eines Unpolitischen* is an apocalypse only in the sense that Mann thought there were no longer great men to be found, tying this to the argument that mankind is made up of individuals (112–15). Bertram's interpretation of these arguments, and his application of them to the politics of the time, is a clear invitation to their further interpretation as arguments in favor of the fascism that was beginning to spread in academic circles, as is described by Joachim Fest in his chapter " 'Professor NSDAP': Die Intellektuellen und der Nationalsozialismus," in *Das Gesicht des Dritten Reichs.*[3] Bertram stresses the importance of Heinrich as the real target of Mann's wrath — not France, but the German traitor, whose determination was to undermine, and thus to destroy, the true character of Germany (102–4).

As early as 1910 Mann and Bertram were close friends and described as "aus einem Holz geschnitzt" as true expressions of the German character (*TMUB*, 55). Hübinger says that both Bertram's *Nietzsche* and Mann's *Die Betrachtungen eines Unpolitischen* were written while their authors were in constant consultation with each other, and it can be said that they were coauthors of both (53). This is confirmed by Mann's comment in his diary on 11 September 1918 that Bertram's *Nietzsche* is a sibling of *Die Betrachtungen eines Unpolitischen*, and that it makes the same central point.[4] It is clear from the surviving diaries of these years that Mann and Bertram were indeed very close friends. However, one gets the impression that during these years immediately after the war Mann was beginning to have reservations about Bertram and about the reception of *Die Betrachtungen eines Unpolitischen* in general, although he does not elaborate. His silence is eloquent.

Intellectual circles adopted the view that *Die Betrachtungen eines Unpolitischen* represented the true conservative spirit of the German people, expressing German rejection of democracy as incompatible with the German character, continues Hübinger. The professors at Bonn agreed with Mann's view that politics as the expression of 1789 were thoroughly unsavory, unsuitable for spiritual persons, and they seconded his praise of war, hatred of France, and hatred of "civilization." The book was seen as a definition and justification of the German rejection of the enlightenment era and its view of humanism and human rights (*TMUB*, 46). It was widely felt in Germany by the middle class and particularly by academics, both professors and students, that neither the military defeat nor the domestic political upset at the end of the First World War was acceptable. They found that, unlike Bismarck's work, the Weimar constitution had little German spirit (37). The educated middle classes thought that it was simply vulgar. According to Hübinger, the attitude was that "die Ausübung von Macht und der Anspruch auf politische Vorherrschaft ohne geistige Grundlage und kulturelle Leistung seien pure Rohheit" (43). These opinions could well be based on Bertram's interpretation of the book and do not necessarily reflect any acquaintance with the book itself.

Thomas Mann had indeed criticized French-style politics in the most vehement and absolute terms. *Die Betrachtungen eines Unpolitischen*, says Hübinger, was taken as an ideological national patriotic message. It was an expression of the eternal protest against the Roman world, an expression of humanity and the justification of the German soul against cold reason (48). Hübinger says that it was widely accepted at the time that in *Die Betrachtungen eines Unpolitischen* Mann was arguing that Germany had to find something new in politics, other than democracy: he did not want the rule of the proletariat (51). However, as shown above, to interpret his stand against Rousseau's democracy as a rejection of democracy itself reflects a complete misunderstanding of Mann's argument in *Die*

Betrachtungen eines Unpolitischen. Mann's only comment on governmental form is to dismiss it as not relevant. It is political approaches and attitudes that Mann discusses, not form. Kurt Sontheimer underlines this emphatically in his *Thomas Mann und die Deutschen* (Sontheimer, 43). In spite of its title, *Die Betrachtungen eines Unpolitischen* was taken as political dogma, says Hübinger (86). Nobody expected Mann to support the new democracy:

> Wem damals in Deutschland das Revolutionäre widerstand und wer dem Bewahrenden zuneigte, fand in jenem Buch sein geistiges Arsenal . . . Daß Thomas Mann sehr bald einen anderen Weg einschlagen sollte, konnten wir jungen Studenten es vermuten? Zahlreichen, wenn nicht den meisten Lesern der 1919/20 rasch bis zum 18. Tausend aufeinanderfolgenden Auflagen der "Betrachtungen" paßte es ausgezeichnet, dort haltzumachen, von wo aus der Dichter weiterging. (*TMUB*, 63)

However, in my opinion, the book was not understood as simply an argument against democracy. There is a strange and disturbing mystical, religious character given to its interpretation, as can be seen in Litzmann's words in 1920. According to him, Thomas Mann had been compelled to write the book, by a force he could not have resisted; in addition he had had a revelation that would be their salvation and a guide for the future. However, in Litzmann's opinion, Mann had misinterpreted this revelation:

> Es ist etwas über den Menschen gekommen, das zwang ihm die Feder in die Hand, und es erhob ihn über seine Zeit hinaus. Er sagte Dinge, wie der Mann in der Offenbarung, Dinge, die dunkel waren und die er falsch gedeutet hat. Aber er sah in diesem Dunkel Kräfte, die sich durchringen, die für uns Erlöser waren und für die kommenden Zeiten Erlöser sein werden. (*TMUB*, 69)

The misunderstanding, or misinterpretation, as it is usually called, appears to contain an element of deliberate reinterpretation and this is inherent right from the beginning. The following statement about Catholic support for Mann shows that the central point about Protestantism expressed in *Die Betrachtungen eines Unpolitischen* has been ignored: "Sie haben uns eine Geisteshaltung gezeigt, die in erbitterter Gegnerschaft gegen den aufklärerischen Geist und seine Nützlichkeitsmoral eine so hoch konservative und positive ist, daß wir, katholische Jugend, Sie im Kampfe gegen den modernen Geist ganz als den unsern beanspruchen können" (*TMUB*, 64).

Both of these comments show distortions of Mann's views. Litzmann talks about dark powers that will be the salvation of Germany. There are no dark powers mentioned in *Die Betrachtungen eines Unpolitischen*. It is preposterous to associate Mann's work, or even his very being, with dark powers, unless (remembering Nietzsche's observation, mentioned above) men of genius, or of outstanding intellect, have some magic ability that enables them to acquire knowledge through supernatural channels. Possibly the comment refers to *Innerlichkeit*, that much-used and rarely explained term describing some inner quality that distinguishes the Germans from other peoples, perhaps what Bertram describes as "die Musik als die metaphysische und damit als die deutsche Form der Freiheit, der 'Freiheit von der Welt.'"[5] However, what Mann means by the term is specifically, and nothing more or less than, the Protestant consulting his conscience to determine what is right and what is wrong as compared with the Roman Catholic consulting a priest, or dogma. If Litzmann, as he says, thinks Mann misinterpreted these dark powers, there is nothing left of Mann's argument. The Catholic comment transfers the pragmatic approach that Mann advocates as suitable for government to the very political enlightenment tendencies that he opposes and substitutes some kind of obscurantism for Mann's pragmatism. Mann does not define music as metaphysical, but as form. He rejects the application of metaphysics to politics. Today we would describe this as the separation of Church and State. Here we have a concrete example of the play with oppositions that underlies *Doktor Faustus* and *Die Betrachtungen eines Unpolitischen*. Mann's opposition between Rousseau's enlightenment democracy and a democracy based on individual freedom has been read as an opposition between enlightenment and obscurantism. Mann was assumed to be a spokesman for the incipient fascist movement that would eventually crystallize as support for National Socialism.

Right from the beginning in 1905 this group had revered Mann in quite an extraordinary way, and with the appearance of *Die Betrachtungen eines Unpolitischen* he was raised to an unreasonable level of religious adoration and treated as a national hero. In other words, he was looked on as the equivalent of a saint. He was put in a flattering position, which he very soon realized was based on a misunderstanding. Although he did say much of what they said he had said, their interpretation reflects a very selective, somewhat fanciful reading of the book. His arguments were taken out of context and enthusiastically, if diabolically, carried forward.

* * *

In 1922, in the speech "Von Deutscher Republik,"[6] Mann publicly advocated supporting the Weimar Republic and warned of the dangers inherent in fascism. In this speech he specifically addresses the prevailing misinterpretation of his *Die Betrachtungen eines Unpolitischen*, but it is apparent from the tone of this speech that Mann is facing a very hostile audience. After four years of misinterpretation and extrapolations based on this misinterpretation, an atmosphere had been created that was not receptive to reconsideration. As Erich Kahler points out, the book is too abstract for ordinary comprehension. It reached the public through filters and its arguments became half-truths. Also, it arrived on the scene too late to be effective, because political and social developments had already taken another course. The distinction between what he said and what they said he said became blurred and nobody would listen to him.[7]

In fact, Mann did not say anything different in this speech from what he had said in *Die Betrachtungen eines Unpolitischen*. It does, however, certainly sound different. He has used a whole new set of illustrations of his point, but, most important, he has changed his use of the word "democracy." Here he uses the word to apply clearly to the kind of government he described as the natural sort of government for Germany in *Die Betrachtungen eines Unpolitischen*, while he continues to differentiate it from Rousseau's "democracy." The initial idolizing of Mann and his political writings essentially derives from the combination of his rejection of France and everything French, together with an identification of the Weimar Republic with French-style democracy. It is this identification that Mann refused to make. He saw the principal danger for Germany in the probability that people would think that Rousseau's democracy was the only possible kind of democracy, which is exactly what happened in this circle.

Mann's defense of democracy is now based on the American model, and no longer on his own abstract theories. In *Die Betrachtungen eines Unpolitischen* he seems to have been quite ignorant about the nature of democracy in the United States. In the interval his friend Hans Reisiger had translated Walt Whitman into German.[8] As can be seen from his article, "Hans Reisiger's Whitman Werk," Mann recognized the similarities of what Whitman says about democracy with what he himself says in *Die Betrachtungen eines Unpolitischen* about the form of democracy that would be desirable for Germany: a pragmatic, non-ideological system of order, based on individualism, and he refers to these arguments in "Von Deutscher Republik."[9] As he had argued in *Die Betrachtungen eines Unpolitischen*, it is a question of attitude, not of form. He argues that the only alternative for Germany is to cooperate in the development of the Weimar Republic to make it truly reflect German values, looking to the future rather than to the past. He warns specifically against the reactionary nationalist movement developing in France. To oppose the new Republic is vulgar obscurantism and reaction, he says. It is sentimental, a combination of Romanticism with enlightenment raised to the level of terrorism (VDR, 818). This is, of course, also a synthesis of "the word" with "the music," of the eighteenth with the nineteenth century.

Mann's speech was made to a very hostile audience, largely university students and professors. There was some hope that he would return to the fold at first, says Hübinger (*TMUB*, 87), but the aversion to Thomas Mann started then. It was personal hatred; he was considered to be unreliable. Most of this hatred was centered in Munich circles, where Mann was considered to be a renegade (89–91). Aversion to Mann was not specifically National Socialist, but came just as much from right-wing nationalists, and during the 1920s the major newspapers in Munich were overwhelmingly against him. Opposition reached its highest point when he was awarded the Nobel Prize in 1929.[10] Hitler nurtured a particular hatred of Thomas Mann. This hatred was carried to such an extreme that, in 1937, the fact that Ida Herz was one of his admirers was considered to be sufficient reason for the withdrawal of her citizenship (*TMUB*, 179).

Mann was naturally not very pleased with the situation he was placed in. He interpreted it as a moral obligation to participate actively on the political scene. On 25 May 1926 he wrote to Ernst Fischer:

> Ich glaube, daß ein Künstler nicht verpflichtet ist, . . . ein Lehrer und Führer zu sein. Ich sagte schon, daß ein Künstler gelegentlich in diese Rolle gedrängt wird und sie dann, so gut es gehen will, ausfüllen und darin genügen muß. Sein Beruf, seine Natur, besteht aber nicht im Lehren, Urteilen, Wege weisen, sondern im Sein, im Tun, im Ausdrücken von Seelenlagen.[11]

In 1925 Mann declared the Social Democratic Party Germany's most suitable party; in 1928 he described himself as a socialist, and at the 1930 election he asked the German public to support the Social Democrats. However, his apparently non-political activities were much more important in feeding this personal hostility. During these years, Mann gave speeches all over Germany, using every opportunity to put forward his arguments against fascism, no matter what the purported subject of his talk. In these speeches he countered the fascist reinterpretation of German literature. He made several trips abroad participating in cultural exchange programs for the promotion of German reintegration to Europe. He found such activities distasteful, but did them, nevertheless, out of a sense of responsibility. He resented the time it took away from his work. It was these activities abroad that were the main cause of the hostility against him. He was considered to be presenting himself, not as Thomas Mann, but as the personification of German culture, and this portrayal was deemed to be false.

The hatred came to its predictable peak in 1933 after Hitler became chancellor. Mann gave a speech on Wagner, which was well received, for a festive occasion in Munich.[12] However, he was attacked in the Munich press when he gave the speech abroad. In February, before Hitler had become chancellor, there had been favorable reviews of this same talk (*TMUB*, 128). In April 1933, following his presentation of the talk in Amsterdam, the "Protest der Richard-Wagner-Stadt München" was published in the *Münchner Neuesten*, a conservative nationalist, not a National Socialist, newspaper. Karl Voßler reacted by describing the protest, which claimed the speech defamed Wagner, as vulgar opportunism, partly stupid and partly against the better knowledge of the protestors. He had heard

Mann's talk and praised it (*TMUB*, 129). Rolf von Hoerschelmann said it was "kaum glaubliche Tragikomödie" because the talk had been given to an overfull auditorium and received with enthusiastic applause. Mann claimed that the attack was a great injustice since they had taken sentences out of context. He expressed doubt that they had even read the text and concluded that the attack was a personal attack against his character.[13]

In Hübinger's view the protest was a calculated political move against Mann's person and had nothing to do with his so-called defamation of Wagner. The evidence of the speech itself fully supports this conclusion. There is virtually nothing in it that can be politically interpreted, and this at a time when Mann was speaking out very strongly against National Socialism in his other speeches. The originators of the protest were members of the Munich intellectual group of which Mann was a member. The text of the protest included the following statement: "Herr Mann . . . hat das Unglück erlitten . . . , seine früher nationale Gesinnung bei der Errichtung der Republik einzubüßen und mit einer kosmopolitisch-demokratischen Auffassung zu vertauschen" (*TMUB*, 130–32). The protest revived the old charge that Mann had "purged" *Die Betrachtungen eines Unpolitischen*, and the repetition of this charge in the spring of 1933 can only be understood as a clear denunciation, for the purpose of declaring Mann an enemy of Germany. Certainly it had nothing to do with Wagner. Mann, on the advice of his children, wisely stayed out of Germany, and in August his property was confiscated (*TMUB*, 130–32). Hübinger believes that the intention of the protest was to have Mann arrested and sent to Dachau, an opinion shared by Mann. In a letter to Otto Basler, he said: "[Es] könnte . . . leicht sein, daß man in einem deutschen Konzentrationslager exerzieren müßte" (133). The following year he wrote in a petition to the Ministry of the Interior: "die furchtbare Denunziation [des] Protests [hätte mich], wäre ich zufällig an Ort und Stelle gewesen, . . . Gesundheit und Leben kosten können" (133). Hübinger concludes that this protest, which was signed by many of Mann's previous good friends, was the decisive factor in the denunciation of Mann as an enemy of the people.[14]

* * *

The probability that Mann would have ended up in a concentration camp is in all likelihood not exaggerated, since it was a common consequence of opposing National Socialism. For example, Carl von Ossietzky, a journalist who spoke out very strongly against National Socialism in *Die Weltbühne* in the summer of 1930, was arrested and tortured. This was long before Hitler became chancellor. Ossietzky was later set free, but effectively silenced, since his health was destroyed in the prison camp, and he died, a weak and broken man, a few years later. There were many similar cases, but Mann isolated Ossietzky and made an example of him, writing in 1932 that the judgment against Ossietzky was terrible and humiliating, because justice was corroborating in the forceful silencing of opposition to the fascist dictatorship.[15] In 1936 he wrote to the Nobel Prize Committee in Oslo supporting Ossietzky's candidature for the Nobel Prize, on the grounds that he was a martyr to freedom. Mann said that, unfortunately, after three years in a concentration camp he was no longer presentable and would not be able to receive the prize personally.[16] In 1938, on Ossietzky's death, Mann wrote that he had become a symbol for the suffering of the free intellect. His death was accelerated by the revenge taken against him and it was possible that in time his struggle for humanity would become legendary.[17]

* * *

The explanation given by his contemporaries for Mann's opposition to fascism is that he was arrogant, deceitful, and an opportunist. They claimed that with *Die Betrachtungen eines Unpolitischen* he had provided a sound basis for the movement and been honored for it. Then, for no rational reason, he had turned against the very movement he had contributed to creating and become a traitor to the cause. He was simply lying for his own personal advantage and giving himself airs. Joseph Roth wrote the following to Stefan Zweig in August 1933:

> Es ist doch nicht richtig. . . . Ich habe Thomas Manns über den Wassern Schweben nie gemocht. Ein Goethe ist er nicht. Er hat nicht das Recht zu solchen Aussprüchen. . . . Thomas Mann ist ein Usurpator der "Objektivität." Er ist imstande, mit Hitler sich auszusöhnen, unter uns gesagt. Es ist ihm nur unmöglich gemacht, vorläufig. Er ist einer jener Menschen, die Alles erlauben, unter dem Vorwand, Alles zu verstehen.[18]

It is also clear that hindsight, based on the outrage of his former associates at his opposition to fascism, led to a retroactive negative reinterpretation of his entire life. The following appeared in a literary journal in 1933: "Der große Aufbruch deutschen Geistes im Jahre 1933 [hat] ihn in rettungslose Einsamkeit geworfen [und er ist — schon seit seinen Anfängen] dem Organisch-Synthetischen echter deutscher Art immer fremd geblieben [— nun hat er] jede Verbindung mit seinem Volke verloren" (*TMUB*, 135).

Such a fall, from the heights of sainthood to the depths of treason, requires a further explanation. How can a saint become the Devil's advocate? There must have been an outside cause. In the 5 December 1936 issue of Cologne's *Der Westdeutsche Beobachter*, these lines appeared:

> In dem Augenblick, da Thomas Mann mit seinen "Unpolitischen Betrachtungen" anfing, politisch zu werden, horchten wir auf und wurden

uns klar, daß hier etwas nicht stimmen könne. [Später sei dann Thomas Mann,] der mittlerweile eine Jüdin geheiratet hatte, vollends zum Stammgast literarischer Verbrecherkeller geworden. (*TMUB*, 183–84)

In the same year another newspaper contributor wrote: "An dem Beispiel der dekadenten halbjüdischen Literatenfamilie Mann wird uns der Abstand klar, den unser Volk heute von dieser Art Aesthetentum genommen hat. . . . Thomas Mann hat sich . . . heute auf seinen ureigentlichen geistigen Nährboden, das Judentum, zurückgezogen" (*TMUB*, 184).

Ernst Krieck, a prominent National Socialist educator, writing in 1937, was even more denunciatory:

> Thomas Mann lügt vor sich selbst, vor der Welt und vor der Geschichte. Wer ist der Gott, bei dem Thomas Mann schwört? Nach seinen Josephs-Romanen und andern Bekenntnissen muß angenommen werden: er schwört bei Jehova, er schwört bei jenem Widergott, der heute im jüdischen Bolschewismus zum bösen, zum zerstörerischen Prinzip der Menschheit geworden ist. Thomas Mann schwört bei Beelzebub, der nicht der Gott des deutschen Volkes ist. Thomas Mann schwört beim Gott der Verwesung und der Lüge. Was Thomas Mann in letzter Zeit unternommen hat, das ist die Selbstenthüllung des von Jugend auf in ihm wohnenden zerstörerischen Prinzips. Am Tun eines Menschen erkennen wir die Art seines Gottes, zu dem er betet und bei dem er schwört.[19]

This last comment made a very profound impression on Mann. In his 1945 article "Warum ich nicht nach Deutschland zurückgehe"[20] he mentions it specifically as an answer to this question. One simply could not live in a society where there were people who thought in this way.

In the end, for most German commentators of the time, opposition to National Socialism was tantamount to Judaism. Hitler, as we know, called the Jews a syphilitic contamination of the Aryan people.

✳ ✳ ✳

In the context of Mann's life and works, the argument cannot be sustained that *Die Betrachtungen eines Unpolitischen* is nothing more than an insignificant polemical tract against his brother Heinrich and that it is irrational. In fact, it is the expression of Mann's basic political philosophy and the source of most of the arguments he used in his fight against fascism. His contemporaries considered it very important, so much so that he was looked on as a national hero when it appeared and the book was used for educational and propaganda purposes. Its greatest impact on Mann's life, however, derived undoubtedly from the repercussions of its original enthusiastic reception and misuse. It became the major factor determining his life from then on. The persecution of Mann by National Socialism was not primarily because he was a political opponent, but rather because he was deemed to have betrayed the cause. He lived for years in a hostile environment of hatred, vilification, isolation, and ultimately the threat of death at the instigation of his former friends, an experience that undoubtedly greatly colored his impression of the period.

Mann's story, as described above, cannot really be interpreted as a cause of fascism, but is rather more an illustration of its effect. It is an illustration of how fascism led to irrational and emotionally determined behavior on the part of the academic community, releasing a degree of barbarism that is inconceivable in sane circumstances. It is all very well to consider Mann's attitude hypocritical and self-seeking. It is of quite a different order to consider that either hypocrisy or a difference of opinion, whichever it was, justifies the kind of persecution that these people clearly perpetrated.

Notes

[1] Paul Egon Hübinger, *Thomas Mann, die Universität Bonn und die Zeitgeschichte* (Munich: Oldenbourg, 1974). Subsequent references to this book will be indicated in the text with a page number and, if necessary, the abbreviation *TMUB*.

[2] A reprint of this article can be found in Ernst Bertram, *Dichtung als Zeugnis* (Bonn: Bouvier, 1967), 99–118.

[3] Joachim Fest, *Das Gesicht des Dritten Reiches* (1963; rpt., Munich: Piper, 1993), 338–55.

[4] Thomas Mann, *Tagebücher, 1918–21* (Frankfurt am Main: Fischer, 1977), 3.

[5] Bertram, *Dichtung als Zeugnis*, 106.

[6] Thomas Mann, "Von Deutscher Republik," in *GW*, 11:809–52. Subsequent references to this work will be indicated with a parenthetical page number and, if necessary, the abbreviation VDR.

[7] Erich Kahler, *The Orbit of Thomas Mann* (Princeton: Princeton UP, 1969), 11–12.

[8] Thomas Mann, *Tagebücher, 1918–21*, 524, entry for 31 May, 1921.

[9] Thomas Mann, "Hans Reisigers Whitman-Werk," in *GW*, 10:626–27.

[10] Hübinger gives a list in a footnote of the extraordinary number of articles that appeared in the press in the 1920s attacking Mann (91). It is almost an entire page long.

[11] Thomas Mann, *Briefe, 1889–1936* (Frankfurt am Main: Fischer, 1961), 256.

[12] Thomas Mann, "Leiden und Größe Richard Wagners," *GW*, 9:363–428.

[13] Thomas Mann, "Erwiderung," in *GW*, 11:785–87.

[14] "[Der] Protest der Richard-Wagner-Stadt München . . . hatte die — von dem nationalsozialistischen Regime in unzähligen Fällen ähnlich virtuos aufgebaute oder ausgenutzte — publizistische Kulisse geschaffen, die ein totalitäres

Herrschaftssystem für seine Verfolgungsmaßnahmen und Gewaltstreiche als öffentliche Legitimation schätzt" (*TMUB*, 135).

[15] Thomas Mann, "Zum Urteil des Reichsgerichts, Leipzig, im 'Weltbühnen'-Prozess gegen Carl von Ossietzky," in *GW*, 12:677–78.

[16] Thomas Mann, "An das Nobel-Friedenpreis-Comité, Oslo," in *GW*, 12:779–83.

[17] Thomas Mann, "Zum Tode Carl von Ossietzkys," in *GW*, 12:825.

[18] Joseph Roth, *Briefe, 1911–1939* (Berlin: Kiepenheuer & Witsch, 1970), 276–77.

[19] Ernst Krieck, "Agonie: Schlußwort zu Thomas Mann," *Volk im Werden* 5 (March 1937): 121–25; here, 122.

[20] Thomas Mann, "Warum ich nicht nach Deutschland zurückgehe," in *GW*, 12:958–59.

3: The Significance of *Die Betrachtungen eines Unpolitischen* for *Doktor Faustus*

O NE OF THE OUTSTANDING CHARACTERISTICS OF *Doktor Faustus* is the violence of the emotions expressed, a much greater violence than in any other of Mann's novels. Mann tends, when discussing emotions, to be analytical and detached, but not here. *Doktor Faustus* expresses extreme degrees of hatred, frustration, anguish, and helplessness. The atmosphere is heavy with misunderstanding and innuendo, the emotion immediate and personal. Mann is experiencing his suffering and frustrations of the 1920s and 1930s all over again in his portrayal of Adrian's suffering. He is anything but kind in the novel to his former friends.

The relationship of *Doktor Faustus* with *Die Betrachtungen eines Unpolitischen* is not limited to the use of the same metaphors — music and theology as expressions of politics — to the same underlying disagreement on the nature of humanism, and to the parallel between the misinterpretation and misuse of Adrian's music in *Doktor Faustus* and that of Mann's *Betrachtungen eines Unpolitischen* in real life. In *Die Betrachtungen eines Unpolitischen* the two opposing social philosophies are presented in the form of personification. Mann describes them as individuals with different attitudes towards life and society. They are personalities, caricatures of types we all see every day (and not just in Germany), and they are opposites in almost every respect. The context in which Mann has presented these personalities is political, and he describes these characteristics — not necessarily political in themselves — as determining their political stand. He is quite specific about this: the *Zivilisationsliterat*, or the Catholic humanist, is the potential totalitarian and the Protestant artist is the liberal democrat, the advocate of the open society. Thus, when we see these characters in Mann's work, we know, because we have been told, what their politics will be, should politics come into question. There are innumerable small details in the novel that point to this parallel. The same characters with all their identifying idiosyncrasies, described in details illustrative of their political inclinations, are carefully reproduced in *Doktor Faustus*. In fact, in this sense, Zeitblom and Adrian are stock characters, symbols of two important intellectual approaches to politics prevalent in Germany at the time portrayed in the novel. A closer look shows that not only are their characteristics the same, but the relationship between them is also almost the same as their relationship in *Die Betrachtungen eines Unpolitischen*. Zeitblom, an associate who is almost as close to Adrian as a brother, has replaced Heinrich, the *Zivilisationsliterat*.

I posit that the characterizations in *Die Betrachtungen eines Unpolitischen* can be shown from the text to apply accurately to the characterizations in *Doktor Faustus*. These characterizations are established in the early part of the novel. The importance of this parallel does not become apparent until the events turn political, when the differences between the two determine their different reactions to historical events. The following summary of these oppositions in character, as found in *Die Betrachtungen eines Unpolitischen*, is expressed here as an opposition between Zeitblom and Adrian, using the definitions of the *Zivilisationsliterat* and the Protestant artist from the earlier work. It makes statements about the two that will later be substantiated in the textual analysis. However, the truth of these statements is not a particularly controversial point. What is controversial is their significance. The application of these parallels and of the significance to Mann of these differences in worldview for the interpretation of *Doktor Faustus* leads to an interpretation of the novel that diverges radically from the standard interpretation and that resolves many of the contradictions that have confounded critics in the past.

Zeitblom is a humanist, but Adrian finds his kind of humanism inhuman. Adrian expresses his dislike of Zeitblom's humanism clearly and describes it as medieval. Zeitblom, on the other hand, describes this rejection of his humanism as evidence of Adrian's inhumanity. Zeitblom is a literary man, a philologist, a classicist, a specialist in rhetoric, whereas Adrian is clumsy with speech (*BeU*, 50). Zeitblom considers Adrian's frequent difficulty with speech a symptom of sickness and is forever stressing his own ability with language. Adrian is a musician and Zeitblom is distrustful of music and musicians. His tastes are French eighteenth-century, whereas Adrian's are German nineteenth-century (391–93). Besides the very symbolic viola d'amore, this is a recurring motif and is emphasized in chapter 24. Everything surrounding Adrian is modeled after Dürer, Mann's model for the true German character (114). Zeitblom interprets these Dürer associations as manifestations of psychological disorder. Zeitblom is a moralist, basing his morality on abstract concepts and the fashionable views of the moment (491–92). He takes no personal responsibility and is not concerned about truth (387). Adrian, on the other hand, is moral, as distinct from being a moralist. He lives in a state of doubt and guilt, taking on everybody's guilt as his own and, at the end of the novel, is presented as a Christ figure (295–96). Zeitblom is self-righteous and respectable, always has an opinion about everything, and is always right, whereas Adrian reserves judgment and observes (490). Zeitblom assumes that Adrian shares his judgments, whereas there is clear evidence throughout the novel that this is rarely the case. Zeitblom does not like deviation from the norm, which he regards as immoral, and sees German Protestant culture, as illustrated in Adrian, as a deviation from the norm, which for him is Latin. Adrian values individualism and the right to be himself above all things. That is what he means by freedom. Zeitblom is extremely critical of this individualism, describing it as anti-social and arrogant. Finally, Zeitblom has a great aversion to the elementary, except in one respect — sex. He has a sexual explanation for everything (464–65). The main ingredients of his philosophy are rhetoric, psychology, and eroticism (303). He considers himself an expert on human nature and is constantly making psychological analyses to explain the behavior of those around him, virtually always in erotic terms. The characteristics that Zeitblom does not like in Adrian are the characteristics of the German Protestant artist, such as having a sense of humor, being dedicated to his work, and protecting his solitude and individualism and above all his freedom, not to mention Adrian's inhuman disregard of the erotic. Zeitblom finds these characteristics suspicious or indications of immorality. The character described as the *Zivilisationsliterat* does not like the specifically German characteristics of the German Protestant artist: "Man ist nicht Literat, ohne von Instinkt die 'Besonderheit' Deutschlands zu verabscheuen" (56). Most critics agree with Zeitblom that Adrian is unacceptable, yet understand Adrian's Protestant characteristics as indications of his pact with the Devil and with fascism.

Zeitblom does his best to paint Adrian black, but in fact the Protestant artist does not much like the *Zivilisationsliterat* either. He tolerates him, because he does not feel it is his role to change mankind. It is an unequal struggle, because the *Zivilisationsliterat*, while posing as respectable and a moralist, is in fact intolerant and imposes his views with little regard for truth or reality. Mann makes it very clear in *Die Betrachtungen eines Unpolitischen* that he does not like the *Zivilisationsliterat* (21). In chapter 1 of *Doktor Faustus* Zeitblom makes it clear that Adrian does not like him (*DF*, 12). This is, of course, very obvious throughout the novel. The fact that Zeitblom sees this as a criticism of Adrian rather than of himself does not change the fact that Mann has made this dislike the starting point of the novel. It does not seem to occur to anyone to ask why he does not like him.

Nevertheless, it is one thing to accept Zeitblom's view that it is a sign of immorality to have a sense of humor, that living moderately and getting on with your work is asceticism, and that Dürer melancholy is a symptom of madness, but quite another to go so far as to ascribe such views to Mann. Mann's characterizations of the *Zivilisationsliterat* and the German Protestant artist, as expressed in *Die Betrachtungen eines Unpolitischen*, appear clearly in *Doktor Faustus*. The difference is that Mann expresses these opinions in *Doktor Faustus* from the point of view of the *Zivilisationsliterat*, who expresses his own character positively rather than negatively and the opinions of the Protestant artist negatively rather than positively. Zeitblom has not been defined as representing views that Mann held, but as representing those views that Mann thought destroyed Germany as he anticipated would happen. This characterization is established very clearly in the novel up to the period of the end of the First World War and the appearance of Adrian's *Apocalipsis cum figuris*, parallel with the time when Mann published *Die Betrachtungen eines Unpolitischen* in his own life.

* * *

As early as 1934 Mann showed his determination to wreak literary revenge on National Socialism for its treatment of him. On April 2 of that year Mann wrote to René Schickele that he was thinking of writing a novel that, as Hübinger says, would be a counterpart to *Die Betrachtungen eines Unpolitischen* (245–46). On 10 August 1934 he again wrote to Schickele that he was tempted to immediately throw all reservations to the wind and write a book against the regime that it could not ignore. This book would be "Revanche für alle . . . erlittene geistige Unbill."[1] Mann's fury at National Socialism came to a peak with the withdrawal of his citizenship in 1936 and of his honorary doctorate by the University of Bonn in 1937 and was particularly directed against those who had adopted and distorted *Die Betrachtungen eines Unpolitischen*, then turned on him, the members of the Bonn Literary Society. However, he did not write his book at that point. He decided to put it off, since it would undoubtedly have resulted in the banning of his books in Germany and his complete severance from his German readers (*TMUB*, 245–46). In 1934 there was no way of knowing if or when National Socialism would come to an end in Germany. On January 13, 1934, Peter Suhrkamp reported that Mann had written:

> Es ist mein dringender Wunsch, mit Deutschland und meinen deutschen Lesern verbunden zu bleiben, und ich würde es für einen Fehler der deutschen Machthaber halten, wenn sie mich durch die Forderung unmöglicher Bekenntnisse ins Emigrantenlager drängten. (*TMUB*, 246)

Not until May 1943, when Germany surrendered in North Africa, opening the way for the Allied landing in Sicily and the foreseeable defeat of Germany and, consequently, the collapse of National Socialism, did Mann begin to write *Doktor Faustus*. He is very specific about the date.

The above statements of intention are clearly a far more important indication of what *Doktor Faustus* is about than Mann's 1904 diary entry to the effect that he was mulling over the idea of a syphilitic Faust. The experience of the First World War, the events of the 1920s and 1930s, the collapse of German society, the advent of fascism, and the deliberate, specific, and public rejection of Mann by his own friends and colleagues completely changed the significance of the idea and made it political, rendering the syphilis quite redundant in its original sense and endowing it with a totally different meaning. Michael Mann argues that the story obviously has nothing to do with the original idea of the diabolical and destructive freeing from inhibitions through intoxication.[2] At the time of the 1904 entry in his diary, Mann may or may not have been thinking of Nietzsche's life, highly probable though this may be. One can see that a study of the diabolical reversal of moral values as a result of madness induced by syphilis would have appealed to Mann in 1904. However, in *Die Betrachtungen eines Unpolitischen* Mann expresses concern that the *Zivilisationsliterat* of the twentieth century was basing many of his political ideas on an acceptance of Nietzsche's later work, on statements that were probably to some extent influenced by his approaching madness. It is the political application of this understanding of Nietzsche that Mann associated with fascism (210). There is no doubt that Nietzsche and his effects, both positive and negative, were very important to Mann's understanding of the period. There is no doubt that this ambivalent shadow of Nietzsche hovers over the novel. In *Doktor Faustus* both Adrian and Zeitblom are Mann's contemporaries and the society they live in has become politicized, which completely changes the importance of Nietzsche. Like Mann's and Nietzsche's work, not to mention Wagner's, Adrian's work was interpreted politically, completely changing its nature, and used by National Socialism in a corrupted form. Mann wrote *Doktor Faustus* not simply about Nietzsche, but about his own similar and much more immediate case, having learned, from bitter personal experience, that it was not necessary to have syphilis or to go mad to write things that could be turned on themselves and become their opposites. Mann did not consider himself mad, but many of his contemporaries did. This is not to say that the character of Adrian as presented in the novel does not reflect the influence of Nietzsche, but his political opinions, professional activities, and relationship to Munich intellectual society represent Mann specifically, as one version of the modern product of these influences. Zeitblom, I propose, also represents Nietzsche, but in a different interpretation. The proposed Faust novel about Nietzsche was overtaken by events and became something very different from what it was to have been in the beginning. Mann makes the point in his essay on Lessing that you cannot extrapolate anything about how a person would react outside his epoch on the basis of arguments formulated in his own time.[3] The atmosphere of rising fascism in Germany during the 1920s cannot be compared with the political environment Nietzsche knew. We can view the novel as being about Nietzsche only insofar as it is a novel about Nietzsche's influence.

* * *

The importance of *Die Betrachtungen eines Unpolitischen* in Mann's life cannot be overestimated. It is the decisive factor in his own story throughout the period portrayed in the novel. It is my argument that the glorification of Mann and of the book and the subsequent conflict between Mann and the Munich academic community, generated by the disagreement on the interpretation by the Bonn Literary Society of *Die Betrachtungen eines Unpolitischen* and ending in the attempt to have him arrested as politically undesirable, is reflected in the plot of *Doktor Faustus*. All Zeitblom's comments about what Adrian says and does in the second part of the novel — and what he is doing is supporting the Weimar Republic — are accompanied by some expression of his conviction that Adrian is saying the opposite of what he really believes. The first part of the novel establishes what Adrian believes and shows that Zeitblom does not understand him but interprets his views as their opposites, or, when he cannot explain them away, as a reflection of demonic influence or a psychological disorder.

Adrian's arguments are found in *Die Betrachtungen eines Unpolitischen*, reflecting Mann's views as expressed in the person of the Protestant artist. It seems to me evident that Adrian's arguments represent Mann's view of nineteenth-century liberal humanism as distinct from Catholic humanism. Underlying virtually all interpretations of *Doktor Faustus* is the assumption that Zeitblom and not Adrian represents liberal humanism, which is simply not the case, if the argument is based on Mann's understanding of the word. Zeitblom represents the Catholic humanist, the character condemned by Mann in *Die Betrachtungen eines Unpolitischen* as an intolerant pedant. Mann has not been subtle about this in *Doktor Faustus*. Zeitblom defines his own principal characteristics in chapter 2, where he presents himself as a Catholic, a humanist, and a philologist, a pedant. He says his thinking has been influenced by his Catholic training and that there is no contradiction between his Catholicism and his humanism (*DF*, 15). The humanists Zeitblom mentions as his models (*DF*, 10) are those who opposed Luther.[4] Zeitblom's humanism is, therefore, Catholic humanism. These characteristics in Zeitblom are not figurative, but literal, and they are stressed, much more unequivocally than are Adrian's characteristics. The significance of Zeitblom's Catholicism and humanism is completely misunderstood by critics, since Mann clearly means these to be understood as negative, not as positive characteristics.

Implicit in the general assumption that humanism is a "good thing" is the absolute rejection of any relationship between humanism and fascism. That is all very well, but Mann did not think so, and, while disagreement on this point may be a legitimate reason for rejecting the message of the novel, it is not a legitimate reason for misinterpreting it. In fact, surprising though it may perhaps seem to today's reader, most German Freemasons did support National Socialism.[5] Freemasonry is the archetypal humanist organization, as described by Mann in *Der Zauberberg*, in the person of Settembrini. It was not humanism that was rejected by the German

Freemasons, but the idea that this could be achieved through internationalism. The goals of humanism would have to be realized by Germany alone and National Socialism was seen as the true road to this noble end. It was not, in the eyes of the German Freemasons, Germany that abandoned humanism, but the Entente countries, which had, out of self-interest and a narrow racist view, abandoned the basic precepts of humanism with their vindictive behavior against Germany.[6] The hostility of the major lodges of the Freemasons against opponents of National Socialism was specifically directed against those involved in the very activities that Adrian and Schwerdtfeger participate in:

> Wir würden den Deutschen verachten, dem die Ehre seines Volkes so wenig gilt, daß er die Schmach und die Unbill, die Deutschland durch und nach dem Versailler Diktat erlitten hat, so vergessen kann, daß er mit Angehörigen eines anderen Volkes in Verkehr treten kann, ehe dieses nicht das uns zugefügte Unrecht rückhaltlos anerkennt. Für die Erneuerung und die Wiederherstellung der Ehre unseres Volkes zu kämpfen, ist eine der ersten sittlichen Pflichten unseres Bundes.[7]

* * *

There are still today those, such as Hermann Kurzke, who are convinced that *Die Betrachtungen eines Unpolitischen* is an argument against democracy and attribute Mann's support for democracy during the Weimar Republic to a reversal of his original argument out of arrogant self-interest, in spite of the fact that it was not in his own interest, was very time-consuming, and made his life extremely unpleasant.[8] Kurzke is convinced that Mann's later antifascist stand was hypocritical.[9] The present study is based on an understanding of Mann's views and behavior that is in contradiction to the view of Kurzke and others. Mann always claimed that he had been arguing for democracy and that *Die Betrachtungen eines Unpolitischen* had been misinterpreted, a claim I find to be fully substantiated. This situation provides the basis of the novel in my argument. However, the position taken by Kurzke and Mann's contemporaries — that Mann's views were fascist and that he was hypocritical and self-interested in supporting the Weimar Republic, and had betrayed those who had trusted him for guidance — is equally the basis of the novel. It is the position of the narrator. Therefore Kurzke's interpretation of *Die Betrachtungen eines Unpolitischen*, although directly opposed to the interpretation offered here, should not affect the interpretation of *Doktor Faustus*, except in the specifically relevant point: is Adrian advocating democracy or is his later defense of democracy hypocritical? In *Doktor Faustus* Mann plays with these two points of view. He gives his/Adrian's opponent, his close associate Zeitblom, the predominant voice, and Zeitblom's view of Adrian is very similar to Kurzke's view of Mann. In the interpretation offered here, Adrian remains isolated and frustrated in the background and in the end he is silenced, as was Mann. Interpretations based on understanding Adrian's views as fascist do not explain the events of the novel, because they do not follow through the nature of his association with Zeitblom, and they ignore what is actually going on. This seems to be the result of the refusal to consider that it may be Zeitblom who represents fascism. The story that Zeitblom is telling in his hagiography is the story of the promising genius who went wrong. There is a strong element of personal revenge in Zeitblom's account. He feels his hero has betrayed him. This is very apparent towards the end of the novel. In *Doktor Faustus* it is Zeitblom who ultimately supports National Socialism and Adrian who opposes it. This story is consistent with either interpretation of *Die Betrachtungen eines Unpolitischen*, but only if it is understood that Zeitblom supports fascism on what he deems to be Adrian's authority and that what Zeitblom describes as Adrian's ultimate madness is his rejection of National Socialism. Contrary to commonly accepted opinion, I contend that *Doktor Faustus* is essentially the story of the rejection of the most German of all Germans by the Germans themselves. The academics who supported fascism deliberately rejected traditional German liberal values, as represented by Adrian, and destroyed them. I see no evidence in the novel to suggest that it was these Protestant values that led to fascism, but what seems to me to be very clear and unambiguous evidence in chapter 34 (*Fortsetzung*), which Mann himself has described as pure fascism,[10] that the rejection of these values was essential to fascism. It is well known that the principle academic support for fascism was from literary scholars like Zeitblom, such as Ernst Bertram, who were deliberately rewriting the history of German literature to bring it into line with fascist thought. What could not be adapted was burned.

I suggest that the message of *Doktor Faustus* has suffered the same fate as the message of *Die Betrachtungen eines Unpolitischen*: it is understood as its opposite. Adrian and his works do not represent fascism, but democracy. The novel *Doktor Faustus* is not primarily a profound statement of the cause of National Socialism. It is not an explanation, but rather the portrayal of the mental process leading to its justification and of its effect. Mann shows how the Munich intellectual crowd came to accept the idea of National Socialism and turned on him because he opposed it. The ambiguity of the novel lies in the underlying subject matter, the opposing interpretations of Adrian's music, not the novel itself. It is not ambiguous, but it is about ambiguity. However, the central theme is the return of the concept of heresy, of the idea that dissent is a threat to society. The process, as he shows through Zeitblom, the "flower of his times," is based on Mann's fundamental understanding of political thinking, as described in *Die Betrachtungen eines Unpolitischen*. *Doktor Faustus* is his revenge for the way he was treated. He understood the battle between the *Zivilisationsliterat* and himself as a form of civil war:

Auf deutschem Boden, sage ich, sogar als deutsche Bürger- und Bruderkriege werden europäische Kriege geführt, und zwar mit Waffen, die an fortgeschrittener Grausamkeit denen nichts nachgeben, die an den Fronten wüten. Da stehe ich im Erdgeriesel, Eisenhagel, gelben Stickqualm einer Giftgasbombe und weiß nicht, ob ich noch lebe. Doch, ich lebe wohl noch. Und so gälte es denn nun Erwiderung, Heimzahlung, schreckliche Gegenrechnung? Es eilt nicht. Eine allgemeine moralische Betrachtung stehe voran. (*BeU*, 194–95)

* * *

Starting with chapter 33 there is a shift in the novel. Up to this point, Mann has been at pains to establish the differences between the philosophies of Zeitblom and Adrian. He has turned *Die Betrachtungen eines Unpolitischen* into a novel. The rest of the novel shows what happens after the First World War as a result of these differences. The relationship between the two becomes strained and Zeitblom becomes very critical of Adrian. *Doktor Faustus* is a historical novel. From this point on, the novel is based on Mann's experience during the 1920s and the influence of *Die Betrachtungen eines Unpolitischen* in Germany. The apparently innocuous Catholic humanist of pre-First-World-War Germany, so beloved of critics, becomes a supporter of fascism after the war, and eventually of National Socialism. This is inherent in his philosophy, according to Mann. It is not he who has changed, but the situation in which he finds himself. His fascism is the result of a predisposition, just as Adrian's rejection of fascism is the result of a predisposition. In the second part of the novel the public facts of Mann's life in Munich are the facts of the novel, with Adrian representing Mann's position and Zeitblom representing those who turned against him with the advent of National Socialism. Zeitblom apologizes for not actively participating in this persecution, on the grounds that he loves Adrian, but he understands and shares the views of this group. Zeitblom's account puts a gloss on it out of delicacy, but he is shown to consider Adrian's fate to have been his own fault, the result of his stubborn insistence on maintaining nineteenth-century liberal values. However, since the *Zivilisationsliterat* does not believe in guilt, he calls it predestination. Predestination is not the same as predisposition.

Notes

[1] Thomas Mann, *Briefe, 1889–1936* (Berlin: Fischer, 1961), 371.
[2] Michael Mann, "Adrian Leverkühn — Repräsentant oder Antipode?" *Neue Rundschau* (1965): 202–6; here, 203.

[3] Thomas Mann, "Rede über Lessing," in *GW*, 9:229–45; here, 243.

[4] Lieselotte Voss, *Die Entstehung von Thomas Manns Roman* Doktor Faustus: *Dargestellt anhand von unveröffentlichten Vorarbeiten* (Tübingen: Niemeyer, 1975), 132.

[5] Allan Oslo, *Die Freimaurer* (Düsseldorf: Albatross, 2002).

[6] Oslo, *Die Freimaurer*, 348.

[7] Oslo, *Die Freimaurer*, 351.

[8] Hermann Kurzke, *Thomas Mann: Epoche — Werk — Wirkung* (Munich: Beck, 1991), 149–52.

[9] Hermann Kurzke, *Thomas Mann: Das Leben als Kunstwerk* (Munich: Beck, 1999), 272.

[10] Thomas Mann, *Die Entstehung*, 243.

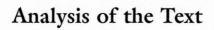

Analysis of the Text

4: Going to Leipzig

ADRIAN'S DECISION IN CHAPTER 15 to change the center of his approach to life from theology to music is the most significant decision in his life and must, therefore, be analyzed very carefully. It is this decision that he defines in his Faust story in chapter 47 as the beginning of his Faust's association with the Devil (*DF*, 662). When the argument for this decision is read in the context of *Die Betrachtungen eines Unpolitischen*, the significance of the fact that Mann's Faust is a musician becomes clear. Music, Protestant theology, and German nineteenth-century liberal humanism are virtually synonymous to Mann, and speaking of one is speaking of the others. This is literally the case in *Doktor Faustus*, and Adrian's sometimes cryptic and sometimes trivial remarks about music often make better sense when understood as about German Protestant culture, or liberal humanism, or politics. The relationship between politics and music in the novelis made clear by Hanns Eisler's comment that "a certain social situation leads to a certain musical technique which, in turn, when applied in practice makes this particular social situation possible."[1] Adrian's political argument in the novel is presented through his discussions of music, which are political analogies during the entire course of the novel.

It is important to distinguish between what he says about his music and what Zeitblom says about it. It is generally assumed that Adrian's music is meant to represent fascism, but this assumption is based primarily on Zeitblom's descriptions. It is necessary to trace Adrian's argument separately and in its totality, to study the sequence of the logic that shows the relationship of these remarks to the political context in which they are expressed. To understand Adrian's arguments about music it is certainly necessary to have a general knowledge of what the musical terms mean and also to have a general notion of the kinds of argument that were prevalent in musical circles during the nineteenth century and the beginning of the twentieth century in Germany; this is not necessary to understand Zeitblom's commentaries. These arguments are provided in the novel by Kretzschmar and Adrian, but not by Zeitblom. The music arguments are simplified, but still legitimate in themselves. However, it is the political sense of the arguments that makes the novel coherent and explains the relationships between the characters. Faust as musician is simultaneously Faust as Protestant, Faust as liberal humanist, and Faust as democrat.

In chapter 15, where Adrian decides to turn from theology to music, Mann gives the first clear indication of where the novel is going. Adrian is primarily concerned with the fundamental problems of his society and this concern will be the primary motivation and subject matter of his art. His decision is triggered by the reactions of Zeitblom to the content of the lectures at Halle and immediately by the political views expressed by the students. Mann has shown this connection through juxtaposition of the events and by illustrating Adrian's concern about the direction political thought is taking in Germany. The whole discussion surrounding his decision is elucidated by the application of concepts Mann developed in *Die Betrachtungen eines Unpolitischen*. Adrian's intellectual development is biographically roughly parallel to Mann's in that he is beginning, at this time, to become aware of political tendencies in Germany. So as not to leave any doubt in the reader's mind, Mann has anachronistically used much more explicitly political arguments for this discussion than were current in Germany in 1905.[2]

In the political discussion in chapter 14 the young theology students see fascism and communism as the only political options available. Their argument is centered basically on whether it is better to take the "national" or the "international" road. Adrian rejects both alternatives. The Winfried political discussion is one of the few points in the first part of the novel where Zeitblom specifically reveals Adrian's political position. Adrian rejects the political arguments of the students, a rejection that Zeitblom and the others ascribe to arrogance and lack of interest in the community. However, what chapter 14 shows is the opposite, that Adrian is intensely interested in politics, or the community, and concerned about the developing tendency to potentially totalitarian political thought. Zeitblom tries to assure the reader that, despite appearances and his statements to the contrary, Adrian really shares the views of the nationalists. He dismisses Adrian's position and says that he rejects their arguments simply to be in opposition and to show his superiority. Zeitblom expresses no opinion of his own on the political argument in this chapter. His opinion is revealed later, in chapter 30, where he is shown to have been on the side of the national approach (*DF*, 409).

The political problem Adrian sees is most clearly illustrated by the Kierkegaard episode, where the Winfried club discusses the essential subjectivity of Protestant Christianity (*DF*, 160–61). This is the basis of the religion and of traditional German liberal social values. It is the opposite in France: "Seit Jahrhunderten ist Frankreich von der Geschichte zur antichristlichen Sendungsmacht in Europa ausersehen. Von Deutschland gilt das Gegenteil" (*DF*, 160). Kierkegaard has questioned the need for the continued existence of the church, but Adrian finds this position too radical, too dangerous for society. He says it would mean denying the distinction between madness and religiosity:

Ich weiß ja, daß es die Begabtesten von euch sind, die Kierkegaard gelesen haben, die Wahrheit, auch die ethische Wahrheit, ganz ins Subjektive verlegen und alles Herdendasein perhorreszieren. Aber ich kann eueren Radikalismus, der übrigens bestimmt nicht lange vorhalten wird, der eine Studentenlizenz ist, — ich kann euere Kierkegaard'sche Trennung von Kirche und Christentum nicht mitmachen. Ich sehe in der Kirche auch noch, wie sie heute ist, säkularisiert und verbürgerlicht, eine Burg der Ordnung, eine Anstalt zur objektiven Disziplinierung, Kanalisierung, Eindämmung des religiösen Lebens, das ohne sie der subjektivistischen Verwilderung, dem numinosen Chaos verfiele, zu einer Welt phantastischer Unheimlichkeit, einem Meer von Dämonie würde. Kirche und Religion zu trennen, heißt darauf verzichten, das Religiöse vom Wahnsinn zu trennen. (*DF*, 160–61)

Unlike Roman Catholicism, Protestant theology in itself, argues Adrian, does not provide a sufficient basis for the maintenance of order. Since it is entirely subjective and based on individual personal responsibility, its logical tendency is towards absolute anarchy. It follows that the development of a German democracy based on Protestantism and individualism will require an external framework, a set of rules. The form of the social order has traditionally been derived from theology, but it cannot be deduced from Protestant theology, which is individualist by nature. Society must, nevertheless, be subjected to rules of procedure to prevent anarchy. The political discussion is shown to confirm this, since both the political alternatives put forward are French, based on Roman Catholicism, on the principle of the suppression of individuality, and are, therefore, not appropriate for Germany. The distinction that Mann makes in *Die Betrachtungen eines Unpolitischen* between French politics and the kind of politics suitable for Germany has been established in the novel as based on the distinction between Protestant subjectivity and Roman Catholic objectivity.

An important negative characteristic of Rousseau's democracy, or "enlightenment," as Mann describes it in *Die Betrachtungen eines Unpolitischen*, is that it is pure abstract intellect, as is mathematics, and has nothing to do with humanity. In his letter to Kretzschmar discussing his move, Adrian says he enjoys mathematics, but sees it as only a form of entertainment and cannot imagine identifying himself with it. Music, however, is the union of theology and mathematics (*DF*, 176). If theology represents Protestant morality and individualism, and mathematics, being pure intellect, represents Rousseau's democracy, or "enlightenment," then music provides the key characteristic necessary to accompany the development of a German democracy: it is a synthesis of both. The individual does not identify himself with his government. Adrian likens this effort to unite theology and mathematics in music to the Renaissance, a preparation for another German Reformation, another breaking away from Roman totalitarianism:

Item, sie hat viel von dem Laborieren und insistenten Betreiben der Alchimisten und Schwarzkünstler von ehemals, das auch im Zeichen der

> Theologie stand, zugleich aber in dem der Emanzipation und
> Abtrünnigkeit, — sie *war* Abtrünnigkeit, nicht vom Glauben, das war gar
> nicht möglich, sondern im Glauben. (*DF*, 176)

Utopian, or "enlightenment," democracy, secularized Roman Catholicism,
is abstract intellectualism expressed in words, whereas German democracy
must be a synthesis of abstract intellectualism, or "enlightenment," with
Protestantism, and this synthesis is expressed through music. Adrian has
decided that the political solution is to be found through music and not
through theology.

The Devil says that Adrian's intention to develop this synthesis is what
drew his attention to him:

> Denn deine Hoffart verlangte es nach dem Elementarischen, und du
> gedachtest es zu gewinnen in der dir gemäßesten Form, dort, wo's als
> algebraischer Zauber mit stimmiger Klugheit und Berechnung vermählt
> und doch zugleich gegen Vernunft und Nüchternheit allzeit kühnlich
> gerichtet ist. (*DF*, 331)

The Devil is associating music with the elementary, or the emotions,
and accusing Adrian of using magic and cleverness to argue against intellect. This is the same as Zeitblom's reaction to Adrian's *strenger Satz*.
Zeitblom, being a *Zivilisationsliterat*, thinks that music is politically suspect,
and right from the beginning of the novel he tries to persuade his readers
that Adrian is therefore, by implication, also politically suspect. We know,
however, that Mann himself did not think that music is suspect in itself; on
the contrary, he thought musicality was a defining German characteristic in
the positive sense. He defines music as a gift of God. Clearly, Zeitblom's
message is not Mann's message. Not only is his view in direct opposition to
Mann's own view, but being suspicious of music is an important characteristic of Mann's favorite *bête noire*, the *Zivilisationsliterat*. This is clearly
established in *Die Betrachtungen eines Unpolitischen* and clearly stated in
Der Zauberberg by Settembrini, Mann's clearest caricature of the
Zivilisationsliterat.[3] Events in the novel show, however, that there are circumstances where music can be politically disastrous: specifically, when the
Zivilisationsliterat, whose proper realm is words, misuses it politically.

The Devil's definition of music reflects Catholic cultural values. Music,
in this tradition, is seen as a tool in the service of an ideal, as a means to an
end, not an end in itself. In this sense, music appeals to the emotions, and
these are essentially irrational. In Mann's philosophy, on the contrary,
music is the art of giving form to ethics, which is an end in itself. A government based on music, therefore, will be shaped by ethics, or individual
moral decisions, and will have no other purpose beyond this. In contrast
to a government based on dogma, or "the word," where social organization
is directed to some abstract goal, music, the essentially German art, allows
the overall imposition of order while retaining subjectivity, or individual

morality, and dispensing with this abstract determining goal. This is why Adrian is trying to eliminate the cadence, or absolute determining goal of music. If there is no set key, as there is not in twelve-tone music, there is no predetermined obligatory close. In terms of establishing a democratic social order, this means incorporating into music, that is, into nineteenth-century German Protestant culture, an element of Rousseau's democracy, that is "enlightenment," but in such a way as to preserve the essential German individualism. The introduction of "enlightenment," or of politics, to German music, or Protestant society, without sacrificing its particular German character is Adrian's intention. Mann is talking about music as a creative, intellectual process, the writing of new music. This has nothing to do with passively listening to music without thinking about it, using music in the background to create a mood, or mass singsongs to develop a sense of solidarity, or enthusiasm for a cause. Nor does it have to do with revering the musical heritage as an achieved cultural good. It is specifically the use of a set of fixed, but at the same time flexible, rules of procedure that the composer follows to arrive at a new, contemporary expression of the eternally human.

This difference in understanding of the nature of music is one of the fundamental dichotomies of the novel. Adrian is a composer, a creator of new music. Zeitblom is a casual musician, and both the music and the instrument he plays, the viola d'amore, are museum pieces. This fundamental breach in communication is central to the novel. Distrust of new music, based on this different understanding of the nature of music, is equally distrust of all nineteenth-century German humanist achievements based, as they are, on subjectivity, which is proper to nineteenth-century music. One cannot understand the arguments in the novel if one does not appreciate the use in the novel of this difference of opinion about what music is.

Mann says in *Die Betrachtungen eines Unpolitischen* that literature and politics are one and the same thing in France. The typical French literature is social criticism, an awakening of the social conscience and a call for social change through politics. The typical German art is music, not literature. By implication, in Germany music and politics are one and the same thing. Zeitblom says: "In Deutschland genießt doch die Musik das populäre Ansehen, dessen sich in Frankreich die Literatur erfreut" (*DF*, 170).

Adrian hesitates to give up theology for music. That is, he is conservative, nervous about social change, which is the coming move to democracy that the students have been discussing. His concern is to discover a philosophical basis for the development of a specifically German type of democracy. When this is done through Protestant theology either it results in anarchy or it reverts to Roman Catholicism. He describes giving up theology as similar to leaving a cloister: "Es hat seine absurden und lächerlichen Seiten, dies wissenschaftliche Klosterleben, aber wollen Sie verstehen, daß ein geheimer Schrecken mich abmahnt, es aufzugeben, die Heilige Schrift unter die Bank zu legen und in die Kunst zu entlaufen" (*DF*, 175).

Adrian leaves the abstract contemplation of the ideal German society for art, which is the observation of reality. The replacement of ideals with reality is the philosophical move from the eighteenth into the nineteenth century. This subtle difference from the "enlightenment," or the utopian, approach is significant. Finding a philosophical basis for social organization is traditionally associated with Rousseau, Roman Catholicism, and literature. It is not based on reality, but on wishful thinking, on an abstract notion of what should be. "Enlightenment" was the secularization, or "leaving the cloister" of Roman Catholicism. However, it carried the cloister with it: the idea of an intellectual elite contemplating abstract values. The result was a great impulse to the development of literature. Adrian, through studying theology, has been contaminated with "enlightenment," but he is going to apply this "enlightenment" to reality. The German departure from the cloister, the Reformation, led to the development of music and the expression of the word through music.

The move to Leipzig is the turning point in Adrian's life in another way. By becoming a musician he represents the idea of the modern Protestant humanist artist, as described in *Die Betrachtungen eines Unpolitischen*, and, previously, in *Buddenbrooks*. This is the true modern German, in Mann's view, the specifically German transition from the nineteenth to the twentieth century. Whereas in France the *bourgeois* became a *Literat*, in Germany the *"Bürger"* became an artist. The decision for change only served to make Adrian aware of his own fate, says Zeitblom, and he wipes his hands of any participation in it. He dissociates himself from this musical character of the liberal Protestant German and presents Adrian's decision as suspect and fatalistic. The reason Adrian's change in profession is inevitable is that it is, logically, the ultimate achievement of Protestant German humanism, which is what Adrian represents. Expressed positively, Adrian's decision to study music means that he has come of age and recognized that he is the true German, musical and Protestant — and an artist.

Zeitblom sees the move to Leipzig as representing a full break from Kaisersaschern, where life was not much different from that in Halle. The move to Leipzig and Kretzschmar, however, is not a break from Kaisersaschern; it is a moving on. This is what artists do. The facts of the story show that in Adrian's life Kaisersaschern and Kretzschmar are virtually synonymous, as are Kretzschmar and Leipzig. It is Halle that is different in this all-important aspect. It lacks "the music," as is shown in the reaction of the students to Adrian's improvisation. They have no understanding of music as a creative act. Zeitblom's early memories of Adrian's association with music are of singing canons, and grasping the principles of harmonic modulation under the *Lindenbaum*. This is, of course, the basic German idea, the reconciliation of polyphony with harmony, as achieved by Bach. It represents, symbolically, the move from the eighteenth to the nineteenth century and the beginning of modern German culture. By calling the decision to study music instead of theology an annulment of the time in between these early musical experiences and the present (*DF*, 184–85), Zeitblom discounts the entire Kretzschmar episode, which is nineteenth-century and the development of subjectivity, or individualism. It is clear in the novel that Adrian's association with Kretzschmar was by far the greatest influence on his formation, yet Zeitblom denies the significance of this influence. Here we see Zeitblom's crucial misunderstanding of Adrian's position. It is the general misunderstanding that occurred in Germany of Mann's position in *Die Betrachtungen eines Unpolitischen*: it is the interpretation of nineteenth-century values as the German expression of the values of the eighteenth century, an obscurantist muddling. It is reactionary, going backwards, not forwards. Subjectivity, or individualism, and personal responsibility, or morality, are interpreted as irrational, as arbitrary reliance on emotion instead of objective reason. Zeitblom's description of the farmyard canon singing is associated in his mind with the erotic. Not only does Zeitblom not understand Adrian; he is offering false explanations of what he is doing. He is coloring his account with value judgments that are the opposite of Mann's and making statements that contradict the evidence of his own account, thereby misleading the reader about what Adrian is doing.

Adrian's decision to change career is in fact developed under the influence of Kretzschmar, who is an American. There is no direct explanation given in the novel of why Mann decided to make him an American. However, in *Die Betrachtungen eines Unpolitischen* Mann refers exclusively to Rousseau's democracy as undesirable. He does not seem to have become familiar with the nature of American democracy and understood that it was not based on French attitudes until he read Reisiger's translation of Walt Whitman in 1922 and was favorably impressed by Whitman's exuberant praise of democracy.[4] Mann has given Adrian an advantage over himself in that he has made this familiarity with American democracy part of his development through the close contact with Kretzschmar during his youth. Kretzschmar is the musical German who has flowered under democracy. However, the argument remains intellectually autobiographical and essentially the same as the argument in *Die Betrachtungen eines Unpolitischen*. Making Kretzschmar an American is an intensification of Mann's own development, reflecting the further clarification of his ideas during his exile in the United States and his appreciation of Roosevelt's political philosophy. By using Kretzschmar Mann has eliminated from Adrian's argument in *Doktor Faustus* both the ambiguous use of the term "democracy" and the polemic against France that are characteristic of *Die Betrachtungen eines Unpolitischen*. Adrian's argument for democracy will be positively expressed and not, as was Mann's, qualified by the rejection of French democracy. Kretzschmar serves his purpose and then disappears from the novel. Adrian refers to him much later in the novel, in chapter 38, as having had an important influence on his views (*DF*, 547). The move to Leipzig is, therefore, a move from the Winfried crowd, which, like Zeitblom, has an eighteenth-century approach to music and to politics, forward to Kretzschmar in Leipzig, a move from naïve political utopianism to liberal democracy. It is Adrian's recognition that Kretzschmar's road is the correct road. Kretzschmar says, according to Zeitblom, that Adrian does not yet write because he is too proud to produce something imitative (*DF*, 171). It is not an adaptation of American democracy that he is to produce, but a truly German democracy, a musical democracy.

Adrian's letter to Kretzschmar in chapter 15, where he is laying down conditions about his decision to make the change from theology to music, is metaphorical from beginning to end. His arguments are more applicable to politics than to art and reflect arguments against politicians and political life found in *Die Betrachtungen eines Unpolitischen*. He is talking about music, but equally he is talking about politics, when he says he will not become a soloist or a director and have to persuade the masses and win applause. He will become a theorist behind the scene, a composer. Politically, he is talking about demagogy; culturally, he is talking about innovation rather than interpretation. He anticipates that, although he will not have trouble figuring out how it is done, he will find it difficult to set up a framework for it that will be accepted by the culture, and this will give him headaches (*DF*, 178). It is difficult to understand what he means by this in terms of music. The artist just creates; he does not explain his work. That is what the critics try to do. In political terms, he means that it will be difficult to express himself in such a way that he will be correctly interpreted, a problem that did indeed cause Mann severe headaches. In *Die Betrachtungen eines Unpolitischen* he explained the theoretical premises for what he considered a democracy acceptable to the educated middle class. The elaboration of the idea would necessarily be the work of political leaders and politicians, not of the theoretician, based as it is on evolution and the application of fundamental values in specific circumstances. When he found that he was being misunderstood about what these values were, he went to great pains to explain himself, futilely, as it turned out, and to his detriment. As we shall see, in chapter 25 the Devil is talking about precisely this, about how he is elaborating Adrian's original idea and turning it into National Socialism by eliminating these underlying fundamental values.

This is the way it is done, says Adrian in his letter to Kretzschmar. The way what is done? His explanation is simply a lengthy description of the overture to act 3 of Wagner's *Die Meistersinger von Nürnberg*.[5] However, a summary of his description, leaving out the elaborate diversions on the orchestration, shows that the content has little to do with the technique of musical composition but is instead a discussion of politics. First, he says, it is necessary to ask in popular philosophical terms about the nonsense going on in the world, about the purpose of all the agitation and persecution. The main point has to be suggested, but avoided. Then another simple, popular point is shown as significant. The various points are separated from each other and discussed. Finally, the main point is taken up again and is presented as though it had always been there and carried to its conclusion, amazing everyone by its emotional effect. It is difficult to see this as a technical discussion of music, although it is expressed in musical terms. This paragraph is the basic statement of Adrian's intentions, of his purpose in studying music:

> So geht es zu, wenn es schön ist: Die Celli intonieren allein, ein schwermütig sinnendes Thema, das nach dem Unsinn der Welt, dem Wozu all des Hetzens und Treibens und Jagens und einander Plagens biederphilosophisch und höchst ausdrucksvoll fragt. Die Streicher verbreiten sich eine Weile weise kopfschüttelnd und bedauernd über dieses Rätsel, und an einem bestimmten Punkt ihrer Rede, einem wohl erwogenen, setzt ausholend, mit einem tiefen Eratmen, das die Schultern emporzieht und sinken läßt, der Bläserchor ein zu einer Choral-Hymne, ergreifend feierlich, prächtig harmonisiert und vorgetragen mit aller gestopften Würde und mild gebändigten Kraft des Blechs. So dringt die sonore Melodie bis in die Nähe eines Höhepunkts vor, den sie aber, dem Gesetz der Ökonomie gemäß, fürs erste noch vermeidet; sie weicht aus vor ihm, spart ihn aus, spart ihn auf, sinkt ab, bleibt sehr schön auch so, tritt aber zurück und macht einem anderen Gegenstande Platz, einem liedhaft-simplen, scherzhaft-gravitätisch-volkstümlichen, scheinbar derb von Natur, der's aber hinter den Ohren hat und sich, bei einiger Ausgepichtheit in den Künsten der orchestralen Analyse und Umfärbung, als erstaunlich deutungs- und sublimierungsfähig erweist. Mit dem Liedchen wird nun eine Weile klug und lieblich gewirtschaftet, es wird zerlegt, im einzelnen betrachtet und abgewandelt, eine reizende Figur daraus wird aus mittleren Klanglagen in die zauberischsten Höhen der Geigen- und Flötensphäre hinaufgeführt, wiegt sich dort oben ein wenig noch, und wie es am schmeichelhaftesten darum steht, nun, da nimmt wieder das milde Blech, die Choral-Hymne von vorhin das Wort an sich, tritt in den Vordergrund, fängt nicht gerade, ausholend wie das erste Mal, von vorne an, sondern tut, als sei ihre Melodie schon eine Weile wieder dabei gewesen, und setzt sich weihsam fort gegen jenen Höhepunkt hin, dessen sie sich das erste Mal weislich enthielt, damit die "Ah!"-Wirkung, die Gefühlsschwellung desto größer sei, jetzt, wo sie in rückhaltlosem, von harmonischen Durchgangstönen der Baßtuba wuchtig gestütztem Aufsteigen ihn glorreich beschreitet, um sich dann, gleichsam mit würdiger Genugtuung auf das Vollbrachte zurückblickend, ehrsam zu Ende zu singen. (*DF*, 178–79)

This description is both too specific and too vague to be a program of study in musical composition, and it does not discuss the significant points of interest in the construction of a piece of music. It is also based on something already written and therefore not new. However, when one looks at the libretto of the opera, at the argument that the music is meant to express, the meaning becomes clear. In the third act of *Die Meistersinger*, the new triumphs over the old, but it does not break away from the old; rather, it absorbs it and continues the tradition in a new form.

Die Meistersinger form an essentially democratic group:

> SACHS
> Wie längst von den Meistern beschlossen ist,
> ob Herr, ob Bauer, hier nichts beschließt:
> hier fragt sich's nach der Kunst allein,
> wer will ein Meistersinger sein.
>
> Act 1, scene 3[6]

The story of the opera is that Walther von Stolzing is in the process of liquidating his estate to become a citizen of Nuremberg. He is the aristocrat resigning his privileged status to become just another member of society. He has learned to write poetry by studying Walther von der Vogelweide:

> WALTHER
> Am stillen Herd in Winterszeit,
> wann Burg und Hof mir eingeschneit, —
> wie einst der Lenz so lieblich lacht',
> und wie er bald wohl neu erwacht, —
> ein altes Buch, vom Ahn vermacht,
> gab das mir oft zu lesen:
> Herr Walther von der Vogelweid',
> der ist mein Meister gewesen.
>
> Act 1, scene 3 (57–58)

One cannot get much older in the German tradition. However, Walter von der Vogelweide is pre-Reformation, not in the German Protestant tradition, as Beckmesser points out:

> BECKMESSER
> Doch lang schon tot;
> Wie lernt' ihn der wohl der Regel Gebot'?
>
> Act 1, scene 3 (58)

To win the hand of the beautiful heiress, Walther has to be accepted as a member of the *Meistersinger* and win the song competition. He is rejected out of hand on his application for membership because he does not follow the prescribed rules. Hans Sachs, the hero of the story and a recognized poet — and undeniably middle-class — is impressed with this new approach and suggests that they should not reject the new out of hand, just because it is unfamiliar to them:

SACHS
(der vom Beginn an Walther mit wachsendem Ernst
zugehört hat, schreitet vor)
    Halt, Meister! Nicht so geeilt!
    Nicht jeder eure Meinung teilt. —
    Des Ritters Lied und Weise,
    sie fand ich neu, doch nicht verwirrt:
    verließ er unsre Gleise,
    schritt er doch fest und unbeirrt.
    Wollt ihr nach Regeln messen,
    was nicht nach eurer Regeln Lauf,
    der eig'nen Spur vergessen,
    sucht davon erst die Regeln auf!
                       Act 1, scene 3 (63)

He calls Walther's style "the old in the new":

SACHS
    Kein' Regel wollte da passen, —
    und war doch kein Fehler drin.
    Es klang so alt — und war doch so neu, —
    wie Vogelsang im süßen Mai!
                       Act 2, scene 3 (73)

Adjusting to the new is a question of recognizing the need:

SACHS
    nun sang er, wie er mußt';
    und wie er mußt', so konnt' er's, —
    das merkt' ich ganz besonders.
                   Act 2, scene 3 (73)

It is also a question of giving innovation some consideration and not
rejecting it out of hand:

SACHS
    Herr Merker, was doch solch ein Eifer?
    Was doch so wenig Ruh'?
    Eu'r Urteil, dünkt mich, wäre reifer,
    hörtet ihr besser zu.
                  Act 1, scene 3 (63)

Sachs rewrites Walther's song, retaining his new idea, but correcting it
to conform to the essential *Meistersinger* tradition. Walther competes in
the contest and wins the girl. Sachs' argument is that the people should
have the right, once a year, to question the rules themselves:

SACHS
Vernehmt mich recht! Wie ihr doch tut!
Gesteht, ich kenn' die Regeln gut;
und daß die Zunft die Regeln bewahr',
bemüh' ich mich selbst schon manches Jahr.
Doch einmal im Jahre fänd' ich's weise,
daß man die Regeln selbst probier',
ob in der Gewohnheit trägem Gleise
ihr' Kraft und Leben nicht sich verlier'.
Und ob ihr der Natur
noch seid auf rechter Spur,
das sagt euch nur,
wer nichts weiß von der Tabulatur.

Act 1, scene 3 (55)

SACHS (eifrig fortfahrend)
Drum möcht' es euch nie gereuen,
daß jährlich am Sankt Johannisfest,
statt daß das Volk man kommen läßt,
herab aus hoher Meisterwolk'
ihr selbst euch wendet zu dem Volk.
Dem Volke wollt ihr behagen;
nun dächt' ich, läg' es nah,
ihr ließt es selbst euch auch sagen,
ob das ihm zur Lust geschah!
Daß Volk und Kunst gleich blüh' und wachs',
bestellt ihr so, mein' ich, Hans Sachs!

Act 1, scene 3 (56)

The *Volk* find Beckmesser's opposition to Walther stupid:

VOLK
Seid still! 's ist gar ein tücht'ger Meister!
Still! Macht keinen Witz!
Der hat im Rate Stimm' und Sitz.
Ach! der kann ja nicht 'mal stehn!
Wie soll es mit dem gehn?
Er fällt fast um.
Gott! ist der dumm!
Stadtschreiber ist er, Beckmesser heißt er.

Act 3, scene 5 (132)

Beckmesser, however, objects to Sachs' position as populist, the rule of the masses:

BECKMESSER

Singet dem Volk auf Markt und Gassen!
Hier wird nach den Regeln nur eingelassen.
Act 1, scene 3 (63)

So do some of the other *Meistersinger*:

KOTHNER

Der Kunst droht allweil Fall und Schmach,
läuft sie der Gunst des Volkes nach.
Act 1, scene 3 (56)

Beckmesser accepts at the end that he does not understand the new rules and disappears in the crowd. Walther is accepted as a *Meistersinger*, and the people are pleased:

VOLK

Das ist was andres, wer hätt's gedacht!
Was doch recht Wort und Vortrag macht!
Act 3, scene 5 (138)

The grand finale is a tribute to the *Meistersinger* for their glorious achievement in preserving traditional German culture, thus preventing its disappearance in the general Latin culture:

SACHS

Daß unsre Meister sie gepflegt
Grad' recht nach ihrer Art,
nach ihrem Sinne treu gehegt,
das hat sie echt bewahrt:
blieb sie nicht adlig, wie zur Zeit,
wo Höf' und Fürsten sie geweiht;
im Drang der schlimmen Jahr'
blieb sie doch deutsch und wahr:
und wär' sie anders nicht geglückt,
als wie wo alles drängt und drückt,
ihr seht, wie hoch sie blieb im Ehr': —
was wollt ihr von den Meistern mehr? —
Habt acht! Uns dräuen üble Streich': —
zerfällt erst deutsches Volk und Reich,
in falscher welscher Majestät
kein Fürst bald mehr sein Volk versteht,
und welschen Dunst mit welschem Tand
sie pflanzen uns in deutsches Land;

> was deutsch und echt wüßt' keiner mehr,
> lebt's nicht in deutscher Meister Ehr'.
> Drum sag' ich euch:
> ehrt eure deutschen Meister!
> Dann bannt ihr gute Geister;
> und gebt ihr ihrem Wirken Gunst,
> zerging' in Dunst
> das heil'ge röm'sche Reich
> uns bliebe gleich
> die heil'ge deutsche Kunst!
>
> Act 3, scene 5 (138–39)

The specific defect in Beckmesser's song, based on the old rules, is that the music requires the stress to be put on syllables of the words that are not stressed in ordinary speech. This is a clear sign that art is out of step with the culture. "The word" has been subjected to "the music" to the extent that it has become meaningless. It is this that Sachs corrects by accepting Walther's new idea and making it otherwise conform to the traditional rules.

The reference to Wagner's *Meistersinger* in Adrian's letter is understood by reference to the text, which explains the music. Music in itself does not explain anything. The theme of the opera is one of the infinite number of possible variations on the basic theme of *Doktor Faustus*: Adrian means to try to develop a democracy that is not based on French Roman Catholic humanism, but on nineteenth-century Protestant humanism. He is to do this through the incorporation of "the word" in "the music" — a point that Mann made 1922 in "Von Deutscher Republik":

> Hörtet ihr kürzlich die "Meistersinger"? Nun, Nietzsche äußert zwar sprühenderweise, sie seien "gegen die Zivilisation" gerichtet, sie setzen "das Deutsche gegen das Französische." Unterdessen aber sind sie Demokratie, durch und durch, demokratisch in dem Grade und auf so beispielhafte Art, wie etwa Shakespeare's "Coriolan" aristokratisch ist — sie sind, sage ich, deutsche Demokratie und beweisen mit biederstem Pomp, auf romantisch innigste Art, daß diese Wortverbindung, weit entfernt, naturwidrig zu sein oder die Logik des hölzernen Eisens zu verraten, vielmehr so organisch richtig gefügt ist wie außer ihr vielleicht nur noch die andere: "Deutsches Volk." (*VDR*, 825)

Thus he is making the story of *Meistersinger* analogous to the need to accept the Weimar Republic, the introduction of democracy to Germany, through adjusting it to respect traditional German values, rather than French values.

Why Mann has clothed his reference to *Meistersinger* in such an elaborate description of the orchestration can perhaps be explained by Hanns Eisler's remark on the importance of orchestration to nineteenth-century music: it serves the specific function of providing contrast and variety: "This style is appropriate, as no other, for appealing to the individual experience and to the individual imagination. The listener is not forced to take a predetermined attitude but an attempt is made to excite him, to entertain him and to create associations for him."[7]

Adrian's definition of his political aims is clothed in an appeal to individualism. Thus the description of the orchestration is an integral part of his argument.

Kretzschmar's answer to this letter can also be interpreted as about politics. To some extent he repeats the same remarks and uses the same images as Adrian does in his letter. He uses the image Mann uses in *Die Betrachtungen eines Unpolitischen* to describe his kind of democracy: the people are the subject as well as the object, or government by the people, for the people, a slogan undisputedly associated with democracy: "Objektive und subjektive Motive [verbinden] sich bis zur Ununterscheidbarkeit." (*DF*, 181).

When Kretzschmar refers to Adrian's future work he does not mention harmony, the metaphor for the traditional German hierarchical society of the nineteenth century, but only counterpoint, the system with voices of equal value. It is better for Adrian to concern himself with the problems of polyphony, or equality, than with arguments about the final end: "Es ist besser, von Kanon-, Fugen- und Kontrapunkt-Exerzitien Hauptweh zu bekommen als von der Widerlegung der Kant'schen Widerlegung der Gottesbeweise" (*DF*, 182).

The dichotomy Kretzschmar is talking about is not harmony versus polyphony, but the problem of democracy, or polyphony, that is not directed to an ideal.

It is clear from this that Adrian plans to carry on from where Wagner left off, to continue the job of making "the word" compatible with "the music" and to modernize Wagner, in keeping with the new times, in order to save Germany from being absorbed in the iniquitous Latin culture. This is Mann's mission, as expressed in *Die Betrachtungen eines Unpolitischen* and in his subsequent statements and activities. It is in contradiction to fascism, which is based on the Latin concept of government and the rejection of liberal Protestant values.

The story, or the action, of the novel first becomes obvious here, with Adrian's decision to counteract the tendency to consider totalitarianism that he sees developing at the core of German society, among the young Protestant students of theology, and particularly in Zeitblom, who, as a Catholic, is highly susceptible. He is going to do this through his music, as Wagner did. "The word," the tool of the *Literat*, is by its nature political, the tool of the politician. The "politician" in *Die Betrachtungen eines Unpolitischen* is a demagogue in the Rousseau tradition of political "enlightenment." Adrian's decision to study music is tied to his accepting a certain amount of this political "enlightenment" philosophy, but rejecting demagogy, and developing a synthesis of "the word" with "the music." This decision is discussed by the Devil at length in chapter 25.

In chapter 15 Adrian is putting forth the idea that, since German cultural and social progress is properly expressed through music, then democracy in Germany must originate in music and be musical. Music in Germany reflects the state of the culture and Adrian is becoming aware that the present form of the State is not consistent with the present state of the culture. He is seeking a synthesis of German musical culture with French literary culture to prevent the destruction of traditional German liberal society, Protestant values, and music through their absorption into a system of government based on French Catholic values. From this point on, Adrian is concerned with finding the right combination of "the word" with "the music," otherwise expressed as the combination of polyphony and harmony. To repeat the quotation from Eisler, "a certain social situation leads to a certain musical technique which, in turn, when applied in practice makes this particular social situation possible."

Notes

1 Hanns Eisler, *A Rebel in Music* (New York: International, 1978), 42.

2 Hans-Joachim Schoeps, "Bemerkungen zu einer Quelle des Romans *Doktor Faustus* von Thomas Mann," *Zeitschrift für Religions- und Geistesgeschichte* 22 (1970): 324–55. The political discussion is a montage of an actual political discussion that took place in 1931 (324).

3 Thomas Mann, *Der Zauberberg*, GW 3, 132.

4 Thomas Mann, "Hans Reisigers Whitman-Werk," in *GW*, 10:626–27.

5 Thomas Mann, *Die Entstehung*, 213.

6 Richard Wagner, *Die Meistersinger von Nürnberg* (Reinbek bei Hamburg: Rowohlt, 1981), 57.

7 Eisler, *A Rebel in Music*, 46.

5: Adrian's Studies in Leipzig

THE DESCRIPTION OF ADRIAN'S STUDIES contributes to the reader's understanding of how Adrian is sorting out his basic approach to creating a democratic music. This is in fact what Adrian is doing, as he reports to Zeitblom in his letter from Leipzig in chapter 16. The account of his visit to the brothel is a funny anecdote that precedes a serious discussion of his intellectual development. Zeitblom diverts the attention of the reader from this important discussion by the simple expedient of devoting the entire following chapter to a fanciful elaboration of the visit to the brothel. The episode in chapter 17, where Zeitblom implies that Adrian contracts syphilis, falls into the category of Zeitblom's speculations about things he cannot know and is not part of the story from Adrian's point of view. It is necessary, as always, to follow what Adrian is doing separately from what Zeitblom says he is doing.

As he writes to Zeitblom in chapter 16, Adrian is beginning his further study with Kretzschmar and finds that harmony bores him, because it is not socially relevant: ". . . da das Dominospiel mit den Akkorden ohne Thema mein Bedünken nach der Welt weder zu sieden noch zu braten taugt" (*DF*, 188).

At this point in the novel, the metaphorical game predominates. The discussion, which uses musical vocabulary, can be read as about politics with the simple replacement of the musical vocabulary by its political equivalent. Adrian finds it much more interesting to work with polyphony and is making good progress. Polyphony, or counterpoint, refers to the horizontal movement over time of individual voices of equal value, all saying virtually the same thing. What they say is determined by the first voice, as in a canon or round. Polyphony is democratic in the Rousseau sense of equality of voices with uniformity. The authority is the leading voice. However, Adrian is aware that it is foolish to separate harmony from counterpoint: it is the combination of the two that makes music.

Harmony is vertical simultaneity of voices that move over time together according to rules determined on the basis of a hierarchy. The value of a voice depends on its relative position in the hierarchy. The relative positions change, but only to fall into a different hierarchy. The voices do not all say the same thing. In fact, they do not say anything at all in themselves, and can exist without a melody, or a dominant voice. Everything depends on the relationship of the voice to the system, as Adrian says at the end of chapter 7, and any particular combination of notes has, therefore, more than one meaning. However, this ambiguity is resolved by understanding the context. "Beziehung ist alles. Und willst du sie näher bei Namen nennen, so ist ihr Name 'Zweideutigkeit'. . . . Musik [ist] die Zweideutigkeit als System" (*DF*, 66).

Harmony is aristocratic in that it is hierarchical but allows for individual voices. These, however, have no authority; the authority is the system, the set of rules. It is necessary to understand the role of the melody, or of the individual voice, in building good relationships, he says. He means, of course, to make the specific new kind of music that he intends to write. This is the beginning of his attempt to combine democracy with the German cultural tradition, expressed metaphorically now as combining harmony (predominant in the nineteenth century) with polyphony (predominant in the eighteenth century).

Mann is using these terms throughout the book in a sustained metaphor referring to social organization. These definitions can easily be understood as political and Mann has used this inherent double meaning throughout the novel. Adrian is talking about music as politics. When the argument is understood in its political sense, it corresponds to the basis of the political arguments in *Die Betrachtungen eines Unpolitischen*, where eighteenth-century means Utopia and nineteenth-century means liberal humanism.

Under Kretzschmar's guidance, Adrian is doing theoretical work on the significance of the transition from the eighteenth to the nineteenth century. He finds that the separation of counterpoint from harmony is artificial and leads to an incomplete whole. It is simply boring. To find harmony without polyphony boring is to find a set of rules that do not allow each voice an equal right inadequate. The rules must allow for democracy. The "melody" is the individual voice and the problem is that introducing the individual voice will undoubtedly lead to dissonance, or dissent. "Kretzschmar gibt mirs auch zu und sagt selbst, daß man von allem Anfang der Rolle gerecht werden soll, die das Melodische bei der Entstehung guter Verbindungen spielt. Die meisten Dissonanzen, sagt er, sind gewiß eher durch das Melodische in die Harmonie gelangt als durch harmonische Kombination."[1]

Adrian's approach, under Kretzschmar's guidance, is organic, not dogmatic. He is learning by starting from the given basics and working it out for himself. He is also studying the history of philosophy, the encyclopedia of philosophical sciences and logic, an "enlightenment" study.

This discussion of Adrian's studies continues the political metaphor. The specific problem to be solved is making polyphony compatible with harmony — that is, making democracy compatible with traditional German culture. Adrian's remarks following this discussion have identifiable political content. Romantic music, he says, is "ein[e] aus dem bloß Musikalischen ins allgemeine Geistige hinaustretende Kunst" (*DF*, 191). That is, music is becoming a vehicle for the expression of intellectual problems that are not specifically musical. For this reason, people who are against the Romantic, that is, are stuck in eighteenth-century Utopianism, are always against late Beethoven, where the individualization of the voices is much more significant than in the older music. The key word here is individualization. Utopian philosophies are based on suppressing individuality, to make the individual subordinate to the whole. Eighteenth-century music had no difficulty with polyphony, whereas it was much more difficult in the nineteenth century, when Beethoven was beginning to succeed with it, because it had to be combined with subjective harmony, that is, traditional German culture, or individualism. Adrian's remark can be interpreted as meaning that it is easy to develop a theory of democratic government based on utopian ideals, but not at all easy to develop a liberal democracy that preserves the nineteenth-century respect for the individual. Adrian's train of thought was triggered by the remark of a critic that Schumann's third symphony showed an "umfassende Weltanschauung" (*DF*, 191). This is a deliberate pointer to the political implications of Adrian's remarks.

The basic problem that Adrian sees in establishing a system of government — how to maintain order and at the same time to maintain subjective freedom, to accommodate dissent — is introduced in chapter 20. Here Zeitblom says that Adrian is dedicating himself almost exclusively to the combination of words with music. Adrian insists that music and language are one and the same thing, that they belong together, that music and language are interchangeable (*DF*, 218). The goal of German music, says Adrian, is the union of the word with the music, as occurred with Wagner. Zeitblom says about Adrian's Brentano song cycle that it is music studying itself, that the notes support each other (*DF*, 245). Adrian represents the artist who adapts a certain amount of the literary approach of the *Zivilisationsliterat*, or "the word," or "enlightenment," to German culture, which is "the music." Adrian is giving "the word" more weight than has been done before, carrying this tradition forward, in keeping with the times. He has begun to work on the reconciliation of polyphony and harmony, on combining counterpoint with expressiveness, and is developing an interest in oratorio, where the orchestral harmony is subordinated to polyphonic vocal music, that is, to the words (*DF*, 201). Adrian's greatest difficulty in achieving this reconciliation is the inevitability of dissonance resulting from the imposition of polyphony on harmony, a problem, Zeitblom tells us, that he will largely overcome by the time he writes his *Weheklag Dr. Fausti* (*DF*, 207). Dissonance is, in political or religious terms, dissent, and a system that will accommodate dissent is the opposite of totalitarianism. Adrian's purpose is, in political terms, to solve the problem of the accommodation of dissent, or individualism, while introducing equality, which French political philosophies do not do, making them, in Mann's view, inherently totalitarian.

In terms of music, the combination of strict counterpoint with extreme expressiveness is a technical point. Most musicians consider it in bad taste and incorrect to play baroque music with what is called expression, dropping and increasing the intensity of the sound, intensifying and relaxing the pulse. These subjective intrusions are, however, essential to nineteenth-century music: they are what bring it to life. Zeitblom calls applying this nineteenth-century technique to eighteenth-century music as putting feeling, or subjectivity, into the objective. This is another way of saying that Adrian is combining the musical values of the eighteenth century with the musical values of the nineteenth century to make twentieth-century music. In its political interpretation, it is combining democracy with German human values, particularly individual expression, or subjectivity. Zeitblom says that a person of his own education, that is, a *Zivilisationsliterat*, a Catholic humanist, would reject the Romantic if it were not for its inherent musicality, but that it can easily be revived by someone with a mission (*DF*, 246). Zeitblom, as a Catholic humanist, rejects individualism and subjectivity, which, like music, he understands as expressions of emotion. This statement is a reference to the nature of the use by National Socialism of the Romantic, which, Zeitblom implies, is justified on emotional grounds, because it serves a higher goal.

Polyphony was first reconciled with harmony by Bach, thus introducing the development of harmonic music, which was not possible before that for technical reasons. Harmony offered infinite possibilities of musical invention and virtually replaced polyphony in western musical development. Citing Kretzschmar, Zeitblom claims that it is not a legitimate ambition for Romantic music to use polyphony on the authority of Bach, because it gives the middle voices an authority of their own, when they are meant only to be fill:

> Bei Brahms, den er [Kretzschmar] sehr hochachtete, demonstrierte er ihm [Adrian] die Bezugnahme auf Archaisches, auf alte Kirchentonarten, und wie dies asketische Element bei ihm zum Mittel eines düsteren Reichtums und dunkler Fülle werde. Er gab seinem Schüler zu bemerken, wie in dieser Art von Romantik, unter vernehmbarer Berufung auf Bach, das stimmenmäßige Prinzip dem modulatorisch-farbigen ernst entgegentrete und es zurückdränge. Und doch handle es sich dabei um einen nicht ganz legitimen Ehrgeiz der harmonischen Instrumental-Musik, Werte und Mittel in ihre Sphäre mit einzubeziehen, die eigentlich der alten Vokal-Polyphonie angehörten und auf die wesentlich homophone Instrumental-Harmonik nur übertragen wurden. Polyphonie, kontrapunktische Mittel würden herangezogen, um den Mittelstimmen, die doch im Generalbaß-System nur Füllung, nur akkordische Begleiterscheinung seien, höhere Eigenwürde zu verleihen. Wahre Stimmen-Selbstständigkeit, wahre Polyphonie sei das aber ja doch nicht, sei es auch schon bei Bach nicht gewesen, bei dem man zwar die kontrapunktischen Künste der Vokalzeit überliefert finde, der aber doch von Geblüt ein Harmoniker

und nichts anderes gewesen sei, — schon als Mann des temperierten Klaviers sei er das gewesen, dieser Voraussetzung für alle neuere harmonische Modulationskunst, und sein harmonischer Kontrapunkt habe mit alter vokaler Mehrstimmigkeit im Grunde nicht mehr zu tun gehabt als Händels akkordisches al fresco.[2]

Zeitblom explains the basis of Adrian's argument for democracy, paving the way for his future objection to Adrian's scheme. He has already dismissed Adrian's efforts as *a priori* naive and demonic and also in bad taste. Kretzschmar is saying that using counterpoint in Romantic music results in a change in the nature of the original counterpoint; it is only an adaptation, not the real thing. The reason is that it would give weight to nineteenth-century values, giving authority to the middle voices (that is, classes), which in medieval polyphony was not the case.

Some of the songs that Adrian was working on at this time anticipate his *Apocalipsis cum figuris*, says Zeitblom (*DF*, 215). This is particularly the case, he says, when Adrian chooses the text from Dante's lines about the damnation to hell of the innocent and of those who have not been baptized. This is an expression, in religious terms, of totalitarianism. Zeitblom objects to it as inhuman. However, the reason he gives for its being inhuman is that those who have not been baptized have not been exposed to the opportunity to believe (*DF*, 216). Apparently damnation would be legitimate, in Zeitblom's view, if the opportunity to believe were indeed offered but nevertheless rejected. He dislikes the automatic exclusion from society of dissenters and provides a humane, an inquisitorial, solution to the problem: dissent cannot be tolerated, but it is only humane to persuade the dissenter to see the error of his ways and give him the opportunity to repent before he is excluded. This is, in the context of National Socialism, a rejection of racism, but not of anti-Semitism, and Zeitblom makes it clear that he disagrees with Hitler on his policy towards the Jews.[3] However, the Jews were not the only people excluded by National Socialism. Zeitblom's argument justifies the concentration camps for the torture, — or persuasion — of political dissidents.

Zeitblom likes the image of the man with the light on his back to guide those following, although he himself is not "enlightened" (*DF*, 217). This is a clear reference to the attitude of a great many followers of Hitler. As Mann pointed out in "Von Deutscher Republik," such people were supporting the developing National Socialist movement with no idea of where it was leading them (VDR, 820). This man did not expect to be understood, but simply appreciated for his beauty, says Zeitblom, a reference to the charismatic effect of Hitler (*DF*, 217). They are following obscurantism, under the impression that they are "enlightened." This is aesthetic politics, based on irrationality.

Mann very subtly confuses the information vital to an understanding of Adrian's activities with Zeitblom's exposure of himself as having fascist tendencies. A careless reading could easily identify this fascist tendency with Adrian, since Zeitblom's self-exposure is always associated with his implication that Adrian is saying something questionable. The fact that today's reader unthinkingly assumes that all honorable persons reject fascism leads to the assumption that Zeitblom, who presents himself as an honorable person, is rejecting fascism. This is not, and was not, the case. Mann is showing here, once again, Zeitblom's susceptibility, in spite of the fact that he is an honorable man, to National Socialism. In theory, he likes the idea of following a leader for aesthetic reasons, without questioning where he is going. In theory, he solves the problem of dissent through brainwashing. These are Zeitblom's responses to the problems, not Adrian's, and Adrian shows his dislike of these comments. Adrian is clearly studying the problem of dissonance, or dissent, of allowing everyone an equal voice and at the same time protecting subjective freedom. The problem of protecting subjective freedom is synonymous with the problem of accommodating dissent. This early song cycle can be seen as analogous to Mann's own writings before the First World War, which anticipated *Die Betrachtungen eines Unpolitischen*. Adrian is studying the nonsense going on in the world, asking the purpose of all the agitation and persecution, which as he said was the first task in the problem of combining "the word" with "the music" (*DF*, 178).

A problem in interpreting *Doktor Faustus* is Mann's use of anticipation. Information necessary to the interpretation is given, but its relevance is often not noticed on a first reading and, through neglecting this information, critics have made careless and erroneous assumptions about important aspects of the story, and these assumptions have been perpetuated, unquestioned in the literature. The novel must be read as a whole, because interpretation depends on familiarity with the whole. The ultimate outcome of the story is the result of the thought patterns and predispositions of Adrian and Zeitblom, which determine their reactions when placed in a particular situation, and these thought patterns and predispositions are defined long before this situation occurs.

In his later interpretation of Adrian's *Apocalipsis cum figuris*, Zeitblom does not mention the accommodation of dissent. Mann informs the reader, for purposes of interpreting the novel, that combining "the word" with "the music" is synonymous with combining polyphony with harmony, with combining the subjective with the objective, with combining the eighteenth century with the nineteenth century, and with combining freedom with order. The problem facing all these combinations is the accommodation of dissonance, or dissent, which is the necessary condition for freedom, or the valuing of individualism, in democracy. The reader has been told that this is the subject matter of Adrian's *Apocalipsis cum figuris*. It is this problem that Adrian is addressing with the invention of his *strenger Satz*.

Mann has also informed the reader that Zeitblom interprets subjective freedom, or individualism, as "feeling," or "emotion" and understands it as incompatible with rationality. By extension, he also understands music, harmony, and the Romantic, as "feeling" or "emotion." However, subjective freedom, or individualism, is synonymous with *Innerlichkeit*, the inner sense of personal responsibility and consulting one's conscience that forms the basis of modern Lutheranism and German humanism. Zeitblom, therefore, will also interpret *Innerlichkeit* as relying on emotion. All of these concepts are the result of the Reformation and also quite undeniably "German." It has been made clear that Zeitblom will inevitably interpret Adrian's arguments as meaning something quite different from what Adrian is actually saying. For Zeitblom, a synthesis of "the word" and "the music" means a synthesis of politics and irrationality.

This information, which is so necessary to understanding the story, is not taken into consideration, so far as I am aware, in any analysis of the political argument in the novel.

Notes

[1] Thomas Mann, *Doktor Faustus* (Stockholm: Bermann-Fischer, 1947), 218–19. There are a few significant passages in this 1947 edition that do not appear in the standard *GW*, vol. 6 edition.

[2] Mann, *Dr. Faustus*, 1947 ed., 123–24.

[3] Helmut Neuberger, *Winkelmaß und Hakenkreuz: Die Freimaurer und das Dritte Reich* (Munich: Herbig, 2001), 80–81. In his study of Freemasonry and National Socialism, Neuberger shows that, although the majority of Freemasons rejected all their traditional humanist views in favor of National Socialism, most of them were absolutely against racism.

6: Adrian's *Strenger Satz*

Einen Systemherrn brauchten wir, einen Schulmeister des Objektiven
und der Organisation, genial genug, das Wiederherstellende, ja das
Archaische mit dem Revolutionären zu verbinden. (*DF*, 252)

THIS REMARK INTRODUCES Adrian's explanation of his *strenger Satz*. It is
a reference to Beißel, who invented a new and simplified musical
system for his congregation, since the traditional melodies are far too
complicated. As in Wagner's *Meistersinger*, his music is guided by the
accentuation of normal speech. The harmony is according to a set tabula-
tion, and it is an open system that can be expanded to include everything.
Thus the entire congregation could and did participate in both the creation and the performance of the new music. The result was surprisingly
effective. Zeitblom thought the system naïve and silly. Adrian, however,
admires Beißel for his independence of mind, sense of order, and lack of
sentimentality, an objective attitude that Zeitblom considers a sign of
unacceptable arrogance and makes him fear for Adrian's soul (*DF*, 88–96).
It is with this essentially conservative and closed attitude that Zeitblom
receives Adrian's explanation of his *strenger Satz*. The reader is not
required to adopt the same attitude. The entire argument is expressed in
musical terms.

Adrian says that freedom is another word for subjectivity, and it eventually becomes untenable in itself and needs the protection of objectivity.
Freedom itself recognizes that it has to be subject to laws and rules. This
does not mean that it is not still freedom (*DF*, 253). The purpose of the
objectivity, or laws and rules, that Adrian has in mind is to protect, not to
suppress, subjectivity, or individualism. Adrian has already made the same
point in chapter 14 about Kierkegaard's suggestion that the church is no
longer necessary. Mann made the same point in 1939 in "Maß und Wert":
anarchy is individualism that is not socially restricted.[1] Whether the conversation is about theology, music, or politics, the same principles apply, so
talking about one is talking about the other.

Zeitblom openly interprets Adrian's musical argument in political
terms. He objects that freedom subject to laws and rules would no longer
be freedom, any more than the totalitarianism resulting from revolution is
freedom. Adrian disagrees. He says Zeitblom is talking about political freedom and he himself is talking about subjective freedom. It is, of course, not
only political freedom but also subjective freedom that totalitarianism
attacks. Zeitblom is not recognizing the distinction. Adrian, as did Mann,

is differentiating between the approach to politics that is based on the protection of subjective freedom and one that precludes it in the name of "political" freedom. The revolution and its totalitarian result stems from the French Revolution and Rousseau's democracy, the "political," or "enlightenment," position that claims to be arguing for freedom but tends, in fact, to the sacrifice of subjective freedom to the demand for equality, or uniformity. To put it another way, it leads to the damnation of dissenters, to the destruction of all opposition. Adrian is talking about the accommodation of dissent, the problem he has been working on all along. He is looking for a way to make equality compatible with freedom. Zeitblom has told us that this is also the subject of Adrian's *Apocalipsis cum figuris.*

Adrian argues that the conventions that are crumbling today were fixed at a time in history when they were based on social reality and for a long time fulfilled their purpose, the purpose of organization. Without organization there can be nothing, least of all art (*DF*, 254). He cites Beethoven as an example of someone who took a fixed set of rules and, through subjectivity, regained freedom. Beethoven achieved freedom through the use of the variation. The variation in music is the elaboration of a simple theme, giving it a specific character. There are infinite possibilities of variation, often resulting in passages that are not immediately recognizable as being based on the same simple theme. It is the individualization of the general, expressing the general through the specific. This is the specific defining characteristic of German culture — individualism — that differentiates it from the medieval concept of defining the culture as a unit. The variation was taken up by Brahms — that is, the next generation — continues Adrian, and turned into a fixed, an objective rule. Mann is making a parallel between Brahms and Bismarck here, in the parallel of the development of music with the development of nineteenth-century German political culture. At this point Mann introduces the basic argument of *Die Betrachtungen eines Unpolitischen*: this makes freedom the principle of overall economy, the principle that infinite variety is possible, based on the same fixed material. *Der strenge Satz* is the total integration of all musical dimensions through total organization: "Ich werde dir sagen, was ich unter strengem Satz verstehe. Ich meine damit die vollständige Integrierung aller musikalischen Dimensionen, ihre Indifferenz gegeneinander kraft vollkommener Organisation" (*DF*, 255). In social terms, Adrian's *strenger Satz* is the modern, German, liberal democracy that it is necessary to develop as a continuation of the existing nineteenth-century form of government, now that the form of the State no longer corresponds to the culture. The important phrase that distinguishes this total organization from totalitarianism is "ihre Indifferenz gegeneinander." This refers to the absence in Adrian's system of the compulsion of the *Zivilisationsliterat* to conformity. His system precludes arbitrariness at the same time as it allows individualism. It is not revolutionary, but ties the revolutionary idea with what has always been:

> Bei ihm [Brahms] entäußert sich die Musik [German society] aller kon-
> ventionellen Floskeln, Formeln und Rückstände und erzeugt sozusagen
> die Einheit des Werks jeden Augenblick neu, aus Freiheit. Aber gerade
> damit wird die Freiheit zum Prinzip allseitiger Ökonomie, das der Musik
> nichts Zufälliges läßt und noch die äußerste Mannigfaltigkeit aus iden-
> tisch festgehaltenen Materialien entwickelt. (*DF*, 254–55)

Adrian goes on to explain that historically all the different elements
developed independently of each other and arbitrarily. The more developed elements depreciated the elements that had not developed. This is
what has happened to society: the lower classes were depreciated, because
they had not developed, but now they have and have earned the right to
participate in their government. The fact that they are not included is the
indication that the State does not reflect the present state of the culture.
Adrian is developing a framework for a dialectic interplay of all social elements for constant adjustment to ever changing needs.

In the following argument it is necessary to remember that harmony
refers to a fixed, aristocratic, hierarchical organization and counterpoint to
a system of equal weighting of voices. Mann means this to be understood
politically, while it is also true of music.

> — Die Musik ist ein Wildwuchs, sagte er. — Ihre verschiedenen Elemente,
> Melodik, Harmonik, Kontrapunkt, Form und Instrumentation haben sich
> historisch planlos und unabhängig voneinander entwickelt. Immer, wenn
> ein isoliertes Materialbereich geschichtlich vorwärtsgebracht und höher
> gestuft wurde, blieben andere zurück und sprachen in der Einheit des
> Werkes dem Entwicklungsstand Hohn, der durch die fortgeschrittenen
> behauptet wurde. Nimm etwa die Rolle, die der Kontrapunkt in der
> Romantik spielte. Er ist dort bloße Dreingabe zum homophonen Satz.
> Entweder ist er eine äußerliche Kombination homophon gedachter
> Themen oder die nichts als ausschmückende Umkleidung des harmoni-
> schen Chorals mit Scheinstimmen. Aber wahrer Kontrapunkt verlangt nach
> der Simultaneität selbständiger Stimmen. Ein melodisch-harmonisch
> angelegter Kontrapunkt, wie der spätromantische, ist keiner . . . Was ich
> meine, ist: Je weiter die einzelnen Materialbereiche entwickelt und manche
> sogar verschmolzen werden, wie in der Romantik Instrumentalklang und
> Harmonie, desto anziehender und gebietender wird die Idee einer ratio-
> nalen Durchorganisation des gesamten musikalischen Materials, die
> aufräumte mit anachronistischen Mißverhältnissen und verhinderte, daß ein
> Element zur bloßen Funktion der anderen wird, wie zur romantischen Zeit
> die Melodik zur Funktion der Harmonik wurde. Es gälte alle Dimensionen
> gleich zu entwickeln und alle so auseinander hervorzubringen, daß sie kon-
> vergieren. Auf die universale Einheit der musikalischen Dimensionen käme
> es an. Ganz zuletzt geht es um die Aufhebung des Gegensatzes von poly-
> phonem Fugenstil und homophonem Sonatenwesen.[2]

For instance, says Adrian, in the nineteenth century, the Romantic
period, harmony, or vertical organization, was the rule, and counterpoint,

which requires simultaneous, independent voices, was used only decoratively or incidentally. The melody, the independent voice, was completely subordinated to the harmony, that is, to the system. In the late nineteenth century a hierarchical counterpoint was overlaid, but that is not real counterpoint. He is, of course, talking about Bismarck's introduction of partial democracy, or representation, but not deliberation. So the idea gradually became more attractive, continues Adrian, of a rational and thorough reorganization that gets rid of false anachronistic relationships and prevents one element from being reduced to a function of the other. It has become necessary to develop all dimensions equally and bring each element forth to a point of convergence. It would be a question of overall unity. Finally it is a question of lifting the opposition between eighteenth-century polyphony and nineteenth-century harmony. This is what Adrian is proposing to do: to create a German democracy founded on a fusion of nineteenth-century German values and eighteenth-century French, "bourgeois" democratic values. That is what Mann said was necessary in *Die Betrachtungen eines Unpolitischen.* This is what Adrian has already said he is doing, although he is saying it in musical terms. Zeitblom has identified this with the demonic. Adrian's system is revolutionary and reactionary in that it is a retention of the harmonic values of the nineteenth century together with the reintroduction of polyphony. It is approaching from the other direction the achievement of Bach, who proved that it was possible to combine the two. Politically it is the development of a democracy based on the German Protestant achievement. This argument is the reverse of Zeitblom's argument, reflecting a fundamental difference in approach to music. Adrian is a creator, an artist, making ever-new combinations of what already exists to make the new. Zeitblom regards music as sacred. Existing music is to be interpreted, much as the Bible is interpreted, but it cannot be changed. Zeitblom feels that it is illegitimate to mix subjectivity with objectivity.

Adrian has tried to do it with five tones, his key word h–e–a–e–es, the running motif for transparent structure, but this is too limited. Transparency is not enough. It has to include all twelve tones of the scale or, in other words, it has to include the whole of society. Adrian's problem is finding a suitable organization of tones, a key word so that all can be used melodically and harmonically.[3] In other words, it is one thing to find that this is necessary, it is another thing to figure out how to make it function well, to find a constitutional framework. Adrian says the number of possible combinations in his proposed system is endless (*DF*, 255–57). However, Zeitblom distrusts the system and calls it a "magic quadrangle." He thinks it is too complicated and that you could not be aware of everything that is going on at once. Adrian says that that doesn't matter; the general effect would be pleasing (257). Politically speaking, being aware of everything that is going on implies the need for total control, whereas

Adrian is talking about total order, which is not the same thing. The first requires a system of spies while the second is the rule of law.

Zeitblom does not understand how there can be freedom if everything is subjected to a preordained order. He thinks harmony would then be subject to chance. Adrian says the order is freely established and then the material works itself out according to a set of rules. He calls it a constellation that would protect the worthiness of each tone contributing to the harmony and that the resulting dissonances (dissenting voices) would be justified by being made absolute, and any combination of sounds that can be legitimated by the system would be justified. Zeitblom asks what happens when the constellation produces something banal and traditional and Adrian says the constellation would thereby be revalidating it. This is the means by which the old is retained in the new. The constellation is the ruling constitution that legitimizes discord, or difference of opinion, and channels it (*DF*, 257–58). As Mann said in 1944, in "Schicksal und Aufgabe," there is a tendency to think of the liberal tradition as trivial and banal. The liberal tradition is freedom, progress, humanitarianism, and civilization, which includes appeal to reason and mastery of the dynamic of nature: drive, blood, and the unconscious.[4] Zeitblom's position is the classical totalitarian argument against individualism and the open society.

Suddenly the conversation does not even sound as if it is about music. Zeitblom calls Adrian's scheme a radical Utopia and finds it reactionary. Adrian says it is both progressive and regressive and shows the ambiguity of life and that Zeitblom's objections would not count against the fulfillment of the ancient longing to put things together in an orderly fashion and resolve music (German society) in accordance with human reason. Zeitblom thinks Adrian is talking more about magic than about reason, to which Adrian answers that the combination of magic and reason results in wisdom (*DF*, 258–59).

This discussion of Adrian's *strenger Satz* has to do with politics and is only very thinly disguised in musical terms. It is, however, not about fascism, as Zeitblom understands it, speaking anachronistically, as his interpretation in chapter 34 (*Schluß*) of Adrian's *Apocalipsis cum figuris* confirms. Adrian/Mann is trying to explain that the free working of society, democratically organized under a constitution, a set of carefully worked out, agreed rules and regulations for its proceedings, will produce the best results and reflect the traditional nature of German Protestant society, in that it respects freedom and accommodates dissent. It is at the same time progressive, placing the traditional in an ever new light and making ever new combinations. Zeitblom is very dubious about this. Zeitblom, as a *Zivilisationsliterat*, cannot accept the central point that the sum of freely made individual decisions will result in a smoothly functioning society. This system is often called the middle road in politics and Mann himself referred to it as a middle road, but it is not a middle road

between fascism and communism or between left and right. It is a completely different and radically opposed road, based on a different view of
mankind, a view that trusts in the "magic" results of the open society. At
the time in question, 1910, this view was called conservative in Germany,
as Mann called it in *Die Betrachtungen eines Unpolitischen*. It is political in
that it has to do with government, but antipolitical in that it rejects
polemics and demagogy. It is not based on political speeches and playing
with words, persuading the masses and seeking applause, but is an attempt
to keep society harmonically progressing by means of the resolution of disagreements through deliberation. Zeitblom calls it "magic," partly because
he does not understand it, but primarily because he does not believe it is
possible or desirable. It is contrary to his tradition of Catholic humanism
and his view of mankind. He does not trust that an open society promoting the free movement of individuals could function. What appears by
these means could be banal. The whole point about Adrian's system is that
it is based on the German Protestant tradition. That is the difference
between liberal democracy and fascism or communism, which are both
regressions to medieval Catholicism in secularized form, a rejection of
individualism. The *Zivilisationsliterat* does not trust the people; he thinks
he is a better judge of what is good for the people than the people themselves are. He equates the need for order with the need for control. He
does not tolerate dissent, because there is only one right answer.

Adrian sees that Zeitblom does not understand what he is saying, and
this gives him a headache. It is the problem that Adrian anticipated in his
letter to Kretzschmar: how to present his argument so that he would be
properly understood. Zeitblom is suspicious that the system itself reflects
the headache. What Zeitblom consistently describes as Adrian's pain and
associates with syphilis and the demonic is illustrated in the novel as Dürer
melancholy. It is a sign of the Protestantism of Adrian's true German character, and it is this Protestant character that Zeitblom suggests is suspect
in Adrian's system, as becomes very clear in his analysis of Adrian's
Apocalipsis cum figuris in chapter 34 (*Schluß*). The Devil in chapter 25
attributes Adrian's headaches to his trying to combine his Dürer melancholy with his interest in politics, which is what Adrian is doing here. This
whole discussion is a prelude to the appearance of Adrian's *Apocalipsis cum
figuris*, which is conceived by Adrian in the same state of melancholy.

Zeitblom concludes from this: "In seiner Nähe [war] Sterilität, dro-
hende Lähmung und Unterbindung der Produktivität nur als etwas
beinahe Positives und Stolzes, nur zusammen mit hoher und reiner
Geistigkeit zu denken" (*DF*, 253). He is misdirecting the reader. He is
ignoring Adrian's whole argument and dismissing it as though Adrian had
never spoken and just picked up the premises, Adrian's starting point: the
times are difficult. However, Adrian has not demonstrated sterility, but
the reverse. He has solved the problem of introducing equality without

sacrificing freedom through "the music" by the invention of the twelve-tone system. The problem facing Adrian now is not of solving the problem of how democracy can be made compatible with German values, but of expressing his solution in such a manner that Zeitblom will understand it. The difficulty is that Zeitblom does not share Adrian's values. They are thinking on different planes and assume different meanings for the same words.

In order to talk about democracy in the guise of music, Mann introduces an argument that allows Adrian to say that he is talking simply about music — that is, giving a legitimate contemporary musical argument — and, at the same time, make political interpretation of it possible. Schoenberg's twelve-tone system provides the essential ingredient: the important point about Schoenberg's system for the novel is that all the notes, that is the participants, are of equal value and freed from subjection to hierarchy of any kind. Specifically what Schoenberg was trying to do was to eliminate the need for the resolution, or for a final goal, for "Erlösung." The idea was to create an open rather than a closed system. The use of this system makes it possible to talk about democracy while talking at the same time about music. The system is superimposed on Adrian's declared intention in chapter 15 to follow in Wagner's footsteps. It is a continuation of the same argument. This fusion of Schoenberg's modern system with Wagner's Romantic system is primarily significant for its metaphorical purpose. Adrian's musical system is a reconciliation of the true German tradition with modern equality, making the State compatible with the culture, while defending it against being swept up in the Latin culture. In musical terms, Mann is bringing together the opposing positions of a fundamental musical dispute of the second half of the nineteenth century. The Brahms school argued that musical subjectivity had to be given form by containment in the traditional framework, whereas the Wagner school abandoned this framework entirely in favor of program music, where the formal framework is provided by a text, or by "the word," either explicit — as in songs or operas — or implicit — as provided in explanations in program notes.

Zeitblom, like the Devil in chapter 25, sees Adrian's solution as sterile in its present form, but promising. Zeitblom can only see Adrian overcoming this "sterility" through higher and purer intellect. Zeitblom sees the *strenger Satz* as needing academic elaboration. He is ignoring the essential German Protestant safeguarding of subjective freedom in Adrian's system and accepting only what turns it into a basis for German fascism: the idea of basing politics on music. However, Zeitblom has a completely different understanding of music from Adrian. Adrian sees music as a creative, intellectual activity, as organization and the giving of form, as progress. Zeitblom sees music as sacred, as static, as the expression of pure emotion. As we shall see when he analyses the *Apocalipsis cum figuris* for presentation to the Kridwiß *Kreis*, he interprets and elaborates its argument with the use of his higher and purer intellect as a proposal for a "cult of music" as the basis of government.

Adrian's remark about combining the archaic with the revolutionary can be understood as a definition of fascism, but it is not, or not necessarily. Mann discusses what he means by revolutionary and reactionary in his preface to the first edition of the magazine *Maß und Wert* in 1937. This magazine was founded by literary political exiles for the purpose of keeping true German culture alive during the reign of National Socialism in Germany. Mann quotes Goethe: "Es gibt kein Vergangnes, das man zurücksehnen dürfte, es gibt nur *ein ewig Neues, das sich aus den erweiterten Elementen des Vergangenen gestaltet,* und die echte Sehnsucht muß stets produktiv sein, ein Bessres erschaffen" (*GW*, 12:801). The past is our origin and part of us. It is what we build on to make something better. The new is based on the past, but it is not the past. This, Mann says, is the definition of art: consciously handing on tradition and looking to the future. It is conservative revolution. The fascists have corrupted this and understand it as its contradiction.

Zeitblom says that Adrian's system precludes freedom, and Zeitblom is always right, say so many of the critics, disregarding entirely what Adrian has said (for example: It is total order, therefore it is fascism).[5] However, fascism is not total order, it is total control. Fascism is not rational organization; it is irrational arbitrariness, based on emotion. It is incorrect to parallel Adrian's *strenger Satz* with fascism.

A minority of critics understand what Mann is talking about in *Doktor Faustus*. Significantly, it is made up of those who have studied Mann's political views. Unfortunately, most of them have not specifically addressed the novel to explain the implications of this understanding for its interpretation. It is interesting to look at the argument of one of the exceptions, Gert Sautermeister, about Adrian's *strenger Satz*, which makes the argument presented here seem trivial. He argues that Adrian is advocating economic socialism. His definition of Adrian's *strenger Satz* is essentially correct:

> Mannigfaltigkeit und Vielförmigkeit sind der Beweis dafür, daß die Freiheit dadurch, das sie dem Gesetz und der Regel folgt, vom vororganisierten Material ausgeht, jeder Beschränkung durch den Zufall oder durch die Willkür enthoben ist, keinem "blinden Verhängnis" mehr begegnet und daher voll, auf gesicherter Basis, sich entfalten kann, . . . so wie in einer wirklich demokratischen Sozialordnung die individuelle Würde aller gemeinschaftsbildenden Subjekte durch ihre identische Stellung zur Materialbasis, dem Gemeineigentum, gewährleistet sein würde.[6]

However, calling it economic socialism is carrying the argument too far. Adrian is not talking about economics and property, but about freedom of thought and expression, or subjectivity, and form. Sautermeister bases his argument on Mann's "Bekenntnis zum Sozialismus" (1933),[7] where Mann said that socialism is defined as:

> . . . die rationale Organisation der ungeordneten Materie, ihre "Durchdringung mit Form und Vernunft, mit Freiheit und Gerechtigkeit" — eine Organisation, die ihre Analogie in der Kunst findet: "Kunst bestand immer in dieser Durchdringung und Vermenschlichung, das heißt Vergeistigung. Sie ist das Zünden des Geistes in der Materie, der natürliche Trieb zur Gestaltung und Vergeistigung des Lebens."[8]

At this point in the novel, Adrian is advocating not economic socialism but liberal democracy. Mann's recognition that social problems exist and must be addressed by government lies outside his fundamental conception of the basis and justification of democracy. Whether it is socialism or not is a question of content, not form, and it is form that is in question here. The form of government that Adrian is proposing is liberal democracy, the form that Mann advocated in *Die Betrachtungen eines Unpolitischen* and supported all his life. He did sometimes address questions of content, but he never changed his view on form. Adrian does advocate a kind of socialism in chapter 31, but that is several years later, and later still, in chapter 47, he is clearly advocating socialism. His *strenger Satz* does not preclude socialism; it makes it possible if it is desired. Mann's socialism was akin to Bismarck's social legislation and the modern Welfare State and was opposed to radical left-wing socialism, which sacrifices freedom to equality. In *Die Betrachtungen eines Unpolitischen*, he is arguing for the open society, where social mobility, that is, specifically, education, is not dependent on property (*BeU*, 258). Sautermeister's interpretation blurs the fundamental distinction, important to understanding the novel as a whole, between this kind of democracy and Rousseau's democracy or communism. The basic point of Adrian's *strenger Satz* is that the only restriction on the freedom of the individual note is the equal freedom of every other note. Such a system accommodates dissent by defining subjective freedom as its first principle.

In this respect it is very interesting to compare Adrian's argument likening the development of music to the development of society with Hanns Eisler's 1931 argument on the same subject.[9] The similarity in the phraseology and the development of the argument is striking enough to suggest the probability that Mann has deliberately copied the method Eisler uses in his book, which is clearly, unambiguously, and intentionally about politics.[10] Eisler's explanation of the parallel of the development of music with political history is communist and describes the motor force as the class struggle, whereas Mann describes it as alternating subjectivity and objectivity and their ultimate synthesis. The perspective is radically opposed. Adrian, like Eisler, identifies the variation with individualism and describes it as the distinctive feature of the nineteenth-century development of music. Eisler, however, associates this development with capitalism, and considers it superseded (42), whereas it is Adrian's idea to incorporate it as an indispensable component of his new music.

Eisler argues that the sterility surrounding the development of music was recognized and solved by Schoenberg in 1910 (28–29). However, although he is undeniably the greatest modern composer, he is bourgeois and his music reflects capitalism: "Young composers, and above all young proletarian composers, must not listen to or copy him uncritically, they must have the strength to differentiate the content of his work from the method" (75–76).

In the description of Adrian's *strenger Satz*, Mann is not talking about content, but he is also not talking about method. Adrian has not yet worked out his method, but has been only partially successful. Totalitarianism, whether fascism or communism, is defined by its method, not by its content. Clearly, Adrian is not talking about fascism, if he is talking about totalitarianism, but about communism. However, he is talking about neither. He is talking about liberal democracy. It is the form that is significant.

* * *

That Adrian enters the pact with the Devil to overcome "crippling inhibitions" is virtually universally accepted as a given fact, but there has been little discussion of what these inhibitions are. It seems to be assumed that they have to do with his so-called artistic sterility, which Zeitblom talks about, but does not illustrate, in chapter 22. He does not, however, define what they are. Zeitblom's constant preoccupation with Adrian's chastity strongly implies, as does his whole approach, that he sees these inhibitions as sexual, or, as he describes it, Adrian's lack of humanity. However, these inhibitions are quite clearly defined in chapter 21. Zeitblom begins to cast doubt on whether Adrian, in developing his theory, sees what is going on around him, whether his experience of life influences his work (*DF*, 236). However, he comments later that Adrian has insights that he expresses without thinking and that these could endanger his life. He describes these "insights" as "crippling inhibitions" in the development of his talent (*DF*, 241). Adrian's response to Zeitblom's objection is that in these days art has to take a moral stand, which he means as a contradiction of what Zeitblom says. "Schein und Spiel haben heute schon das Gewissen der Kunst gegen sich. Sie will aufhören, Schein und Spiel zu sein, sie will Erkenntnis werden" (*DF*, 242). In other words, Adrian's inhibitions are moral in nature, not psychological, or sexual, as Zeitblom infers.

Zeitblom thinks that if art is to take a moral stand without destroying itself, morality will end up being a travesty of innocence (*DF*, 242). This travesty of innocence, according to Zeitblom, is reflected in Adrian's efforts to overcome traditional harmony through the incorporation of polyphony. He calls it technically primitive, naive. Zeitblom goes further and says that Adrian's combination of strict counterpoint with extreme expressiveness is demonic (*DF*, 237–38). These remarks about Adrian's inhibitions are rather cryptic when they are made, but take on a quite sinister significance towards the end of the novel. This passage is the summary of the political events of the novel, from Zeitblom's point of view. He is clearly shown to be against what Adrian is doing. He is stating that Adrian's idea of how to express German culture politically is wrong, as Litzmann said of Mann's argument in *Die Betrachtungen eines Unpolitischen*. Adrian is signing his death warrant with this activity. These remarks are in reference to Adrian's development of his *strenger Satz*, the great insight that Adrian expresses without thinking. Zeitblom associates this *strenger Satz*, or Adrian's argument for democracy, with "crippling inhibitions" and says that the danger to Adrian's life will result from his expressing such ideas publicly — that is, society will turn against him (*DF*, 241). This can only be an openly political remark. Zeitblom is stating once again that dissent will not be tolerated. The inhibition that Adrian suffers from in the novel is identified here as listening to his conscience rather than going along with the crowd. This is elaborated by the Devil in chapter 25 and it is inspiration to overcome this inhibition, his Protestant morality, that the Devil offers to Adrian. In Mann's view, there are no conditions under which the artist will succumb to this temptation:

> Der Künstler und Dichter wenigstens wird seiner tiefsten Natur nach immer ein unveräußerliches Recht auf individualistisches Ethos haben, er ist der notwendige und geborene Protestant, der einzelne mit seinem Gott. Es kann und darf um seine Einsamkeit, seine "evangelische Freiheit" auch in Zeiten straffster sozialer Gebundenheit nicht geschehen sein. (*BeU*, 491)

Bernhard Schubert provides an interesting discussion of Mann's position on this question.[11] He argues that Mann firmly believed that stubborn Protestant subjectivity is separated from inner natural powers and that his characters protect themselves from the anarchy of compulsion through social forms and symbolic behavior. They do not need illusions and are not thrown off the track. They reject the Dionysian with their Protestant will to truth and their conscientiousness. In Schubert's view, this is an Apollonian strategy that is based on a denial of reality (574). According to Mann, Aschenbach, in *Der Tod in Venedig*, falls victim not to Dionysus but to aestheticism, an arbitrary betrayal of the Protestant German lifestyle. Mann describes fascism in the same way, as an arbitrary abandoning of the Protestant German lifestyle (575). He sees the ethical, Apollonian armor of German Protestant subjectivity as a protection against the dangerous and pathological yearning for release. The imperative of Christian asceticism inhibits the discharge of the Dionysian impulses that are directed against the principle of identity. Nietzsche, unlike Mann, thought that this repression would ultimately collapse under pressure into Dionysian convulsion (576). However, Adrian does not collapse in chapter 25; he resists to the end.

It has been shown that Zeitblom does not understand Adrian's work and misinterprets it. Adrian is arguing for democracy and Zeitblom will interpret his system as an argument for a new kind of totalitarianism, based on a "cult of the music." The reader has been told that the "crippling inhibitions" that prevent Adrian from developing his talent consist in insisting on the preservation of individual freedom and listening to his conscience. He has also been told how to interpret Adrian's *Apocalipsis cum figuris* for himself, without Zeitblom's dubious assistance.

Notes

[1] Thomas Mann, "Maß und Wert," in *GW*, 12:798–820; here, 819.

[2] Thomas Mann, *Dr. Faustus* (Stockholm: Bermann-Fischer, 1947), 296–97.

[3] This is, of course, nonsense. The use of letters to name musical tones is a meaningless convention. The letters have no significance as letters. This is another one of the difficulties in translating *Doktor Faustus*: the conventions for naming tones vary from language to language and the reference is entirely lost when these names are translated and incomprehensible when they are not. The note names in English would be B, E, A, E, Bb. The translation of the note names completely destroys the allusion to the transparent butterfly, the haetera Esmeralda, that Zeitblom implies.

[4] Thomas Mann, "Schicksal und Aufgabe," in *GW*, 12:918–39; here, 918.

[5] Lieselotte Voss, *Die Entstehung von Thomas Manns Roman* Doktor Faustus: *Dargestellt anhand von unveröffentlichten Vorarbeiten* (Tübingen: Niemeyer, 1975), 149.

[6] Gert Sautermeister, "Zwischen Aufklärung und Mystifizierung: Der unbewältigte Widerspruch in Thomas Manns *Doktor Faustus*," in *Antifaschistische Literatur*, ed. Lutz Winkler (Königstein: Scriptor, 1979), 77–125; here, 121.

[7] Thomas Mann, "Bekenntnis zum Sozialismus," in *GW*, 12:678–84; here, 680.

[8] Sautermeister, "Zwischen Aufklärung und Mystifizierung," 122.

[9] Hanns Eisler, *A Rebel in Music* (New York: International, 1978), 36–58.

[10] Eisler was a well-known figure in the musical world as well as in the political world. Furthermore, he was Mann's neighbor in exile in California.

[11] Bernhard Schubert, "Das Ende der bürgerlichen Vernunft? Zu Thomas Manns *Doktor Faustus*," *Zeitschrift für deutsche Philologie* 105:4(1986): 568–92.

7: Zeitblom's Propensity to Demonology

THE IDEA OF ZEITBLOM'S ESPOUSING demonology appears ridiculous in the light of everyday common sense. However, in the world of the novel, fascism is presented in the shape of demonology and, therefore, requires this image. At the end of the novel, Adrian is presented as a Christ-figure, which is equally ridiculous in the world of reality, but appropriate to the novel. Obviously, in a secular age, no ordinary human beings fall into either of these categories. For most of the novel, Mann has presented both Adrian and Zeitblom as believable members of society. They have their peculiarities, which one may like or dislike, but in the real world of today few of us think in the terms set by the novel. It has to be remembered that *Doktor Faustus* is a work of art, not a sociological study. We do not object to this kind of allegorical imagery in a painting; on the contrary we consider it appropriate. The images in *Doktor Faustus* are allegorical, basic and simple, black and white. Their presentation, however, is not so simple, nor are they so readily identified. Mann has painted his novel in full color, with subtle nuances and grayed areas where statements mean one thing when they are concrete and quite another thing in the abstract context in which they are presented. Mann has, in effect, reversed the medieval practice of illustrating theological truths in real world settings — a man about to fall into the clutch of the Devil is illustrated as hanging desperately on the edge of a cliff with the Devil holding his arms out at the bottom, waiting for him to fall. Abstractions are presented literally as reality. Mann is doing the reverse, presenting the real world to illustrate the theological abstractions that underlie it.

Adrian's predisposition to democracy has been established as based on the fact that he thinks like a musician. His approach to solving the problem of moving ahead with the times and keeping his art in tune with the culture has led to the development of a new musical system that is point for point the parallel of liberal democracy. Zeitblom, as a Catholic humanist, a *Zivilisationsliterat*, will derive his politics from his theology and his idea of theology is essentially Roman Catholic. Humanism is, in its origin, a secularization of medieval Catholicism. In chapter 22, during the conversation on the Zionsberg after Ursula's wedding, during the very same conversation and immediately before Adrian reveals his *strenger Satz*, Zeitblom expresses his views on marriage and sex as based on what sounds very much like Nietzsche's celebration of life. This in itself sounds innocuous, but earlier in the novel Zeitblom has described the combination of this philosophy with Roman Catholic theology as dangerously approaching demonology: "Denn die Theologie, in Verbindung gebracht mit dem Geist der Lebensphilosophie, dem Irrationalismus, läuft ihrer Natur nach Gefahr, zur Dämonologie zu werden" (*DF*, 123).

In *Die Betrachtungen eines Unpolitischen* Mann says that the political expression of this combination is fascism. He argues that the *Action française*, the French Catholic fascist movement, is based on the politicizing of Nietzsche's philosophy of life, sacrificing "truth" to "life" in the interests of the State. This is a corruption of Nietzsche, since Nietzsche's philosophy is based on individualism (*BeU*, 210–11). Mann considered that to apply Nietzsche's argument that procreation is the holy way to life and the road to the future to politics is an effort to identify the national with the anti-human and a barbarous misuse of Nietzsche. It is to identify Nietzsche with the mystical, dark and introverted, type of Romanticism that was associated with Catholicism in the nineteenth century and with National Socialism in the twentieth century. In Mann's view, as he said in his report on his trip to France, "Pariser Rechenschaft," Nietzsche represents the reverse of this: overcoming this tendency. Using Nietzsche in this way is essentially reactionary in that the problem that Nietzsche was addressing no longer exists.[1]

Nietzsche was not the only source of ideas that can have a negative effect when irresponsibly used to justify a disregard for the intellect in collective matters. The nineteenth century also produced several other ideas questioning the absolute domination of the intellect, such as Schopenhauer's theory of the domination of will and Freud's theory of the importance of subconscious drive. The development of these theories of drive and will was simultaneous with, but not related to, this tendency to a return to medieval theology, as Zeitblom tells us in chapter 11 (*DF*, 122–23). These concepts are certainly not related to this tendency; they are in contradiction to medieval Catholic theology. They were developed in the context of individualism, whereas medieval theology was based on a denial of individualism. Zeitblom, however, does not see this incompatibility. He finds that combining these movements gives the modern watered-down nineteenth-century theology more substance (122–23), since Lutheran theology, which insists on relying on commonsense, is shallow and does not reflect the true relationship of human nature and the tragic side of life (122). Zeitblom describes Protestant humanism as replacing the humanistic function of religion with the adaptation of religion to social ideals, turning it into nothing more than ethical progress (122). Ethical progress would seem to be not a "nothing more" but a "sine qua non" of social organization, and Zeitblom is talking about social organization. With this definition, he is reversing the causal relationship established by Mann in *Die Betrachtungen eines Unpolitischen*, where he describes German humanism as the development, not the origin, of modern

Lutheran theology, whereas Zeitblom implies that German humanism is not theology, but opposed to it: it was a fundamental error for theologians to accept that rationality be applied to the dogma, because it left them having to defend indefensible contradictions and this destroys belief (*DF*, 121). In other words, there is a fundamental contradiction between rationality and belief, and Zeitblom is favoring belief. In *Die Betrachtungen eines Unpolitischen* Mann attacks this tendency of the *Zivilisationsliterat* to revert to the medieval concept of belief. Zeitblom is doing just this. He is, in effect, denying that Lutheran theology and German humanism are expressions of religion, on the grounds that they are based on individualism. He is in the process of restoring the medieval concept of religious belief, basing it on a glorification of these mysterious, irrational powers of will and drive and on Nietzsche's glorification of life. He is turning the individual subconscious into a collective subconscious. The Devil explains in chapter 25 that this process has occurred. The result is secularized demonology, or fascism.

The question of the influence of the erotic in the early part of the twentieth century, very clearly represented in the novel by Zeitblom, is very complex and beyond the scope of this study. It is clear in the novel that Zeitblom is preoccupied with the erotic and, for purposes of interpreting Zeitblom, the existence of this element cannot be neglected. As the novel moves on, Zeitblom increasingly describes sex as the motivation behind all human decisions, and his tendency is to collectivize, or politicize this, rather than leave it in the realm of individualism where it belongs. He does this by interpreting individual reactions as manifestations of pseudo-scientific generalizations about human behavior, making unjustified assumptions that are not supported by fact and are at times contradicted by his own evidence. Mann has defined this influence as being Nietzsche's in the case of fascism. In chapter 22 Zeitblom espouses the view that procreation is the holy way to life and the road to the future in his interpretation of the meaning of marriage. It is this image that establishes Zeitblom's predisposition to fascism in the simplified imagery of the novel.

Mann dismisses as nonsense the suggestion that the political influence of Nietzsche is reflected in the fact that some persons used his philosophy as an excuse for licentious behavior. This is, of course, very much part of the Munich environment portrayed and criticized by Zeitblom in the novel.

> Will man es als politische Wirkungen Nietzsche's ansprechen, daß er einige Grubenbesitzer oder Großbörseaner bewog, sich für Renaissancemenschen zu halten, oder daß ein paar dumme Jungen und Fräulein ihn dahin verstanden, sie müßten sich amoralistisch "ausleben," — in Gottes Namen, das ist nicht ernst. (*BeU*, 210)

Therefore, Zeitblom's criticism of such behavior is not a criticism of fascism or a reflection of Mann's views in this context. Neither do the characters described as living this way in the novel, most particularly Clarissa and Ines, represent fascism. Their behavior is an expression of individualism, of going against the current. It is also an expression of their suffering. On the other hand, those in the novel who enthusiastically believe in this philosophy in the abstract, such as Institoris and Zeitblom, are shown as behaving not eccentrically, but conventionally — and also as ultimately espousing fascism. In his discussion of the proposed marriage between Ines and Institoris Zeitblom says that the problem is that they have opposite views of life. They are in fact personifications of the main oppositions of the time, the opposition between aestheticism and morality, or between the uninhibited theory of the glorification of life and a pessimistic honoring of suffering with its depths and wisdom. This difference, in its creative origin, had been an expression of individualism, a personal unity, and had only recently become an opposition, he explains. Ines and Institoris are prime examples of these extremes (*DF*, 383–84). It is this same difference that is revealed between Adrian and Zeitblom in the discussion of marriage that follows.

During the conversation on the Zionsberg, Zeitblom says, referring to Adrian, that if you believe in the Devil, you already belong to him. It is because Adrian has identified sex with the Devil that Zeitblom describes him as belonging to the Devil. Adrian says that he has simply used a theological metaphor. However, theology is the origin of the secularized values of the community and Mann is describing politics as a secularized version of theology. The same values, or measures of good and evil, apply to both areas. Adrian is, in fact, speaking of the Devil, but it is a secularized Devil, removed from religion to the area of civilized social order, or social organization. It is in this context that Mann is putting the question. What is the place of the erotic, or the expression of subconscious will, in social decisions? Zeitblom does not consider it demonic.

Adrian does not believe in the existence of the Devil in any religious sense. The German Lutheran tradition has not only made the Devil metaphorical; it has made the values associated with God and the Devil relative, through the defining of good and evil as a question of conscience, based on social utility. The fact that Luther believed in the Devil, which Mann introduces through Kumpf, is a red herring. It is not Luther who defined modern German Protestantism. Luther was a thoroughly medieval man who, by breaking away from the totalitarian authority of Roman Catholic Church dogma, opened the door to the gradual development of modern German, secularized, Protestant subjectivity. Luther belongs to his times, not to the present, and the term Lutheran refers to the historic development of what he introduced. In his essay on Lessing, Mann makes the point that one cannot extrapolate from what Luther said and did anything about what Luther would say or do outside of the context of his own historical period.[2] In fact, Zeitblom specifically mentions that Kumpf rejects the duality of early Protestantism. In Kumpf's view, it is the intellect that the Devil corrupts, quite a different concept from Zeitblom's (*DF*, 130–31). Kumpf is, therefore, making a joke when he refers to the Devil in connection with wine, women, and song, and Adrian laughs at it. Zeitblom does not find it funny.

In general, Zeitblom shows Adrian as remarkably little interested in sex. Of course, the main reason that Mann has done this is to counterweight and emphasize Zeitblom's excessive interest in sex. Zeitblom has already told us that Adrian does not talk about sex. This discussion is, in fact, the only time in the novel that he does. Zeitblom, on the other hand, finds a sexual explanation for everything. As for what Adrian actually does in the sexual vein, Zeitblom does not know, because Adrian does not talk about it. It could be argued that it is none of Zeitblom's business. Zeitblom is also relatively reticent about his own sexual activities. It is the activities of others that he fantasizes on.

However, a closer look at this conversation shows that, in fact, even here Adrian is not really talking about sex at all, but dismissing it as secondary. The conversation, having established Zeitblom's theoretical enthusiasm for the erotic, which I take to be symbolically Nietzsche's glorification of life, thus throwing up a flag to identify his predisposition to fascism, moves on to establish the metaphor of marriage. This association is as misplaced chronologically in the novel as are Adrian's arguments for democracy and the political discussion of the Winfried group. The events in the novel are chronological and are often placed specifically by exact date. There is, however, no chronology whatsoever in the presentation of the ideas, or thought patterns. What is new in this chapter of *Doktor Faustus* is the introduction of marriage as a metaphor for political organization. It is this metaphor that underlies the story of Marie. As gradually becomes clear, but is certainly not obvious at this point in the novel, all the discussions of marriage are about politics.

Zeitblom and Adrian are discussing the institution of marriage, and Adrian says that, theologically speaking, calling marriage Christian is intended to remove sex from the Devil, although it does not change anything, because calling it Christian is just a game with words. The important thing is that it domesticates sex, which is a good thing, in Adrian's view. Adrian's theology is Lutheran, the same as Kumpf's. Nature is subsumed in the human and the abuse of natural instincts is controlled by individual conscience, convention, good manners, love, and of course, rationality. In the case of sex, this is marriage, or commitment, which is the recognition of personal and social responsibility. A marriage is the founding of a community, a basic social unit involving more than one individual. Sensuality cannot be separated from love, says Adrian, because sensuality is a meaningless word in itself. All sensuality implies tenderness, the taking and giving of pleasure, and is an expression of love. Since sensuality and love mean the same thing, the Christian dogma of man and wife becoming one flesh is nonsense, argues Adrian. Sex takes two people and is based on love, so the Christian dogma is meant to remove love from marriage. The dogma denies the association of sex with love. It does so by denying individualism, removing the possibility of spiritual interchange, turning marriage into a collective unit. Adrian rejects this dogma energetically. Adrian does not identify sex with the Devil; he rejects the barbarism of associating sex and marriage simply with procreation. Sex is not associated with the Devil when it is an expression of love. It is the identification of the erotic as the determining factor in the decision to marry that Adrian associates with the Devil.

Ursula's wedding is a quiet family ceremony in the light of day — that is, nothing to do with exorcising the Devil — for the purpose of establishing a new family, the basic social unit. When Adrian discusses the marriage, he refers to her new husband with reference to his suitability for assuming this role. He does not speculate on his sexual prowess as does Zeitblom when he discusses the marriage of Ines with Institoris, briefly in chapter 29 (*DF*, 395) and extensively in chapter 32 (438–39). The whole description is a play on the motif of eyes, which is always in reference to point of view, or of observing reality, despite Zeitblom's association of eyes with sexual attraction. Both images are taken from Shakespeare's *Love's Labour's Lost*. Schneidewein is an optician, a maker of spectacles and optical instruments. He was trained in Switzerland, the democratic country. Adrian says he has "good eyes" and is therefore suitable. The ultimate outcome of this marriage will be an angel, the blonde, blue-eyed, German Nepomuk, who speaks German in the Swiss, or democratic, way.

Zeitblom says that Adrian's views on marriage make him uncomfortable about discussing his own marriage plans (*DF*, 250). This remark only makes sense if Zeitblom has a quite different view of the meaning of marriage. He excuses Adrian from attending his own wedding, to be celebrated with dancing and ceremony. However it is not the party aspect that he thinks Adrian would object to. Adrian participates in the "Faschingsfest," which is a great party based on religious tradition. It is not Adrian but his father who suffers from headaches at parties. Zeitblom attributes Adrian's headache at Ursula's wedding to his revulsion at the orgiastic celebration of the sacrifice of his sister's virginity, this "Opferfest der Magdschaft" (248). Adrian, he says, conceals this disgust by praising the subdued good taste of the ceremony — so much for Zeitblom's understanding of Adrian's argument. Adrian, as always, according to Zeitblom's account, does not mean what he says. The reason he thinks Adrian will not want to go to his wedding is ultimately because he thinks Adrian associates the Devil with sex and has dishonestly and hypocritically constructed a justification for his sister's marriage that leaves sex out. Zeitblom's wedding will not be celebrated on this hypocritical basis.

The two interpretations of the purpose of marriage are different. As concerns sex they are opposites. Adrian's interpretation is that marriage is the intellect and the spirit controlling nature and turning evil into good. Zeitblom's interpretation is that marriage is celebrating the irruption of evil — in the traditional theological sense — and calling it good. They also differ in that Adrian's view of marriage is as of something directed to the future, whereas Zeitblom's view is that it is an end in itself. Zeitblom's argument, which amounts to saying that marriage is based on a celebration of sex, seriously questions the humanity of his humanism. His humanism is not German Protestant humanism. There is a difference between seeing sex as an expression of love and describing it as sensuality and the human basis of a social unit, and seeing the fundamental basis of social organization in sex, a manifestation of irrational drive and simply for purposes of procreation. Perhaps this attitude towards sex can indeed be associated with the Devil. It is certainly devoid of intellectual or spiritual content. The result of Zeitblom's marriage is three not very prepossessing children who blindly follow their *Führer*. It is important to see not simply Zeitblom's view of marriage in itself, but also his dislike of Adrian's view. He is not describing Adrian as not liking parties. He is describing his own rejection of rationality as the criterion for marriage, or for social organization looking to the future.

Adrian, in fact, is not talking about sex at all, but of the basic difficulty in political organization, the inviolability of the individual: "Die Lust zu fremdem Fleisch bedeutet eine Überwindung sonst vorhandener Widerstände, die auf der Fremdheit von Ich und Du, des Eigenen und des Anderen beruhen" (*DF*, 250). This argument sounds very much the same as the argument put forward by Martin Buber in *Ich und Du*.[3] Martin Buber, the very influential German Jewish Zionist theologian, had as a main concern the development of a way to organize a humane new society, where the individual cooperates with the community in his own and the community's interest. This is only possible, without destroying the individual, if his own personal idiosyncrasy and sense of self and personal responsibility are neither questioned nor threatened but enhanced. Buber's argument was the original argument forming the basis of the Kibbutz. At the time, he was considered an anarchist. Buber bases his political arguments on his theology, which explains why Zeitblom remarks that he has the impression that there is something explicitly foreign about the way Adrian expresses himself (*DF*, 251). The recurring motif of Adrian's difficulty with "du" is used in this sense, to illustrate his insistence on maintaining his independence as an individual, as Arzt points out in chapter 14 (156–57). He can only address another as "du" when he trusts that their working together to build a society for the future will reinforce his own individualism. This he achieves in his association with Rudi Schwerdtfeger.

Zeitblom's remark about Adrian's believing in the Devil immediately precedes Adrian's beginning to develop his twelve-tone theory, thereby associating the two and implying that there is something demonic in Adrian's system. What we have seen, however, is that the relationship of Adrian's *strenger Satz* with this discussion is his preoccupation with the problem of combining personal morality and individualism with government. It is the same argument as before, beginning in the marriage discussion with two individuals and developed by Adrian in the application of his *strenger Satz* to include five notes/individuals and a theory for further development (*DF*, 255). This time, instead of using his disagreement with Kierkegaard as his basis, he has used his agreement with Martin Buber, a Jew.

Zeitblom says he does not like to identify sex with the Devil, since that is insulting the source of life, advocating nihilism. Adrian denies that there is anything about the source of life to insult, but Zeitblom ignores this remark. However, the reader should not. Adrian is rejecting the Christian dogma on which social organization is based, that sex belongs to the Devil unless sanctioned by dogma, and he is replacing dogma with love, mutual respect, and trust between two individuals. He is also rejecting Zeitblom's argument, which amounts to an irresponsible glorification of a permissive clause in the dogma, theologically speaking. Zeitblom sees the question of "good" or "bad" as revolving around sex itself. In Adrian's argument sex is neither good nor bad. The moral question revolves around how the fact of sex is managed, how a natural function, or drive, can be turned to benefit society. Adrian is associating sex with individualism. In fascist thought, individualism, Protestantism, and pre-Roman Christianity are synonymous with Judaism, as Mann's use of Buber's *Ich und Du* symbolism throughout the novel indicates. What Zeitblom is pointing out is not that Adrian associates sex with the Devil, but that he associates social organization based on the inviolability of the individual with Judaism.

Zeitblom clearly does not understand Adrian's argument about domesticating sex. He separates the characteristic of man as part of nature from his spiritual nature, then makes the irrational aspect of human nature the main theme of his theory. He is giving religious status to the celebration of procreation — that is, the crude natural, or instinctive, act. Not only that, he says that it has always been the humanist view that sex is not associated with the Devil., but rather that procreation is virtuous, and it is true that all the incidents in Schleppfuß's lectures and in the *Gesta Romanorum* illustrate this point. It is not sex that is shown as evil, but any action or attitude that interferes with sex as the instinct to procreation. Sex as a manifestation of love is rejected in these stories, quite specifically in Schleppfuß's story of Heinz and Bärbel. Bärbel, says Zeitblom, crippled Heinz, not through the Devil, but through love (*DF*, 147–48). He clearly rejects the idea that love humanizes sex. In his account of Adrian's trip to Graz, where he, Zeitblom implies, irreparably damaged his brain through the deliberate contraction of venereal disease, he attributes Adrian's downfall to the fact that his motivation must have been love. The problem is that he crudely fixed his instinctive sexual drive on a specific individual (204). The result was a deadly chemical synthesis of love and poison (205–6). This is a flat rejection of Adrian's argument. Zeitblom is associating individualism with madness.

In his puppet opera Adrian defines this preoccupation with procreation as an erotic farce and a tool of totalitarianism. Zeitblom rejects Adrian's opera as unjustified derision of the moral message of the priest (*DF*, 426). The moral message of the priest in these stories can be summed up as "procreation is the holy way to life." In any event, in these stories, putting obstacles to procreation certainly leads to death. Zeitblom's position is a rejection of Adrian's Protestant humanism in favor of a Catholic humanism that has been turned on its head through secularization. As Kumpf has told us, the Devil can corrupt the intellect but not morality, and, as Schleppfuß has illustrated, his favorite tool is sex. The question in these stories is: "Whose mind has been corrupted by sex, the priest's or his victims"? In the context of the argument of the novel, it would seem to be that the problem originates in the attempt to apply an ideal — in this case chastity — to social organization, or to politics. It results in a reversal of the ideal, a barbaric manipulation of the masses.

In the Christian tradition, as has been amply illustrated in chapter 13 and in the *Gesta Romanorum* in chapter 31, sex is the preferred tool of the Devil for enticing man to abandon God and, as Adrian has stated here, this is the accepted theological stand. By deciding to reverse this, Zeitblom is showing that he is confusing theology with demonology. He is accepting the values of the Devil as good, rather than evil. Does not demonology mean sharing the Devil's values, rather than God's? Is this compatible with Zeitblom's Catholic humanist values? Mann suggests that it is indeed. The glorification of procreation is nothing more than a revival of medieval Catholic values. All these medieval stories are about the application of religion for control of the masses, which is politics, and it is being done through the glorification of procreation. There is no reference to chastity and higher values in these stories. Heinz's and Bärbel's association of sex with love, which results in a natural desire for chastity, is condemned as corrupt, anti-natural, and associated with magic and the Devil. Zeitblom associates Adrian's *strenger Satz* with magic, a property of religion, but redefined by dogma as a contradiction of the dogma. When it is deemed not to contradict, it is a miracle, not magic.

Zeitblom believes in the Devil. Although his Devil is also largely secularized and metaphorical, his Catholicism had not undergone the same moral metamorphosis as had Lutheran Protestantism and had simply become, as he erroneously describes Protestantism, a weak adaptation to social morality. That the adaptation was weak is illustrated by his use of modern German philosophy and scientific discoveries to fill the gap left by the lack of objectivity that was provided by the Church. It is a corruption of the already corrupt Roman Catholic application of metaphysics to politics through the distorting influence of these Protestant values and scientific discoveries. This requires that Zeitblom redefine the Devil, taking away his most prominent characteristic approach to mankind, corruption through sex. Instead of identifying the Devil with sex, he associates him with dissenters, again in the medieval fashion. This is, in fact, a radical departure. Sexual abuse is normally considered a heinous crime and generates much more revulsion at all levels of society than most other crimes. In other words, it is the general view that the misuse of sex has to do with the Devil. On the other hand, the attitude towards dissent had long been radically reversed in Germany. It was considered not only a right, but in some circumstances a moral obligation, to oppose what one thinks is wrong, and all scientific advance is based on dissent from established ideas. It is precisely this subjective freedom that Mann felt was under threat with the introduction of Rousseau's democracy. Adrian's answer to this problem, given in his *strenger Satz*, is to develop a democratic system, to find a means of adjusting "the music," to redefine the system in such a way that it not simply tolerates dissent but is based on dissent as a principle. The argument of his *strenger Satz* is fundamentally the same as the argument in his reflections on Ursula's marriage to a Swiss. They are both about the incorporation of democracy to German humanity and based on the principle of the inviolability of the individual. Zeitblom associates this idea with the Devil. If dissenters, or individualists, are associated with the Devil, then tolerating dissent, or individualism, is tolerating the Devil. The Devil has corrupted Zeitblom's mind through sex.

The identification of marriage with social order, or politics, comes from Bachofen's theory of mother-right. His book, *Das Mutterrecht*, published in 1861, was rediscovered around 1900.[4] It is, like Spengler's *Untergang des Abendlandes*, a scientific theory of the inevitable development of history according to immutable natural laws.[5] According to Bachofen's theory, society develops through three stages: the elemental, or hetaerism, the lunar, or conjugal mother-right, and the solar, or spiritual stage, where pure father-right prevails.

Hetaerism is a primitive matriarchal system of social organization, based on the concubine with political influence. This stage is unregulated, with a purely natural and elementary relationship between the sexes, and is essentially corrupt. The second, or middle, stage of evolution is conjugal matriarchy. Its emergence is the realization of a natural law and represents emancipation from sensual animal life. During this stage society develops a decorous system of manners, and specific cultures are founded and protected. Conjugal matriarchy presupposes exclusive marriage, in that it legitimates regulated sex, not based on passion, and introduces the necessity of the father in the superior mother-world, with a balanced acceptance of the father-world in service to the mother-world. The culture of this period is humanity, reconciliation, peace, rectitude, and morality.

This period of conjugal mother-right is, however, a transitional stage, between hetaerism and patriarchy. Bachofen sees this stage as inferior, because in it the woman is more important than the man, and, since the woman represents materialism and corruption, it is necessary to strive for the victory of father-right. The realm of the father is the highest cultural stage, because the woman is completely dominated. The emphasizing of paternity means the freeing of the intellect from nature and bodily existence. Only the spiritual principle pertains exclusively to the man. He breaks free from the elementary and is joined to the heavenly light. His world is repression, war, power, and struggle, with logical thinking dominating over irrational emotionalism. In Bachofen's view, the Roman political system is the embodiment of triumphant father-right (63, 221, 436, 962, 983). He saw the patriarchal world as the most perfect and expressed in the Roman political system and medieval Christianity. Bachofen lumps hetaerism and conjugal matriarchy together and describes Christianity as arising out of the ruins of the mother-world.

As scientific and useful as this study may be in its factual content and in its deciphering of myths, Bachofen's fascist conclusions are based on personal value judgments that are radically opposed to Mann's values. However, Bachofen's description of the period of conjugal matriarchy is virtually the same as Adrian's description of marriage and of the fundamental Protestant values that he represents and that Zeitblom rejects. Bachofen explains the emergence of these values as the result of the sexual union of pure intellect with the "hetaere," which explains why Zeitblom associates Adrian's developing mental confusion, as he sees it, as the result of a sexual union with a corrupted prostitute, whom he calls Hetaera Esmeralda. Zeitblom's own marriage is, by Bachofen's logic, of a much higher order. Further, Bachofen associates the social goal of a higher political order with a combination of the Roman political system with medieval Christianity, a position Mann condemns as totalitarian in *Die Betrachtungen eines Unpolitischen*. Zeitblom represents this fascist position.

Zeitblom is using the intellect to argue against intellect, one of the fundamental contributions to the rise of intellectual fascism, as Joachim Fest points out in his chapter on Intellectuals.[6] Zeitblom's eroticism is not reflected in his own behavior, as presented in the novel. It is an eroticism of the mind. However, his behavior does represent a rejection of Adrian's argument. His own marriage, celebrated publicly in conformity with this barbarous tradition, he describes as a need to conform to convention. The appeal of his Helene is symbolic, based on her name, not on her person. It is a celebration of the Greek ideal of beauty, which is not, as Zeitblom himself says, reflected in reality (*DF*, 18). Zeitblom never describes his own motivations as sexual, yet he is obsessed by sex and finds a sexual motivation to explain everybody else's behavior. I have seen few studies of this aspect of the novel, which is peripheral to the intention of this study. This is very interesting, given the general preoccupation of more recent critics with Mann's sexual orientation. It is mentioned here as an illustration of the discrepancy between what Zeitblom says and the reality he describes. Essentially Zeitblom is viewing life as a fairytale. The virtue of the woman is her beauty and the marriage ends the story: they live happily ever after.

What is clear, and must be stressed, is that Adrian is not advocating fascism. He is advocating democracy. Equally clear and equally important is Zeitblom's interpretation of Adrian's *strenger Satz* as advocating totalitarianism and the basis of this misinterpretation: his dismissal of the components based on the autonomy of the individual. This is expressed in the above discussion as distrust of Adrian's argument for individualism as the basis of marriage, rather than sexual compulsion. He attributes what he considers Adrian's confusion to the migraine headaches. Adrian is describing social organization as a rational decision and Zeitblom is describing it as an irrational expression of will.

In order to understand the latter part of the novel, which is openly political, it is necessary to understand the underlying political content of the beginning of the novel. It lays the basis for how the various characters react to the political upheaval at the end of the First World War and during the 1920s and for Adrian's ultimate destruction. Both early critics, Holthusen and Becher, rejected the theology but liked the music, and Becher identified the theology as demonology. However, they did not distinguish who was talking. Adrian talks about democracy through talking about music. Zeitblom talks about fascism through talking about theology. His theology, like all his ideas, is based on sex. Sex, whether defined as evil, nature, will, or drive, or as a positive good, is fundamentally a manifestation of irrationality.

Although the political situation has yet to present itself in the novel, sides have already been taken. Zeitblom and Adrian have been revealed as representing opposing political predispositions. Whereas Adrian has decided to dedicate himself to salvaging German Protestant values, Zeitblom has exposed to the reader his rejection of German Protestant society and his belief that a return to the Catholic values of the High Middle Ages is inevitable and desirable. Both arguments in chapter 22, Zeitblom's fascist glorification of life and Adrian's musical democracy, are paraphrases of arguments taken from *Die Betrachtungen eines Unpolitischen.*

On a more mundane level, Mann's aversion to public eroticism and the glorification of the sexual is well known. This aversion was one of the major contributions to his lifelong disagreement with his brother Heinrich, the original model for the *Zivilisationsliterat.* Returning to the superficial argument about marriage, it is interesting to compare it with

Mann's 1925 essay "Über die Ehe."[7] In relation to Zeitblom's marriage, based on aesthetic symbolism, Mann says aesthetics has nothing to do with ethics, usefulness, or fruitfulness (*GW*, 10:196). And in relation to Adrian's argument, he says that you should not marry for sex. You marry to form a community (*GW*, 10:206). It simply cannot be maintained that Zeitblom's position is representative of Mann. It is undeniably Adrian who represents Mann's position.

Notes

[1] Thomas Mann, "Pariser Rechenschaft," *GW*, 11:9–97; here, 48–51.

[2] Thomas Mann, "Rede über Lessing," *GW*, 9:229–45; here, 243.

[3] Martin Buber, *Ich und Du* (Leipzig: Insel-Verlag, 1923).

[4] See Edmund Remys, *Hermann Hesse's* Das Glasperlenspiel: *A Concealed Defense of the Mother World* (New York: Lang, 1983).

[5] Oswald Spengler, *Untergang des Abendlandes* (Munich: Beck, 1920).

[6] Joachim Fest, *Das Gesicht des dritten Reiches* (1963; rpt. Munich: Piper, 1993).

[7] Thomas Mann, "Über die Ehe," *GW*, 10:191–207.

8: Interlude

THE FIRST WORLD WAR IS THE decisive break in the development of the events that are significant for the story of the novel. The change in the economic and political environment resulting from Germany's defeat leads to a realignment of forces and relationships, based primarily on the suddenly extreme importance of whether each of the characters is a Catholic humanist, a *Zivilisationsliterat*, or a Protestant artist. Before proceeding with the discussion of the development of Adrian's and Zeitblom's political thought in the new situation, it would be well to pause and look at some examples of Mann's light-hearted illustration of the fundamental differences between them in chapter 24, Zeitblom's report on Adrian's stay in Italy. This report establishes the date of the stay and the physical setting, but this is only marginally necessary to the development of the novel. The real purpose of the chapter lies elsewhere. For most of the chapter Zeitblom talks about himself and about his view of his relationship to Adrian, his theory of art, and various other matters. In this sense it can be described as Zeitblom's *Zwiesprach*, the counterpart to Adrian's observations in chapter 25.

The visit to Italy is the only occasion in their adult lives on which Adrian and Zeitblom live in close proximity for an extended length of time. In chapter 24, as always in the novel, events work both ways. If Zeitblom has the opportunity to observe Adrian and to develop his theory of Adrian's "predestination" to "damnation," basing it on Adrian's true German artist character, then Adrian has equal opportunity to observe Zeitblom's "predisposition" to fascism, based on his character as a *Zivilisationsliterat*. In chapter 24 Zeitblom is defensive and self-justifying, as he is nowhere else in the novel. This gives the impression of self-consciousness, as though he felt that he was being observed.

He expresses many opinions and also makes categorical statements that are questionable, not only for their validity in themselves, but for the grounds he bases them on. Zeitblom exposes himself in an accumulation of detail and, although none of the points is decisive in itself, it is the very accumulation of detail that makes the point. The chapter is not very long, but in it Mann has summed up for the reader the various indications of Zeitblom as a *Zivilisationsliterat* that can be inferred from previous chapters. Mann particularly draws attention to his interpretation of Zeitblom's humanism. It is this character that explains his behavior in the second half of the novel. All in all, chapter 24 forms a tight résumé of the views that

define Zeitblom as a *Zivilisationsliterat.* Zeitblom obscures the significance of Adrian's stay in Italy and its importance to the development of his
ideas. A further very important point culled from this chapter is the clear
indication that Adrian actually actively dislikes Zeitblom's views, another
point generally overlooked, although it is apparent in every chapter where
Adrian is allowed to express his view. Zeitblom's ability to interpret
Adrian's music is put seriously in question. Finally, Zeitblom's discussion
of Shakespeare's *Love's Labour's Lost,* ending with Frank Harris's interpretation of the play, explains the use of some of the leitmotifs and considerably illuminates the plot of the novel. It is a very revealing discussion of
Zeitblom's underlying motives in his biography. This is a very curious passage, seemingly quite irrelevant to the novel at a first reading and largely
ignored by critics. It is unlikely that Mann included it merely for comic
relief, although it is very funny.

* * *

Zeitblom dwells on the behavior of the daughter of the house, who swings
her spoon and repeats words, questioning them. Zeitblom considers this
behavior to be eccentric and concludes, therefore, that she is subnormal in
intelligence. He is puzzled that nobody else thinks anything of it (*DF,*
283). This is, of course, another example of the criticism of schoolteachers
who depreciate imagination and questioning and, above all, deviation from
the norm, criticism that crops up time and again in Mann's works, starting
with *Buddenbrooks* and coming to its peak in *Doktor Faustus.* It was not an
arbitrary decision to make Zeitblom a schoolteacher. It is, taking the context
of Mann's works as establishing the norm, another labeling of Zeitblom as
a *Zivilisationsliterat,* the humanist pedagogue, but, more important, it is a
way of putting Zeitblom in a position of influence on the younger generation. Mann was very distressed at the extent of potential fascist support
among young university students after the First World War. This must necessarily be a comment on their teachers. In *Doktor Faustus* Mann has
extended this criticism to the university and applied it particularly to the
Catholic School of Theology. It is not legitimate, in analyzing the novel,
to forget Mann's dislike of schoolteachers.

What Zeitblom specifically associates with lack of intelligence in this
case is the questioning of the reliability of words. Pride in his facility with
words is one of his prominent characteristics, yet he makes comments that
show that he does not like people questioning words or casting doubt on
their reliability. Here he shows that he considers reflecting on words to
show a lack of intelligence. Just as he did not grasp Schleppfuß's point
about the nature of the ambiguity of the concepts of good and bad when
they are seen as objective and not subjective values, he is unable to grasp

the use of words here. This reaches its peak in Zeitblom's discussion of the views of the Kridwiß *Kreis*, where Zeitblom is quite happy to accept that the meanings of words are turned on their heads. He says that it is the duty of men to seek perfection through the intellectual study of the absolute, of abstractions like truth, freedom, and justice, rather than to study nature (*DF*, 363). However, his ultimate conclusion, the result of his humanistic reflections, is expressed in his favorable view of Swift's proposal to eliminate abstract words altogether by making them concrete (*DF*, 491). It is the uneducated, the *Volk*, who disagree with Zeitblom.

* * *

As throughout the novel, in chapter 24 Zeitblom stresses Adrian's insistence on solitude and exaggerates it out of all proportion. His attitude is that to want solitude is immoral and antisocial. He describes Adrian and Schildknapp as living like recluses in Italy, while reporting that they lived in Palestrina with an extended family, that when in Rome they attended receptions for visiting international artists, went to the opera and to open-air concerts, played dominoes in a local coffee-house, and so on (*DF*, 291). They also had Zeitblom and his wife as houseguests for three weeks. If they were ever recluses, it seems to have been only in the mornings when they were working, and even then they were together.

The question is whether Adrian's solitude, which Zeitblom objects to so strongly, should be taken literally, in the social sense. In fact, he is annoyed that Adrian — who, he repeatedly insists, lives in antisocial solitude — is always surrounded by other people when he goes to visit him. Clearly, on the surface of the novel, this resentment can be explained as simple jealousy and a feeling that he is excluded, but there is a more serious explanation lurking behind this. The solitude that disturbs him is directly related to Adrian's work, or to what goes on in his mind. Adrian's distance from society and lack of interest in what is going on, which Zeitblom mentions time and again, refers to the divergence of his views from those accepted by Zeitblom's circle of friends. Adrian's friends are all individuals whose relation to each other is largely through him. They are all artists and intellectuals. Zeitblom's friends are a crowd and are largely academics. It is in this sense that Adrian is a lone sheep. What Zeitblom means by Adrian's insistence on solitude is his insistence on individualism, on subjective freedom, or dissenting opinion. That he does not object to solitude in the literal sense is revealed in his argument in support of Ludwig of Bavaria, where he says that withdrawing from society to live in rural isolation cannot be seen as a sign of madness (*DF*, 572). It is the price of being an artist that one sees more clearly looking through a glass than participating, as Tonio Kröger does literally, but other people often do not like what the artist sees. This hostility is projected to the person of the artist. That this is the case becomes very clear towards the end of the novel. Solitude is a variant on individualism and, as Zeitblom points out, individualism is not considered acceptable by the fascist academics of the Kridwiß *Kreis*.

* * *

Elsewhere in the novel, on several occasions, Zeitblom complains that he himself has to work, always in the context of having to miss some event. It is clear that he considers that work that is self-imposed is immoral, since he always expresses it negatively. This is essentially an anti-intellectual attitude. It is also anti-individualism. Behind his comments is the assumption that in Italy Adrian should be on holiday. He sums it up: "Kurzum, in der Stadt wie in der Abgeschiedenheit des Gebirgstädtchens führten die beiden das Welt und Menschen vermeidende Leben gänzlich von den Sorgen ihrer Arbeit beanspruchter Menschen. So wenigstens kann man es ausdrücken" (*DF*, 292).

Mann's way of expressing Adrian's approach to work shows admiration, not contempt: "Wenn ich irgend etwas von meiner Zeit sympathetisch [*sic*] verstanden habe, so ist es ihre Art von Heldentum, die modern-heroische Lebensform und -haltung des überbürdeten und übertrainierten, 'am Rande der Erschöpfung arbeitenden' *Leistungsethikers*" (*BeU*, 144–45).

Mann also commented on Zeitblom's attitude: "Wo ist der abgeschmackte Tor, der glaubt, ein produktiver Trieb könne je unsozialen, antisozialen Wesens sein?" (*BeU*, 314).

* * *

Some of the statements Mann puts into Zeitblom's mouth are preposterous from the point of view of the artist and of the sort that would particularly annoy him. For instance, Zeitblom states categorically that artists pay little attention to their surroundings, except insofar as they are relevant to their work environment: "Diese Künstler geben wenig acht auf eine umgebende Gegenwart, die zu der Arbeitswelt, in der sie leben, nicht in direkter Beziehung steht, und in der sie folglich nicht mehr als einen indifferenten, der Produktion mehr oder weniger günstigen Lebensrahmen sehen" (*DF*, 285–86).

This statement is made in the context of Zeitblom's enthusiastic description of the landscape, the appreciation of which he describes as a manifestation of his humanism. What he describes is classical eighteenth-century taste: Italian scenery with its clear blue sky and shepherds portrayed as Pan

(*DF*, 285–86). All this, he says, is antiquity and beautiful, which is an unrealistic and sentimental view, according to Mann in *Die Betrachtungen eines Unpolitischen* (*BeU*, 392). It is comparable with Hans Castorp's vision of antiquity in the snow scene in *Der Zauberberg*, which represents Settembrini's unrealistic utopian vision of society, and Aschenbach's delirium in *Der Tod in Venedig*, which is symbolic of his fall into decadence. It is eighteenth-century idealism, which, as expressed repeatedly by Mann in his essays and his stories, and stressed in *Die Betrachtungen eines Unpolitischen*, is not German and must be rejected. It shows once again that Zeitblom's humanism has nothing to do with humanity.

First of all, Zeitblom's statement that artists pay little attention to their environment is misleading. How can choosing an environment because it is a favorable framework for one's work mean indifference to the environment? Each of the environments Adrian has chosen for his life, which is his work, has been described through Zeitblom as carefully chosen. This does not mean indifference. Adrian's study at Pfeiffering is a replica of Dürer's workshop. The important thing, however, is that Adrian has modernized it, brought it up to date, and accommodated it to his needs. Adrian's preferred environment is a thoroughly modern and efficient expression of the German Protestant tradition. This is the focus of Adrian's choice of Pfeiffering, not, as Zeitblom says, because it is similar to Hof Buchel. There are undoubtedly innumerable farmsteads in Germany with a tree in the courtyard. In *Die Betrachtungen eines Unpolitischen* Mann describes Dürer as the symbol of the German Protestant tradition. This modernized German Protestant environment is symbolic of Adrian's work. Further, Adrian's environment is defined by its human content, not just his study. He lives among the *Volk*, represented by the Schweigestill family.

Zeitblom repeatedly, throughout his account, is at pains to point out that Adrian is also indifferent to nature, in circumstances where it is Adrian whose lifestyle leaves room for nature, whereas Zeitblom's life is entirely social when he is not at work. Adrian, on the other hand, lives in the countryside and uses long walks as the means of collecting his thoughts and restoring his energy for working, as did Mann.

Zeitblom's expressed perception of Adrian bears no relationship at all to the reality he portrays. The reader should see this, because it becomes very important indeed as the novel progresses. If Zeitblom's predisposition as a *Zivilisationsliterat* leads him to make untrue statements to support his argument in trivial matters, there is reason to question his statements in other matters. The untruths of the *Zivilisationsliterat* are not usually deliberate, conscious falsehoods; they result from a problem of perception. The *Zivilisationsliterat*, when he is critical of reality, does not see reality as it is, but as what he wants it to be so that it fits in with his theories. As in the case of the charge of solitude, when Zeitblom says that Adrian pays no attention to the environment, he is not referring to the physical environment:

he means that he does not accept, but rather opposes, the intellectual environment. This is a serious defect that Zeitblom anticipates will cause Adrian grief in the end. It is the great inhibition that the Devil in chapter 25 thinks Adrian should overcome. It is what Mann calls having a conscience, another manifestation of Adrian's individualism.

Mann ends Zeitblom's description of the sunset with Schildknapp ridiculing his tourist sentimentalism and Adrian laughing. Zeitblom interprets this evidence that Adrian does not share his views and enthusiasms, and above all his sentimentality, as a distortion in his view of reality: "Denn mir schien, daß er die Gelegenheit wahrnahm, über meine und Helenens Ergriffenheit und über die Herrlichkeit der Naturerscheinung selber gleich mit zu lachen" (*DF*, 286). Zeitblom is suggesting that sentiment makes the reality and that Adrian, through rejecting the view of reality through sentiment, is rejecting the reality itself. Ultimately, he will not admit that Adrian really does not agree with him: "Es versteht sich, daß Adrian nur mit lächelndem Kopfnicken, nicht ohne Ironie, das Entzücken meines Humanistenherzens teilte" (*DF*, 285). Such evidence that Adrian has different views from those imputed by Zeitblom recurs in nearly every chapter of the novel, and Mann always has Zeitblom treat this as evidence either of Adrian's immorality or of his sense of humor, which is also immoral in Zeitblom's view. This insistence that Adrian does not express his real views, which Zeitblom insists are really the same as his own, becomes increasingly important as the novel progresses. It underlies the whole development of the novel from chapter 34 to the end. This particular example in chapter 24, and the way it is expressed, suggests that it is at this moment that Adrian realizes that Italy is not the right environment for his work. It also suggests that Adrian is recognizing the real significance of the difference between himself and Zeitblom. Zeitblom laughs in the wrong places. He takes literally what is supposed to be ironic and sees what is meant seriously as ironic. His appreciation of reality is sentimental, not realistic. Zeitblom is looking at his environment, but he is seeing the wrong aspects of it.

Zeitblom's comment on the ruins is a delightful illustration of the contrast between the conflicting points of view, summing it up and throwing it back into the context of the nineteenth-century Romantic artist versus the eighteenth-century *Zivilisationsliterat*. At the top of the hill are a few Roman ruins. Zeitblom frequently goes, as on a pilgrimage, to look at them, whereas Adrian is not interested and never goes further than the monastery garden where he works every day. Zeitblom says this is because Adrian never wants to look at anything (*DF*, 281). Three pages later he says they went walking every afternoon. Once again, Zeitblom's commentary is not consistent with the information he provides. Not only does this again illustrate Zeitblom's association of Adrian's work with lack of sociability and interest in his environment, but it does so by a visual image of the eighteenth-century man skipping over the middle ages to antiquity and the nineteenth-century artist enjoying the peace and tranquillity of the monastery garden. It brings to mind Mann's argument that Catholics do not recognize the Reformation as a break (*BeU*, 511–14). For Adrian the monastery is, at this point in his life, a relict of a past time, the equivalent of the Roman ruins for Zeitblom. It is a foreign curiosity and has no significance in modern German Protestant culture. Zeitblom does not see the Middle Ages as dead, but as lurking in the background, not as something overcome, but as something suppressed, as he has already shown us in his account of Kaisersaschern. The incident also reflects Mann's own dislike of handbook tourism (*BeU*, 480). All these points are discussed in *Die Betrachtungen eines Unpolitischen* as illustrations of the differences between the two types. There is also the question of what relationship there is between looking at Roman ruins and observing the actual environment in which we live. The *Zivilisationsliterat* pines for the return of the ideal of the Roman Empire. This is a fascist ambition.

* * *

Mann has firmly established at the outset of the novel that Zeitblom's humanism is fundamentally medieval Catholic in origin. In chapter 24 he gives various examples of Adrian's dislike of this humanism. However, it is not until chapter 27, in the Capercailzie episode, that he makes it quite clear that Adrian rejects Zeitblom's Catholic humanism absolutely. Mann leaves no doubt in the reader's mind that this is the case. In chapter 27 Adrian clearly and unequivocally says about Zeitblom's humanism exactly what Mann says in *Die Betrachtungen eines Unpolitischen*. Zeitblom rejects the study of natural science as not contributing to the glory of mankind. He distinguishes the intellect in man from the natural and says it is the duty of men to seek perfection through the study of absolute abstractions, like truth, freedom, and justice. Adrian says Zeitblom's position is untenable, because it denies the physical nature of the origin and ultimate destination of man, including his intellect. Man is primarily a piece of disgusting nature, with a certain measure of spiritual potential. All humanism tends to medieval geocentricism and anthropocentrism. It is popularly held to be in favor of science, but it cannot be, because one cannot depreciate the material that natural science studies as the work of the Devil without also seeing natural science itself as the work of the Devil. The Catholic Church has preserved this view and insists on ignorance in the name of humanity. Humanism is medieval (*DF*, 363–64). Adrian's viewpoint is reminiscent of Kumpf's argument that the human intellect is not a reliable guide in the service of mankind. This is the Lutheran position, and it is opposed to asceticism, or the denial of human nature, and is therefore also opposed to humanism and totalitarianism. The unity of body and intellect is fundamental to Mann's thought. Zeitblom's implication that Adrian's interest in the creatures at the bottom of the sea is evidence of Adrian's association with the Devil is valid only from the Roman Catholic point of view. The Protestant tradition teaches specifically that "all creatures, great and small" are in the realm of God. The separation of body and intellect underlies all of Zeitblom's philosophical comments — with the exception of sex.

* * *

A substantial part of chapter 24 is Zeitblom's interpretation of Shakespeare's *Love's Labour's Lost*. Mann has made this very funny indeed. This should not, however, divert attention from its content. Mann has jumbled up Zeitblom's discussion of the play to the extent that it is very difficult to sort it out, mixing Zeitblom's interpretation of the argument of the play together with his comments on both Adrian's music and Adrian's own interpretation of the text. Mann has used the play in the context of the argument of the novel, emphasizing aspects that are not central to Shakespeare's supposed intentions. He has, however, simply changed the focus, not the message. Basically, he has modernized it.

The basic plot of *Love's Labour's Lost* is simple. The king of Navarre has his court swear an oath to live three years in the pursuit of higher learning. The purpose is "to know that which else we should not know." This will make them "heirs of all eternity," "the wonder of the world." This is parallel to the aspiration of the original Faust, the aspiration that Goethe's Faust rejects as misguided. The conditions of the king's oath are that they mortify the flesh, eat only one meal a day, sleep only three hours in the night, and see no women. The king has adopted for his court a form of what can be anachronistically described as ascetic political "enlightenment." These conditions can be seen as either monasticism or the cult of militarism, depending on whether they are directed outward or inward. All forms of ascetic "enlightenment" are based on the assumption that man is composed of two incompatible elements, intellect and nature, and that only one can operate at a time.

The general view seems to be that Shakespeare was not thinking in political terms, or in religious terms, either, for that matter, but simply socially and in the broader sense of human nature. However, the political dispute about whether England was to be a Protestant or a Roman Catholic country dramatically colored the times he lived in, and to be on the wrong side could mean imprisonment and torture, or death — and which was the right side could change over night. The possibility of a secular State had not yet seriously crossed anyone's mind and the monarch had virtually absolute and arbitrary power. Shakespeare was in a very dangerous and vulnerable position, a position not unlike the position of the writer in National Socialist Germany. John Palmer points out that the play touches on various points that were considered questions of high treason, or heresy, and that several contemporary dramatists were arrested and tortured for expressing views such are expressed in *Love's Labour's Lost*.[1] In other words, in Shakespeare's times, as Mann is suggesting for his own times, such questions were indeed political questions. Mann is reading the play in this context. In the play the dual view of human nature, which Mann associates with Catholic humanism and totalitarianism, is demolished. It is a comical repetition of Adrian's attack on Zeitblom's humanism.

In *Love's Labour's Lost*, the princess of France turns up on an embassy and, for reasons of State, the court is obliged to receive her and her entourage. Of course, the men immediately fall in love with the women and want to break their oath. This is what Zeitblom says happens to Adrian in his extraordinary account of the Marie episode. As punishment for having taken such a stupid oath, and Shakespeare makes it clear that he intends to have the oath understood as nonsense, the women require the men to stick to the conditions of asceticism for a year, not studying, but caring for the sick. The point of the women's proposal is that the men are to abandon abstractions and ideals and the pursuit of a life removed from humanity in order to attend to the human needs of the moment. They are to turn from utopian dreams of conquering the world to preoccupation with problems at home. Shakespeare's argument is a light-hearted version of Mann's argument in *Die Betrachtungen eines Unpolitischen*: the pursuit of ideals is not in the interests of mankind, because it is counter to human nature; the purpose of government is to attend to the human needs of the moment, not to build Utopias. Adrian says at the end of *Doktor Faustus* that it was the reversal of this process that led to fascism (*DF*, 662). Berowne's role in the play is that of ridiculing the whole idea that learning that is not in the service of life has any value or is indeed humanly possible, because asceticism is contrary to human nature. This role is parallel to Mann's purpose in writing *Die Betrachtungen eines Unpolitischen* and to the role he gives to Adrian in *Doktor Faustus*. *Love's Labour's Lost* is rollicking good fun, laughing at the French Catholic approach to government for the delight of the Protestant English. Nowhere in the play is the original monastic ideal held as tenable or even taken seriously. It is set up for the purpose of destroying it. Couching the women's alternative ideal in monasticism is meant as a joke, a punishment of the men for having entertained the idea of "enlightenment" monasticism in the first place. *Love's Labour's Lost* is a comedy. By reversing the outcome in *Doktor Faustus*, Mann has written a tragedy.

Parallel with this central plot is a secondary plot, whose center is Don Armado. His principle characteristic is excessive verbosity without much substance, and a comically pretentious misuse of words. His role is to parody the way the main characters play with words. He is in favor of love. However, when he himself falls in love, his brain ceases to work and he is struck speechless. It is to be noted that Zeitblom's analysis does not reflect his report on what Adrian said he was intending to show in his interpretation of the play. Adrian claimed that the purpose of the opera was to ridicule, through parody, the affected asceticism that was the result of classical studies, by paralleling it with the vulgar "natural" and to illustrate the ridiculous aspects of each through the other (*DF*, 218–19). Zeitblom does not mention Don Armado in his own analysis. This is a serious distortion in his interpretation of Shakespeare's play and of Adrian's operetta, in that it removes the dialectic from the argument.

In *Doktor Faustus*, the story of *Love's Labour's Lost* represents yet another variation on the central theme of the novel, anachronistically interpreted as an argument for a welfare democracy, based on a correct appreciation of human nature. It is another expression of the definition of humanity, or of the kind of humanism that, in Mann's view, is necessary for the development of a humane society. Zeitblom declares himself a humanist and, with his peculiar interpretation of *Love's Labour's Lost*, he is showing that his humanism is opposed to humanity, as Mann understands the term. He sees everything that is not intellect as barbarism, because he has a mistaken, an essentially medieval, view of the relationship between intellect and nature. He is upset at Shakespeare's making fun of studying antiquity by presenting such studies as opposed to love in the play and particularly at his identifying specifically love with barbarism, as Berowne, the hero of the play does (*DF*, 289). Berowne, however, is being ironic and is, in fact, opposing this opposition, but not for the same reason as Zeitblom. Berowne is objecting to the idea that nature and intellect are seen as oppositions. Zeitblom is not objecting to this opposition; he is objecting to including sex on the wrong side. A large part of this chapter is dedicated to showing precisely this: if sex is involved, it is not barbarism in Zeitblom's view. Therefore he can and does condone barbaric behavior, as in the cases of Ines and Clarissa, for instance, as he interprets their stories. One of the characteristics of the attitude of the German intellectuals who supported the development of fascism was to be indulgent in the face of irrational emotionalism, as Zeitblom shows himself to be. Logically, if sex can be used to explain a motivation, it belongs clearly on the side of intellect, rather than on the side of nature. This is putting the preferred tool of the Devil into the brain. As Kumpf says, the Devil can corrupt the intellect, but not morality.

As we have seen in *Die Betrachtungen eines Unpolitischen*, the despicable *Zivilisationsliterat* is the German who takes French political "enlightenment" seriously, which is what Zeitblom does here. He thinks Shakespeare's views are expressed by the king and not by Berowne, and he identifies their falling in love as the punishment Shakespeare metes out to his gentlemen for breaking their vow to prefer wisdom and to live ascetically (*DF*, 289). Zeitblom's interpretation of the play is absurd. The punishment Shakespeare metes out is to make the men continue with their vow of asceticism while directing their attention to humanity instead of to conquering the world. Zeitblom is distorting Shakespeare's message in a very devious way. He starts by eliminating the principal argument that seeking the light of knowledge can lead to a disregard of wisdom, that the academic approach is blind to reality, because it is based on authority rather than on observation.

The central argument of the play, the association of eyes with perception, understanding, point of view, or the observation of reality is presented by Berowne:

> To seek the light of truth; while truth the while
> Doth falsely blind the eyesight of his look:
> Light seeking light doth light of light beguile:
> So ere you find where light in darkness lies,
> Your light grows dark by losing of your eyes.
> (Act 1, scene 1, 75–79)[2]

Palmer insists, as seems to me the only interpretation in the broader context, that the meaning of Berowne's criticism is directed to the fundamental defect of "enlightenment," using basically the same argument as Mann, or Adrian. Palmer illustrates the multiple use in the play of the word "light": "light of the eyes, light in the printed word, light of the intelligence, and a light beyond even that — a light divine that may be lost in following its earthly reflection" (8). This multiple use of the "light" motif is fundamental to Mann's argument in *Doktor Faustus*. It occurs in various forms. His rejection of Berowne's argument is behind Zeitblom's argument that Adrian does not "observe" the world around him, whereas he himself does. Agreement with Berowne's argument is behind Mann's portrayal of Zeitblom: he has "blinded" himself to the "perception of reality" through too much study of antiquity. As I argue throughout, Adrian's position reflects the opinions Mann expressed in *Die "Betrachtungen" eines Unpolitischen*, his "observations." Later in *Doktor Faustus*, Adrian blames the Devil's use of "his own evil eye" to explain his nephew Echo's death. The most important use of this play on the meanings of the word "light" is Adrian's contamination with "*Illumination*." These images are central to the interpretation of the novel. Of course, Berowne's comment can also be interpreted as meaning simply that too much reading can lead to "physical blindness." Palmer quotes Dr. Johnson, the famous British *Literat* and compiler of dictionaries, as allowing only this literal interpretation of Shakespeare's discussion of eyes (7). Zeitblom points out that he himself is "myopic," meaning that he has to wear glasses (*DF*, 182), but does Mann mean something more?

Zeitblom's association of eyes with love is also taken from the play, where Berowne attributes falling in love to the irresistible appeal of a woman's eyes. Zeitblom recurs frequently to this image to explain Adrian's preferences in his choice of friends. He is always implying emotional, irrational appeal, rather than intellectual appeal. Shakespeare is using this play with words to support his argument that "light" comes from other sources than simply books and studying the stars, that both have to be taken into account, and that one modifies the other. Zeitblom is using this association with "love" as an intensifier and complement to the academic approach, not as a qualifier. It also appears to me to be clear that Zeitblom is referring rather to sexual compulsion than to love, a distinction that Shakespeare did not make. Love generated through an appreciation of the other's eyes is spiritual in that it is a recognition of similar ways of looking at the world. One does not fall in love with eyes that are "lumps of coal." What attracts Berowne to Rosaline is her wit and acute observation. Zeitblom dismisses this attraction, saying that she is "nothing but" a saucy and witty girl. Rosaline's argument that Berowne, with his "enlightenment" pretensions, is a wise man playing the fool he condemns as based on a lack of loyalty (*DF*, 288). This is an entirely inappropriate remark in the context of Shakespeare's play, but the suggestion that it is disloyal to point out that the pursuit of Utopia is foolish is apt in the context of the implied parallel with National Socialism.

Love's Labour's Lost is a caricature of humanism, claims Zeitblom. He does not like this. In *Die Betrachtungen seines Unpolitische*n Mann says that the goal of the *Zivilisationsliterat* is to come up with the formula for installing heaven on earth, which is what Zeitblom admires in Shakespeare's play. Specifically, and it bears repeating, the only thing he objects to is including sex on the side of barbarism. Not only is Zeitblom disagreeing with Berowne's criticism of Catholic humanism, but he is also dismissing this criticism as not meant seriously. It is my impression that critics of Shakespeare take for granted that this criticism is meant seriously; indeed, it is the point of the play. Adrian interprets it in this way. However, what Berowne is criticizing is not wisdom but the definition of wisdom as a combination of asceticism and abstract knowledge. It is a characteristic of the *Zivilisationsliterat* that he removes the human from the intellect and, therefore, from politics. This is a recurring point in the novel. Zeitblom is making the wrong association. He is taking the two polar images of eyes offered by Berowne — the "light" of a woman's eyes and "enlightenment" through study — and summing them, rather than averaging them out. He is, so to speak, combining sex, or Nietzsche's glorification of procreation, with the "enlightenment" approach to knowledge. Shakespeare, on the other hand, is combining knowledge with love to find the human, as does Adrian in chapter 22.

Berowne's criticism of wisdom as absurd is not meant seriously, says Zeitblom, because it is made by means of ridicule. Through these comments Zeitblom is offering one of the reasons why he does not believe that

Adrian means what he says: it is Zeitblom's inability to understand irony, as he lacks a sense of humor, with the result that he takes everything literally. Mann is illustrating the danger of irony when Zeitblom takes seriously what is meant to be ironic and dismisses the underlying serious argument as irony. If Adrian uses parody to express something humorously, Zeitblom takes him to mean the opposite of what he says. However, parody is not irony, which does often mean the opposite of what is said. Parody means what it says. Zeitblom is interpreting parody as irony. This is only one of the many illustrations of this aspect of Zeitblom's character, which is very important to the novel.

Zeitblom has got himself tied up in a very complicated misinterpretation of the play, which is really quite simple and straightforward, because he has misunderstood which side Shakespeare is on, has got it backwards, so to speak. Such a misunderstanding of the author's position is exactly what happened in the reception of *Die Betrachtungen eines Unpolitischen* and, by extension, of Adrian's *Apocalipsis cum figuris*. Zeitblom's discussion of *Love's Labour's Lost* must be interpreted as an illustration of the whole way in which Zeitblom misinterprets Adrian. He has him backwards.

* * *

Having given up the idea of writing the opera with the original text in English, Adrian is very proud of being able to write it so it could be sung in either language, says Zeitblom. This was a great tour de force, a clever trick, and very difficult. To Zeitblom's surprise, Adrian was far prouder of this achievement than of the music itself. Zeitblom finds this unsettling:

> Ich hätte wohl froh sein sollen, daß er schließlich davon abgekommen war, meine dramaturgische Bearbeitung des Stückes nur im sprachlichen Original zu vertonen. Er hatte es sich aber statt dessen zur Aufgabe gemacht, sie auf englisch und deutsch *in einem* zu komponieren, will sagen: er hatte es auf sich genommen, die Melodie in beiden Sprachen mit den Harmonieen übereinstimmen zu lassen und dafür zu sorgen, daß sie in beiden ihr eigenes melodisches Profil besaß und korrekt deklamiert war. Auf dieses Kunststück, eine wahre Tour de force, schien er stolzer zu sein, als auf die musikalischen Eingebungen selbst, von denen das Werk lebte, und um deren unbefangenes Blühen jener Zwang mich ein wenig besorgt machte.[3]

In fact, musically, such a feat is not a novelty; it is not very difficult to write music that can be sung either in German or in English, particularly with Shakespeare — Schubert did it. Handel did it with the Bible in the Messiah, and it is still disputed which version of the text is the original. This is, in its political analogy, a reference to the possibility of accommodating "the music" to "the word" in such a way that it fits either cultural peculiarity, to developing a German democracy that is in harmony with the American model and at the same time respects the unique character of each culture. Zeitblom is concerned that this condition may interfere with the uninhibited blooming of the music, or of German culture. It can also be read as a comment on the novel itself, which can be read from either Zeitblom's or Adrian's point of view. This is indeed quite a remarkable achievement.

Zeitblom then goes on to criticize Adrian's music for not defending the triumph of feeling. Music, by its very nature, says Zeitblom, should lead men out of the sphere of absurd artificiality into the world of nature and humanity, but Adrian's music did not. Adrian gave the spontaneous world of emotion and nature the same weight as its presumptuous denial (*DF*, 289–90). Once again Adrian, like Shakespeare, is describing human nature as a synthesis of natural and intellectual components. Adrian is presenting his operetta in modern dress and once again reconciling German Romanticism with French "enlightenment," the running metaphor for democracy. Zeitblom does not understand Adrian's synthesis. He seems to think that Adrian should be illustrating the triumph of the erotic, an achievement he attributes to music, as does the Devil in chapter 25.

In chapter 34 (*Schluß*) Zeitblom says, when he interprets Adrian's *Apocalipsis cum figuris* as an argument for fascism, that he has finally learned how to understand Adrian's music (*DF*, 503), a statement that is shown here to be false. It is not surprising that critics ignore this passage. Mann is laying the basis in this discussion for the misunderstanding and misuse by Zeitblom and the other members of the Kridwiß *Kreis* of Adrian's *Apocalipsis cum figuris*. Zeitblom's interpretation of *Love's Labour's Lost* is the description of his role in the novel. He interprets Adrian and he gets him wrong. He is identifying Adrian with Berowne and he is interpreting Berowne as wanting to conquer the world, as an abstract intellect who has finally discovered that it is necessary to add sex to find the light.

* * *

Zeitblom's reflections illustrate that he does not understand the character of the German artist as described by Mann in *Die Betrachtungen eines Unpolitischen* and as illustrated in *Doktor Faustus* in Adrian. He has a French appreciation of art and artists. This is significant for Zeitblom's interpretation of Adrian's works. French art is political, according to Mann; it takes a moral stand on social issues, whereas German art is descriptive and does not advocate a course of action.[4]

The most remarkable statement Zeitblom makes about the artist is his quotation of Holofernes, one of the characters in *Love's Labour's Lost*. Holofernes, in Shakespeare's play, is a schoolteacher, a pompous, pedantic ass who prides himself on his Latin. He fancies himself a critic of poetry and he is also a meddler, attempting to betray Berowne to the king. He is meant by Shakespeare to be a figure of fun and placed at a distinctly lower social and intellectual level than the main protagonists of the play. He and what he says are not to be taken seriously, but as nonsense. Mann very clearly shows that Zeitblom is a parallel to Holofernes: not only is he a teacher of Latin and a pompous pedantic ass, but he adopts Holofernes' opinions as his own. This alone casts doubt on how seriously the reader is meant to take Zeitblom and his opinions. Holofernes' comment, according to Zeitblom, is the unsurpassable, full description of the mind of the artist, slipped by Shakespeare into a purely incidental jocular part of the play. This definition must be applied to Adrian, says Zeitblom.

> Dies ist eine Gabe, die ich besitze, einfach, einfach! Ein närrisch extravaganter Sinn, voll von Formen, Figuren, Gestalten, Gegenständen, Ideen, Erscheinungen, Erregungen, Wandlungen. Diese werden empfangen in dem Uterus des Gedächtnisses, genährt im Mutterleibe der pia mater, und geboren durch die reifende Kraft der Gelegenheit. (*DF*, 289)

> This is a gift that I have, simple, simple;
> a foolish extravagant spirit, full of forms, figures,
> shapes, objects, ideas, apprehensions, motions,
> revolutions: these are begot in the ventricle of
> memory, nourished in the womb of *pia mater*,
> and delivered upon the mellowing of occasion.
>   (Act 4, scene 2, 67–72)

This bears little relationship to Adrian's approach to his art. Mann insists that art is intellect; it is stressed that Adrian's approach is intellectual. Adrian, like Mann, is primarily concerned with form. Adrian's art approaches the mathematical, with a theological component, which is morality. It is ironical, and irony is intellectual. It is dialectic, which Zeitblom does not understand. Holofernes' definition of the artist is, however, a description of Zeitblom's biography of Adrian, in every particular: largely a fantasy, based on a memory.

This remark, which Mann has slipped into a seemingly inconsequential bit of nonsensical business in *Doktor Faustus*, is tantamount to a bald statement that Zeitblom has misinterpreted Adrian in the manner of the *Zivilisationsliterat*. It dismisses the role of intellect in art, reducing art to talent and inspiration with a degree of magic. At the same time Zeitblom describes Adrian as a serious intellectual. The musical intellect is in Zeitblom's view, therefore, talent, inspiration, and magic. Zeitblom exposes himself as having a foolish, deprecating view of what an artist is, then describing Adrian as fitting this mould, even though the evidence shows that Mann has designed Adrian to his own mould of the nature of the artist, an intelligent, responsible, hard-working creator of form. It was

Mann's view that talent is an insignificant starting point for artistic creation and inspiration has nothing to do with it. Zeitblom, however, misinterprets the intellectual content of Adrian's work. He has, of course, been doing this from the beginning with his attributions of magic to portrayals of mathematical truisms, such as the magic quadrangle, and to Adrian's *strenger Satz*. Zeitblom is moving steadily towards replacing intellect with emotion, inspiration, and magic and falsely using Adrian as his model. He does not see his view of Adrian as foolish or deprecating.

In this respect, what Zeitblom says about the music for *Love's Labour's Lost* is revealing. It contradicts his previous statement by showing that Adrian's art is calculated. The success of the music, reports Zeitblom, is due to its being tied together as a whole through anticipation and reminder and repetition of the same motifs: "Das bedeutend Wiederkehrende und schon Vertraute, die geistreiche oder tiefsinnige Anmahnung [ist] immer das Sprechend-Eindrucksvollste" (*DF*, 287).

This is Mann's view of what he himself has tried to do in his own work, what he calls the self-quote. He has certainly done this in *Doktor Faustus*, which is why analyzing its content leads to always repeating the same arguments. The novel is based on a few basic ideas that are repeated over and over again in the form of variations. The simple statement of these basic themes is always to be found in the novel, but usually in a context that obscures its overall significance. It is a technique Mann says he learned from Wagner for the purpose of giving his work coherence, and it pertains to his epic theory. It applies not only to the individual work, but also to his work as a whole. This technique can be found in a simpler form as early as in *Buddenbrooks*. It contradicts the quotation from Holofernes.

Then Zeitblom says the music is about politics. He suggests that a connoisseur of music would be in favor of Adrian's rejection of "Romantic democracy and moral demagogy" in favor of self-centered cool esoteric, which Zeitblom calls art for the sake of art, art for connoisseurs alone. Unfortunately the music is sad because it implies hopelessness, he says, because the self-centered cool esoteric is a parody of itself (*DF*, 290). Once again, Zeitblom shows that he does not understand that parodying something is showing it to be ridiculous. The political relevance of this particular statement is found elsewhere. Mann argues at length in favor of Wagner and Romantic ideals in many of his essays, just as he rejects the self-centered cool esoteric of the eighteenth-century. Mann states specifically in "Von Deutscher Republik" that it is a misinterpretation of the nineteenth-century democratic revolution, favored by sprouting fascists, to call it self-centered cool esoteric (*GW* 11:820). This is what Adrian is saying here.

Here, as virtually everywhere, Zeitblom shows a completely subjective view of things. Mann's approach to writing is always objective, or so he claims. This is certainly very basic to his theory of art, and he considered himself an artist, not just a writer. His objectivity in his portrayal of Zeitblom has been very successful, to judge from the almost total acceptance of Zeitblom's interpretation of Adrian by the critics. The discussion of Adrian's works and theories of art, once they have been purged of Zeitblom's judgments, reflect what Mann considered to be his own approach. However, let us look again at Zeitblom's commentary on Holofernes' theory of art:

> Dies ist eine Gabe, die ich besitze, einfach, einfach! Ein närrisch extravaganter Sinn, voll von Formen, Figuren, Gestalten, Gegenständen, Ideen, Erscheinungen, Erregungen, Wandlungen. Diese werden empfangen in dem Uterus des Gedächtnisses, genährt im Mutterleibe der pia mater, und geboren durch die reifende Kraft der Gelegenheit. (*DF*, 289)

> This is a gift that I have, simple, simple;
> a foolish extravagant spirit, full of forms, figures,
> shapes, objects, ideas, apprehensions, motions,
> revolutions: these are begot in the ventricle of
> memory, nourished in the womb of *pia mater*,
> and delivered upon the mellowing of occasion.
> (Act 4, scene 2, 67–72)

When he wrote *Doktor Faustus* Mann was an experienced writer, had made his reputation, and was an old man. Holofernes' remarks could well apply to Mann's approach to *Doktor Faustus*: a facility for giving shape to things and an account of memories that, over time, have lost their sharp edges. This does not contradict the fact that, in form, *Doktor Faustus* is absolutely calculated. Nor does the subjectivity of its subject matter contradict the absolute objectivity of its portrayal. Mann claimed that he wrote the book from Zeitblom's point of view to make it humorous, to soften the impact of its dreadful message.[5] It is humorous. It is rolling-in-the-aisles funny in chapter 24. It is also, by the same argument, deadly serious. A character who misinterprets things, who gets things wrong, particularly a narrow, self-righteous character like Zeitblom, is a stock comic character. However, when the context is politics, comedy can turn into tragedy. Zeitblom's assessment of Holofernes is slipped into a purely jocular part of the story, as is the original remark in *Love's Labour's Lost*.

* * *

Zeitblom feels an outsider in the company of Adrian and Schildknapp, who seem to him to form a closed society, where there is no place for him. This particularly bothers him when he visits Adrian in Italy. Mann's explanation in *Die Betrachtungen eines Unpolitischen* for the rejection by the intellectual — that is, the Protestant artist — of the *Zivilisationsliterat* explains Adrian's rejection of Zeitblom in *Doktor Faustus*. According to Mann, the

Zivilisationsliterat thinks there is only one right opinion and that sharing this right opinion is, for the *Zivilisationsliterat*, the basis of the solidarity of intellectuals. Certainly Zeitblom has an opinion about everything and always assumes that Adrian agrees with him, whether he does or not. Zeitblom is, in fact, an extreme example of the narrow-minded moralist who recognizes only one right opinion. On the occasions when Adrian actually expresses disagreement, or qualification, Zeitblom assumes he is being ironic, or he implies that there is some demonic influence warping Adrian's view.

In *Die Betrachtungen eines Unpolitischen* Mann says he thinks the idea of intellectual solidarity is nonsense, because intellectuals, being individualists, always disagree with one another, and that the solidarity of intellectuals has nothing to do with right opinion. He considers that there is, however, a kind of solidarity of intellectuals and that it depends primarily on the similarity of their ways of existence. His argument is as follows. It is a comradeship in nobility and suffering, which is the source of all tolerance, conscientiousness, courtesy, and chivalry. This solidarity is also the source of the disgust of the intellectual at all dogmatism. The *Zivilisationsliterat* is not familiar with this disgust, which is a reason for questioning his humanity. An intellect that thinks with the will rather than with observation is not an intellect, since it is not intellectual to consider all contradiction and doubt a sign of immorality. The *Zivilisationsliterat* puts an abyss between his kind, those with principles, and the others, the aesthetes, the self-seeking, the egocentrics, the bad citizens. He is not interested in humanity but in right opinion. He keeps the company of those who do not contradict him, because he needs to be right. This dulls his conscience, his sense of truth and justice, and he becomes a bigot. This is his intellectual freedom, but it is stiff and cold, hypocrisy preaching humanity (*BeU*, 321–25). This is Mann's view of people like Zeitblom. This characteristic of the *Zivilisationsliterat* describes Zeitblom from Adrian's point of view. On the other hand, it is the explanation of the association of Adrian with Rudi Schwerdtfeger. It is a comradeship in nobility and suffering, which is the source of all tolerance, conscientiousness, courtesy, and chivalry.

Zeitblom wants to be with Adrian because he loves him. In other words he is thinking with his will, not with his mind. Actually he disapproves of Adrian as an aesthete and ascetic. He admires, but does not like, or understand, his music. Zeitblom considers himself to be a man of principle and is outrageously dogmatic about his opinions, but he does not realize that Adrian rejects him because of his opinions. Certainly, Zeitblom does not share Adrian's lifestyle; he does not like Adrian's lifestyle. He does not like Adrian's friends. He considers Schildknapp to be self-seeking and egocentric and resents his presence. He puts an abyss between himself and Schildknapp and dislikes having to associate with him.

Zeitblom stresses that, when Adrian gave a foretaste of his operetta, he played parts of his work for them once, and only once. In other words, Zeitblom wanted to hear the music again, but Adrian decided not to repeat it. Zeitblom did not come very well out of the discussion of the music:

> Ich vermochte nicht viel zu sagen; Schildknapp, der immer ein sehr gutes, empfängliches Publikum abgab, kommentierte das Gebotene viel schlagfertiger und intelligenter als ich, — der ich noch nachher, beim Pranzo, benommen und in mich gekehrt am Tische der Manardis saß, von Gefühlen bewegt, denen die Musik, die wir gehört, sich so völlig verschloß. (*DF*, 291)

Ultimately, the appeal to Zeitblom is to the emotions. He has told us he did not like the argument of Adrian's operetta, but he clearly dismisses discussion of the content as irrelevant because of its overall emotional appeal. He has told us what the content of the argument is in his own interpretation and dismissed all deviations in Adrian's interpretation from his own as not meant seriously.

* * *

Mann has concocted a delightful justification for Zeitblom to explain his sense of rejection by Adrian. What Zeitblom is doing here, as Orlowski has shown from the form of the narrative,[6] is giving Adrian the ideal medieval attributes of a saint. He is describing Adrian as pure intellect with no natural instincts. Falling from these saintly medieval values is, traditionally, giving in to sex. However, in Zeitblom's modern secularized world, sex is no longer in contradiction to sainthood, but a necessary attribute. If Adrian is to keep up with the times, achieve perfection, and see the light, he will have to accept sex. After the First World War, in chapter 33, in conjunction with the appearance of his *Apocalipsis cum figuris* and its adoption by the Kridwiß *Kreis*, Zeitblom reports that he did, in his alliance with Rudi Schwerdtfeger. Adrian has at that point, in Zeitblom's account, achieved full sainthood.

However, Zeitblom says Adrian makes him feel his own sexuality is shameful. The reason he feels so uncomfortable and out of place, he says, is that he is married, that he pays tribute to nature, and this makes him feel ashamed and depressed. Nobody else in the house does that. He has, of course, once again forgotten about Helene. Adrian and Schildknapp live like monks, he says. He dismisses Schildknapp's abstinence as part of his general miserliness, but says it is their chastity that is the basis of their living together. He will not go so far as to call it friendship. The intellectual tie does not even enter his head: everything has a sexual explanation. Then he says that it was specifically this bond of chastity that made him jealous of Schildknapp: "Ich vermute, daß es mir nicht gelungen ist, dem Leser eine gewisse Eifersucht auf das Verhältnis des Schlesiers zu Adrian zu verbergen; so möge er denn auch verstehen, daß es dieses Gemeinsame, das Bindemittel der Enthaltsamkeit war, dem letzten Endes jene Eifersucht galt" (*DF*, 293).

Zeitblom's statement is not true. He is not ashamed of, but proud of, his sexual activities. They define him as normal, put him in the right camp. In chapter 22, only two chapters earlier, Zeitblom has expressed quite different views on sex. Zeitblom implies throughout the novel that Adrian's intellectual capacity and sexual reservation come from the Devil, thus standing the Christian tradition on its head. Further, he has made it clear that he himself does not associate sex with the Devil. In Zeitblom's view, it is the lack of a sexual relationship that makes Adrian inhuman and he has been arguing all along that this abstinence is not natural. What he objects to about Schildknapp's association with Adrian is that he is intellectually a bad influence. What Zeitblom is arguing once again is demonology. His modern, secular, Catholic humanism is ascribing attributes of God to the Devil and describing Adrian as being in the service of the Devil in that his values are the fundamental Christian values. It is an outright lie that Zeitblom finds indulgence in sex shameful. It is in direct contradiction to what he says elsewhere. What he means, and he resents it, is that he senses that Adrian is critical of him. Zeitblom does not like criticism.

Zeitblom lists evidence that Adrian does not like physical contact and deliberately keeps people at a distance, particularly in his analysis in chapter 17 of Adrian's account of his visit to the brothel, and again here. Now, says Zeitblom, he feels it is not just a backing off from an advance, but an avoidance of making an advance himself. This is a strong statement that Zeitblom now sees active dislike in Adrian's attitude towards him. However, Zeitblom interprets it as the result of Adrian's chastity. The improbability of this is accentuated when Zeitblom explains the fact that nobody else sees this by stressing the closeness of his friendship with Adrian, which he himself has just put in question. What Zeitblom senses is Adrian's active dislike of his views, which he refuses to recognize. He says that Adrian had always lived the life of a saint, except for his visit to Graz, or it could have been Preßburg, and its repercussions. Zeitblom makes the preposterous remark that he thinks Adrian's chastity resulted from the ethos of purity, before the visit, and, after the visit, from the pathos of impurity (*DF*, 294). Zeitblom, however, specifically remarks that he observes no outward change. This is the second unobservable change that Zeitblom says he senses in Adrian in this chapter. If the narrator himself sees no change, does the reader have to accept that there is a change?

Zeitblom, by the time of writing, has finally figured out what was wrong with Adrian. He is reaching back for an explanation of Adrian's mad behavior at the end. What Mann is showing, with Zeitblom's comments on things that he sees in Adrian that nobody else sees, is that Zeitblom has changed his perception of Adrian. It is not Adrian who has changed, but Zeitblom's retrospective perception of him. Zeitblom's values have changed. He is describing Adrian's chastity, or status as a saint, as he then saw him, as impure, or negative, as coming from the Devil. Zeitblom has thus reconciled his self-respect with his lack of chastity and put Adrian in the wrong.

* * *

Zeitblom explains why there are inconsistencies in his biography of Adrian. In *Love's Labour's Lost*, says Zeitblom, the real character of Berowne is expressed in his soliloquy at the end of act 3, where he is shown as a serious intellectual who is the victim of a shameful passion. This is not the interpretation usually put on this soliloquy. It is true that Berowne is raging against Rosaline and his love for her, but most commentators see nothing of the outraged intellectual in the speech. As pointed out above, Zeitblom is mistaken to interpret Berowne as an ascetic intellectual to whom falling in love is a punishment. Harold Bloom describes Berowne's attitude as offended male narcissism (136),[7] which is more to the point. Zeitblom continues, however, by saying that Rosaline, therefore, is quite wrong to describe Berowne as an example of the wise man playing the fool and using all his mental ability to give foolishness the appearance of worth. Rosaline's comment refers to the foolishness of Berowne's "enlightenment" pretensions at the beginning of the play, which Berowne has already himself pointed out are nonsense, but not in her presence. Zeitblom does not accept Rosaline's remark as valid, although it is the point of the play. However, Zeitblom has also told us that Berowne has also misrepresented Rosaline: that she is in fact nothing more than a saucy and witty girl. Zeitblom's remark, of course, invalidates the authority of her opinion.

Today Frank Harris is not taken seriously or remembered as a critic of Shakespeare.[8] In fact, his lasting fame is due to his pornography, or his obsession with sex. Mann uses Frank Harris's argument, that the negative characterization of Rosaline in the play is to be found only in Berowne's speeches, as the basis for Zeitblom's next comment: there is nothing in the play except Berowne's remarks that supports this characterization of Rosaline, says Zeitblom (*DF*, 288). Berowne is deliberately distorting the truth, says Zeitblom. Shakespeare has Berowne do this from a compulsion to fly in the face of all artistic criteria and bring in his own personal experience for purposes of revenge, says Zeitblom, again following Harris. This is rather a strange commentary. Mann is basing this passage on Harris's questionable search in Shakespeare's plays for inconsistencies that help us to understand Shakespeare the man. Zeitblom concludes, again following Harris, that Berowne represents Shakespeare himself, that Shakespeare is deliberately distorting Berowne's character in order to seek revenge on a woman who betrayed him. By inference, the distortions in Zeitblom's account are deliberate. They reveal his intention to seek revenge. All critics agree that there are inconsistencies in Zeitblom's account. Mann is telling the reader here that the inconsistencies in his story are important, that they reveal Zeitblom's intentions. In the context of the novel, Zeitblom is writing biography, not fiction. He has not invented his characters and a great deal can be inferred about Zeitblom from the way he portrays them. There are, of course, no other sources for information about Zeitblom. He has misinterpreted both Shakespeare's message and Berowne's position, in the same way that he has misinterpreted Adrian. Zeitblom is, in other words, like Frank Harris with Berowne, in defiance of the aesthetic perfection of the whole, applying his own interpretation, dismissing what is actually said, which contradicts his interpretation, by substituting a sexual explanation for Adrian's perversity.

Zeitblom further argues, once again following Harris, that Rosaline represents Shakespeare's dark lady of the sonnets who betrayed Shakespeare with the beautiful young friend (*DF*, 288). Zeitblom is explaining the source of his invented story of Marie. He says that Rudi stole Marie, thus betraying Adrian. However, in his account, Adrian does not take his revenge on Marie, but on Schwerdtfeger. It must be admitted that the argument of who is betraying whom with whom does get out of hand here. However, Mann's story is clear. Mann is telling us here that by misrepresenting the beautiful young Schwerdtfeger, Zeitblom is seeking revenge on him for having stolen Adrian from him. His interjection of Marie in the guise of Rosaline is a red herring. She is no more than a clever and witty girl. The argument that Zeitblom misrepresents Rudi out of revenge is not as far-fetched as it may at first appear. It may seem contrived, but no more so than much of the novel. This all becomes clear in the story of Marie.

Of course, Mann is stating his intentions in *Doktor Faustus*. Just as Berowne loves Rosaline, Zeitblom loves Adrian. Zeitblom is portrayed as, as Rosaline says of Berowne, a serious intellectual playing the fool and using his mental ability to give foolishness the appearance of worth, using his intellect to argue against intellect. Mann is himself portraying personal experience for purposes of revenge.

* * *

Although superficially chapter 24 is not directly political, there is in fact a heavy political element in the atmosphere in Palestrina. This is a change. The only openly political discussion in the novel to this point, that of the

Winfried outing in chapter 14, is presented in an idyllic, pastoral, but German environment. The students are on a healthy romp through the countryside, without a serious care in the world. This has the effect of making the discussion appear abstract and theoretical and of no particular importance. In Palestrina the specific politics under discussion are Italian politics. Zeitblom reports on this, making it seem a bit of quaint local color. The issues being discussed by the Italians are not significantly elaborated in this chapter; Zeitblom simply reports that they are talking about politics. He gives this background little importance, seeing his Italian surroundings as idyllic. However, this sinister lurking political environment forms the background enveloping Adrian's account of his encounter with the Devil, which shows that Adrian gives it a great deal of significance. Mann has couched Adrian's reflections in chapter 25 between the invitation to attend a meeting at the club in Palestrina and Schildknapp's report on this visit: "die Biedermänner haben das governo durch die Hechel gezogen" (*DF*, 333). It is in this context of rising political unrest and Zeitblom's appreciation of it that chapter 25 is to be understood. This is what Adrian observed in the environment in Italy, a much more profound observation than Zeitblom's observation of the sunset or of some Roman ruins.

The protagonists of the political scene in Palestrina are the brothers of the hostess, again apparently introduced as background local color. However, they are in fact Mann's conventional prototypes: the conservative inarticulate man and the polemical political man, that is, the nineteenth-century *bourgeois*, the individualist, and the twentieth-century version of the eighteenth-century "enlightenment" political theorist, the *Zivilisationsliterat*. The lawyer is conservative, which, in Mann's terms, means apolitical, or not revolutionary. His brother Alfonso is political, a radical freethinker and critic, against Church, King, and government. His main preoccupation is to discredit the government by charges of corruption, which he does at every opportunity. He is very eloquent. The lawyer, on the other hand, is somewhat eccentric, has no pretensions, and sits reading the newspaper in his underwear, to the embarrassment of his petit-bourgeois, uneducated brother. Mann has briefly described the basic political argument of his times, as he saw it, and placed it in Italy where, of course, the broader implications of the new political trends first became apparent. It is a miniature variation on the basic theme of the novel. One is reminded of another political story by Mann, *Mario und der Zauberer*, which clearly draws a parallel between what was happening in Italy and what was happening in Germany.

Zeitblom, as we have now come to expect, sympathizes with Alfonso, although he does not express any specifically political opinions. Zeitblom presumes an ambiguous hostility towards the educated brother on the part of Alfonso. The grounds for this sympathy are that, although education is a good thing and something to be proud of, it does not give the right to go against social convention. Zeitblom apparently does not see advocating revolution as going against convention. Mann is again demonstrating Zeitblom's identifying the norm with the *Zivilisationsliterat* and objecting to the conservative individualism of the middle class. Zeitblom gives precedence to following the crowd over informed, independent opinion. The lawyer is informed: he spends his time reading the newspaper.

* * *

Chapter 24 does not advance the plot any more than chapter 25 does. Nothing happens. The importance of both chapters is to clarify points of view, to comment, in a very muddled way, on the leitmotifs, and to explain the intentions of the novel. Chapter 24 is, in miniature, the novel itself. It sums up what has been established in the first part of the novel, showing that Zeitblom is indeed a *Zivilisationsliterat* and that this is the cause of the underlying conflict between him and Adrian. Zeitblom's early view of Adrian as a saint is reinforced, as well as the basis of Zeitblom's interpretation of the events in the second half of the novel. It anticipates and explains the story of Marie and suggests, as will be shown, that Zeitblom has subjective motives for his strange account of this episode, where both Adrian and Schwerdtfeger appear suddenly so very out of character. It introduces the political and intellectual environment that constitutes the background to Adrian's conversation with the Devil in chapter 25 and, indeed, the rest of the novel. Most important, it shows that Zeitblom misinterprets Adrian's music. Zeitblom has tried to create a spooky atmosphere in his account with his ghost story (*DF*, 283), suggesting that it is supernatural powers that set the scene in Palestrina. In chapter 25 Adrian sets the scene very much within this world and not in the supernatural.

The concept of a dichotomy between nature and intellect sums up Zeitblom's humanism and, consequently, the false picture that he paints of Adrian. He describes Adrian as an extraordinary intellect and a saint, as living an ascetic life. He describes Adrian as using his sanctity and intelligence to produce his music, which, although there may be incompatible elements in his argument, ultimately appeals simply to the emotions. As we shall see, it is in this way that he interprets Adrian's *Apocalipsis cum figuris*. Zeitblom's long discussion of *Love's Labour's Lost* is an anticipation and explanation of the strange interpretation he makes of the story of Marie. In Zeitblom's account, Adrian's tragedy, like Berowne's, is to fall in love with the wrong girl, the French girl with black eyes, a tragedy he passes on to Rudi. Adrian's evil in Zeitblom's account is to reject Rudi, the blonde, blue-eyed German, for having temporarily conquered his refusal to accept the dominance of emotion over intellect.

There are three completely separate illustrations in chapter 24 of the fundamental differences between the German Protestant artist and the *Zivilisationsliterat*. There is the running commentary showing the difference between Zeitblom's view of the world and Adrian's, particularly the fundamental difference in their attitudes towards intellect, nature, and mankind, where Zeitblom's humanism is shown to have little to do with humanity. There is Zeitblom's tortuous discussion of the similar argument found in Shakespeare's *Love's Labour's Lost*. And there is the illustration of the Italian political background, personified in the Manardi brothers, who represent the political manifestation of these two basic positions. This lighthearted chapter describes as idyllic the same environment that Adrian describes as sinister in chapter 25. As Zeitblom says in chapter 30, things take on quite a different meaning, just because the lighting changes. Just as tragedy can be seen as comedy, comedy can be seen as tragedy. In both examples, Zeitblom is seeing as comedy what Adrian is seeing as tragedy.

Notes

[1] John Palmer, *Comic Characters of Shakespeare* (London: Macmillan, 1949), 23.

[2] William Shakespeare, *The Complete Works of William Shakespeare*, ed. W. J. Craig (London: Oxford, 1965).

[3] Thomas Mann, *Dr Faustus* (Stockholm: Bermann-Fischer, 1947), 336.

[4] Palmer points out, in his discussion of *Love's Labour's Lost*, that it is specifically this that distinguishes Shakespeare from Molière. *Les Précieuses Ridicules*, which deals with a related theme, is satire, intended to criticise and correct, whereas Shakespeare's *Love's Labour's Lost* is parody, inviting his audience simply to look at themselves (*Comic Characters of Shakespeare*, 2–3).

[5] Thomas Mann, "Humor und Ironie," in *GW*, 11:801–5.

[6] Hubert Orlowski, "Prädestination des Dämonischen: Zur Frage des bürgerlichen Humanismus in Thomas Manns *Doktor Faustus*" (diss., University of Posen, 1969).

[7] Harold Bloom, *Shakespeare: The Invention of the Human* (London: Fourth Estate, 1998), 124.

[8] Frank Harris, *The Man Shakespeare and His Tragic Life-Story* (New York: Frank Harris, 1921), 220.

9: The Outbreak of the First World War

IN CHAPTER 30 MANN ILLUSTRATES how Zeitblom takes the final step in the development of his predisposition to fascism. In order for the political approach of the Catholic humanist *Zivilisationsliterat* to shift from advocating communism to advocating fascism, three factors are necessary. First, he must be literally a Roman Catholic; second, his eroticism must espouse Nietzsche's glorification of life, the sacrifice of truth to life; and third, he must be an enthusiastic nationalist. Zeitblom has been shown to fulfill the first two requirements. However, there is, as yet, no political situation. All that has been established is Zeitblom's theoretical predisposition to fascism. The third factor, the concept of the ideal of "the nation," the emergence of an enthusiastic emotional nationalism that will serve as the focus for the development of the movement, is now being tentatively introduced. Nationalism is not a characteristic of the principal *Zivilisationsliterat* in *Die Betrachtungen eines Unpolitischen*, who is a pacifist and advocates radical democracy, but of a variant *Zivilisationsliterat*. The views expressed by Zeitblom are among those that prompted Mann to start work on *Die Betrachtungen eines Unpolitischen*, where he analyses why such views are not an alternative to radical democracy. Mann's conclusion was that this variety equally reflects a disregard of individualism and subjective freedom, which are the fundamental values of German Protestant humanism, and those that distinguish it from Roman Catholic humanism.

At the beginning of the First World War, Zeitblom calls on Adrian to take his leave as he excitedly goes off to war. Schildknapp is also present. Zeitblom chatters on extensively about his aggressively nationalistic views on the war, and rounds off his exposition with a statement of his ambitions for Germany. The whole chapter illustrates considerable friction between Adrian and Zeitblom, because Adrian objects seriously to his stand.

Zeitblom's argument in chapter 30 centers on the purpose of the war. He assumes in his whole discussion that Germany is the aggressor in the First World War, fighting for change and to achieve world power. He sees this as a very positive indication that Germany is coming of age and asserting its right to equal power in the world. Mann's views on the First World War, as found in *Die Betrachtungen eines Unpolitischen* and in other works, such as *Friedrich der Große*, are very patriotic, but they are not the nationalistic views that Zeitblom expresses. On the contrary, they are radically opposed to these views. Germany is not fighting the First World War in order to become a world power, but simply to prevent its own destruction.

* * *

Schildknapp specifically rejects Mann's argument in *Friedrich der Große* by parodying it. Zeitblom reports that he made them all laugh about the situation,

> ... denn er nahm meine einigermaßen gerührte Darstellung wohl an, zog aber all diese gemütvolle Brutalität, würdige Zerknirschung und biedere Bereitschaft zur Untat durch die Parodie des langen Denkers, der einen längst festgelegten strategischen Plan mit moralischer Poesie umkleidete, ins unwiderstehlich Komische, — noch mehr ins Komische als das fassungslose Tugend-Gebrüll einer Welt, der dieser trockene Feldzugsplan doch längst bekannt gewesen war. (*DF*, 405–6)

Zeitblom finds this funny and says that he sees that tragedy can be made into comedy just by changing the lighting: "So stimmte ich gern in die Heiterkeit ein, nicht ohne anzumerken, daß Tragödie und Komödie auf demselben Holze wüchsen und ein Beleuchtungswechsel genüge, aus dem einen das andre zu machen" (*DF*, 406).

"Tugend-Gebrüll" is the term Mann uses in *Die Betrachtungen eines Unpolitischen* to refer to the moral outcry of the Entente countries against Germany's invasion of Belgium, a neutral country, at the beginning of the First World War. Schildknapp rejects Mann's view as immorality disguised as Protestant morality and the view of the Entente powers as confused. Specifically, he is rejecting Mann's argument that Germany's participation in the First World War was defensive and not aggressive.

* * *

Zeitblom's starting point in his discussion is a modification of the position of the *Zivilisationsliterat*:

> Zwar waren die Fuchteleien jenes im Grunde völlig unsoldatischen und für nichts weniger als für den Krieg geschaffenen Tänzers und Komödianten auf dem Kaiserthron dem Gebildeten peinlich — und seine Stellung zur Kultur die eines zurückgebliebenen Dummkopfes gewesen. Aber sein Einfluß auf diese hatte sich in leeren Maßregelungsgesten erschöpft. Die Kultur war frei gewesen, sie hatte auf ansehnlicher Höhe gestanden, und war sie von langer Hand an ihre völlige Bezugslosigkeit zur Staatsmacht gewöhnt, so mochten ihre jugendlichen Träger gerade in einem großen Volkskrieg, wie er nun ausbrach, das Mittel sehen zum Durchbruch in eine Lebensform, in der Staat und Kultur eines sein würden. (*GW*, 6:400)

He says that before the war the educated classes, that is the *Zivilisationsliteraten*, thought that the aristocracy had to be got rid of, and that they wanted to use the war to create a new State that reflects the state of the culture. The *Zivilisationsliterat* in *Die Betrachtungen eines Unpolitischen* wants to do this by sabotaging the war effort through pacifism so that Germany will lose the war and be forced to adopt Rousseau's democratic values, because adopting Rousseau's democratic values would mean the destruction of German values. Zeitblom is not a pacifist; on the contrary, he is aggressively nationalistic. His criticism of the Kaiser is not that he is militaristic, but that he is not. Zeitblom does not want Germany to lose the war, although, as will be seen in the discussion of chapter 34, he later found that the destruction of German society as a result of losing the war was an advantage. In chapter 30 he associates the need to destroy nineteenth-century German values, not with losing the war and defeating militarism, but with winning the war and introducing militarism. He is using the war for political purposes, as does the radical left-wing *Zivilisationsliterat*, for the purpose of achieving a State that reflects the culture. Zeitblom, like his left-wing brother, wants to achieve this correspondence by rejecting the culture. Mann argues the reverse, that not the culture, but the State must be adjusted to preserve these values in a democracy. The role of the *Zivilisationsliterat* has been adapted in *Doktor Faustus* to apply to fascism, rather than to communism.

Zeitblom claims to have pangs of conscience, on reflection, about his enthusiasm for the First World War and questions whether Germany had the right to go to war. However, he did enjoy going along with the crowd: "Und doch ist es für das höhere Individuum auch wieder ein großer Genuß, einmal — und wo hätte dies Einmal zu finden sein sollen, wenn nicht hier und jetzt — mit Haut und Haar im Allgemeinen unterzugehen" (*DF*, 402). This is a retrospective denial of his clear enthusiasm for the war, which is what chapter 30 is all about. He later denies this enthusiasm, thereby refusing to take personal responsibility for his actions and opinions, and deflecting the blame to others. This is irresponsible and immoral in Mann's view, but typical of the *Zivilisationsliterat*. Zeitblom is saying here, as he says in chapter 34 (*Fortsetzung*), that he enthusiastically goes along with the crowd, even when he does not entirely agree with what the crowd is doing. He explains that the individual likes to be subordinated to the community.

Zeitblom argues that it is Germany's destiny to be a world power. Destiny, he says, is a pre-Christian German concept, a tragic, mythological motif for an opera (*DF*, 401). It is not a pre-Christian German concept. It is a medieval concept, taken from the classics, and completely contrary to Mann's philosophy. Mann was hostile to the view that things happen because they are the result of unavoidable destiny. This hostility was the basis of his opposition to Oswald Spengler. In Mann's view, the belief in fate is irresponsible and inhumane, because believing that events occur as the result of some power outside this world makes it futile to do anything to prevent their happening. The concept of fate is central to Zeitblom's account in *Doktor Faustus*. Zeitblom repeatedly uses terms in the category of fate, such as predestination and destiny, and indeed demonic, to refer to Adrian and to many events in the novel.[1]

Adrian is contemptuous of Zeitblom's idea that Germany could break through to become a world power and says (wrongly) that Zeitblom thinks Kaisersaschern, meaning German Protestant culture, should rule the world (*DF*, 409). Adrian's comment reflects Mann's view that German culture was unsuited to imperialism. Imperialism is a British characteristic and Germany would make a mess of it (*BeU*, 507). However, that is not what Zeitblom means. He sees Germany's breakthrough to world power as requiring a rejection of the Protestant, individualist character of German culture, which he describes in negative terms:

> Ästhetische Erlöstheit oder Unerlöstheit, das ist das Schicksal, das entscheidet über Glück oder Unglück, über das gesellige Zuhausesein auf Erden oder heillose, wenn auch stolze Vereinsamung, und man muß nicht Philolog sein, um zu wissen, daß das Häßliche das Verhaßte ist. Durchbruchsbegierde aus der Gebundenheit und Versiegelung im Häßlichen, — sage mir immerhin, daß ich Schlafstroh dresche, aber ich fühle, habe immer gefühlt und will es gegen viel derben Augenschein vertreten, daß dies deutsch ist kat exochen, tief deutsch, die Definition des Deutschtums geradezu, eines Seelentums, bedroht von Versponnenheit, Einsamkeitsgift, provinzlerischer Eckensteherei, neurotischer Verstrickung, stillem Satanismus. (*DF*, 411)

Adrian does not like Zeitblom's remark. He gives him one of his rejecting looks, "stumm, verschleiert, kalt distanziert bis zum Kränkenden," followed by his sneering smile (*DF*, 411). Zeitblom's statement is a rejection of Protestant values — that is, of Adrian, as Zeitblom sees him.

In chapter 31 Adrian gives his considered response to Zeitblom's position, arguing that medieval Roman Catholic social organization is based on the control of the masses by a priesthood, or a cultural elite, for the purpose of preventing freedom of thought and that, in effect, this is done by turning social organization into an erotic farce. Adrian likens this medieval theology to Zeitblom's demonology in chapters 11 and 22. The alternative he offers is a complete inclusion of the masses in the determination of the culture and the deliberate rejection of the idea of a cultural elite. Adrian's ambition for Germany is now social democracy. Zeitblom not only rejects Adrian's views as offensive, but dismisses them on the grounds that Adrian really means the opposite of what he says.

The sum of Mann's argument in *Die Betrachtungen eines Unpolitischen* is that Germany rejects the very changes that Zeitblom says Germany is fighting for. The novel does not show that Mann changed his views, as some critics have claimed. In *Doktor Faustus* Mann shows that he thought that the rejection of these Protestant values in Germany and their replacement with the views Zeitblom expresses was a major cause of fascism. Mann's stand is reflected in Adrian's rejection of Zeitblom's arguments. However, he has completely eliminated all his own anti-French sentiment in his portrayal of Adrian, restricting his comments, at this point, to only those in favor of liberal democracy. Adrian's comment is limited to pointing out that, because of the war, his planned cultural trip to France has been cancelled in favor of Zeitblom's aggressive trip. The shift in enemy from radical democracy to fascism has made it necessary to leave the argument against France aside, as did Mann in real life. In Mann's view the argument was not between radical enlightenment and reactionary obscurantism, but between both these positions and liberal democracy. These shifts away from *Die Betrachtungen eines Unpolitischen* do not reflect a change of view but a shift in the target of Mann's attack. In chapter 30, the radical left-wing *Zivilisationsliterat* of *Die Betrachtungen eines Unpolitischen* is transformed into his counterpart, the nationalist *Zivilisationsliterat*. The underlying argument remains constant, but France has become irrelevant.

* * *

In answer to all Zeitblom's comments, Adrian says that there is only one important question, the question of freedom. This is Adrian's opposing view of the necessary breakthrough: "Es gibt im Grunde nur *ein* Problem in der Welt, und es hat diesen Namen: Wie bricht man durch? Wie kommt man ins Freie? Wie sprengt man die Puppe und wird zum Schmetterling? Die Gesamtsituation ist beherrscht von der Frage" (*DF*, 410). Adrian points out that this is a reference to Kleist's essay on marionettes, which, he argues, is speaking only about aesthetics (410). Adrian, however, is using it to answer Zeitblom's political comments. His argument contradicts everything Zeitblom has said. It can be read as a *non sequitur*, since Zeitblom has not been talking about freedom, but in the context of Mann's thought it is not. The sum of the views of the *Zivilisationsliterat*, when applied to politics, will mean the end of freedom. This is the conclusion of *Die Betrachtungen eines Unpolitischen*, the conclusion Mann came to when he reflected on opinions such as Zeitblom has been expressing here. It is the conclusion Adrian comes to. In chapter 31 Adrian again uses the image of marionettes to make the point that demagogic militarism, like medieval Catholicism, is the denial of freedom.

Zeitblom says that aesthetics is everything, distorting Adrian's remark by transferring the goal of the breakthrough from the individual to the community. The Protestant German is an aesthete and requires freedom within his society, as Kleist argued. Zeitblom is arguing for the aesthetic State, which denies subjective freedom in the name of the State as a whole. Adrian is restating the argument of the *strenger Satz*: the only important principle in the establishment of a State is the protection of subjective freedom. In both cases, Zeitblom interprets the argument in the manner of the *Zivilisationsliterat*, transferring this freedom to the State. He is describing the true German goal, the purpose of the war, as a desire to break out of the fetters of nineteenth-century society, that is, Protestant morality and individualism. Zeitblom's argument is not only radically opposed to Adrian's view but is a deliberate rejection of it. Zeitblom, however, thinks he has expressed the same view as Adrian.

Zeitblom's definition of the deep German character, quoted above, is his interpretation of *Innerlichkeit*. Protestantism, with individualism and reliance on personal conscience and refusal to participate in the broader Roman community — Mann's definition of *Innerlichkeit* — is described in terms of a psychological sickness to be overcome. The standard interpretations of the novel agree with Zeitblom's interpretation of the true German Protestant as psychologically disturbed, but Mann certainly did not. Neither does Adrian. Zeitblom's definition of the German character is, presumably, a reference to the "dark powers" that Litzmann claimed to have seen in *Die Betrachtungen eines Unpolitischen*, a distortion of the Protestant *Innerlichkeit* that Mann defined as the uniqueness of the German character. By some peculiar twist of the fascist mind, Mann's defense of *Innerlichkeit* in *Die Betrachtungen eines Unpolitischen* was interpreted by Catholic intellectuals as the description of an inhibition that had to be overcome and at the same time as a true definition of the German character (*TMUB*, 69). The term *Innerlichkeit* has been transformed into meaning that the powers of the night should rule politics instead of the intellect. This exaggerated intellectualizing of *Innerlichkeit* is scholasticism, using the intellect to argue against intellect, turning it into a philosophy that is irresponsibly propagated by academics. It was appropriate to the nineteenth century, but not to the political situation of Germany immediately after the First World War.[2] In its extreme manifestation it was a deliberate rejection by the individual of nineteenth-century Protestant values and participation in the community in favor of a withdrawal into the service of an ideal, a return to nature or to antiquity, a complete anti-social withdrawal from the world into subjectivity. Zeitblom's definition of the necessary breakthrough is not only that Germany should take over the world but that Germany must do so by rejecting its Protestant, individualist culture. He does not think that Kaisersaschern should rule the world, as Adrian suggests. He thinks that Kaisersaschern has to be overcome in order for Germany to rule the world. Zeitblom and Adrian are arguing from contradictory premises, reflecting the two opposing tendencies of nineteenth-century Romanticism, extreme individualism and a tendency to return to Catholicism. Ironically, Mann did say that for totalitarianism to be successful in Germany it would have to overcome Protestantism. He said that Protestant *Innerlichkeit* was the greatest obstacle to totalitarianism.

The image of marionettes that Adrian uses is indeed political. His opera is a parody of a totalitarian system of government, where the individual is being led around on strings. Having expressed a variation in chapter 30 on his view of the basic political problem to be solved, the preservation of nineteenth-century Protestant humanism, he is now elaborating his view of the results of not solving this problem, the return of Catholic humanism and totalitarianism. The account of Adrian's activities during the war in chapter 31 shows that Adrian is working on yet another variation of this basic theme. Adrian and Schildknapp are working on medieval materials for Adrian's puppet opera. They find them outrageously hilarious, which offends Zeitblom. Anything funny about them is due to the translation, he says (*DF*, 420). He thinks that Adrian maliciously misrepresents the Middle Ages. These stories are similar to Schleppfuß's stories, and Zeitblom takes them seriously. He is outraged that Adrian is parodying them and says that Adrian has turned the moral lesson of the priest into an erotic farce:

> Das musikalische Drama hatte seine Stoffe der romantischen Sage, der Mythenwelt des Mittelalters entnommen und dabei zu verstehen gegeben, daß nur dergleichen Gegenstände der Musik würdig, ihrem Wesen angemessen seien. Dem schien hier Folge geleistet: auf eine recht destruktive Weise jedoch, indem das Skurrile, besonders auch im Erotischen Possenhafte, an die Stelle moralischer Priesterlichkeit trat, aller inflationärer Pomp der Mittel abgeworfen und die Aktion der an sich schon burlesken Gliederpuppen-Bühne übertragen wurde. (*DF*, 425–26)

Adrian would seem to be interpreting the moral lesson of the priest in these stories to be that procreation is the holy way to life. By using puppets, Adrian shows that the priest is leading people around on strings. This is what Adrian has just argued, in chapter 30, that it is necessary, above all things, to oppose. In *Die Betrachtungen eines Unpolitischen* Mann calls the priestly moralizing of the *Zivilisationsliterat* "pfäffischer Dünkel" (535). Zeitblom is objecting to this objection and implying, by extension, that Mann's/Adrian's parody of Catholicism and the *Zivilisationsliterat* are irony, that is, that they mean the opposite of what they say. It is Zeitblom's position that, in making fun of this moralizing, Adrian is saying he does not really mean to criticize it, but to affirm it. Zeitblom interprets everything Adrian says as meaning the opposite of what he thinks, turning all Adrian's disagreements with his own views into confirmation of them. Zeitblom is a school teacher and he has told us that Adrian is childish, and that the expression of this childishness is his schoolboy tendency to irreverence and blasphemy in bad taste; of course he does not mean what he says. Zeitblom's view of Adrian is doubly negative: not only does he describe all of Adrian's characteristics as negative, but he also describes everything Adrian says as meaning its negation.

In chapter 31, Adrian implicates Zeitblom's father as a contributor to Zeitblom's unacceptable views when he comments that he gets the puppets from Catholic apothecaries (*DF*, 426). Zeitblom's father is a Catholic apothecary, a secularized Roman Catholic, who, nevertheless, maintains the values of his community (14). Zeitblom has already implicated Adrian's father as a contributor to what he considers Adrian's unacceptable views in chapter 3.

* * *

This discussion of Adrian's view of the Middle Ages is placed beside a discussion of his view of the future he is striving for in his art. He says that it is necessary to eliminate the growing gap between the culture and the people (*DF*, 427). To achieve this, a new organization must be found that incorporates the new, without losing sight of tradition. It is necessary to do this in such a way that the effect is simple and does not betray the effort that went into achieving it. This is the argument of Wagner's *Die Meistersinger*, of *Die Betrachtungen eines Unpolitischen*, and of Adrian's *strenger Satz*. The ideas are Adrian's, says Zeitblom, and, although his arguments are sporadically produced, he is very eloquent. This facility with words is, of course, the result of his having incorporated a degree of "enlightenment" thought into his views. He is repeating his argument that music, or the expression of German society, must be organized in terms of its relationship to the whole of society, not just to an intellectual elite. It is for the sake of preserving the culture in a mass society that he wants to do this, not for the sake of the State. The breakthrough is to escape the intellectual coldness of today's technical intellectuality, or of the utopian approach of the *Zivilisationsliterat*, and find a world of new emotion, or subjectivity. Whoever manages to do this will be the savior of culture, which has become isolated from the people and will die out if it does not find its way back. This new organization is to make music, the expression of German humanism, the servant of a community that is perhaps not cultured, but will be a culture. This will be healthy and matter-of-fact, unemotional and reliable.

This is Adrian's plan for a democratic society based on German values. It is an argument for socialism and the democratization of education. Mann presented this same argument in 1927 and described it as cultural democratization.[3] It is once again the argument of combining the eighteenth-century approach with that of the nineteenth century. Instead of using the terms "harmony and polyphony," Adrian is using the terms "Romanticism and technical intellectuality," but he is saying the same thing. It is the argument that the move to liberal democracy is necessary to preserve German cultural values. Schildknapp is skeptical about this. He says that music, or German Protestant society, is too closely tied to the Romantic to be able to remove the Romantic from it without destroying it. Adrian says that this is the task, clearly a statement about what he is doing in the novel. Zeitblom does not like Adrian's idea. He says it is incompatible with Adrian's pride and arrogance. It is out of character. Art is intellect and the intellect is not responsible to the community. Art that serves the needs of the masses and sees itself as having a duty, for the sake of society, to meet these needs will come to grief. It will be the death of intellect. Zeitblom is convinced that in the end intellect will be, although very indirectly, serviceable to mankind, no matter how irresponsible it is (*DF*, 429). All revolutions postpone serving the needs of the masses till after the achievement of the Utopia, as Zeitblom is arguing here.

These arguments, if read as simply about music, sound superficially very much as though Adrian and Zeitblom have reversed roles. Adrian seems to be taking the *Zivilisationsliterat* view that art must be for the purpose of serving social morality and Zeitblom seems to be taking the view that art cannot accept this obligation of preaching social morality without destroying itself. This is not the case. Adrian is not talking about a preaching purpose, of catering to the masses, he is talking about organization and participation. Adrian is talking again of the lost equilibrium of present society, of the isolation of the masses from the culture. He is proposing, not a lower, but a higher form of art, an art in which all participate, as Beißel attempted. Once again, his argument sounds as if it is taken from Hanns Eisler: "In order to check the decay of music and to find a new technique, a new style and thus a new circle of listeners, the modern composer will have to leave his airtight room and find his place in society. It is not a question of sentimentality and kindheartedness but a question of music."[4]

However, Eisler distinguishes between his own Communist movement and the bourgeois movement, which also sees this problem. The problem with the bourgeois movement is that it "tries to combine in some measure tradition and progress [and] expects everything to emanate from the creative power of individual geniuses" (48). He includes Schoenberg in this group.

Zeitblom, in his tortuous way, is justifying the misuse of art by fascism. Adrian's point is that art must be properly understood if it is not to be misused. He is arguing against a totalitarian society run by an interpreting intellectual elite. Zeitblom, on the other hand, has just identified music with intellect and both with politics. He is saying, by implication, that government does not have to serve the needs of the masses and does not have to be responsible. It is a contradiction of the point Adrian has made with his puppet opera. In his puppet opera Adrian is arguing against a totalitarian society run by an elite, whereas Zeitblom is arguing in favor of such a society. All the components have been put in place for the development of German fascism: a nationalistic totalitarian government run by an intellectual elite and based on a cult of music, which is what Zeitblom is arguing would be desirable. Adrian opposes Zeitblom's views on every point. Zeitblom, however, shows again that he does not take Adrian seriously, that he thinks Adrian's opposition to his views is not real. Of course Adrian agrees with him, he says, he is just being contrary, trying to show that he is not arrogant (*DF*, 430).

* * *

Zeitblom's views of the First World War do not reflect Mann's own, but, in each case, views Mann had been arguing against since 1914, arguments he had been formulating and partially expressing for years. Mann came to think these ideas were the underlying source of the support for National Socialism. He makes it very clear in chapter 30 that he means Zeitblom to represent these views and Adrian's position to be understood as opposed to this position. The particular choice of categories Zeitblom uses for expressing his thoughts and the way in which he uses concepts carefully chosen from *Die Betrachtungen eines Unpolitischen* indicate that Mann means the reader to see this connection. Certainly, his friends and contemporaries would have seen the correlation at once. Adrian's hostile reaction is a true representation of Mann's reaction to these views. Mann's reaction, like Adrian's, was to fall into fits of Dürer-type melancholy and feverish writing. The result of Mann's reaction was his apocalypse, *Die Betrachtungen eines Unpolitischen*, and, in the novel, Adrian's is his *Apocalipsis cum figuris*. Both express the fear that the *Zivilisationsliterat* would triumph in Germany after the war and warn that this would mean the end of freedom and the end of German culture. Mann was attacking totalitarianism in the form of communism. Adrian is attacking it in the form of fascism.

It is during this period in the novel, when politics begins to intrude, that the direct parallel with the opinions expressed in *Die Betrachtungen eines Unpolitischen* weakens. Zeitblom does not express pacifist views, but is aggressive. Adrian does not defend Germany's position, nor does he attack France. These are important differences. However, the characterizations and systems of values of the two protagonists are strengthened rather than weakened with these modifications. Adrian's and Zeitblom's positions are diametrically opposed. Adrian sees the necessary "breakthrough" as discovering the means to preserve nineteenth-century Protestant values, whereas Zeitblom sees the necessary "breakthrough" as overcoming these values. Adrian finds his answer in socialism and Zeitblom finds his in aggressive nationalism, expressed here as Germany's destiny to take over the world, and authoritarianism, expressed here as an intellectual elite determining the culture by manipulating the masses. This is identical with the argument of the Kridwiß *Kreis*. Zeitblom interprets Adrian's goals as identical with his own by simply interpreting Adrian's position as its opposite. Zeitblom's arrogance is astronomical.

Notes

[1] This is in accordance with Orlowski's findings, but not with his conclusions (Hubert Orlowski, "Prädestination des Dämonischen: Zur Frage des bürgerlichen Humanismus in Thomas Manns *Doktor Faustus*" [diss., U of Posen, 1969], 176),

according to which Zeitblom's belief in fate crippled his humanism in his attempt to counter fascism. On the contrary, Zeitblom's belief in fate contributes to his justification for his optimistic support of fascism as an extension of his Catholic humanism. He is contributing to the achievement of Germany's destiny. Its use in the novel explains rather that Adrian's defeat was inevitable, in Zeitblom's view: the forces of destiny were against him.

[2] Thomas Mann, "Die Bäume im Garten," in *GW*, 11:861–69.

[3] Thomas Mann, "*Romane der Welt*: Geleitwort," in *GW*, 10:673–77; here, 674–75.

[4] Eisler, Hanns. *A Rebel in Music* (New York: International, 1978), 112.

10: The End of the First World War

IN CHAPTERS 33 AND 34 MANN EXPLAINS the basis of the great gulf that opens up between Zeitblom and his friends and Adrian and Rudi in the second part of the novel. Zeitblom describes six different aspects of the period just after the end of the First World War: his personal attitude towards the political situation; the political theories of the Kridwiß *Kreis* and his explanation of the conclusions reached; Adrian's activities both during and after the war; Adrian's *Apocalipsis cum figuris*; its reception by Zeitblom and his associates; and Adrian's and Rudi's decision to cooperate in support of the Weimar Republic.

There is strong opposition among critics to identifying Zeitblom with National Socialism, and more or less universal agreement among them that Mann does not present him as supporting National Socialism. Certainly, Zeitblom makes a few remarks to the effect that he is not entirely in agreement with Hitler's policies. However, he makes clear statements, glossed over by the critics, that identify him as definitely sympathetic to fascism in the abstract. In these chapters he is clearly and unmistakably shown by Mann to be one of those intellectuals he described in 1931 in "Die Wiedergeburt der Anständigkeit": in the 1920s, says Mann, these people fell into the fashionable sickness of deifying the irrational and are, therefore, guilty of complicity in the triumph of the anti-intellectuality of the political mass movements. They made it easier for its leaders to appeal openly to irrational motivations.[1] This deification of the irrational is symbolically portrayed by Zeitblom's removal of sex from the realm of the Devil. It is illustrated by his deification of Adrian, which is, given his values, irrational. Its most blatant manifestation is his acceptance of fascist arguments.

At the end of the First World War, Zeitblom methodically outlines the various stages in his thought that convince him that totalitarianism is inevitable and not to be feared. He then proceeds to explain that this is based on a cult of the culture, which is what turns totalitarianism into fascism, rather than communism. Adrian specifically warns of the danger of developing a cult of the culture in chapter 31 (*DF*, 428), but it is clear in chapter 34 (*Schluß*) that Zeitblom is interpreting Adrian's *Apocalipsis cum figuris* as the basic argument for this cult. To what extent and how Adrian is responsible for this development is the subject of Adrian's conversation with the Devil in chapter 25. Chapter 34 presents Mann's view of how National Socialism became intellectually acceptable among Catholic academics. It is his explanation of why intelligent, well-educated, well-meaning persons adopted a fascist political philosophy and did not recognize the dangers inherent in Hitler's National Socialism and therefore oppose it. The argument presented is that fascism resulted from a desire to control the masses by a rejection of nineteenth-century humanism in favor of a return to the medieval Roman social order centering on a cult of the culture, as a deliberate alternative to the Weimar Republic. The evidence of chapter 34 does not describe an educated middle class that passively rejected the Weimar Republic out of lack of interest in politics but an educated middle class that actively rejected the Weimar Republic on nationalist grounds and supported fascist arguments as the desirable alternative political approach. However, it is fascism, not specifically National Socialism, that is under discussion by the Kridwiß *Kreis*.

* * *

In chapter 30, at the beginning of the First World War, Zeitblom uses many of the arguments ascribed to the *Zivilisationsliterat* in *Die Betrachtungen eines Unpolitischen*, thus identifying him as having an appreciation of the situation radically opposed to Mann's own position. Zeitblom's views are the particular variation of these views that is colored by emotional and aggressive nationalism, but that is the only difference between him and the basic *Zivilisationsliterat*.

In chapter 33, in contrast, Zeitblom uses the language, not of the *Zivilisationsliterat*, but of the Protestant artist, that is, of Mann's position. Zeitblom talks about his *a priori* rejection of the "Tugend-Suada des Rhetor-Bourgeois und 'Sohnes der Revolution'" when he refers to the politicians trying to run the Weimar Republic. By summing up succinctly the politicians in the same terms that Mann used in his definition of the *Zivilisationsliterat*, he gives the superficial impression that he himself is not a *Zivilisationsliterat*, but that his position is Mann's position, which is not the case. It is not the case because the ideas are taken out of context and illegitimately applied to a completely different situation. In fact, the bulk of Zeitblom's comments suggests that he would welcome the advent of democracy. However, right at the beginning of his commentary Zeitblom says he would have preferred Germany to go communist rather than to fall into the hands of the Weimar politicians, whom he calls oppressive powers. He describes Communism as a historical development and improvement of Rousseau's theory of democracy: "Die russische Revolution erschütterte mich, und die historische Überlegenheit ihrer Prinzipien über diejenigen der Mächte, die uns den Fuß auf den Nacken setzten, litt in meinen Augen keinen Zweifel" (*DF*, 452). In *Die Betrachtungen eines Unpolitischen* Mann is against Rousseau's democracy precisely because it leads logically to Communism.

Zeitblom's argument starts with a confirmation of his status as a *Zivilisationsliterat*. The people of other nations were more conservative, he says, because they had won the war and could just go back as they were, instead of having to face a historical break. He is particularly jealous of France, because of the justification and confirmation through victory of its bourgeois, intellectual frame of mind, the feeling of protection in the classical and rational. He says he would have felt more at home in France than in Germany:

> Ich beneidete insonderheit Frankreich um die Rechtfertigung und Bestätigung, die, wenigstens scheinbar, seiner bewahrend bürgerlichen Geistesverfassung durch den Sieg zuteil geworden war; um das Gefühl von Geborgenheit im Klassisch-Rationalen, das es aus dem Siege schöpfen durfte. Gewiß, ich hätte mich damals jenseits des Rheines wohler und mehr zu Hause gefühlt als bei uns. (*DF*, 469)

France is the spiritual homeland of the *Zivilisationsliterat*, says Mann in *Die Betrachtungen eines Unpolitischen*. The *Zivilisationsliterat*, Zeitblom, has declared himself once again to be against everything German and to belong to the enemy camp, according to Mann's views:

> "Ich — ein Abtrünniger? Ob ich das Vaterland liebe oder nicht: ich bin es selbst!" Aber das ist die offenbare, spiegelfechterische und gedrehte Unwahrheit. Er ist nicht das Vaterland; ist es nicht nur nicht, sondern hat es mit seinem geistespolitischen Kultus des Fremden dahin gebracht, daß er keinen Gedanken, keinen Begriff, kein Gefühl mehr mit dem eigenen Volkstum gemeinsam hat. (*BeU*, 553)

Zeitblom dismisses the entire development of German culture in the nineteenth century, indeed since the Reformation, as an unsuccessful aberration:

> Wurde nicht dort am runden Tisch eine Kritik der Tradition auf die Tagesordnung gesetzt, die das Ergebnis der Zerstörung von Lebenswerten war, welche lange für unverbrüchlich gegolten, und war nicht ausdrücklich die Bemerkung gefallen . . ., daß diese Kritik sich notwendig gegen herkömmliche Kunstformen und -gattungen, zum Beispiel gegen das ästhetische Theater kehren müsse, das im bürgerlichen Lebenskreis gestanden habe. . . . (*DF*, 493–94)

In Mann's view, the development of German culture and art forms depended on the Reformation. It is the Reformation that destroyed the long-standing values of Roman Catholicism in Germany. Mann thought that this was a good thing, not a bad thing, as Zeitblom suggests. Zeitblom has already, in chapter 30, expressed this negative view of Protestant individualism. To be against Protestant values is not incompatible with Rousseau's democracy. It is this very characteristic that Zeitblom calls classical and rational and admires.

Zeitblom rejects radical democracy for no other reason than that it is French, and he takes the alternative *Zivilisationsliterat* position, radical reaction, based on nationalism and a cult of the culture. Ironically, this fascist alternative to Rousseau is also French in origin. In *Die Betrachtungen eines Unpolitischen* Mann says that Barrès, a French advocate of fascism, is a good example of aesthetic politics. The difference between what Barrès advocates and utopian democracy is that he is reactionary and nationalistic. But that is the only difference (*BeU*, 549–50). In 1928, speaking of Barrès and French nationalism, Mann said that nationalism in Germany is barbarism. A curse and metaphysical interdict hovers over it, because it is a sin against the German spirit.[2] Fascism was the alternative generally adopted by German humanists in their opposition to what they considered the French betrayal of humanist principles.

What we find in Zeitblom's account is an illustration of the extent and nature of the influence of *Die Betrachtungen eines Unpolitischen*. Phrases such as *Tugend-Suada des Rhetor-Bourgeois und "Sohnes der Revolution"* cannot really be understood without reference to *Die Betrachtungen eines Unpolitischen*, where this terminology, which is specifically Mann's invention, is explained. Zeitblom is using Mann's arguments against Rousseau's democracy against the Weimar Republic. He simply rejects the goal of Rousseau's democracy: the pursuit of abstract virtues, such as justice and freedom. Mann was rejecting not the goal, but the means, which Zeitblom retains. Zeitblom is using descriptive terms demagogically and changing the goal from justice and freedom to the nation.

In *Die Betrachtungen eines Unpolitischen* Mann describes the *Zivilisationsliterat* as the enemy of German culture. However, Zeitblom identifies this term with the enemy of the German State, that is, with France and everything French. This is an entirely different concept, which drains the term of all philosophical content. Zeitblom uses these terms simply as nationalistic rhetoric to support opposition to the Weimar Republic on the grounds that it is imposed by France. Nationalism is not a characteristic of the *Zivilisationsliterat*. Nationalism is not the same as patriotism; it is essentially a negative concept that has nothing to do with culture. It is irrational, a suspension of all criticism in favor of emotion. At the same time, the values that are rejected by Zeitblom and the Kridwiß *Kreis* in these chapters are the very values that Mann considered the defining characteristics of German culture. These values, as Mann describes them, are Protestant. The important underlying values that make them Protestant — having a conscience, a sense of responsibility and a concern for humanity — are deliberately dismissed as insignificant, as Zeitblom tries to convince the reader in chapter 34 (*Schluß*). The effect of these Protestant values is that the recognition of the fallibility of the human mind, influenced as it is by subconscious powers such as will and emotion, leaves one in a state of doubt about truth, justice, good and evil, and so on. Zeitblom, however, presents all his opinions as statements of indisputable fact, showing that he does not share this view, a view he criticized when Kumpf defended it. In the Kridwiß *Kreis*, the whole of nineteenth-century German culture is rejected, except Adrian's idea of music as being the expression of German culture.

Mann waxed eloquent and vitriolic against France and "politics" and "democracy." He lamented that a government in Germany based on French political philosophy would destroy German culture. However, this is only one part of his argument, the part that he has Zeitblom take literally, with no understanding of the underlying argument. Zeitblom's arguments would lead logically to the acceptance of such a government. However, hostility against France was general in Germany after the war. In fact, Zeitblom's description of the stupid and dangerous way that the French were treating Germany (*DF*, 450–52) comes entirely from Mann's diaries of the period, where the bulk of the comment is outrage against this treatment. Mann's tirade in his diaries, however, is not directed against the German politicians in Weimar but against the government of France, particularly Clemenceau. In his speech "Von Deutscher Republik" Mann pointed out that those politicians whom the nationalists were deliberately impeding in their efforts to develop a German democracy were Germans, not Frenchmen (*VDR*, 826). Hübinger has documented this use of *Die Betrachtungen eines Unpolitischen* as support for this opposition to Weimar by the Bonn Literary Society (see my chapter 2). In the novel, as in real life, the academics do not stop at simple resistance; they turn this resistance into fascism and claim to base their arguments on Adrian's. Zeitblom illustrates this distortion in chapter 34 (*Schluß*), as does the Devil in chapter 25.

* * *

Zeitblom dissociates himself from the criticism of German culture by the Kridwiß *Kreis* by giving the impression that he is only reporting what others said, but he makes it clear that he thought they were right:

> Wird man es verstehen, daß ein Mann bei der Verarbeitung solcher Neuigkeiten vierzehn Pfund Gewicht verlieren mag? Sicherlich hätte ich sie nicht eingebüßt, wenn ich an die Ergebnisse der Sitzungen bei Kridwiß nicht geglaubt hätte und der Überzeugung gewesen wäre, daß diese Herren Unsinn schwätzten. Aber das war ganz und gar nicht meine Meinung. Vielmehr verhehlte ich mir keinen Augenblick, daß sie mit anerkennenswerter Fühlsamkeit die Finger am Pulse der Zeit hatten und nach diesem Pulse wahr-sagten [*sic*!]. (*DF*, 492)

This is a clear and unequivocal statement that Zeitblom agreed with the political analysis of the Kridwiß *Kreis*. These views are put forward in

the context of *a priori* rejection of the Weimar Republic: "Die demokratische Republik [wurde] auch nicht einen Augenblick als ernstzunehmender
Rahmen für das visierte Neue anerkannt, sondern mit einmütiger
Selbstverständlichkeit als ephemer und für den Sachverhalt von vornherein
bedeutungslos, ja als ein schlechter Spaß über die Achsel geworfen" (*DF*,
485).

Zeitblom claims to be disgusted by the general political discussion and
unrest following the collapse of the monarchy and refuses to participate in
events (*DF*, 452–53). However, he means this very specifically, because he
does join in the discussions of the Kridwiß *Kreis*, which is already very
active by 1919. The Kridwiß *Kreis* is a group of eight to ten leading
Munich academics, brought together by a certain Kridwiß, to exchange
ideas about the political and social situation. Zeitblom is clearly a member
of this group, not just an observer. The level of discussion is not always
very elevated, says Zeitblom, because a couple of young princes attend. He
is particularly irritated that the Jew, Breisacher, is included. He cannot tolerate him, but respects his scholarship — in chapter 28 Breisacher preaches
a return to primitive religion, with human sacrifice (*DF*, 375). Zeitblom
also does not like the industrialist, Bullinger, who is only invited because
of his influential position. He is uncomfortable about Unruhe, who
preaches a Darwinism that nobody seriously believes in. He does not know
why he mistrusts him. He also inexplicably mistrusts a literary historian
who explains everything through racial theories. He is uncomfortable
about the poet, Daniel Zur Höhe, who preaches terrorism, poverty,
chastity, unconditional obedience, and conquering the world. In chapter 47,
in 1930, Zeitblom says Zur Höhe does not mean it seriously (*DF*, 661).
Here he says it is poetic license, aesthetic nonsense, that it bears no relationship to anything.

With Zeitblom's description of the members of this group, Mann
provides a nutshell summary of contemporary academic interests (*DF*,
481–83). It sounds like a meeting of a group like the Freemasons, or the
Bonn Literary Society. It is perfectly clear from the text, in spite of the
views of the apologists for Zeitblom, that his reservations are personal ani-
mosities, not reservations about their political opinions and activities. He
thinks what they do academically is harmless. What they do academically is
indeed harmless; nobody should question today the utility of medical studies that show that one racial group is more subject to a particular disease
than others or sociological studies showing that another racial group shows
a distinctly higher mathematical ability than others. The implication is,
however, that they are mixing philosophy with politics. They are applying
these approaches to politics, and that leads to totalitarianism. Mann has left
out the most serious instances of misuse — Nietzsche's glorification of life
and the questionable application of Freud's discoveries, Bachofen's theory
of the superiority of a society with no feminine influence, and undoubtedly

many more — because Zeitblom takes them for granted. It must be remembered that Ernst Bertram, the primary promoter of *Die Betrachtungen eines Unpolitischen* for political purposes, was an expert on Nietzsche, and Zeitblom presents himself as an amateur expert on Freud's theory of subconscious drive. Zeitblom's participation in this group is typical of behavior Mann attributes to the *Zivilisationsliterat*:

> So umgibt er sich mit Subalternen, mit solchen, die zwar nicht seinesgleichen sind, aber der gleichen Gesinnung huldigen, und von denen er daher keinen Widerspruch, keine Störung und Beleidigung zu besorgen hat. Il a besoin d'avoir raison. Auf diese Weise aber wird vollends das Gewissen eingeschläfert, der Sinn für Wahrheit und Gerechtigkeit verkümmert, und rasch ist jener Grad von Entsittigung und Bigotterie erreicht, wo allem, was nicht zur "Lehre" schwört, die Wahl gelassen wird, schurkisch oder idiotisch zu heißen. Dies ist die Geistesfreiheit des Politikers. Dies die "Solidarität aller Geistigen," die er meint. Dies steife und kalte Pharisäertum predigt Menschlichkeit. (*BeU*, 323–24)

Zeitblom is a suitable member of this society. He is a classicist, as were many fascist philosophers, and a medievalist, sympathetic with and informed about the medieval values reflected in fascism. It must always be borne in mind that Zeitblom is professor of history and Latin at the Catholic school of theology at Freising. This is the kind of place where academic support for fascism was developed.

Zeitblom justifies his membership in the Kridwiß *Kreis* on the grounds that he feels an intellectual responsibility to find out what is being said. He reveals, however, that this is not in order to oppose the movement but to keep himself up to date on current right opinion. He felt no intellectual responsibility to listen to the political discussions he mentions at the beginning of his account. He is impressed by the conversations in the Kridwiß *Kreis*, excited at seeing the birth of new ideas. A lot of new, disturbing, and frightening things are said that contradict Zeitblom's worldview, but the remarks are clever and prophetic and confirm these disturbing statements, making them reality, he says (*DF*, 469–70). This is an affirmation of Spengler's theory of the inevitable decline of western culture in *Untergang des Abendlandes*, the first volume of which appeared in 1918.[3] Mann is showing the position to be irrational: it is measuring value by the latest fashion: "Denn wie leicht hat es der bloß Urteilende, immer in den richtigen Kahn zu springen, den Anschluß nie zu versäumen, immer mit der neuesten Jugend Arm in Arm befunden zu werden" (*BeU*, 490). As we have seen in chapter 30, these ideas do not contradict Zeitblom's worldview. What is disturbing and frightening is the boldness of actually applying such ideas outside the context of Rousseau.

Kridwiß found, and he was entirely right, says Zeitblom, that the subjects they discussed were important (*DF*, 484). They discussed questions of social reality, to establish the present and the coming situation, and these realities had to do with Zur Höhe's fantasies. Zeitblom assures us, in the same sentence, that Zur Höhe's poetry is only symbolic (*DF*, 484). Zur Höhe's fantasies consist in the cult of aesthetic "enlightenment" in the form of militarism, for the purpose of conquering the world. Zeitblom has already shown his susceptibility to this kind of thinking in his analysis of *Love's Labour's Lost*. His protestation here is that fascism is not militaristic, even though it sounds as if it is.

They were aware, says Zeitblom, that the destruction of existing values in Germany, as a result of the war, gave them an advantage over other countries (*DF*, 484). This is yet again Mann's *Zivilisationsliterat* speaking:

> Er wünscht also die physische Demütigung Deutschlands, weil sie die geistige in sich schlösse; wünscht den Zusammenbruch — aber man sagt es richtiger auf französisch: die débâcle des "Kaiserreiches," weil durch diese physische und moralische débâcle — die moralische mag übrigens auch vor der physischen kommen — endlich, endlich der heiß ersehnte, handgreifliche und katastrophale Beweis erbracht wäre, daß Deutschland in Lüge und Roheit statt in der Wahrheit und im Geist gelebt hat. (*BeU*, 61)

It was agreed by the Kridwiß *Kreis* that there was a drastic decline in the value given to the individual and a general indifference to his fate (*DF*, 484). This appeared to be, but was not, caused by the war. The war only put in high relief what had already happened. This was not a value judgment, just fact, says Zeitblom. There is a certain satisfaction in establishing facts. The dimensions of this statement are enormous. Limiting it narrowly to the political sphere, it is the statement that the State is dealing not with persons but with "the masses," a great anonymous body. The implication of these facts, says Zeitblom, was that nineteenth-century values were put in question, particularly the function of education for raising the intellectual level of the masses. These criticisms were put forward by academics, the very persons responsible for education, says Zeitblom, lending the opinion weight. Mann refers to these leaders of the young as *Dunkelmänner*[4] — the *Dunkelmänner* are among Zeitblom's humanist models (*DF*, 10). In 1923, in "Geist und Wesen der Deutschen Republik," Mann described the economic situation and the brutality of the French occupation as understandable reasons for a rejection of the Republic and the reversal of traditional values on the part of young persons. However, he said, their desire for a better world is being corrupted by their being driven into the arms of obscurantism (*GW*, 11:859–60). *Duden* defines *Dunkelmann* as "Vertreter des Rückschritts; Feind der Bildung" and the origin of the word as a sixteenth-century satire ridiculing the vulgarity and backwardness of contemporary academics.

Zeitblom had already felt, as the war broke out, he says, that the era of traditional society had ended, a view expressed apocalyptically by Mann in *Die Betrachtungen eines Unpolitischen*. It becomes clear in the course of

Zeitblom's argument, however, that he does not mean that times are changing and the emphasis is shifting, as did Mann. Zeitblom means an absolute break with the traditional social values, a deliberate rejection of the *Bürger* tradition. He has said this before, at the beginning of the war, in chapter 30. Advocating abrupt change is advocating revolution.

Zeitblom continues his argument, basing it entirely on French arguments that Mann attacks in *Die Betrachtungen eines Unpolitischen*. Zeitblom is being selective in his choice of authorities. The collapse of the monarchy in Germany was seen as equivalent to the French Revolution, but everybody rejected the idea of freedom growing out of it, because freedom was already dead, so dictatorship was inevitable, whether one wanted it or not. This argument is de Tocqueville's (*DF*, 485). Zeitblom's claim that "everyone" shares this view is questionable, as is his assumption of inevitability. Sorel had anticipated that there would be war in *Réflections sur la violence* in 1907 and had said that parliamentary discussion was an unsuitable means of governing the masses and that it was necessary to have recourse to myth (*DF*, 486–87). To use myth is to use force for victory over truth. Myth, argues Mann in *Die Betrachtungen eines Unpolitischen*, is an unacceptable tool for home government and pertains exclusively to external politics in time of war. The *Zivilisationsliterat* has this backwards:

> Denn in der *inneren* verbietet er eine menschliche Betrachtung des Politischen aus Opportunitätsgründen völlig und besteht vielmehr auf einer politischen Betrachtung alles Menschlichen. *Genau umgekehrt* verhält es sich bei seinem Gegentyp, dem Nicht-Politiker, den wir noch immer nicht besser, als mit dem Namen des Ästheten zu nennen wissen. Dieser hält dafür, daß in der *äußeren* Politik, wenigstens zuzeiten, der Mythos ein unverbrüchliches Lebensrecht, — ein Vorrecht vor dem Individuell-Menschlichen besitze, und daß in solchen Zeitläuften die außermenschliche, politisch-historische Seite der Dinge entschieden ins Auge zu fassen sei, während die menschlich-kulturelle zwar nicht aus der Welt geleugnet werden, aber doch für den Augenblick zurücktreten müsse. In der *inneren* Politik dagegen ist ihm der Mythos, die Politisierung alles Menschlichen, von Grund aus verhaßt, und hier, wahrhaftig, liebt er die menschliche Aufklärung, wie etwa die Kunst oder die Religion sie betreiben. (*BeU*, 433)

The Kridwiß *Kreis*, however, regarded this situation as already existing or inevitably coming. All this is a not very oblique reference to Oswald Spengler, whom Mann thought subversive, because he, like the members of the Kridwiß *Kreis*, predicted the inevitability of totalitarianism and advocated contributing to bringing it about (*GW*, 10:178).

Zeitblom says he wondered about the wisdom of what was being said, but nobody would have listened had he said so. To say so would be to admit to a worn-out idealism in bad taste and against the spirit of the times. This is why Zeitblom gives up his belief in traditional values — because it is in bad taste. It was better to go along with the inevitable course of the world, says Zeitblom (*DF*, 488–89). Going along is one of the more important characteristics of the *Zivilisationsliterat*:

> Ein Literat also ist ein Wesen, das immer genau weiß: "Man muß jetzt, — —" und immer auch gleich *kann*. Das Weitere ist bloß Kommentar. Der Literat nämlich *ist* nicht, er urteilt nur, — ein lustiges, neidenswertes Los, wie ich oft empfand. Denn wie leicht hat es der bloß Urteilende, immer in den richtigen Kahn zu springen, den Anschluß nie zu versäumen, immer mit der neuesten Jugend Arm in Arm befunden zu werden. Man kann aber "rückständig" sein und doch eben *mehr* sein, oder um ein Wörtchen hinzuzufügen und den Ton darauf zu legen, mehr *wert* sein, als manch ein urteilend an der tête Marschierender, — einfach, weil man überhaupt etwas ist und also schwerer, langsamer, weniger behend-mitläufig, voranläufig ist als so ein windiges Nichts von literarischer Orientiertheit. (*BeU*, 490)
> Epochen vorwiegend individualistischen und sozialen Denkens, zum Beispiel, wechseln in der Geschichte. Aber nur literarische Wetterhähne verkünden und fordern unbedingt eins oder das andere, je nachdem der Wind weht, und verdammen den Sünder gegen den Zeitgeist zum Pfuhl.[5] (*BeU*, 491)

Zeitblom does not doubt that his friends in the Kridwiß *Kreis* are right in what they say. What he does not like is that they are so pleased about the coming of the inevitable (*DF*, 486). Zeitblom does not like taking things lightly and making jokes about serious matters. They made games of supporting lies with academic evidence and arguments. They thought the whole thing was a joke, says Zeitblom, illustrating that they recognized the irresponsibility of what they were doing. They said the purpose of justice was to represent the wishes of the people and not the truth. These reservations on Zeitblom's part do not amount to a rejection of what is said. He thinks they are right and accepts their views as scientific and inevitable.

* * *

It must be kept in mind that Mann is presenting Zeitblom's arguments justifying fascism in the form of gross parody. He is presenting them in the form of their logical implications and their specific eventual historical results, not as were presented in 1919. It is Mann's point that people like Zeitblom did accept arguments whose implications were those of the arguments presented in the novel. It is a misuse of philosophy, or science and aesthetics, to apply them to the solution of social problems, as it is a misuse of society to attempt to solve its problems by applying philosophical, scientific, or aesthetic theories. This is an important point in Mann's argument against Catholic humanism.

It must also be kept in mind that Mann is having Zeitblom put forward these arguments at a moment in German history when nobody has heard much of National Socialism; they are not new ideas, but, in this context, untried, abstract ideas. Mann shows that there is a marked tendency to irrationality in the approach of the Kridwiß *Kreis*, with the use of intellect and science in its service. This is also neither new nor unique, but it is irresponsible intellectual utopianism from Mann's point of view. Zeitblom suggests at the time of writing that it was irresponsible to accept such arguments, but not very seriously. He has no intellectual weapons to fight against these views, because they do not contradict his fundamental values as a Catholic humanist. They contradict only details of his overall view of mankind. He assumes that the fundamental responsibility of government is to determine the values of society as a unit. He questions articles of content, specifically racism, but does not question form. It is this form of government that Mann rejects in *Die Betrachtungen eines Unpolitischen*. Zeitblom does not like this new situation, but facts are facts and you cannot fight against the inevitable, he says. Besides, going against the trend isolates you from your fellows and, in Zeitblom's view, this is immoral. Mann is demonstrating the fact that Zeitblom's morality is Catholic and not Protestant like Adrian's. Adrian, by contrast, refuses to go along with the current intellectual fashion, and this is what costs him his life, as Zeitblom predicts in chapter 21 (*DF*, 241). The intellectual fashion in Munich in the 1920s was fascism.[6]

Zeitblom's explanation for the arguments of the Kridwiß *Kreis* sounds very much like Adrian's argument in chapter 22 about his *strenger Satz*. He uses the same vocabulary, but the whole thing is shifted, and not very subtly, to reverse the meaning. This new view blurs the distinction between the old and the new, says Zeitblom. It is revolutionary and reactionary.

Zeitblom's next remark, however, has nothing to do with Adrian's system: this is not reactionary, says Zeitblom, but a modern return of mankind to a situation similar to the theocratic Middle Ages. Everything is based on the higher authority of force, the dictatorship of belief (*DF*, 489):

Doch braucht man noch kein entschlossener Misanthrop zu sein, um den Verdacht nicht ganz ungerechtfertigt zu finden, daß die Mehrzahl der Menschen im stillen die Freiheit von Scham und Anstand meint, wenn sie nach Freiheit schreit. Die Negativität des Freiheitsbegriffes ist durchaus grenzenlos, es ist ein nihilistischer Begriff und also nur in geringsten Dosen heilsam, ein offizinelles Gift. Ist, nochmals, dies Mittel indiziert in einem Augenblick, wo das innerste Verlangen der Welt, der ganzen Welt, durchaus nicht auf weitere Anarchisierung durch den Freiheitsbegriff, sondern auf neue Bindungen gerichtet ist und der Glaube an den Glauben, wie wir gesehen haben, bis zum psychologischen Obskurantismus geht? (*BeU*, 515)

> Es ist der pfäffische Dünkel, durch den Glauben was Besseres zu
> sein, die selbstgerechte Bigotterie des Missionars und Pharisäers, verbun-
> den mit beständiger Aggressivität gegen die Elenden, welche nicht
> "glauben." Das versteht unter "Humanität" ein Vernunftprinzip, starr-
> moralisch, moralisch-starr. Das ist niemals sozial im Grunde, nicht fre-
> undlich aus individueller Menschenfreundlichkeit, welche das Gute
> hervorlockt und macht, daß jeder ihr seine beste und edelste Seite
> zeigt. Das weiß nichts von Toleranz, sondern ist hart, trennend, doktrinär
> bis zur Guillotine, humorlos, ohne Liebe in Wahrheit trotz alles
> Liebesgeschreis, ohne Musik, ohne Weichheit, zelotisch-schönrednerisch,
> — abscheulich. (*BeU*, 535–36)

This is not reaction, but progress around a ball, which always comes
back to the same place again, says Zeitblom. This can equally be described
as regression. It is a lifting of the distinction between past and future and
a fusion of the political left and right (*DF*, 489). This image has been taken
from Maurras, the leading French fascist theorist.[7] Mann directly attacked
such a philosophy of history in "Von Deutscher Republik," saying that
it is only too true "daß die Geschichte sich nicht wiederholt, daß es
höchst lebenswidrig sein kann, in historischen Analogien zu denken und
zu fühlen! Mir graut zuweilen vor den Irrtumsgefahren solches Spiels!"
(*VDR*, 820).

The lack of presuppositions in research, or free thought, has become
retrograde and boring, continues Zeitblom. Freedom serves to justify
force, just as reason once served to justify belief and to prove the dogma.
That is the purpose of its existence. Research is based on the assumption
that it is for the purpose of protecting the authority of the community.
This is taken for granted. Academic research is entirely subjective within
the created, seemingly natural framework ruling it, so that it in no way
feels restricted. It must be understood, insists Zeitblom, to rid oneself of
foolish fears of this, that the absoluteness of specific assumptions and
sacred conditions has never hampered human fantasy or individual audac-
ity. On the contrary, because the intellectual uniformity and consistency of
the medieval Church was taken absolutely for granted, people were a lot
more imaginative then than they were in the individualistic nineteenth-
century era. One could give in to one's imagination without worrying
about it (*DF*, 489–90). The arguments put forward by Zeitblom parallel
so closely the description of the ideas of the intellectuals at the time, as
recounted by Joachim Fest, that, had Mann written *Doktor Faustus* after
Fest had published his book, one would assume it to be the source. Fest says:
"Indem sie allen nationalen, konservativen oder völkisch-revolutionären
Ideengebilden breiten Raum ließ, war sie überwiegend das, was die Vorste-
llung jeweils erheischte."[8]

Zeitblom is talking here about the freedom from moral restraint and
the lack of personal responsibility inherent in the system. This denial of

truth in favor of total subjectivity is a variation on Adrian's argument against Kierkegaard's proposal that the Church is no longer necessary. It is Adrian's point that the lack of a set of rules of procedure leads to total madness and irresponsibility and for this reason the Church is necessary. Adrian is talking about the Protestant teaching of personal morality, responsibility, and the search for truth. Zeitblom is pointing out that the medieval Church, or the establishment of dogma, does not serve this purpose of curbing madness but rather fosters it.

This is Zeitblom's justification for his support of fascist views that developed into support for National Socialism. It is, of course, gross parody, but nonetheless an accurate description of the underlying philosophy of totalitarianism, as Mann saw it. Martin Swales argues that Zeitblom's account of the Kridwiß *Kreis* is a caricature that is founded on an accurate understanding of the attitudes of the 1920s.[9] It cannot be reasonably argued that Zeitblom is just reporting the views of others. He is reporting the views of others, but he is accepting these views as legitimate and appropriate to the times. Mann gives these views to Zeitblom, not as originator, but as political supporter, and his tendency to these views has been amply illustrated. Such views were anathema to Mann.

This justification by Zeitblom is different from a passive continuation of the war against France through refusing to cooperate with the Weimar Republic. It is no longer the irrationality and irresponsibility that he apologizes for at the beginning of his discussion of his position at the end of the war. It is very specifically the expression of the wish to return to the social values of the medieval Catholic Church and a defense of these medieval values. It is fascism. It is 1919 in the novel, the year in which *Die Betrachtungen eines Unpolitischen* was published. Zeitblom's views represent not Mann's views but a denial of them. However, the very people who shared the views expressed in the novel by Zeitblom gave Mann an honorary doctorate. This is not inconsistent. In *Die Betrachtungen eines Unpolitischen* Mann describes the break from medieval Catholic values as the fundamental factor making the development of nineteenth-century German society possible and identifies its uniqueness as a culture with the fact that it is based on Protestant values of personal morality and individual responsibility. The purpose of *Die Betrachtungen eines Unpolitischen* was to demonstrate the importance of these values and to show that they were necessary to the continuation of German culture and German art and to the development of a humane democracy. Logically, according to Mann's thinking, to introduce fascism it will be necessary to undo this development.

Mann has done a masterful job of developing Zeitblom's justification of fascism. The variable is freedom, which has suddenly taken on a third dimension. It is no longer political freedom, or the right to have a voice in government. It is no longer subjective freedom, or the right to follow one's conscience undisturbed. It is theological freedom: the right to subject oneself to dogma and gain freedom from the inhibitions and restraints of personal responsibility, as the Devil in chapter 25 tries to persuade Adrian. It is the rejection of individualism in favor of the community. Zeitblom does not mention the consequences of rejecting the dogma here, but he has already expressed his view that dissenters are to be excluded from society after an effort has been made to persuade them of the error of their ways. The Devil confirms this. Indeed, in chapter 30, Zeitblom stated that it is desirable to subject oneself to the community. This is all neatly fused with a fatalistic doctrine of inevitability.

Zeitblom's arguments give a fascist twist to general arguments. There is always the old in the new, but not as deliberate reaction. Science is never free from assumptions, but the assumptions are not dictated. Truth, freedom, justice, and reason are not absolute terms, but subject to circumstance and discussion, not simply redefined. However, theological freedom makes them meaningless as abstract terms; they cease to exist as such and take on the characteristics of things that you can point to. Arguments of this type were adopted before it became stark reality that Hitler actually meant what he said — when it was too late — but this does not make the arguments any more acceptable — unless you agree with them of course, as many people do. Mann did not. However, these views, though necessary components, do not constitute National Socialism in themselves: they are a crystallization of the views of the reactionary *Zivilisationsliterat* in a concrete situation, the real situation in Germany in 1919. They are an expression of Maurras's fascist philosophy.

Zeitblom has solved the problem of freedom that he had questioned in Adrian's *strenger Satz*. In Adrian's system, individual freedom is no less free for having subjected itself to a self-imposed set of external rules that prevent the freedom of one from restricting the freedom of the other. Zeitblom sees no difference between the subjection of freedom to Adrian's rules of procedure and the loss of both political and subjective freedom under a fascist dictatorship, or the subjection of freedom to dogma. Adrian, in his *strenger Satz*, is talking about subjective freedom, united with political freedom in a liberal democracy that is based on the Protestant view of personal responsibility. Its specific characteristic is that it accommodates dissenting views. In chapter 22 Zeitblom's view is the view of the *Zivilisationsliterat*. It is Catholic and does not distinguish between these two freedoms — or value them either — and it precludes dissent. In chapter 34 it is medieval Catholic freedom that Zeitblom is arguing for. He is sacrificing both subjective and political freedom to theological freedom. He sees his theological freedom as analogous to Adrian's subjective freedom, in that he expresses it in the same terms:

> Es waren die Gewalt, die Autorität der Gemeinschaft, und zwar waren sie
> es mit solcher Selbstverständlichkeit, daß die Wissenschaft gar nicht auf

den Gedanken kam, etwa nicht frei zu sein. Sie war es subjektiv durchaus — innerhalb einer objektiven Gebundenheit, so eingefleischt und naturhaft, daß sie in keiner Weise als Fessel empfunden wurde. (*DF*, 490)

And Adrian's words:

> Aber Freiheit ist ja ein anderes Wort für Subjektivität, und eines Tages hält die es nicht mehr mit sich aus, irgendwann verzweifelt sie an der Möglichkeit, von sich aus schöpferisch zu sein, und sucht Schutz und Sicherheit beim Objektiven. Die Freiheit neigt immer zum dialektischen Umschlag. Sie erkennt sich selbst sehr bald in der Gebundenheit, erfüllt sich in der Unterordnung unter Gesetz, Regel, Zwang, System — erfüllt sich darin, das will sagen: hört darum nicht auf, Freiheit zu sein. (*DF*, 253)

It is a question of context. As Adrian says, "Beziehung ist alles" (*DF*, 66). Zeitblom has left out the dialectic.

What Zeitblom likes about his new political philosophy is that it is not abstract; it provides a sound footing (*DF*, 490). Zeitblom finds that it is a good thing to get rid of abstract concepts and stick to the concrete. He gives the example of Swift's satire about getting rid of words that are by their very nature abstract by carrying objects around on your back to simply point to. He finds Swift's account funny, not because the idea is absurd, as do most readers, but because the uneducated, or non-intellectuals, don't accept it: "Die Stelle ist sehr komisch, besonders noch dadurch, daß es die Weiber, der Pöbel und die Analphabeten sind, die sich gegen die Neuerung auflehnen und darauf bestehen, in Worten zu schwatzen" (*DF*, 491). Zeitblom thinks the idea is sound. He does not like ambiguity, as he has shown several times previously. The fixing of abstract concepts such as good and bad and declaring them unchanged appeals to him. This has been his attitude in the discussion of Adrian's *strenger Satz*, in his discussion of Schleppfuß's lectures, and in his analysis of *Love's Labour's Lost*. Dogma is good in itself, and is not open to interpretation. It is not legitimate to question the meanings of words. Zeitblom wants objectivity instead of subjectivity in the definition of words just as, in chapter 13, he preferred objectivity in the definition of good and bad. In "Von Deutscher Republik" Mann says this is childish:

> Jugend und Bürgertum, euer Widerstand gegen die Republik, die Demokratie ist Wortscheu, — ja, ihr bockt und scheut vor diesen Worten wie unruhige Pferde, abergläubische Nervosität raubt euch die Vernunft, sobald sie nur ausgesprochen werden. Aber es sind Worte, Relativitäten, zeitbestimmte Formen, notwendige Werkzeuge, und zu glauben, es müsse landfremder Humbug sein, was sie bedeuten, ist nichts als Kinderei. Die Republik — als ob das nicht immer noch Deutschland wäre! Die Demokratie — als ob das nicht heimlichere Heimat sein könnte als irgendein strahlendes, rasselndes, fuchtelndes Empire! (*VDR*, 824–25)

In a system where the application of abstract concepts such as truth and justice is determined by their contribution to the maintenance of a belief or doctrine, these concepts in fact cease to exist as abstractions and become concrete. They are simply definitions of what the courts actually do. The values associated with nineteenth-century individualism — freedom, truth, justice, and reason — take on new and different meanings, says Zeitblom, in that they become relative instead of simply theoretical terms. He means that they become relative to a specific overall goal, instead of guidelines for individual behavior in specific situations. He means that the authority decides how to define these words according to its best interests. To find out what they mean it is simply necessary to look at what is being said and done in practice. As Mann said in 1923 in "Geist und Wesen der deutschen Republik":

> *Obskurantismus ist die Gefahr aller Zeiten, deren Begierde das Absolut ist.* (*GW*, 11:859)

Zeitblom has systematically eliminated *Innerlichkeit*, the Protestant basis of nineteenth-century humanism. In this same speech Mann defines *Innerlichkeit* as subjectivity of intellect, individualism, and the result of the traditional system of education, which is designed to cultivate this sense of personal responsibility and understanding of abstract concepts like freedom, truth, justice, and reason (*GW*, 11:854–55). It is often claimed that National Socialism is based on *Innerlichkeit*, but Zeitblom has just shown that fascism rejects this Protestant set of values.

Zeitblom refers to the need to feature hygiene and to get rid of all human weakness in order to strengthen the race, which is a rejection of the sentimental humanity of the nineteenth century. This is necessary because it is instinctive, he says. To say that it is necessary to follow instinct is to propose that we are to allow subconscious drive to predominate over intellect. The Protestant view that Mann insists on is that the correct approach is to apply intellect to natural phenomena, to channel them for the benefit of mankind, thus humanizing them. The example the Kridwiß *Kreis* uses to illustrate this point is of the dentist who pulls teeth out, rather than learning root canal treatment. This is in the interest of hygiene (*DF*, 491–92). The reference is to a private joke between Zeitblom and Adrian, although they clearly understand it differently. Zeitblom understands the dead tooth image in his joke with Adrian as a symbol for a specific type of imitative music, just a funny name for the category of the outdated and, therefore, to be rejected. This removes all philosophical meaning from the image and makes it concrete. Adrian says, in chapter 18, that dentists who do not learn to do root canal jobs, whether or not they actually do them, are an example of people who ignore the achievements of their predecessors, rather than building on them. It is unacceptable not to learn and to understand these advances (*DF*, 201). Ignoring the achievements of our predecessors is the reason given for Echo's death:

> Mit entsetzlicher Wildheit und Wut wurde er gepackt und in wenigen Tagen dahingerafft, durch eine Krankheit, von der kein Fall in der

Gegend seit längerem vorgekommen war, von der aber der gute, von solchem Ungestüm ihres Auftretens ganz betroffene Dr. Kürbis uns sagte, daß Kinder während der Rekonvaleszenz von Masern oder Keuchhusten wohl anfällig für sie seien. (*DF*, 627)

The image is, of course, a variation on Zeitblom's rejection of all achievements since the Reformation. He has replaced *Innerlichkeit* with subconscious drive. Incidentally, the choice of this particular example is undoubtedly due to the fact that Mann underwent two root canal treatments during this period, as he recounts in his diaries.

The reason Zeitblom gives for the need for this toughening up of the race is that they are entering a period when there will be wars and revolutions in a situation comparable to the period between the collapse of Roman civilization and the rise of the Holy Roman Empire.

. . . um ein instinktives Sich-in-Form-Bringen der Menschheit für harte und finstere, der Humanität spottende Läufte, für ein Zeitalter umfassender Kriege und Revolutionen, das wohl hinter die christliche Zivilisation des Mittelalters weit zurückführen und eher die dunkle Epoche vor deren Entstehung, nach dem Zusammenbruch der antiken Kultur zurückbringen werde. (*DF*, 492)

This is the period of early Christianity, which — according to fascist philosophy — was a period of barbarism, because the religion was essentially Protestantism, based on the personal effort to guide one's life by the values of the suffering Christ on the cross. The fascist view is that this religion was not Christianity at all but a variant of Judaism. Zeitblom has defined both classical Roman order and the Medieval Church as his preferred alternatives for government. Now he is describing fascism as developing a policy of brutalizing the population by taking back nineteenth-century humanity and destroying the achievements since the Reformation for purposes of war. The suggestion of this line of associations is clear: implicit in the destruction of traditional Protestant values is bloody and brutal war against the Jews. This whole discussion is, in fact, a parody of the National Socialist education policy, as discussed by Mann in his 1938 review of Erika Mann's book on the subject, *Zehn Millionen Kinder*.[10]

The Kridwiß *Kreis* was criticizing a tradition, says Zeitblom, that was the result of the destruction of values that had long been held immutable. This criticism must necessarily be directed against the art forms of the tradition (*DF*, 494). Zeitblom says here, in effect, that the object is to take back the Reformation and all modern German culture and reject all forms of individualism. It was the Reformation that destroyed the immutable Latin tradition. The Devil repeats this argument in chapter 25. This is the return to Medieval Catholicism, anticipated by Mann in *Die Betrachtungen eines Unpolitischen*, and fundamental to fascist thought. Zeitblom likens this to Adrian's discussion in chapter 22, based on Kretzschmar's teaching in chapter 8, about the opposition of harmonic subjectivity and polyphonic objectivity. Adrian's argument is, however, the need for a synthesis of the two approaches, not the substitution of the one by the other. The reason for this synthesis, in Adrian's argument, is that this would protect the nineteenth-century (harmonic) tradition from being engulfed by the inevitability of democracy (polyphony). Mann, or Adrian in the novel, predicted that democracy was coming and warned that it must be controlled, so as not to destroy this tradition and revert to Catholicism. This is how Mann phrased his intentions with *Die Betrachtungen eines Unpolitischen* in "Von Deutscher Republik": "Es war konservativ — nicht im Dienste des Vergangenen und der Reaktion, sondern in dem der Zukunft; seine Sorge galt der Bewahrung jenes Stockes und Kernes, an den das Neue anschließen und um den es in schönen Formen sich bilden könne" (*VDR*, 829).

This is the opposite of what Zeitblom and the Kridwiß *Kreis* are doing.

Die Verbürgerlichung der Kunst, das heißt ihre Individualisierung und Loslösung aus einem gesicherten Kultur- und Glaubensverbande, vollzog sich zur Zeit der Renaissance. . . . Damals war es, daß Kunst und Geist sich verbürgerlichten und zwar vermöge der Kritik, der Skepsis, des Zweifels, dieses fortschrittlichen Prinzips von einst. Von einst! Denn das ist vorbei: Jetzt, eben jetzt hat alles sich gewendet, und die halbtausendjährige Epoche der bürgerlichen Lockerheit ist zu Ende gegangen. (*BeU*, 496)

It bears repeating that Zeitblom says unequivocally at the beginning of chapter 34 (*Schluß*) that he believed in everything they said in the Kridwiß *Kreis*:

Wird man es verstehen, daß ein Mann bei der Verarbeitung solcher Neuigkeiten vierzehn Pfund Gewicht verlieren mag? Sicherlich hätte ich sie nicht eingebüßt, wenn ich an die Ergebnisse der Sitzungen bei Kridwiß nicht geglaubt hätte und der Überzeugung gewesen wäre, daß diese Herren Unsinn schwätzen. Aber das war ganz und gar nicht meine Meinung. Vielmehr verhehlte ich mir keinen Augenblick, daß sie mit anerkennenswerter Fühlsamkeit die Finger am Pulse der Zeit hatten und nach diesem Pulse wahr-sagten [*sic*!]. (*DF*, 492)

This is because he is a *Zivilisationsliterat*. As Mann said in 1931, in "Die Wiedergeburt der Anständigkeit": "Oder was wären die Wortführer des "Nationalsozialismus" anders als schlechte Literaten?" (*GW*, 12:676). Zeitblom may express reservations as he sees Germany is losing the Second World War, but he is clearly on the side of fascism throughout. He never questions anything about, except one variation in fascist philosophy that was peculiar to Hitler: the extermination of the Jews. However, he has revealed that he is aware of this aspect of fascist thought. His ambiguous style is nothing more than shunning responsibility for his actions.

* * *

The first factor influencing Zeitblom in his philosophical voyage to fascism is his Catholic tradition that leads him to admire the French system of democracy, based on Rousseau's Social Contract. The next factor is his nationalistic hatred of France, together with his hurt pride at having lost the war, which leads him to reject this system absolutely. Then comes his conviction, also a French idea, that totalitarianism is inevitable after a revolution. This is compounded by his lack of a personal sense of responsibility, induced by a belief that events are caused by fate. Added to this is his application of metaphysics and of scientific and aesthetic theories to social problems. Once again, it is his Catholic humanism that influences his willingness to accept the desirability of a social order based on controlling the masses by an intellectual elite through belief in a system of unquestioned dogma, or myth. This again is a French idea. His nationalism makes it difficult to accept communism, which is the obvious extension of French democracy, because it has no soul. Others of the party, but not Zeitblom, are against communism simply because they fear for their property. Last, and certainly not least important, is Zeitblom's compulsion to participate in the latest intellectual fashion. The whole process occurs in the context of Zeitblom's fundamental distaste for and distrust of Protestant humanism, as embodied in Adrian. The question is: what does Adrian have to do with any of this?

* * *

Rudi Schwerdtfeger's definitive move out of Zeitblom's circle into Adrian's, at the end of chapter 33, represents symbolically the turning point in the novel, as the musicians unite against the *Zivilisationsliteraten*. Zeitblom's gratuitous account of the private conversation between Adrian and Rudi, where Rudi talks about his supposed affair with Ines, can be overseen as irrelevant to the course of events. It is one of Zeitblom's suppositions that cannot be confirmed. It is, however, very relevant that Zeitblom gives a sexual explanation for Rudi's change of camp. This is a further illustration of the very important point that Zeitblom gives an erotic rather than an intellectual motivation for everything that happens in the novel, even when the facts he provides clearly point to a different explanation. However, on the factual level within the novel, Zeitblom's account establishes the basic point: Adrian agrees to write a concerto especially for Rudi, and Rudi becomes much closer to Adrian. This results in an increasing estrangement of the two groups, caused by the division of opinion about the situation at the end of the First World War. It becomes very clear in these chapters that Mann meant *Doktor Faustus* to portray historical reality from his own personal perspective. What in effect has happened is that Adrian and Rudi have decided to cooperate in defense of the Weimar Republic. Their decision is just as much a political statement as are

Zeitblom's openly political remarks. We know that this was their decision, because this is what they in fact do. This decision is logically in response to the fascist activities Zeitblom recounts in chapters 34. By placing the events in the wrong order Mann illustrates that Zeitblom does not, or will not, see the causal relationship between his own activities and Adrian's decision. He also confounds the reader.

The consolidation of the agreement between Rudi Schwerdtfeger and Adrian to cooperate in support of the Weimar Republic is a continuation of the marriage motif introduced in chapter 22. Schwerdtfeger says:

> Einverleiben wollte ich es mir, daß ich's im Schlafe spielen könnte, und es hegen und pflegen in jeder Note wie eine Mutter, denn Mutter wäre ich ihm, und Sie wären der Vater, — es wäre zwischen uns wie ein Kind, ein platonisches Kind, — ja, unser Konzert, das wäre so recht die Erfüllung von allem, was ich unter platonisch verstehe. (*DF*, 467)

It always appears in the context of the reconciliation of Germany with France.

Notes

[1] Thomas Mann, "Die Wiedergeburt der Anständigkeit," in *GW*, 12:649–77; here, 657.

[2] Thomas Mann, "Gegen die *Berliner Nachtausgabe*," in *GW*, 11:766–73; here, 769.

[3] Thomas Mann, "Über die Lehre Spenglers," in *GW*, 10:172–80; here, 174.

[4] Thomas Mann, "Geist und Wesen der deutschen Republik," in *GW*, 11:853–60; here, 860.

[5] This is, of course, one of the various alternative interpretations of the cold water pond, where Adrian tries to drown himself after he has been destroyed.

[6] The reader who doubts this is referred to the chapter on intellectuals, " 'Professor NSDAP': Die Intellektuellen und der Nationalsozialismus," in Joachim Fest, *Das Gesicht des Dritten Reichs* (Munich: Piper, 1963).

[7] See Ernst Nolte, *Three Faces of Fascism: Action Française — Italian fascism — National Socialism* (New York: Mentor, 1969), 183.

[8] Fest, *Das Gesicht des Dritten Reichs*, 350.

[9] Martin Swales, "In Defence of Weimar: Thomas Mann and the Politics of Republicanism," in *Thomas Mann*, ed. Michael Minden (New York: Longman, 1995), 70–84; here, 83.

[10] Thomas Mann, "*Zehn Millionen Kinder*," in *GW*, 12:825–29.

11: Adrian's *Apocalipsis cum figuris*

ZEITBLOM HAS EXPRESSED ATTITUDES compatible with fascism and Adrian has rejected these attitudes forcefully. Suddenly, now that politics have entered the scene, Zeitblom is associating Adrian with the extreme fascist position of the Kridwiß *Kreis*. This association is through his *Apocalipsis cum figuris*, not through Adrian as a person. The deliberations of the Kridwiß *Kreis* were particularly convincing, says Zeitblom, because they discussed things in the context of a work of art by a friend of his that was rapidly gaining in popularity in Munich. These discussions amounted to a commentary on the work (*DF*, 493). This is clearly a reference to Adrian's *Apocalipsis cum figuris*.

> Nie hätte ich mir jene Redereien am runden Tisch zu Herzen genommen, wie ich es tat, hätten sie nicht den kaltschnäuzig-intellektuellen Kommentar gebildet zu einem heißen Erlebnis der Entstehung eines befreundeten Kunstwerks — befreundet mir durch seinen Schöpfer, nicht durch sich selbst, das darf ich nicht sagen, dazu eignete ihm zu viel für meinen Sinn Befremdendes und Ängstigendes —, eines Werkes, das, einsam dort in dem allzu heimatlichen ländlichen Winkel fieberhaft schnell sich aufbauend, mit dem bei Kridwiß Gehörten in eigentümlicher Korrespondenz, im Verhältnis geistiger Entsprechung stand. (*DF*, 493)

Zeitblom says that he saw a relationship between the confused ideas of the Kridwiß *Kreis* and the *Apocalipsis cum figuris* and it occurred to him that the incorporation of Adrian's work would add to the creativity of these discussions, contributing to the realization of their views: "[Es handelt sich um ein Werk,] das gewisser kühner und prophetischer Beziehungen zu jenen Erörterungen nicht entbehrte, sie auf höherer, schöpferischer Ebene bestätigte und verwirklichte" (*DF*, 470).

What Zeitblom means is that it would systematize their objectives and provide a theoretical framework within which a political program could be developed. He is not describing Adrian's work as fascism in itself, but as a complement, a catalyst. The implication is that he brought it to their attention, thus channeling what they were saying into an intellectually acceptable political proposition (*DF*, 493). He concludes his remarks with a reference to his academic responsibilities, reminding us of his sphere of influence (*DF*, 470).

The context into which he is drawing the *Apocalipsis cum figuris* is, then, the *Zivilisationsliterat* preference for Latin order, the fascist cultural arguments of the Kridwiß *Kreis*, and the environment of the Catholic

University. Zeitblom is adopting Adrian's *Apocalipsis cum figuris* as a major contribution to the development of fascist thought. It will form the basis of a cult of the culture. The account of the history of Mann's honorary doctorate shows that *Die Betrachtungen eines Unpolitischen* was used in just this way by just such groups, selectively, and distorted to mean its opposite. Zeitblom has told us that doubtless the victory of the French concept of government in Germany — the "Herrschaft des Abschaums" — with its claim to be protecting Germany from Communism in the name of intellect, would lead to the destruction of Adrian's work, that is, of traditional German culture (*DF*, 451). He argues that he had come to realize that the rule of the proletariat is ideal in comparison with the rule of those claiming to represent intellect, because the proletariat is not interested in destroying works of art (*DF*, 451). Those who opposed the Weimar Republic by working within the bourgeois democracy to defeat it were humanists, like Zeitblom (*DF*, 452).

The parallel with Zeitblom's account of Adrian's writing of the *Apocalipsis cum figuris* and Mann's account of the writing of *Die Betrachtungen eines Unpolitischen* cannot be ignored. Paul Egon Hübinger comments on this parallel: "Betroffen fragen wir uns, ob bei ihm [Thomas Mann] ein Vierteljahrhundert später die Parallelisierung der 'Betrachtungen eines Unpolitischen' mit der Apokalypse und deren Verfassers mit seiner Person im Unterbewußtsein nachgewirkt haben könnte."[1]

It is highly unlikely, as Hübinger says, that the parallel was subconscious. It is my argument that it was deliberate and that recognizing this parallel is central to the interpretation of *Doktor Faustus*. The title alone is indication of this: *Die Betrachtungen eines Unpolitischen* can accurately be described as an apocalypse with figures. Adrian's *Apocalipsis cum figuris* is used in the same way; it leads to the same reverence, then ultimate rejection, of its author. This analogy is not specifically stated in the novel; indeed, novels do not state their analogies. However, it is more than probable that Mann used his own experience of the development of fascism as the basis of his novel about fascism. Positing this analogy removes the ambiguity from the novel. Zeitblom says that Adrian is not aware of what is going on at the end of the First World War and that the *Apocalipsis cum figuris* has only a symbolic relationship to the times, as does Zur Höhe's poetry. What this means is that Zeitblom has taken it out of context. The use of Mann's *Die Betrachtungen eines Unpolitischen* was a deliberate and immediate use of philosophy for political purposes. In *Die Betrachtungen eines Unpolitischen* Mann describes this kind of behavior as a misuse of Nietzsche's philosophy and in the novel it is a misuse of Adrian's work. In real life, it was a misuse of Mann's work. Mann comments on his error in accepting the honorary doctorate in chapter 25. It is the starting point of the Devil's argument with Adrian: "Man läßt sie sich ja gefallen, die Popularität, nicht wahr, auch wenn man sie nicht gesucht hat und im

Grund überzeugt ist, daß sie auf einem Mißverständnis beruht. Ist immer schmeichelhaft, ist immer wohltuend" (*DF*, 301).

At the time of writing, Zeitblom thinks he and his Munich friends should have had the wit to warn about what they saw coming and tried to stop it. What they said is:

> Das kommt, das kommt, und wenn es da ist, wird es uns auf der Höhe des Augenblicks finden. Es ist interessant, es ist sogar gut — einfach dadurch, daß es das Kommende ist, und es zu erkennen ist sowohl der Leistung wie des Vergnügens genug. Es ist nicht unsere Sache, auch noch etwas dagegen zu tun. (*DF*, 493)

Adrian, in his *Apocalipsis cum figuris*, says: "Das Ende kommt, es kommt das Ende, es ist erwacht über dich; siehe, es kommt. Es gehet schon auf und bricht daher über dich, du Einwohner des Landes" (*DF*, 474).

Adrian's *Apocalipsis cum figuris* is an announcement of impending doom, an alerting to coming disaster. Zeitblom has used almost the same words to describe the attitude of the Kridwiß *Kreis*, but the difference between seeing something as the end and seeing the same thing as a beginning reflects a severe difference in value judgment. It is the difference between optimism and pessimism, and Mann falls clearly on the side of pessimism.

* * *

In discussing the work, Zeitblom's remarks about the conversations of the Kridwiß *Kreis* turn to remarks about contemporary movements in art, about the changes in form that reflect the social changes they have been discussing (*DF*, 494). These remarks faithfully reflect arguments put forward by Hanns Eisler in support of communism and are analogous to the discussion of art in chapter 25. At the beginning one is reminded of Mann's theory of epic form and the shift in interest from the psychological to the objective concern for form. However, this moves almost immediately into Eisler's thesis that a return to the forms of the old Church music is necessary, rejecting Protestant individualist art on the grounds that it is based on education.[2] Zeitblom expresses this change as an expression of the absolute, the binding, and the obligating, thereby using communist arguments to describe Adrian's *strenger Satz* and Mann's works that reflect the discussion of social tendencies by the Kridwiß *Kreis*, which Zeitblom explains as a return to medieval Catholicism. This, in Adrian's work, says Zeitblom, is the result of using the pre-Reformation musical tool, polyphony, and the lifting of harmony, the tool of the nineteenth century. This is not what Adrian is doing. Zeitblom is once again interpreting Adrian's art politically. And he is misinterpreting it. Adrian has used the specific technique of instrumentation, developing his theme through variation, the tool of nineteenth-century music directed to individualism, to arrive at his resolution in his new musical harmony in part 2. In the first part of his oratorio he has used the medieval polyphonic technique of simply adding voices, without variation, superimposed on the out-of-date Romantic rules, to arrive at hell. As he said, when he outlined his purpose in studying music, it is necessary to first identify the cause of the commotion, then resolve it simply, and the means is orchestration.

* * *

One of the problems, says Zeitblom, was that the *Apocalipsis cum figuris* was so difficult to understand (*DF*, 496). In his diary, Mann comments on this problem of *Die Betrachtungen eines Unpolitischen*. He reports that he read a commentary on it that was not very good, but then that was not surprising, since it really was too difficult to comment on such a confused work. "Freilich ist es sehr schwer, von diesem Buch einen Abriß zu geben."[3] He was asked to make a shorter version of it and declined on the grounds that this would not be possible.[4] In "Das Problem der Deutsch-Französischen Beziehungen" in 1922, he said that criticisms of *Die Betrachtungen eines Unpolitischen* tend to show that the critic has not read it.[5] This problem is, of course, considerably compounded when the work under question is music. Zeitblom admits here that he has difficulty in understanding the work. We have already seen that Zeitblom does not understand Adrian's work, even when he thinks he does. He substitutes his own interpretation for Adrian's and dismisses the differences by explaining them as manifestations of Adrian's perverse character.

Zeitblom tells the reader that, in preparation for a work to bring the message to mankind of what was approaching, Adrian is reading about people who had visited hell, mystics and visionaries, and early Christian and medieval speculations about the other world: ". . . um sich für ein Werk zu stimmen, das alle ihre Elemente in einem Brennpunkt sammelt, sie in später künstlerischer Synthese drohend zusammenfaßt und nach unerbittlichem Auftrag der Menschheit den Spiegel der Offenbarung vor Augen hält, damit sie darin erblicke, was nahe herangekommen" (*DF*, 474).

Zeitblom presents this as though Adrian were predicting an inevitable future event, not warning against it. He gives the impression here that Adrian is espousing these medieval ideas and has surrounded Adrian's activities with an atmosphere of sickness and melancholy in this chapter. However, in chapter 31, Zeitblom recounts that during the First World War Adrian is reading *Gesta Romanorum* and laughing over it with Schildknapp. This activity is simultaneous and synonymous with Adrian's apocalyptic studies, although Zeitblom misleads the reader by discussing it separately, as though it had nothing to do with the *Apocalipsis cum figuris*. The result of these studies was his erotic farce for puppets.

Adrian did not use a particular apocalyptic text, says Zeitblom, but mixed them all together and made additions so he came up with a new one of his own. Zeitblom describes part of it as a very complicated fugue, carried to absurdity and at times not clearly defined, as in the pre-Bach period. This is a funny and very apt remark, when understood as a reference to *Die Betrachtungen eines Unpolitischen*. The book is indeed repetitive and confused, talking about everything at once, switching back and forth between opposing positions — in other words, fugue and counterpoint.

> Die Kunst als tönende Ethik, als fuga und punctum contra punctum, als eine heitere und ernste Frommheit, als ein Gebäude von nicht profaner Bestimmung, wo eines ins andere greift, sinnig, verständig und ohne Mörtel verbunden und gehalten "von Gottes Hand," — dieses l'art pour l'art ist wahrhaftig mein Ideal von Kunst. (*BeU*, 319)

The *Apocalipsis cum figuris* is, then, parallel to *Die Betrachtungen eines Unpolitischen* in this way as well: it is based on innumerable references to other works, all mixed together with direct quotations and modifications by Adrian. Works of art are not self-sufficient, says Mann, they rely on the works of others, everything one has read, to give them authority (*BeU*, 11). However, the important point is that Adrian's *Apocalipsis cum figuris* is dialectic, which Zeitblom does not see. He sees it as absurd and not clearly defined. He speaks of a paradoxical synthesis. He does point out that it is pre-Bach — that is, pre-Reformation — only in parts, but he does not recognize the dialectic opposition that this represents. Adrian's work is not a synthesis in the sense that Zeitblom interprets it.

Fascism used Protestant arguments against Rousseau by ignoring the dialectic — reading out the dialectic is a characteristic of the *Zivilisationsliterat*:

> Denn der Politiker *widersteht* dem Bösen — und ob er ihm widersteht! Müssen wir versichern, daß er schlechterdings kein Zigeuner und Abenteurer ist, vielmehr das Gegenteil davon, ein Pedant, ein Prinzipieller, ein Gefestigter, ein Tugendhafter, ein Mann der geborgenen Seele, der jeder geistigen Vagabondage Valet gesagt hat, der nicht nach rechts noch links blickt, sondern unverwandt *den* Weg, den schmalen Weg der Tugend und des Fortschritts im Auge behält, den man nur an der Hand der Doktrin zu wandeln vermag? Was die Dialektik betrifft, so hat er selbstverständlich eine Höllenangst vor ihr, und hastig nennt er jeden Einwand gegen die "Lehre" ein Sophisma, — ungeachtet man mit demselben Recht jeden seiner eigenen Heilssätze sophistisch nennen könnte. (*BeU*, 403)

The *Apocalipsis cum figuris* seems to be meant to be saying the same thing as *Die Betrachtungen eines Unpolitischen*: that there is a good kind and a bad kind of democracy, and that the bad kind leads to totalitarianism. This is not clear in Zeitblom's discussion of it. It cannot be clear, since it is written from the point of view of Zeitblom, who represents those who did not understand the dialectical character of *Die Betrachtungen eines Unpolitischen*. Zeitblom's interpretation of Adrian's *Apocalipsis cum figuris* is necessarily confused. In the broader context of the novel, however, there is not much doubt. The parallels between Adrian's work and Mann's book are so overwhelming that it is legitimate to assume the parallel is intended. Making this assumption explains what happens in the novel and the arguments presented by Zeitblom, particularly his discussion of barbarism, support this assumption. The Devil in chapter 25 associates "the work" with politics, as Zeitblom associates it with the discussions of the Kridwiß *Kreis*.

* * *

Zeitblom says he was horrified and amazed to see the *Apocalipsis cum figuris* take shape. Adrian worked with unnatural speed, as though he were just copying it down, taking dictation. He worked as though possessed (*DF*, 476–77). Adrian conceived the idea of his *Apocalipsis cum figuris* in a period when he was finding it impossible to work. Then, in spring 1919, he suddenly got better and became very active, writing it down very quickly. He worked as though working against the clock, says Zeitblom. Mann reports that this is how he wrote *Die Betrachtungen eines Unpolitischen*: the early parts of it date from the beginning of the war and the last parts from late 1917 and early 1918 (*BeU*, 10). In chapter 33, Zeitblom describes Adrian's state of depression and lack of productivity. This would be the sterility Adrian anachronistically refers to in chapter 22, a sterility that is the result of living in a time of changing values. It reflects the time during the First World War when Mann did no literary work because he was depressed about the imminence of a democracy he feared would be taken over by the German *Zivilisationsliteraten*. Just before he wrote the theologically negative and merciless end, he fell sick again, says Zeitblom. The theologically merciless end of *Die Betrachtungen eines Unpolitischen* is that totalitarianism, a return to the social values of medieval Catholicism, is threatening. Zeitblom does not tell us what Adrian is lamenting in his apocalypse. He himself is not lamenting the end of traditional German society but is all in favor of rejecting it as a colossal historical error. He is reading it, not as an apocalypse, but as a prophecy.

Zeitblom thinks the depression and the hyperactivity were related, that Adrian's depression led to his activity and was part of it (*DF*, 468). He thinks Adrian hides behind his sickness, that he withdraws to develop his adventurous ideas, and then he describes the periods of hyperactivity as "enlightenment" (*Erleuchtungszustand*; *DF*, 479). This is a very important point for understanding the novel. The term "enlightenment" and all synonyms and variations on the term in the novel refer specifically to political activity. Zeitblom is discrediting the source of the work, Dürer melancholy, as sickness and describing the writing down of it, the expression of these views, as political activity. He is, in fact, making a synthesis of the two opposing positions in Mann's argument. He is fusing Mann's/Adrian's arguments about the incompatibility of the German character with totalitarian government with an argument for what the content of such a German totalitarian government should be. In other words, Zeitblom is identifying the Protestant German character as the origin of fascism. He is depicting Adrian's struggle with his Dürer melancholy, that is, his Protestant character, as a struggle to overcome it. This is Germany's political goal, as Zeitblom has already told the reader in chapter 30 (*DF*, 411). This is because he ignores the dialectic in Adrian's argument. The idea of supernatural interference that he suggests is, in fact, the same as the reaction of Litzmann to *Die Betrachtungen eines Unpolitischen*:

> Es ist etwas über den Menschen gekommen, das zwang ihm die Feder in die Hand, und es erhob ihn über seine Zeit hinaus. Er sagte Dinge, wie der Mann in der Offenbarung, Dinge, die dunkel waren und die er falsch gedeutet hat. Aber er sah in diesem Dunkel Kräfte, die sich durchringen, die für uns Erlöser waren und für die kommenden Zeiten Erlöser sein werden.[6]

Zeitblom claims that the magic result of this process is that Adrian has overcome his Protestant inhibitions.

Zeitblom comments that when Adrian was working on his *Apocalipsis cum figuris* he found it difficult to speak clearly, and Zeitblom thinks it is because Adrian found it suited to the subject matter to speak thus (*DF*, 456). This manner of speaking is, of course, because Adrian represents the Protestant German artist of *Die Betrachtungen eines Unpolitischen*, who is not very good with words. He expresses himself through music:

> . . . und man darf nicht zweifeln, daß weniger der Widerstand selbst, als seine Wortlosigkeit und Unartikuliertheit von der Zivilisation als "barbarisch" und haßerregend empfunden wurde. . . . Wortlosigkeit ist menschenunwürdig, ist inhuman. Nicht nur der Humanismus, — Humanität überhaupt, Menschenwürde, Menschenachtung und menschliche Selbstachtung ist nach der eingeborenen und ewigen Überzeugung der römischen Zivilisation untrennbar mit Literatur verbunden. Nicht mit Musik — oder doch keineswegs notwendig mit ihr. Im Gegenteil, das Verhältnis der Musik zur Humanität ist so bei weitem lockerer, als das der Literatur, daß die musikalische Einstellung dem literarischen Tugendsinn mindestens als unzuverlässig, mindestens als verdächtig erscheint. (*BeU*, 50–51)

Difficulty in expressing himself is, therefore, another reference to the subject matter of Adrian's *Apocalipsis cum figuris*. Stumbling speech is also used symbolically in chapter 47 for Adrian's last address, a reminder of his status as German Protestant artist, and, of course, stumbling speech is used for Kretzschmar, who stutters. Zeitblom, incidentally, shows increasing disdain for Kretzschmar as the book progresses and refers to him as a *Kauz* in the context of his description of Adrian's *Apocalipsis cum figuris* (*DF*, 500). An interesting indication that Mann's diaries are a major source for this part of the novel is the fact that during this period Mann was having a great deal of trouble with his teeth and frequently had difficulty speaking, because of ill-fitting temporary bridges. Events in the novel for this period parallel very closely the entries for the period — even the inessentials are brought in. Implicit in Zeitblom's comment that Adrian does not speak clearly is that it is difficult to understand what he says.

* * *

In *Die Betrachtungen eines Unpolitischen* Mann devotes a large section to *Palestrina*, an opera by Hans Pfitzner. He admires the work and feels that it reflects his own approach to life, which is the approach of the Protestant German artist. In *Palestrina* there is a small repeating leitmotif, quite apart from the motifs representing the various characters, he says:

> Es ist das Symbol für einen Teil seines Wesens oder für sein Wesen in einer bestimmten Beziehung: das Symbol seines künstlerischen Schicksals und seiner zeitlichen Stellung, das metaphysische Wort dafür, daß er kein Anfang, sondern ein Ende ist, das Motiv des "Schlußsteins," der Blick der Schwermut, der Blick zurück. . . . Es ist, alles in allem, die zauberhaft wohlklingende Formel für seine besondere Art der Produktivität, eine Produktivität des Pessimismus, der Resignation und der Sehnsucht, eine romantische Produktivität. (*BeU*, 422)

The small repeating leitmotif in *Doktor Faustus* is, of course, Adrian's Dürer melancholy, which can be described as pessimism, resignation, and yearning. It is present in every description Zeitblom gives of Adrian and his environment. It represents Adrian's — and Mann's — particular kind of productivity. It identifies him as the Protestant German artist. Adrian's personal running leitmotif is his musical combination of notes, h-e-a-e-es, which denotes transparency. Zeitblom sees this motif as the result of a poisonous infection, generally assumed to be syphilis, in keeping with his own running motif, which is sexual motivation, an attributing of everything to the erotic, or interpreting life and society as an erotic farce.

This Dürer melancholy is the condition under which Adrian's best work is produced. It is the background to Adrian's production of his *Apocalipsis cum figuris* and of his *Dr. Fausti Weheklag*. These two works of Adrian's represent what are, in Mann's view, his own two most important works, *Die*

Betrachtungen eines Unpolitischen and *Doktor Faustus.* Zeitblom describes the melancholy humor as a sickness and finds it shocking. On the other hand, he loves and admires Adrian, its representative. In chapter 34, he describes this Dürer melancholy as a necessary component of genius: "Genie ist eine in der Krankheit tief erfahrene, aus ihr schöpfende und durch sie schöpferische Form der Lebenskraft" (*DF*, 472).

However, in chapter 1 Zeitblom suggests that Adrian's genius contains an element of the irrational and implies that, in Adrian's case, this irrationality is the result of a contract with the Devil (*DF*, 11). Later events of the novel clarify the way in which Adrian has corrupted this divine gift, according to Zeitblom. But the irrationality Zeitblom is speaking of is not associated with Adrian's *Apocalipsis cum figuris,* which he admires and sees as the work of a hero, or a saint. Zeitblom's identification of Adrian with Germany is based on his incorrect interpretation of Adrian's work as advocating fascism. If he were a member of the Bonn Literary Society, he would recommend bestowing on Adrian the highest honor in its power, an honorary doctorate.

Adrian describes himself as St. John in Dürer's engraving of the Apocalypse (*DF*, 470–71). St. John is traditionally assumed to be the author of the Apocalypse, or the Book of Revelations.[7] Adrian invites Zeitblom to join the audience in the engraving that is watching him being tortured and places the scene in Kaisersaschern rather than in Nuremberg, as in Dürer's painting. He is clearly identifying himself with the scene in the engraving and making it relevant to the present. He is placing Zeitblom among the observers, a scene to be repeated in chapter 47.

Die Betrachtungen eines Unpolitischen is in a way a tribute to Dürer, as Zeitblom says of Adrian's *Apocalipsis cum figuris* (*DF*, 475). In chapter 25 the Devil asks Adrian whether his work was just an expression of Dürer-type melancholy (*DF*, 315), a clear reference to Adrian's *Apocalipsis cum figuris.* Thus we have the further parallels of state of mind, work habits, subject matter, and correlative dates between Mann's work and Adrian's.

Adrian himself compares the pains he is suffering with those of the little mermaid in H. C. Andersen's story (*DF*, 457–58). She has blue eyes and wants to get a human soul through the love of the black-eyed prince. To do this she has to violate her nature as a mermaid and cut her tail into two legs, which obviously makes walking, or getting on with things, very painful. Clearly, Mann uses this image for the question of whether Germany should make an effort to adapt to the French way of thinking, that is, to democracy. Having blue eyes means having a German perspective and having black eyes means having a Latin perspective. This eye symbolism appears time and again throughout the novel. Adrian is of two minds, says Zeitblom — Adrian's eyes are of indeterminate color. At times Adrian criticizes the behavior of the little mermaid and questions whether she would not have been better off just giving it all up, that is giving up trying to change her nature to be acceptable to the world of Catholic humanism and accept democracy. Adrian says that she was prettier with the tail than with legs: as a mermaid she had an organic reality and beauty, whereas as a human being she was pitiful and degraded and nobody would thank her for her effort.

In chapter 47, Adrian refers again to this image (*DF*, 663–64). In the first case it symbolizes the pains he is suffering in adapting his nature to suit the French — that is, to democracy — in a pitiful and degrading situation. In the second case it refers to the pains Adrian has suffered trying to persuade Germany to accept this democracy.

In chapter 33 he is suffering from depression, or Dürer melancholy, and considering giving up the effort. In chapter 47, Adrian says that he did make the effort, because he decided that he preferred the human form (*DF*, 662–63). Having legs and a soul represents humanity, which is achieved through democracy, which does not have to be Rousseau's democracy, but a democracy appropriate to Germany and that will be accepted as democratic by the French. This is what Mann tried to explain in his 1922 speech, "Von Deutscher Republik."

The problem of the little mermaid is a parable of the exclusion of Germany from Europe because Germany did not conform to the European view of humanism and was not democratic. Adrian, in his *Apocalipsis cum figuris*, is searching for an incorporation of traditional German human values into the newly developing democratic Germany. This he describes as giving German democracy a soul, as did Mann in *Die Betrachtungen eines Unpolitischen*. Zeitblom says here that Adrian is making jokes. He is not. He is speaking in riddles. The problem of the little mermaid is the problem Mann was addressing in *Die Betrachtungen eines Unpolitischen*. It is the problem he was addressing in his efforts to achieve German cultural reconciliation with France after the First World War. In the novel, Adrian is doing the same things and for the same reason.

Adrian is suffering severely from migraine headaches and stomach trouble at the end of the war. Zeitblom denies that this has anything to do with the political events, "keine Rede davon" (*DF*, 454), a gratuitous statement, contradicted by the content of the novel. Adrian's "sickness," as Zeitblom terms it, is parallel with Mann's depression and concern for the turn of events at this same point in history. Mann's diaries of the period speak of little other than politics and his health. He complains of sustained and recurring severe stomach disorders, caused by the nervous stress of events and what he considers the irrational political behavior he sees on all sides, particularly in Munich. He does not actively participate in politics, but he follows events closely and politics is virtually the only subject of the interminable conversations Mann had with family and many friends over the period 1918–1921. In chapter 25 the Devil explains that Adrian's illness is caused by trying to grapple with this same problem.

Both the Dürer and the Andersen analogies specifically state that Adrian is taking an interest in events. Since the *Apocalipsis cum figuris* is dealing with the problem of the end of the war, Adrian is clearly taking an active interest. The lack of participation that Zeitblom refers to, then, is not lack of interest or of participation in the problem, but lack of participation in the activities and views of the Kridwiß *Kreis*. Adrian is conspicuously absent from participation in these meetings. His reaction to Zeitblom's comments on what is going on in the streets and the efforts of the Kridwiß *Kreis* to turn the bad into the good, "dem Unheil das Gute abzugewinnen," was to contemptuously shrug his shoulders, as though he had expected this (*DF*, 454). Zeitblom is pointing out that, as the Devil says, Adrian is not doing his part to further the movement. Adrian demonstrates a clear rejection of and disagreement with Zeitblom's position. Mann says he wrote *Die Betrachtungen eines Unpolitischen* "als Erzeugnis einer gewissen unbeschreiblichen Irritabilität gegen geistige Zeittendenzen" (*BeU*, 10).

It is important to see this relationship between Adrian and the Munich intellectuals: Adrian opposes their views, but they do not oppose his. Zeitblom has identified Adrian's views with theirs. At the time that Zeitblom is participating in the Kridwiß *Kreis*, Adrian is working with Rudi Schwerdtfeger in preparation for their international cultural cooperation activities in support of the Weimar Republic.

Zeitblom has described Adrian's work as the result of sickness. In "Von Deutscher Republik" Mann identifies the sickness of the times quite otherwise: as divorcing the nation from the State:

> Faßt endlich Vertrauen, — ein allgemeines Vertrauen, das für den Anfang nur im Fahrenlassen des Vorurteils zu bestehen braucht, als sei Deutsche Republik ein Popanz und Widersinn, als müsse sie das sein, was Novalis als "verwaltende und charakterisierende fremde Kraft" bestimmt, nämlich Schwäche! Scheidung des nationalen und des staatlichen Lebens, sagte ich vorhin, sei krankhaft. Aber was sich nicht scheiden darf, das darf doch unterschieden werden, und daß das Nationale weit mächtiger und lebensbestimmender bleibt als der staatsrechtliche Buchstabe, als jede positive Form, — das ist eine Gewißheit, die uns zur Beruhigung diene. "Deutsche Republik," — die Wortverbindung ist sehr stark im Beiwort; und sollte jenes Pergament von Weimar nicht völlig das sein, was man eine ideale und vollkommene Verfassung nennt, das heißt die restlos-wirkliche Bestimmung des Staatskörpers, der Staatsseele, des Staatsgeistes, — wo wäre denn auch eine Konstitution das jemals gewesen! Man sollte Geschriebenes nicht allzu wichtig nehmen. Das wirkliche nationale Leben ragt, immer und überall, nach allen Seiten weit darüber hinaus. (*VDR*, 825)

It is, therefore, Zeitblom's rejection of the Weimar Republic that Mann considers to be the sickness of the time, not Adrian's melancholy. In *Die Betrachtungen eines Unpolitischen* he had already identified the lack of correspondence between the State and the nation as a problem requiring the solution of democracy. It is outright sickness, in Mann's view, when people like Zeitblom join those who advocate a denial of the State.

* * *

The starting point for understanding the content of Adrian's *Apocalipsis cum figuris* is Zeitblom's explanation in chapter 20, that the basis of its argument is Adrian's preoccupation with the suffering that results from the damning of dissenters (*DF*, 215–16). Adrian has solved this problem with his *strenger Satz*, a system that accommodates dissent. Zeitblom suggests that the *Apocalipsis cum figuris* is divided into two parts, whereas the *strenger Satz* is a unit. Since all of Adrian's political comments have been variations on his *strenger Satz*, it is legitimate to presume that the *Apocalipsis cum figuris* is a dialectical version of the argument — that is, it presents both Adrian's view and an illustration of the position he is warning against. The first part is obscure and wild, based on nineteenth-century principles of musical composition and presented with twentieth-century technology. He has modernized out-of-date Romanticism through the use of technology — loudspeakers, or demagogy — for his description of hell, the world of banality and commonplaces, which is, of course, another possible definition of German fascism. Part one of the *Apocalipsis cum figuris* starts with one voice, but soon involves the whole choir and orchestra. This can be understood as a modernized version of the mass manipulation described by Schleppfuß in chapter 13 in connection with medieval Catholicism. The environment is portrayed as Renaissance-style decadence modernized as jazz. The narrator has an unnaturally strident voice and tells everything that is happening as a matter of fact (*DF*, 500–1), as does Zeitblom. Then Adrian has choir variations of the elect (*Auserwählten*) where all four voices move in the same rhythm. This sounds like an inquisitorial council and the narrator sounds to be very much like Hitler. Adrian's music would appear to represent, in this part, the coming of fascism as a modern version of the Inquisition. Zeitblom is not sure that it is a paradox, but thinks it is, that dissonance is used for everything elevated, serious, pious and intellectual, represented by an angelic children's choir, whereas the harmonic is used for the world of hell, a world of banality and commonplaces (*DF*, 498). For the pious, intellectual part Adrian has used his modern system of tonal equality, which inevitably produces dissonance and is synonymous with the accommodation of dissent in a liberal democracy. No definitive interpretation can be extracted with absolute confidence from Zeitblom's description, but it is clear that the paradox, as Zeitblom describes it, is not a paradox; it is the dialectic that Zeitblom does not grasp, the description of two opposing views of society, as found in *Die Betrachtungen eines Unpolitischen*.

Zeitblom talks about how much he dislikes the laughter that is associated with hell at the close of part one (*DF*, 501–2). The description he gives of Adrian's portrayal of hell is comparable to the Devil's description of hell in chapter 25. Zeitblom was annoyed when Adrian dismissed the moral message of the priest in his puppet opera with ridicule. In his discussion of *Love's Labour's Lost*, Zeitblom dismisses Berowne's criticism of humanism, on the grounds that he made a joke of it. In both cases Zeitblom interprets this as meaning that the criticism is not meant as such because it is humorously expressed. On both of these occasions, he suggests that the criticism is simply a joke in bad taste. Zeitblom would not have mentioned this laughter associated with hell, he says, if he had not felt that it revealed to him the secret of the music, which, he says, is a secret of identity. This, says Zeitblom, is because part two opens with the cosmic sphere music that is clear and transparent. Even though it contains exactly the same musical substance as the laughter of the Devil, it is a transfiguration. The secret of identity is, therefore, that, by including the laughter, Adrian is saying that what he is saying is not true, that he really means the opposite: the hell Adrian has described is not hell at all, but pure transparency. Zeitblom has resolved the dialectic.

What Adrian has done, then, is removed the frantic rhythm and orchestration, the expressions of emotion and enthusiasm of part one, leaving part two, the dialectic opposition, with exactly the same notes, but put forward soberly and simply and accommodating dissonance, or dissent. That is, Adrian has removed the obscurantism and demagogy and replaced it with transparency. Adrian is distinguishing between two definitions of the same word, democracy: the totalitarian enthusiastic kind and the sober kind that is simply an extension of the franchise. This dialectic is the substance of *Die Betrachtungen eines Unpolitischen*. Zeitblom says that Adrian is an expert at differentiating between like things (*DF*, 502–3), a statement that shows that he does not make this differentiation. This, says Zeitblom, is Adrian, it is the music he represents. The secret of identity that Zeitblom has discovered is that Adrian's description of a truly German democracy is the same as his description of totalitarianism. He has interpreted as paradox what is meant to be dialectical opposition. Adrian has described the coming of totalitarianism as hell and Zeitblom does not like this. He finds it blasphemous and in bad taste. Zeitblom is not criticizing Adrian's prediction of the coming of totalitarianism. He is criticizing Adrian's laughing at it and describing it as hell. However, he likes the music and equates it with the German character.

Adrian does not make the conventional distinction between people and things, says Zeitblom. He has used the human voice as though it were an orchestral instrument. At the same time he has used the trumpets and the saxophone as though they were human voices. Zeitblom considers this dangerous and illegitimate (*DF*, 498). He is rejecting the basis of Adrian's argument that democracy can be based on a reconciliation of polyphony and harmony, as in Bach, and he is doing it on the authority of Kretzschmar:

> Bei Brahms, den er [Kretzschmar] sehr hochachtete, demonstrierte er ihm [Adrian] die Bezugnahme auf Archaisches, auf alte Kirchentonarten, und wie dies asketische Element bei ihm zum Mittel eines düsteren Reichtums und dunkler Fülle werde. Er gab seinem Schüler zu bemerken, wie in dieser Art von Romantik, unter vernehmbarer Berufung auf Bach, das stimmenmäßige Prinzip dem modulatorisch-farbigen ernst entgegentrete und es zurückdränge. Und doch handle es sich dabei um einen nicht ganz legitimen Ehrgeiz der harmonischen Instrumental-Musik, Werte und Mittel in ihre Sphäre mit einzubeziehen, die eigentlich der alten Vokal-Polyphonie angehörten und auf die wesentlich homophone Instrumental-Harmonik nur übertragen wurden, Polyphonie, kontrapunktische Mittel würden herangezogen, um den Mittelstimmen, die doch im Generalbaß-System nur Füllung, nur akkordische Begleiterscheinung seien, höhere Eigenwürde zu verleihen. Wahre Stimmen-Selbstständigkeit, wahre Polyphonie sei das aber ja doch nicht, sei es auch schon bei Bach nicht gewesen, bei dem man zwar die kontrapunktischen Künste der Vokalzeit überliefert finde, der aber doch von Geblüt ein Harmoniker und nichts anderes gewesen sei, — schon als Mann des temperierten Klaviers sei er das gewesen, dieser Voraussetzung für alle neuere harmonische Modulationskunst, und sein harmonischer Kontrapunkt habe mit alter vokaler Mehrstimmigkeit im Grunde nicht mehr zu tun gehabt als Händels akkordisches al fresco.[8]

Kretzschmar argues that, although Bach's music is polyphony, by making it possible for polyphony to be expressed within the harmonic system it loses its character as such. Adrian, however, is imitating Bach in reverse and at a different point in history, which completely changes the character of what he is doing. Bach reconciled medieval polyphony with values that in the nineteenth-century had become the norm. The result of this was that these values carried forward the medieval Christian tradition in the new context, making it essentially German Protestant. Bach is the musical version of the Reformation. Between when Bach did this and when Adrian makes the same technical innovation in reverse, the situation has changed and Protestant values have been consolidated. The new polyphony that Adrian introduces will be polyphony, not nineteenth-century harmony, but it will carry with it nineteenth-century values. Medieval polyphony did not contain these values. Thus Adrian's polyphony will not be real polyphony. It will not reflect progress or regression around a ball, ending up at the starting point, but will be progressive and evolutionary, looking to the future. It will not be concrete and absolute, but flexible.

However, all is not lost, for there is another way to interpret why Adrian has done this. Kretzschmar says that Wagner made no distinction between people and things in his *Ring des Nibelungen*, in order to make the myth of music synonymous with the myth of the world (*DF*, 87).

Mann is making the history of the development of music synonymous with the history of German bourgeois culture in *Doktor Faustus*, as he did in *Die Betrachtungen eines Unpolitischen*. Zeitblom interprets Adrian's version of this identification as a myth. However, a myth applied to politics is a cult. It takes on religious connotations. This is, of course, how Mann's *Die Betrachtungen eines Unpolitischen* was interpreted.

Zeitblom dismisses Adrian's rejection of totalitarianism in his *Apocalipsis cum figuris* and sees only Adrian's statement that the bourgeois era is over. He reads it, not as a lament, but as a statement of fact, a prediction of the inevitable. He reads Adrian's alternative suggestion as an argument for a cult of the culture, based on the myth of music, rather than as democracy. Adrian has seen the potential of these dark powers, but has interpreted them incorrectly. This is the relevance of Adrian's *Apocalipsis cum figuris* to the discussions of the Kridwiß *Kreis*. It is the relevance of Mann's *Die Betrachtungen eines Unpolitischen* to the Catholic supporters of fascist and nationalist political movements in Germany in the 1920s.

Nevertheless, Zeitblom still has some reservations about Adrian's argument: there are clear indications that he may be advocating barbarism. The word barbarism, today, is commonly associated with fascism. The Devil in chapter 25 associates it with fascism, as does Adrian. However, in the fascist mind, barbarism is associated with Protestantism, Judaism, individualism, democracy, and modern technology. Zeitblom gives three different reasons why some people have described Adrian's *Apocalipsis cum figuris* as barbarism. He dismisses these charges, not by disagreeing with the fascist definition of barbarism, but by trying to minimize the importance of these barbaric aspects of Adrian's work. Zeitblom does not make it clear whether he is talking about one or both parts of the music. He blurs this distinction. He is, at the same time, pointing out to the reader that there are elements in Adrian's *Apocalipsis cum figuris* that can be interpreted as anti-fascist.

The first reason he gives for this charge of barbarism is that the work combines the old with the new. He explains this objection away. This combination, he says, is not arbitrary, but in the nature of the thing. It is due to the circular path of the world, which lets the earliest reappear in the latest, the same fascist image as he used for describing the philosophy of the Kridwiß *Kreis* (*DF*, 499). Mann objected to this view. The example Zeitblom gives for this combination of the old with the new is that Adrian's music reflects the natural rhythm of speech as did earlier music, which was not really music, but more like recitative (demagogy), rather than subordinating the words to the set rhythm of the music (*DF*, 499). This is Beckmesser's criticism of Walther's music in Wagner's *Die Meistersinger*. As in *Die Meistersinger*, this image does not represent a return to total domination of the word, as Zeitblom claims. It is designed to prevent that. Zeitblom's remark does not reflect what Adrian is doing.

He does not abandon the music in favor of the word. What Adrian is doing is making the music accommodate the word, as in the story of Wagner's *Die Meistersinger* and in the example of Beißel. This is the old in the new, in the sense that giving power to the word is Latin influence, which has been presumably overcome in Germany by the Reformation and the denomination of music as the vehicle of expression in Germany. However, Zeitblom is suggesting that the Latin influence, or the word, is dominant in Adrian's work, that it has taken over the music. Nevertheless, in his discussion of the *Apocalipsis cum figuris*, Zeitblom does not discuss the text, but only the music. He is describing "the music" as though it were "the word." Zeitblom sees Beißel's ghost in all this. In both Wagner and Beißel, the word is influencing the music, becoming an integral part of the whole. According to Wagner's *Die Meistersinger*, the purpose of doing this is to preserve true German *bourgeois* culture from being absorbed by Latin culture. In *Die Meistersinger* this message is used to defend democracy. Beißel's purpose is to achieve a musical expression of the word, an important Protestant tradition, and to develop a simpler musical system so the entire congregation can participate in its development. Zeitblom rejected Beißel. Zeitblom is eliminating this charge of barbarism — that is of Protestantism — with a fascist theory of history and at the same time contradicting his own evidence. He is presenting the evidence that Adrian is arguing for democracy and explaining it away.

However, says Zeitblom, the charge of barbarism is more likely to do with the intrusion of mass modernism, of streamlining. Adrian's work of religious vision seems to see the theological as nothing more than judgment and instilling fear, says Zeitblom (*DF*, 500), showing that he does not recognize Protestantism as religion, as he said in chapter 11. Zeitblom has just told us that there was no reason to fear the theological in his discussion of the views of the Kridwiß *Kreis* (*DF*, 490), and is now reporting that Adrian is saying the opposite. However, he dismisses this barbaric — and basic — argument as well, on the grounds that it is only an incidental part of the whole, which really has quite a different character. Once again, Zeitblom is ignoring the Protestantism and fusing Adrian's dialectical opposition into a paradoxical unity. He is defending Adrian's *Apocalipsis cum figuris* from a fascist point of view.

Zeitblom does refer to the transparent, Protestant part of the *Apocalipsis cum figuris* in that he says the work actually has more to do with Kaisersaschern than with modern streamlining, that it is somewhat archaic (*DF*, 501). Mann is referring here to Kaisersaschern's defining characteristic, its Protestantism, but Mann describes Protestantism as conservative, not as archaic. Although Zeitblom has stated that Kaisersaschern is Protestant, when he describes it in chapter 6 he leaves the impression that the most important thing about it is its Catholic medieval heritage. He talks about Otto, the medieval Kaiser, whose spiritual home was Rome (*DF*, 51), as though this were characteristic of the Kaisersaschern that Adrian knew. This is Zeitblom's view of Kaisersaschern, not Adrian's. The important thing about Adrian is his Protestant background and this is what Kaisersaschern represents in the novel, not its hidden medieval remnants. It was deliberate fascist policy to revive the medieval relics in towns such as Kaisersaschern, particularly in reference to the medieval persecution of Jews.[9] In "Ansprache in Lübeck" Mann says that Kaisersaschern, described as a medieval city in *Doktor Faustus*, does not exist. Adrian, as does Mann, comes from Lübeck.[10] However, Zeitblom is using Kaisersaschern to dismiss modern streamlining as something out of place, and in chapter 30 he implies that the modern, that is Protestant, character of Kaisersaschern is what has to be overcome. Here he is describing this part of Adrian's work as presented as something that has to be overcome. It is true that, in *Die Betrachtungen eines Unpolitischen*, Mann described this characteristic — Protestantism — as the major obstacle to totalitarianism and to the development of imperialism in Germany. He did point out the problem facing fascism. This is a peculiar interpretation of the argument of *Die Betrachtungen eines Unpolitischen*, but it seems to be the interpretation made by Catholic intellectuals.

Zeitblom's view does not recognize the nature of the change that resulted from the Reformation. In chapter 11, he describes German Protestant culture as simply a secularization of Roman Catholicism, and in chapter 6 he describes Kaisersaschern, or Protestant Germany, as essentially Roman Catholic. Trying to renew the cultural customs of a previous, secular time is dangerous, says Zeitblom, because these values once served religious purposes and also pre-Church, barbarian times. The previous, secular time is the German bourgeois period, which is now dead. Zeitblom does not identify the particular German characteristics that Mann describes as the result of Protestantism as such, but sees them as only specifically German characteristics that make the German different from the Frenchman. This paralleling of Protestant values with pre-Roman Christianity is fascist. Pre-Roman Christianity, in the fascist view, was essentially Judaism. Zeitblom is dismissing the religiosity and moral foundation of Protestantism and defining only Catholicism as religion. He is giving a nationalist, or racial, interpretation to Adrian's description of the Protestant mentality. He sees the characteristics that Adrian describes as Protestant as a recrudescence of the pre-Roman German character, caused by a temporary lapse from Catholicism, which is now, with the views of the Kridwiß *Kreis*, to be reversed. Zeitblom has described both the pre-Roman Catholic period and the post-Roman Catholic period as barbarous. The renewal of the medieval State will, however, accommodate this German character, will make a cult of it. As Mann said, the essential German characteristic is musicality. Zeitblom criticizes Adrian's idea of describing the history of music from pre-musical times to its perfection as barbarism and intellectualism (*DF*, 496). This remark makes no sense at all if what is being talked about is music. Zeitblom is describing Protestantism, or traditional German society, as barbarism and intellectualism. He is "correcting" Adrian's interpretation of German society and turning it into fascism. This argument is paralleled by the Devil in chapter 25.

Then Zeitblom gives a third charge of barbarism. When they say the work is barbaric, the critics mean that it lacks soul, says Zeitblom, when actually the work is a constant seeking for soul (*DF*, 501). It is one of Mann's main criticisms of totalitarianism in *Die Betrachtungen eines Unpolitischen* that it is based on a concept of mind as pure intellect and ignores the spiritual. Reminiscent of the little mermaid, in *Die Betrachtungen eines Unpolitischen* Mann is trying to include the concept of soul in the new democracy for Germany; it is what he calls humanity. That Adrian is doing this is a running motif in the novel. It is not the case that Zeitblom describes this yearning for a soul as though it were Adrian looking for his own soul, as critics usually understand this. Zeitblom is nullifying Adrian's argument that there is no soul in the concept of humanism of the *Zivilisationsliterat*. Zeitblom sees the yearning for a soul, that is, not having one, as synonymous with having one (*DF*, 501). He sees Adrian's search for an alternative to totalitarianism, because totalitarianism has no soul, as a statement of the objective of totalitarianism.

In all of these arguments Zeitblom equates barbarism with Protestantism and traditional German society. This is a fascist position and is consistent with his explanation of the discussions of the Kridwiß *Kreis*. It is wrong to see these arguments as evidence that Adrian is arguing for fascism. Zeitblom is defending Adrian against charges that he is not arguing for fascism by explaining the evidence away. Mann is pointing out to the reader that this evidence is there.

Zeitblom sees a further problem with the *Apocalipsis cum figuris*: he does not know how seriously to take Adrian's work. The Devil comments on this ambivalence (*DF*, 314). Zeitblom suspects Adrian of aestheticism, of preaching barbarism to replace traditional culture instead of community, in contradiction to the opinion Adrian had earlier expressed that community was the opposite of culture. "Kurz, es bestand in dem liebenden und angstvollen Verdacht eines Ästhetizismus, der meines Freundes Wort: das ablösende Gegenteil der bürgerlichen Kultur sei *nicht* Barbarei, sondern die Gemeinschaft, dem quälendsten Zweifel überlieferte" (495). Mann certainly said, in *Die Betrachtungen eines Unpolitischen*, that the community would destroy traditional German culture in the sense that the community, in the political sense, is the denial of individualism. Adrian's remark in chapter 14 that he is not an individualist but in favor of the community is refuted by Arzt as not true in the political context (157). In chapter 8 Adrian argues that the salvation of the culture depends on more barbarism and that this is in contradiction to medieval culture (82–83). It is comparable to Adrian's argument in chapter 31 that culture has to become more accessible to the people as a whole and not reserved for an intellectual, interpreting elite (428–30). Zeitblom's remark assumes that the *Apocalipsis cum figuris* is to be interpreted politically. He is talking about its political content and dismissing his disturbing doubt about Adrian's argument as aestheticism. Artists are not to be taken seriously, as the Devil says. Zeitblom is using yet another argument for dismissing the arguments he does not like in Adrian's work.

Mann said that the genuine bourgeois is the genuine aesthete. However, he was very specific about what aestheticism is and equally specific about what aestheticism is not.

> Ja, in Jahren, die zur Verachtung sonst wenig geschickt machen, hatte ich den ästhetizistischen Renaissance-Nietzscheanismus rings um mich her zu verachten, der mir als eine knabenhaft mißverständliche Nachfolge Nietzsche's erschien. Sie nahmen Nietzsche beim Wort, nahmen ihn wörtlich. . . . sie sahen nicht, daß dieser Abkömmling protestantischer Geistlicher der reizbarste Moralist, der je lebte, ein Moralbesessener, der Bruder Pascals gewesen war. Aber was sahen sie denn überhaupt! Sie versäumten kein Mißverständnis, zu dem sein Wesen nur immer Gelegenheit bot. Das Element romantischer *Ironie* in seinem Eros, — weit gefehlt, daß sie ein Organ dafür gehabt hätten. Und wozu sein Philosophieren sie denn also begeisterte, das waren recht nüchterne Schönheits-Festivitäten, Romane voll aphrodisischer Pennälerphantasie, Kataloge des Lasters, in denen keine Nummer vergessen war. (*BeU*, 539–40)
>
> Die "Schönheit," wie jene Dionysier sie meinten und mit steiler Gebärde verherrlichten, erschien mir von jeher als ein Ding für Romanen und Romanisten, als ein "Stück Süden" ziemlich verdächtiger, verächtlicher Art; . . . der Nietzsche, der mir eigentlich galt und meiner Natur nach erzieherisch am tiefsten auf mich wirken mußte, war der Wagnern und Schopenhauern noch ganz Nahe oder immer Nahegebliebene, der, welcher in aller bildenden Kunst *ein* Bild mit dauernder Liebe ausgezeichnet hatte, — das Dürer'sche "Ritter, Tod und Teufel"; der . . . seinem natürlichen Behagen Ausdruck gegeben hatte an aller Kunst und Philosophie, worin "die ethische Luft, der faustische Duft, Kreuz, Tod und Gruft" zu verspüren sei: ein Wort, das ich sofort als Symbol für eine ganze Welt, *meine Welt*, eine nordisch-moralistisch-protestantische, id est *deutsche* und jenem Ruchlosigkeits-Ästhetizismus strikt entgegengesetzte Welt erfaßte. (*BeU*, 541)

As a *Zivilisationsliterat*, Zeitblom rejects what Mann considered true aestheticism. He has not accused Zur Höhe of aestheticism, although his work, as described, clearly falls into what Mann calls the kind based on the misinterpretation of Nietzsche. Zeitblom sees this barbarism as just a joke and his friend Institoris admires it. Zeitblom, of course, is not very reliable on jokes. He sees Adrian's aestheticism as a joke, too, but as a joke in bad taste. The *Zivilisationsliterat*, says Mann in *Die Betrachtungen eines Unpolitischen*, does not like aesthetes (323), meaning what he considers the correct definition of the aesthete, which Mann himself sees as positive.

Aestheticism is not appreciation of or dedication to beauty, says Mann. It is not a criterion of aestheticism to make sentimental hyperbolic remarks about beauty. An aesthete could find these in bad taste. Neither is it the typically modern clever and intellectual mixing of triviality and refinement or brutality and refinement. What it is, is the opposite of demagogical political agitation. It is much more, but today this is its determining characteristic (223). This disregard for politics is described negatively by the *Zivilisationsliterat*. "Und die Kunst hat Propaganda zu treiben für Reformen sozialer und politischer Natur. Weigert sie sich, so ist ihr das Urteil gesprochen. Es lautet kritisch: Ästhetizismus; es lautet polemisch: Schmarotzertum" (*BeU*, 27).

The specifically German artist is a moralist and his art has nothing to do with beauty, says Mann. It is ethical and ethics is ugliness, sickness, and decline (*BeU*, 106). The rescuer from this genuine aestheticism is the *Zivilisationsliterat*, the opponent of the specifically German (232). This is precisely what Zeitblom is doing, rescuing Adrian's *Apocalipsis cum figuris* by eliminating the parts that suggest true aestheticism. Mann has presented Zeitblom's values as the reverse of his own. It is Zeitblom's view that it is aestheticism (read bourgeois) and barbarism (read Protestantism) to oppose the community. Zeitblom is showing that Adrian is doing precisely this and presenting it as a negative, suspicious, and demonic characteristic of his work. Zeitblom has read Adrian's (Mann's) anti-totalitarian stance, based on the pure German character, as aesthetic, and therefore as something not to be taken seriously. He is once again dismissing the evidence of Adrian's disagreement with fascism. Zeitblom says it is aestheticism that led to the barbarism in his own, that is, in Zeitblom's own, soul (*DF*, 495). Barbarism, to repeat, is the rejection of the civilizing effects of Roman organization. Zeitblom has come to understand that it is wrong to hold bourgeois values.

Adrian is indeed preaching barbarism — Protestant morality — not to replace, but to continue traditional culture in modern form. This does not contradict his earlier statement but confirms it.

* * *

In chapter 34 Zeitblom explains why he rejects the Weimar Republic. In chapter 34 (*Fortsetzung*) he illustrates the adoption of fascist values in a Munich academic circle. In chapter 34 (*Schluß*) he explains how he convinced this circle that Adrian's work provides the necessary myth for the intellectual development of a specifically German fascism. The myth is that the Reformation was simply a secularization of Christianity. Protestantism, as pure subjectivity with no dogma, is not religion, but pure emotion, a release from the moral restraints of religion. As Adrian says, referring to the

Protestant Church as a stabilizing factor in traditional German society, removing the Church will make it impossible to distinguish religiosity from madness. It is precisely this that Zeitblom is doing. This cult of the culture is based on music by Catholic humanists, who see music as pure emotion and, traditionally, as belonging in the realm of the Devil. Zeitblom has changed his mind about music belonging to the Devil, as he has about sex. Music is a parallel of traditional Protestant society in Mann's view, and in Adrian's discussions about music, but Zeitblom does not see this parallel. Zeitblom does not associate music with Protestantism, but simply with Germany. He reads the "barbarism, individualism, moral responsibility, and intellectualism" — Protestantism — out of Adrian's work and reads Adrian's new system as a way of overcoming these nineteenth-century, or "harmonic," restrictions that developed in this secularized period. To build a truly German State it is necessary to restore all the totalitarian character-istics of the Catholic State, or civilizing Roman order, that is, objectivity, but based on German values, that is, based on subjectivity and music, which is emotion. The Church, which is for preventing madness, is to be replaced by the State as representative of German culture. In Zeitblom's interpreta-tion Adrian, with his music, has broken through, out of these traditional restraints into a new social order where the music will be supreme.

The argument, as expressed above, sounds a bit far-fetched. However, as reported by Hübinger, *Die Betrachtungen eines Unpolitischen* was taken up and developed as a cult of German uniqueness, requiring a rejection of all rational thought about social organization. The nature of this unique-ness, as Mann described it in his argument, was rejected. Litzmann said that Mann had identified the depths of the German character but had mis-interpreted them. Catholic students identified Mann's work with the nationalist movement. The situation in the novel is an exact parallel of this situation. Zeitblom is implying here, not only that he was one of those who interpreted Adrian's *Apocalipsis cum figuris* in this way, but also that he was instrumental in convincing the Kridwiß *Kreis* to adopt it. He accepts this cult for emotional reasons, not intellectual reasons, although he provides an intellectual argument to support it. It is at this point that he puts Adrian on a pedestal and calls him a saint. Zeitblom is clearly iden-tified in these chapters as a leading member of that group in the novel that represents Mann's friends in Munich, some of whom later turned against him for speaking against fascism, as a similar fictitious group of people is shown to turn against Adrian in the novel.

At the conclusion of his account of the end of the First World War, Zeitblom says that Adrian is identical with his work.

Das ist Adrian Leverkühn ganz. Es ist ganz die Musik, die er repräsen-tiert, und die Stimmigkeit ist als Tiefsinn, die zum Geheimnis erhobene Berechnung. So hat eine schmerzhaft auszeichnende Freundschaft mich die Musik zu sehen gelehrt, obgleich ich, der eigenen schlichten Natur nach, vielleicht gern etwas anderes in ihr gesehen hätte. (*DF*, 503)

Zeitblom has identified music, that is Germany, with his interpretation of Adrian. His interpretation of Adrian is negative, but in a peculiar way. He does not approve of Adrian, but he loves him. It is this love for Adrian that constitutes his nationalism. Specifically, what he does not approve of in Adrian is what he sees as his sense of humor. This, in Zeitblom's view, leads Adrian to say the opposite of what he really means. This is the secret of Adrian and his music: they mean the opposite of what they say. The Adrian Zeitblom sees as a saint and builds a cult around is an invention in his own mind, not at all the Adrian he actually portrays.

Zeitblom identifies Adrian with Germany, and he identifies Adrian, and specifically his struggle to overcome this Dürer melancholy, as he understands it, with fascism. This is the great breakthrough that Germany needs, as identified by Zeitblom in chapter 30, and that he predicts in chapter 22 that Adrian will discover. Because of his Catholic assumptions, he cannot understand that the State can be other than the absolute expression of this character:

> Als deutscher Mann hege ich ungeachtet einer universalistischen Tönung, die mein Weltverhältnis durch katholische Überlieferung erfährt, ein lebendiges Gefühl für die nationale Sonderart, das charakteristische Eigenleben meines Landes, seine Idee sozusagen, wie sie sich als Brechung des Menschlichen gegen andere, ohne Zweifel gleichberechtigte Abwandlungen desselben behauptet und nur bei einem gewissen äußeren Ansehen, im Schutz eines aufrechten Staates sich behaupten kann. (*DF*, 449)

What he means here is that, as a Catholic, he thinks that everybody should be the same. However, the German way is different and better and can only be expressed collectively as an idea and through the State, which must protect this difference. He is using Mann's argument in *Friedrich der Große*. However, the specific German character that Friedrich was defending was Protestant individualism, the very thing that Zeitblom is eliminating, which is why Mann has him mention his Catholicism in the same sentence.

Zeitblom tells the reader that he sees Adrian's sickness as symbolically parallel with Germany's misfortune (*DF*, 454–55). The misfortune he is talking about is Germany's defeat in the First World War. Adrian's sickness, in Zeitblom's view, is his Protestant, Dürer melancholy, the source of all personal responsibility. It is his insistence on individualism. Zeitblom's statement that Adrian's sickness is parallel with Germany's misfortune is explained by his statement that Germany's error, and the cause of her misfortune at losing the First World War, was the Reformation and the resulting bourgeois society and its artistic achievements (*DF*, 493–94). This is what Adrian represents in the novel, and it is the objective of the Kridwiß *Kreis* to correct this. Adrian represents this "error" symbolically in Zeitblom's account, which he is writing after ten years of experience of National Socialism, during which Adrian's presence was extinguished. It is incorrect to interpret Adrian's works as representing National Socialism in the novel. Yet Zeitblom considers that they do.

The sum of Zeitblom's argument is that Adrian's struggle in writing his *Apocalipsis cum figuris* was to overcome his Protestant, German, Dürer melancholy, his sickness, and that he did this through "enlightenment," through a flash of genius. He was sitting around wallowing in this sickness when suddenly he wrote the answer down as though inspired. Adrian is synonymous with Germany in Zeitblom's mind in that, in writing his *Apocalipsis cum figuris*, he discovered the way to throw off these Protestant inhibitions. In 1919, Adrian earned the status of saint and became the savior of the German people. Zeitblom, in contradiction to the evidence he has given, identifies Adrian's opinion with his own opinion, expressed in chapter 30, at the beginning of the war:

> Durchbruchsbegierde aus der Gebundenheit und Versiegelung im Häßlichen, — sage mir immerhin, daß ich Schlafstroh dresche, aber ich fühle, habe immer gefühlt und will es gegen viel derben Augenschein vertreten, daß dies deutsch ist kat exochen, tief deutsch, die Definition des Deutschtums geradezu, eines Seelentums, bedroht von Versponnenheit, Einsamkeitsgift, provinzlerischer Eckensteherei, neurotischer Verstrickung, stillem Satanismus. (*DF*, 411)

Adrian's *Durchbruchsbegierde* was to find a way to preserve these characteristics, although he, of course, had he been given the opportunity, would have expressed them differently.

Nothing positive has been retained of Adrian's *Apocalipsis cum figuris*, or of its prototype, *Die Betrachtungen eines Unpolitischen*, in Zeitblom's reading. It has been turned into its opposite. It is not Adrian who makes a cult of the culture but Zeitblom and the Kridwiß *Kreis*, just as the Devil explains in chapter 25. Zeitblom and his friends have appropriated Adrian's *Apocalipsis cum figuris*, with a dangerously distorted interpretation, to use it as the basis of a myth about German culture and the German character. As Adrian pointed out, although he did not mean it quite this way, the solution would come from academia: "Einen Systemherrn brauchten wir, einen Schulmeister des Objektiven und der Organisation, genial genug, das Wiederherstellende, ja das Archaische mit dem Revolutionären zu verbinden" (*DF*, 252).

A myth needs a high priest and an interpreter to become a cult. At this point in the novel, Zeitblom is not talking about this. His attitude is found in chapter 20, where he admires the idea of following a leader without knowing where he is leading him and who himself does not know where he is going (*DF*, 217). Mann pointed this out in "Von Deutscher Republik":

> Denn was wäre Demagogentum, wenn nicht der platte Trick, das gegenwärtige äußere und innere Elend des Landes zur Verherrlichung des Abgewirtschafteten auszunutzen, ohne übrigens im mindesten Mittel und Wege zu wissen, wie denn die vormalige Pracht wieder herzustellen sei, noch auch nur für den erlassenen Thron, um den man sich schützend schart, einen Prätendenten aufweisen zu können? (*VDR*, 820)

The trouble with the Romantic period, says Adrian, is that it made a cult out of culture. In the modern age, says Adrian, this will lead to the defeat of culture (*DF*, 427–28). This is what National Socialism did.

In chapter 22, in his *strenger Satz* Adrian gives Zeitblom an outline of what he thinks is a desirable and logical system, suited to the times. Zeitblom misinterprets it, as Adrian points out. In chapter 30, Zeitblom makes the same mistake and Adrian is furious. In chapter 34 Adrian writes an emotional lament about the imminent threat to the culture and warns of disaster. This basically Protestant argument is turned upside down through a Catholic interpretation. From then on Adrian's life is one of being misunderstood in the same way and persecuted until he is destroyed. There are optimistic interludes, as Adrian tells his audience in chapter 47. The *Apocalipsis cum figuris* was performed in Frankfurt am Main in 1926, the year in which *Die Betrachtungen eines Unpolitischen* was republished. This performance was sponsored by the International Society for New Music, says Zeitblom (*DF*, 500). 1926 was also the peak period of the flourishing of the Weimar Republic. Zeitblom gives the reader this information, which clearly indicates that Adrian was involved in activities opposed by fascism. Such information is entirely ignored by critics.

In fact, Adrian's refusal to participate in the fascist movement is, in Zeitblom's opinion, the cause of his misfortune. Adrian's refusal is caused, in Zeitblom's view, by all the characteristics Zeitblom identifies as demonic, specifically his intelligence, his arrogance, or refusal to go along with the crowd, and his sense of humor, which leads him to say the opposite of what he means. Zeitblom does not recognize the Protestant arguments about personal responsibility, morality, and individualism, which are the real reasons that Adrian refuses to participate.

The *dénouement* in the novel is slow, but it begins in 1919, in chapter 33 and in the three chapters 34. The turning points are the publication of Adrian's *Apocalipsis cum figuris* and its adoption, through Zeitblom, by the Kridwiß *Kreis* as the basis of a cult of the culture, and Rudi's and Adrian's decision to cooperate as cultural ambassadors in support of the Weimar Republic.

Notes

[1] Paul Egon Hübinger, *Thomas Mann, die Universität Bonn und die Zeitgeschichte* (Munich: Oldenbourg, 1974), 69.

[2] Hanns Eisler, *A Rebel in Music* (New York: International, 1978), 45.

[3] Thomas Mann, *Tagebücher 1918–21* (Frankfurt am Main: Fischer, 1977), entry for 22 March 1921: 495.

[4] Mann, *Tagebücher 1918–21*, entry for 17 Sept. 1921: 546.

[5] Thomas Mann, "Das Problem der Deutsch-Französischen Beziehungen," in *GW*, 12:604–24; here, 608.

[6] Hübinger, *Thomas Mann, die Universität Bonn und die Zeitgeschichte*, 69.

[7] Donald Attwater, *Penguin Dictionary of Saints* (Harmondsworth: Penguin, 1995).

[8] Thomas Mann, *Doktor Faustus* (Stockholm: Bermann-Fischer, 1947), 123–24.

[9] Joshua Hagen, "The Most German of Towns: Creating an Ideal Nazi Community in Rothenburg ob der Tauber," Annals of the Association of American Geographers (2004) 94:1: 207–27.

[10] Thomas Mann, "Ansprache in Lübeck," in *GW*, 11:533–36; here, 534.

12: Adrian's Devil

WHAT ZEITBLOM CALLS "THE DOCUMENT," which he claims to have found in Adrian's papers after his death, is the account Adrian wrote of his conversation with the Devil and is found in chapter 25. This "document" and its counterpart, Adrian's final address in chapter 47, appear to constitute the only evidence in the novel that Adrian has sold his soul to the Devil. As I argue below, this is not an accurate reading of the text. "The document" is part of the subtext of the novel, not part of Zeitblom's story. It must be read with an open mind and a cautious resistance to, rather than a blind acceptance of, Zeitblom's influence. It is an intrusion, Adrian's alternative explanation of what happens.

The conversation is Adrian's revision of the implications of what is happening around him and his role in these events. He recognizes the opposition to his situation as demonic and dramatizes his account, personifying his opponent as the Devil. Zeitblom is puzzled by this, because he rejects the possibility that such views are those of the Devil (*DF*, 295). Therefore he suggests the idea that, since Adrian is clearly speaking with someone, it is not the Devil at all, but someone else, removing the Devil from the scene entirely. In chapter 1 he makes the point he so often makes, but applies only here, that Adrian never knew the name of the person he was talking to (13). In other words, Zeitblom denies that the views expressed in "the document" are the views of the Devil. Zeitblom is not expressing doubt about the existence of the Devil. He states in chapter 1 that Adrian was influenced by the Devil, when he speaks of all genius being demonic and resulting from a disgusting contract (11). Moreover, his whole discussion in chapter 13 depends on his assumption that the Devil exists. Zeitblom is not questioning the existence of the Devil; he is refusing to accept the legitimacy of the argument presented by "the document." Clearly, Adrian and Zeitblom disagree on what constitutes the views of the Devil. "The document" expresses Adrian's interpretation of events, not Zeitblom's, and this must be understood if the novel is to make sense. It is Adrian's own opinion that is under discussion here, not Zeitblom's account, and it is radically different. It does, however, sound very familiar.

In the modern Lutheran tradition, the Devil is often presented as a figure of fun. Mann illustrates this in chapter 12 where Professor Kumpf finds throwing a bun at the Devil sufficient protection against him. Kumpf says the Devil is a spoilsport, since his presence is a reminder of the consequences of wine, women, and song, of losing control of reason and giving in to irrationality and emotion. Kumpf's Devil represents personal irresponsibility.

It is as this Devil that he first appears to Adrian. Since he represents the Devil as Adrian understands him, it can be argued that he could be simply a psychological manifestation. In any event, the starting point of the discussion is the Devil's accusation that Adrian has behaved irresponsibly, a charge that Adrian accepts.

However, the Devil changes his character in the course of the conversation. From representing personal irresponsibility he moves into a discussion of politics, presenting arguments that he attributes to one of Adrian's compositions. These arguments, which are presented as Adrian's, are taken from *Die Betrachtungen eines Unpolitischen*. Adrian recognizes these arguments as a distorted reflection of his own. This Devil is in no way a psychological manifestation of Adrian's psyche. He is taking Adrian's arguments out of context and carrying them further, out of the context of individualism, and applying them to politics:

> Wir schaffen nichts Neues — das ist andrer Leute Sache. Wir entbinden nur und setzen frei. Wir lassen die Lahm- und Schüchternheit, die keuschen Skrupel und Zweifel zum Teufel gehn. Wir pulvern auf und räumen, bloß durch ein bißchen Reiz-Hyperämie, die Müdigkeit hinweg, — die kleine und die große, die private und die der Zeit. (*DF*, 315)

It could be argued that, in this manifestation, the speaker is not the Devil at all, but an illustration of the misinterpretation by the *Zivilisationsliterat* of what the Devil is talking about. The passage can be seen as a presentation of the political arguments based on *Die Betrachtungen eines Unpolitischen* as it was interpreted by the Bonn Literary Society when Mann was given his honorary doctorate. This distortion reflects, and to a startling degree, Hanns Eisler's argument in his 1931 article, "The Builders of a New Music Culture," about how and why music can and should be composed in such a way as to bring about a communist revolution.[1] Adrian's remark about his competence is the kind of remark one would expect Mann to have made about Eisler: "— ein Intelligenzler, der über Kunst, über Musik, für die gemeinen Zeitungen schreibt, ein Theoretiker und Kritiker, der selbst komponiert, soweit eben das Denken es ihm erlaubt" (*DF*, 317). As Adrian begins to realize the implications of this argument, when coupled with his own work, the Devil returns. As he says, he is an opportunist. He claims the right to the system, as developed by this argument, on the grounds that it is a musical system and that music is in the realm of the Devil. He shows Adrian how, with this starting point, the result will be the horrors of National Socialism. He offers Adrian the choice of going along with this madness or of being destroyed. This Devil does not tolerate dissent. In chapter 25 Adrian gradually becomes aware of the real return of evil to Germany, as the Devil goes through this metamorphosis from the socially harmless theological remnant of Lutheranism to the Devil of medieval Catholicism, in his modern secularized — political — form.

The Devil in chapter 25 is real in that he represents the underlying logic of what Adrian sees is beginning to prevail in Munich society. He is in no way a psychological part of Adrian, but a real and deadly opponent, representing views radically opposed to his own. Adrian thinks these views are evil and that they are, therefore, an expression of the Devil. Just as Zeitblom does not recognize the dialectic in Adrian's *Apocalipsis cum figuris* and Mann's admirers in Germany did not recognize the dialectic in *Die Betrachtungen eines Unpolitischen*, the critics who argue that the Devil is a psychological manifestation of Adrian's character are not recognizing the dialectic in the discussion between Adrian and the Devil. Adrian is not arguing with himself. The views expressed by the Devil are not Adrian's views.

Just as Mann, in *Die Betrachtungen eines Unpolitischen*, personifies the ideas of the *Zivilisationsliterat* to represent a point of view that he rejects, Adrian personifies the Devil to represent a point of view he rejects. The Devil represents the metamorphosis of traditional German society to fascism. He is taking back the achievements of the Reformation. Mann quoted Carlyle in 1916: "Die Reformation, das heißt des Himmels Stimme und Gottes Wahrheit contra des Teufels Lüge, wie Carlyle puritanisch sagt, — die Weigerung, 'Unglaubliches zu glauben, feierlichen Trug zu adoptieren oder angeblich von geistlichem Mondschein zu leben.'"[2]

The Devil is the personification of National Socialism, just as the *Zivilisationsliterat* in *Die Betrachtungen eines Unpolitischen* is the personification of radical left-wing politics. National Socialism was real. Adrian, in the discussion, is at absolute odds with the Devil. He agrees with him on most points of fact, but rejects the Devil's prognosis entirely as it applies to himself and disociates himself from it utterly.

The image of National Socialism as associated with the Devil is not exclusively Mann's. As Heinrich Böll said: "Was mag es sein, dieses Untier, ganz sicher ist, daß es aus der Hölle kommt, Gott möge uns behüten!"[3] Hitler himself was not adverse to this relationship. Daniel Goldhagen reports him as saying: "To achieve our aim we should stop at nothing, even if we must join forces with the Devil."[4] Mann says, in a letter to Karl Kerényi in 1936, that he secularizes religious concepts by psychologically translating them into their profane moral manifestations.[5] There is nothing superstitious or otherworldly or super- or subhuman in Mann's identification of the Devil with National Socialism. It is very much part of this world. Zeitblom rejects this association, but in "the document," the person identified as the spokesman for the Devil is the *Zivilisationsliterat*.

The relationship between the exposition of fascist theory by the *Zivilisationsliterat* and the Devil's elaboration of it into National Socialism is clear. The *Zivilisationsliterat* is interpreting Adrian's work as fascism and assumes that Adrian agrees with this interpretation, which he does not. The relationship of this theoretical fascism with the first part of "the document" is that this fascist philosophy is the result of something irresponsible that Adrian has done, some work he produced four years ago. He produced this work because he had allowed himself to become infected by *Illumination*. The Devil associates Adrian with himself from the date of the irresponsible work, not from the date of the infection. Virtually all interpretations of *Doktor Faustus* accept, without question, that the *Illumination* that the Devil is referring to is syphilis. There is no doubt that Zeitblom attributes Adrian's association with the Devil to syphilis, but he has not accepted that this is the Devil. Zeitblom is, therefore, making another association. The Devil in "the document" could be talking about some other infection, as I believe he is. He associates the infection with Adrian's decision to give up theology for music.

* * *

A problem confusing interpretation of "the document" is that Zeitblom misplaces it chronologically, as is indicated in his introduction to it — "das Dokument weist kein Datum auf" (*DF*, 296). He places it in 1911 or 1912. He does not give a reason for this decision, except the clearly false statement that what is said in "the document" has nothing to do with him: "Soll meine Überzeugung etwas gelten, so ist es keinesfalls nach unserem Besuch in dem Bergstädtchen oder während unseres Aufenthaltes dortselbst abgefaßt" (*DF*, 296). It is difficult to imagine why Mann has him make these comments about the date and the relationship of "the document" to himself, if he is not issuing an invitation to the reader to question Zeitblom's decision. Where it should be placed in the chronology of events, by logical inference based on the evidence of the novel as a whole, is after the First World War. The substantial content only makes sense if it is placed in conjunction with the discussions in chapters 34. The Devil offers essentially the same arguments for fascism as does Zeitblom, not as a participant, as does Zeitblom, but as an observer. Further, as in these chapters, the discussion with the Devil centers on a specific work by Adrian that he associates with fascism. At the time where Zeitblom places "the document" Adrian has not yet produced a work that can elicit the interpretation given to the work in question by the Devil. The logic of events in the novel demands that it be placed after the end of the First World War, after the writing of the *Apocalipsis cum figuris* and Zeitblom's report in chapters 34 on the way it can be interpreted to develop a cult of the culture in support of fascism. Zeitblom identifies the *Apocalipsis cum figuris* as the work that contributed substantially to the coming period (*DF*, 419). Chapter 25 is Adrian's — and the Devil's — response to this situation.

The Devil is talking about the use of the *Apocalipsis cum figuris* by fascism. The argument reflects Mann's own preoccupations with the development of fascism and his particular sense of guilt at having provided the movement with arguments in *Die Betrachtungen eines Unpolitischen*. In his introduction to his account of the conversation, Adrian considers the question of keeping quiet about what he has discovered and going along with the crowd and decides that this would be a violation of respectability and reason: "Werde schon schweigen, wenn auch schamhalben bloß und um die Menschen zu schonen, ei, aus sozialer Rücksicht. Habe es willens steif und fest, daß mir die Anstandskontrolle der Vernunft bis aufs letzte nicht locker werde" (*DF*, 296). In *Die Betrachtungen eines Unpolitischen* Mann identifies as one of the greatest advantages of those committing abuse and injustice the tendency of those who see this and recognize it for what it is to keep quiet about it (*BeU*, 193). Mann himself did not keep quiet about it. He did, however, like Adrian later in the novel, present his arguments largely in positive terms, rather than in the negative terms of chapter 25. His insulting and condemning remarks in the 1920s and 1930s are found in his letters and diary entries rather than in his public speeches.

The Italian setting would seem to contradict this chronological setting. However, as we have seen, the chronology in the portrayal of the ideas in the novel is unstable. The room in Palestrina where Adrian sets these reflections is the room in which Mann started to write *Buddenbrooks*.[6] When the Bonn Literary Society decided to bestow an honorary doctorate on Mann, they said it was for *Buddenbrooks* when in fact it was for *Die Betrachtungen eines Unpolitischen*. The reason they did this was to conceal the political implications of the award. The setting thus associates the Bonn Literary Society and *Die Betrachtungen eines Unpolitischen* with Adrian's work. Mann's story "Mario und der Zauberer" also discusses the rise of fascism in Germany under the pretext of writing about fascism in Italy. Adrian is doing the same thing: he is talking about the horrors of fascism in Germany under the pretext of an Italian setting, thereby protecting himself politically. Ultimately, in the literary tradition, the Devil virtually always comes from Italy. The Italian setting notwithstanding, the discussion with the Devil cannot be understood as occurring before the publication of Adrian's *Apocalipsis cum figuris* and its adoption by the Kridwiß *Kreis* in 1919. It is Zeitblom who does not see — or will not see — the relevance of the discussion with the Devil about fascism to Germany and to himself.

* * *

The Devil asks Adrian whether his existence has anything to do with Adrian's incipient intoxication:

> Ich bin nicht das Erzeugnis deines pialen Herdes dort oben, sondern der Herd *befähigt* dich, verstehst du?, mich wahrzunehmen, und ohne ihn,

freilich, sähst du mich nicht. Ist darum meine Existenz an deinen inzipi-
enten Schwips gebunden? Gehör ich darum in dein Subjekt? (*DF*, 313)

He is forcing Adrian to accept responsibility for the fact that the Devil
has come back on the scene. The assumption that this *Schwips* refers to
syphilis is unwarranted. Mann has written "the document" in such a way
as to make it superficially compatible with this assumption, but it does not
have to mean this and does not make much sense with this interpretation.
The sentences make sense, but not the sequence of the argument, because
it provides no causal relationship. The intoxication occurs only in the first
part of the conversation — it disappears entirely when this first manifestation of the Devil evaporates — and interpreting it as syphilis provides no
link to the rest of the argument. It is a deliberate red herring. The role of
the supposed syphilis in Zeitblom's account is to explain the existence of
the supposed pact with the Devil. As Mann said in his 1939 discussion
of Goethe's *Faust*, Goethe only included the pact because Mephistopheles
is enough of a medievalist to feel uncomfortable leaving it out (*GW*, 9:604)
and Zeitblom is a medievalist. However, Zeitblom makes it clear in his
account that this Devil is in his view not the Devil. Furthermore, it is quite
clearly stated by the Devil in chapter 25 that no pact is necessary for the
Devil to do his work (*DF*, 331). The argument is that what Adrian has
done leads to the fascist interpretation of his work that follows. Although
one might argue that what Adrian has done was due to syphilis, the more
important question is: what has he done? It is the deed that makes the
association with the Devil, and the cause of it is irresponsibility, according
to the Devil. Adrian's irresponsible deed is not infecting himself with
Illumination but what he has done as a result. Whether it is syphilis, or
something else, there is no causal relationship between the infection and
the Devil. Theologically speaking, the only sin serious enough to constitute a pact with the Devil is the intellectual rejection of God, and it is a
serious intellectual argument that is presented in "the document."
Whether or not Adrian has syphilis, as Zeitblom implies, is theologically of
no interest whatsoever to the Devil.

In *Die Betrachtungen eines Unpolitischen* Mann describes a typical
remark made by a writer like Zeitblom, a *Zivilisationsliterat*. He would, he
says, give his hero the hint of a suspicion that he was suffering from
syphilis, to distract from the fact that he is really writing about politics. He
would do this to protect himself:

O nein, junger Mann, Sie verlangen Falsches von mir. Ich meine einigen
Grund zu haben, auf meine persönliche Sicherheit Wert zu
legen . . . Meine Gesundheit, welche der jungen Generation immerhin
teuer zu sein scheint, wäre, wie ich befürchten muß, einer längeren
Untersuchungshaft nicht gewachsen. Ich habe den "Robespierre"
geschrieben, bei dessen Premiere Sie und Ihre Freunde so jubelten,

obgleich ich nicht versäumt hatte, meinen Helden in den Verdacht eines luetischen Gehirnleidens zu bringen . . . Obgleich? Gerade deshalb! Sie würden weniger gejubelt haben, hätte ich Ihnen diesen Verdacht nicht freigestellt. Aber eine Konstitution, aus welcher Werke von so melancholischer Tiefe hervorgehen, kostbare Manifeste der vertu sans y croire, — eine solche Konstitution ist nicht dafür geschaffen, sich politisch bloßzustellen. Malen Sie sich aus, daß die Macht Hand an mich legte . . . Nein, nein, lieber Freund, leben Sie wohl! Sie unterbrachen mich in einer bewegten Seite über die Freiheit und das Glück, die ich beenden möchte, bevor ich ins Bad reise. (*BeU*, 581)

Zeitblom frequently comments on his concern that he could be arrested for writing his biography of Adrian and he tries to implant the suspicion of syphilis firmly in the reader's mind before he reaches "the document." Zeitblom relates the syphilis, not to the Devil, but to the position Adrian takes in "the document." Adrian's position is not the Devil's position.

The evidence of syphilis is all tenuous. As Orlowski's argument has made clear, all Zeitblom's accounts of things he does not witness or have clear indisputable evidence to support are based on his supposition of what must have been, in the tradition of hagiography. They are filling in the gaps in the story to make it conform to dogma. Moreover, Zeitblom never actually says that Adrian has syphilis; he only hints at it. It says specifically in "the document" that Adrian is not sick and has no cause to be, in itself a statement that can be understood as raising doubts about the syphilis. Fever is a symptom of physical sickness and syphilis is a physical sickness: "Du hast keine Spur von Fieber, und ist gar kein Anlaß, daß du je welches haben solltest" (*DF*, 300).

In fact, Zeitblom reports that Adrian developed no secondary symptoms, a fact that, he says, contradicts medical evidence of syphilis (*DF*, 211). It is clear that Zeitblom finds the hypothesis of syphilis important to explain Adrian's behavior, but it is important to remember that Zeitblom does not think that Adrian is talking to the Devil.

It is the common wisdom that Adrian's supposed syphilis serves as intoxication, which in turn provides Adrian with artistic inspiration. However, the Devil himself says specifically in chapter 25 that there is no such thing as inspiration (*Einfall*). It is not the original idea, which the Devil freely attributes to Adrian's independent achievement, but the elaboration of it that counts (*DF*, 316). The Devil is offering Adrian an elaboration of his idea through intoxication, but Adrian rejects this offer. Mann, moreover, largely restricts any portrayal of intoxication in the novel to the character of Ines and through the general enthusiasm of Munich society for the Renaissance, which Adrian does not share. Adrian lives a measured, methodical life, with the possible exception of smoking. In Zeitblom's account of Adrian's life, he is hard put to find evidence of any kind of intoxication on Adrian's part, although he tries. He does belabor the cigarettes, an addiction to which Mann confessed. Zeitblom associates intoxication with Adrian's working methods, but these are methodical, and the only thing Zeitblom has to say about this that could at all be related to intoxication is that it is inhumanly fast and, Zeitblom felt, impulsive. This has been explained by Adrian's description of his method in chapter 22, which is to completely organize the material in his mind, then just to write it down, since it is already composed. Inspiration is, therefore, ruled out, since Adrian's composing is based on organization and a mathematical precision that precludes bolts out of the blue. It is a mistake to attribute intoxication to Adrian. The real intoxication in Munich at the time is the fanaticism surrounding the rise of fascism and the mobilization of the masses. The Devil talks about this, but Zeitblom does not. The Devil makes it analogous with the fanaticism preceding the Reformation. Why does Zeitblom leave out such a prominent and defining characteristic of the environment? Ultimately, it is Adrian's rejection of the erotic that Zeitblom associates with the Devil. The Devil does not talk about this.

The Devil says that he does not have any particular outward appearance, but can adapt himself to the situation, like the butterfly that takes on the color of its environment (*DF*, 304). This image is usually considered by the critics to refer to syphilis. For some obscure reason, critics assume that the Hetaera esmeralda is the poisonous butterfly described in chapter 3 and read it as a symbol for syphilis. However, the butterfly that takes on the color of its environment is not the Hetaera Esmeralda. The Hetaera esmeralda represents the transparency, or democracy, that characterizes Adrian's music. Transparency is a condition of "enlightenment." In politics, "enlightenment" is the opposite of obscurantism, and obscurantism is Mann's definition of fascism. The Hetaera Esmeralda is not poisonous. It is the Blattschmetterling that is poisonous and that the Devil refers to, the butterfly that adapts itself to whatever is popular at the moment. In any case, the reference is not to Adrian: it is to the Devil himself, who is insidious.

Die Hetaera esmeralda:
Es waren da Glasflügler abgebildet, die gar keine Schuppen auf ihren Schwingen führen, so daß diese zart gläsern und nur vom Netz der dunkleren Adern durchzogen erscheinen. Ein solcher Schmetterling, in durchsichtiger Nacktheit den dämmernden Laubschatten liebend, hieß Hetaera esmeralda. Nur einen dunklen Farbfleck in Violett und Rosa hatte Hetaera auf ihren Flügeln, der sie, da man sonst nichts von ihr sieht, im Flug einem windgeführten Blütenblatt gleichen läßt. (*DF*, 23)

Der Blattschmetterling:
Es war da sodann der Blattschmetterling, dessen Flügel, oben in volltönendem Farbendreiklang prangend, auf ihrer Unterseite mit toller Genauigkeit einem Blatte gleichen, nicht nur nach Form und Geäder, sondern dazu noch durch minutiöse Wiedergabe kleiner Unreinigkeiten, nachgeahmter Wassertropfen, warziger Pilzbildungen und dergleichen

mehr. Ließ dies geriebene Wesen sich mit hochgefalteten Flügeln im Laube nieder, so verschwand es durch Angleichung so völlig in seiner Umgebung, daß auch der gierigste Feind es nicht darin ausmachen konnte. (*DF*, 23–24)

The supposed syphilis is said to be the cause of Adrian's later collapse into madness. However, this is again a Zeitblom interpretation. Adrian does not go mad in the medical sense; he falls into despair. Why is that to be interpreted as madness?

Many critics draw a parallel between Adrian and Nietzsche. However, it is not the fact that Nietzsche suffered from syphilis that constitutes the parallel in the novel. The relevance of Nietzsche to chapter 25 arises from Mann's concern with the fact that fascism is an illegitimate application by the *Zivilisationsliterat* of Nietzsche's philosophy to politics (*BeU*, 210–11), as the Devil says:

> Eine ganze Horde und Generation empfänglich-kerngesunder Buben stürzt sich auf das Werk des kranken Genius, des von Krankheit Genialisierten, bewundert, preist, erhebt es, führt es mit sich fort, wandelt es unter sich ab, vermacht es der Kultur, die nicht von hausbackenem Brote allein lebt, sondern nicht weniger von Gaben und Giften aus der Apotheke "Zu den Seligen Boten." (*DF*, 324)

In this passage he is talking specifically about Nietzsche, not about Adrian, and he is talking about Nietzsche in relationship to Zeitblom, whom he describes negatively. Mann specifically says that only a Roman Catholic *Zivilisationsliterat* would make this political use of Nietzsche. Nietzsche's comments were being taken out of context, misinterpreted, and used to form part of the intellectual environment that allowed National Socialist ideas to flourish. This was, of course, unintentional on Nietzsche's part. Indeed, how could he have conceived of such an aberration as future fascism? Mann points this out in his 1933/34 diary extracts published as "Leiden an Deutschland."[7] He was primarily concerned, with reference to the relationship between Nietzsche and National Socialism, about the question of moral responsibility for well-intentioned behavior that leads to negative results. Adrian is specifically accused of this kind of irresponsibility by the Devil (*DF*, 314–16). Mann's concern about Nietzsche's position with respect to National Socialism was first and foremost a concern about the fact that his own expressed opinions in *Die Betrachtungen eines Unpolitischen* were being abused in the same way as were Nietzsche's opinions. The misuse of Adrian's opinions is what the Devil is talking about, not syphilis.

It is significant that Zeitblom is shown to have no idea of how Adrian could have contracted syphilis and is forced to invent an explanation. He insinuates that it must have occurred secretly, in the distance, as some subversive infection from the east, or from Austria. In chapter 19 Zeitblom recounts Adrian's trip to, he is not sure where, maybe Preßburg or Graz, in pursuit of the girl he saw a year earlier in the brothel, in order to deliberately infect himself with syphilis. Adrian had said he went to Graz to hear Strauß's *Salome*, but Zeitblom does not believe him (*DF*, 205). It is not only perfectly believable but probable that a person such as Adrian would have gone to Graz for this purpose. This performance was an important event in Adrian's professional environment. As Robert Craft pointed out in 1975, historically, Mahler, Schoenberg, and Berg, major contemporary composers, were there.[8] Zeitblom has invented this episode with the prostitute to support his thesis: it must have happened. He does begin his account of this trip with an appeal to the muses (*DF*, 204), a good indication that it is a fabrication. There is no corroborating evidence in the text to support this account, except for the occasional sentence in chapter 25 that can be, but does not have to be, interpreted as such. One important reason for Zeitblom's thinking it must have happened is that, as Mann said, the *Zivilisationsliterat* finds a sexual explanation for everything.

It is true that as early as 1904 Mann was planning a book about a syphilitic Faust. At that time Mann did some considerable research on syphilis with this project in mind. In *Die Entstehung des Doktor Faustus* Mann comments that, when he was doing this research, the bookseller thought he had syphilis,[9] pointing obliquely at the ease with which this false assumption can be made. However, in the Germany of the time of the novel, the syphilis theme had taken on quite a different significance from any meaning it might have had in 1904. In 1904 there was no obvious suggestion of fascism in Germany, and *Doktor Faustus* is clearly about National Socialism.

Syphilis, it must be remembered, was one of Hitler's favorite images for describing damaging foreign influence in Germany, and he made it synonymous with Jewry. It is not surprising, therefore, that Mann would have Zeitblom associate the syphilis image with opposition to National Socialism. Zeitblom is, after all, "the flower of his time." It is shown very clearly in chapter 34 (*Fortsetzung*) that Zeitblom adopts all the fashionable views as necessary and inevitable, whether he likes them or not. In any event, Zeitblom's identification of Adrian with syphilis is in contradiction to "the document." To presume that the Devil in "the document" is associating National Socialism with syphilis is to have him contradict one of the basic tenets of National Socialist philosophy.

Doktor Faustus is a novel about ideas. It is not syphilis that came from the east; it is the idea of the Jew as a syphilitic contamination of the German race that came from Austria, in the person of Hitler. Jewish influence, as we remember, was the explanation given in National Socialist Germany for Mann's rejection of National Socialism. In his introduction to "the document" Zeitblom rejects the idea that Adrian could have been talking to the Devil, since in "the document" the Devil is advocating

National Socialism. To Zeitblom, therefore, syphilis, or Jewish influence, would have to be considered in the context of opposition to National Socialism, or opposition to the views of the Devil as expressed in chapter 25. In "the document" it is Adrian's infection that has led Adrian to put forward, not to reject, ideas that are susceptible to fascist interpretation. It is logically impossible in the context of Zeitblom's account of Adrian's life to associate syphilis with a pact with a Devil who is promoting National Socialism.

The erroneous insistence in the critical literature that the Devil in chapter 25 is talking about syphilis has been passed on religiously and unquestioned for over fifty years. It is never discussed, but just taken for granted. What Mann says in *Die Entstehung des Doktor Faustus* is that he meant *Doktor Faustus* to appear on the surface to be the story of a syphilitic artist, but that this is a disguise for the real story:

> Dies eine Mal wußte ich, was ich wollte und was ich mir aufgab: nichts Geringeres als den Roman meiner Epoche, verkleidet in die Geschichte eines hoch-prekären und sündigen Künstlerlebens. (169)
>
> Augenscheinlich handelte es sich um die diabolische und verderbliche *Enthemmung* eines — noch jeder Bestimmung entbehrenden, aber offenbar schwierigen — Künstlertums durch Intoxikation. (155)

There is no doubt that Zeitblom, without actually saying it, is telling the story about his friend, who he thinks must have contracted syphilis, but, as he himself points out, it is incompatible with the interpretation of the Devil's views, as expressed in "the document."

Are we to think that Mann explains National Socialism by the fact that one person contracted syphilis, even assuming that person to be Nietzsche, or even assuming that Adrian represents all those who contracted syphilis at the time? He has certainly not offered this explanation of National Socialism in any other of his writings, and there are a lot of them. Assuming Adrian's syphilis to be a fact completely precludes an intelligible interpretation of chapter 25 and, therefore, of the novel as a whole, because it obscures any central thread for following the argument. Indeed, I have not found a single coherent explanation in the literature of what Adrian and the Devil are talking about in "the document." It is the fact that Zeitblom implies that Adrian is suffering from syphilis that is important to the novel, not the syphilis itself. This implication has nothing to do with what is said in chapter 25, which is one of the few accounts in the novel presented wholly from Adrian's point of view.

The key word in "the document" is *Illumination*, which is commonly, and mistakenly, taken to mean inspiration due to syphilis. However, Adrian's "disease" that the Devil describes as gradually poisoning the mind is an intellectual disease, not a physical disease. *Illumination* is a synonym of *Aufklärung*, or "enlightenment" in the political sense and the "disease" that has infected Adrian is "enlightenment." In *Die Betrachtungen eines Unpolitischen*, "enlightenment" refers to taking an interest in words, an interest that gets out of hand and ends up interfering in politics, and this is precisely what Adrian has been doing all along. It was Adrian's decision to do this that first attracted the Devil's attention. In chapter 22 Adrian devised a democratic system based on musical subjectivity. It is the Devil's argument that by partially controlling the "enlightenment," he has allowed Adrian to retain some German characteristics, and he sees that this combination can be used to deflect the "enlightenment" political solution to obscurantism, from Rousseau to Maurras, or to fascism. Fascism differs from communism in that it is based on an emotional glorification of the national, rather than an intellectual and sentimental glorification of mankind in general. However, as the Devil says, Adrian has not done this; he has just provided the idea. In order to develop his original idea into National Socialism, he has to lose his inhibitions. "Enlightenment" is also seen as infection in *Die Betrachtungen eines Unpolitischen*:

> Es war der deutsche Zivilisationsliterat, der mir das Giftigste und Erniedrigendste gesagt hat . . . War es Gift nur für mich? erniedrigend nur für mich? Es ist seine Sache darüber nachzudenken, — Sache desjenigen, durch dessen lateinisch beredten Mund der Zivilisationsliterat zu mir sprach. (*BeU*, 188)

It is a betrayal of traditional German values, in Mann's view.

The fact that Zeitblom has diagnosed syphilis as the most likely cause of Adrian's association with the Devil is no reason to presume that syphilis has anything to do with this other Devil, who Zeitblom denies is the Devil. In "the document," *Illumination* is described as a disease that gradually goes to the head and results finally in devilish enthusiasm and irresponsibility, if it is not controlled in time (*DF*, 312). This is a recurring point in *Die Betrachtungen eines Unpolitischen*, and Mann is not talking there about madness in the sense that Nietzsche went mad — far from it. He is talking about political fanaticism, about reaction, totalitarianism, and the return to the values of Roman Catholicism and to the social order of the medieval Church. The nature of this madness, in political terms, is that it is based on enthusiasm in defiance of reason, that it knows no limits and, starting from utopian social ideas, ends up in totalitarianism and/or Roman Catholicism (*BeU*, 327–28). Assuming that the novel represents Mann's view of his society during the period leading to National Socialism, it seems reasonable to see political fanaticism as the kind of madness intended by Mann in the novel. Political fanaticism certainly makes more sense than syphilis as an explanation of the description of National Socialism in "the document."

Adrian's sickness, according to Zeitblom, is the traditional German "sickness" of melancholy and pessimism. He presumes that this is the cause of the migraine headaches. The Devil denies this and says that the

Spießbürger cannot be relied on to define what is sickness and what is not (*DF*, 314). The migraine headaches, says the Devil, are a result of Adrian's infection with "enlightenment," which leads Adrian to meddle in politics. The sickness is caused by the clash between this Dürer melancholy and "enlightenment," the contradiction between his Protestant thought and his consideration of the alien, Roman Catholic concept of democracy. The headaches are caused by Adrian trying to be what he is not. This combination of Dürer melancholy and "enlightenment" was the origin of the *Apocalipsis cum figuris*. Unlike the Devil, Zeitblom sees the "enlightenment" as overcoming the sickness, not as causing it.

The part of Adrian's conversation with the Devil that is spiced with medical language is specifically commented on as a playful metaphor:

> *Ich*: "Es steht Euch, wie Ihr sprecht. Der Ludewig scheint medicinam studiert zu haben."
> *Er*: "Nicht mehr als du theologiam, will sagen: fragmentarisch und spezialistisch." (*DF*, 311)

Mann's use of syphilis in this passage is a game. It is to be noticed that the adjectives he uses include some that have nothing to do with syphilis, such as the comparison with heresy, "Flagellum haereticorum fascinariorum" (*DF*, 309), or the paralleling of "Metavenerische, Metainfektiose" with "Metaphysische" (*DF*, 310). Mixing metaphysics with politics is the great sin that leads to totalitarianism, in Mann's view. Also, there is no doubt that the National Socialism of intellectuals in the 1920s was a kind of mass "infection" based on the erotic, a deliberate substitution of intellect with emotion.[10] Adrian describes totalitarianism as an erotic farce.

The result of Mann's infection with "enlightenment" was the conclusion that it is incompatible with Protestant individualism, which modifies pure rationality with subjectivity. Political solutions are not the result of abstract logical reasoning but are largely the expression of wishes. The basis of this argument when applied to politics is its dependence on individualism, which is the basis of Adrian's argument. The Devil is showing Adrian that when this argument is collectivized it is fascism. He is not talking about syphilis but about the erotic, politics as the expression of wishful thinking rather than logic. Ultimately, it cannot be proved absolutely that the infection discussed in "the document" is not syphilis. Mann has written this passage in such a way that it can be so interpreted. However, the improbability of this interpretation is overwhelming. The entire novel is based on Zeitblom's giving an erotic interpretation to everything, and it is he who interprets Adrian's work. It is the potential of Zeitblom's interpretation of Adrian's work that the Devil is talking about: the erotic as poison when it takes over the mind.

* * *

Chapter 25 is specifically about Adrian's relationship with National Socialism from his own point of view. It also quite unmistakably illustrates Zeitblom's relationship with National Socialism. Twice the Devil identifies himself with Zeitblom: Adrian asks him who addresses him as "Du," to which the Devil answers only himself and Zeitblom (*DF*, 298); later, in the course of a repetition of Zeitblom's arguments about religion from chapter 11, he asks Adrian who other than the Devil would speak to him these days about religion (*DF*, 324–25). There are repeated references to intellectuals and variations in the Devil's mouth on points already made, or yet to be made, by Zeitblom. The basic point, that there is no such thing as an enthusiastic inspiration until it has been altered by the Devil, in reference to Adrian's *Apocalipsis cum figuris*, is illustrated by Zeitblom's adaptation of the work in chapter 34 (*Schluß*).

Mann did say, repeatedly, that authors only ever write about themselves. This seems not to have been fully taken into account in interpretations of *Doktor Faustus*. There are several discussions in the literature that make an effort to define the extent to which Mann is describing himself in his fictional characters and innumerable attempts to identify characters with real characters. I have seen none that considers that the argument of *Doktor Faustus* is itself autobiographical.[11] Adrian releases his *Apocalipsis cum figuris* in 1919 and it is this work that the Devil is talking about. As Zeitblom says, it is this work that has a heady influence on Adrian's life (*DF*, 419). Like *Die Betrachtungen eines Unpolitischen*, Adrian's *Apocalipsis cum figuris* is an intrusion into the political arena, according to the Devil, and "enlightenment" is a poison when it appears in political form. In "the document," Adrian becomes aware of the fact that this misuse of his *Apocalipsis cum figuris* for political purposes is a reflection of the Devil. It is the Devil who converts it into poison. In chapter 34 (*Schluß*) it is Zeitblom.

It is necessary to study the whole discussion in detail to show that Adrian's close relationship with fascism that the Devil implies is, in fact, a deadly opposition to it.

* * *

The Devil originally presents himself as representing good old-fashioned Protestant Germany and says he is very popular. This Devil is Mann himself, as he expressed himself in *Die Betrachtungen eines Unpolitischen*. The Devil states Adrian's problem and associates it with himself. He introduces the misunderstanding immediately: "Man läßt sie sich ja gefallen, die Popularität, nicht wahr, auch wenn man sie nicht gesucht hat und im Grund überzeugt ist, daß sie auf einem Mißverständnis beruht" (*DF*, 301). The parallel with Mann's dilemma as discussed above is clear.

The Devil presents arguments about what the traditionally German is and about Adrian's not having the courage to defend this because he lacks style. He uses the same basic images to support his argument as Mann uses in *Die Betrachtungen eines Unpolitischen*: aestheticism, cosmopolitanism, and Dürer melancholy. These are the images used by Zeitblom to define Adrian, and indeed Adrian himself uses them. Adrian feels uncomfortable hearing the Devil express his own views. These characteristics are meant by Mann to be the distinguishing marks of Protestantism. It is these arguments that Mann, in *Die Betrachtungen eines Unpolitischen*, and Adrian, in the *Apocalipsis cum figuris*, support so fiercely. They are the values of individualism. Adrian's refusal to defend these values refers, therefore, to these values as illegitimately adopted by the Kridwiß *Kreis* and by the Devil in chapter 25, as collective values. It is Zeitblom's argument in chapter 30 that Germany must overcome this Protestant apolitical attitude. It is the fascist view that Protestant individualism belongs to the Devil and must be overcome. The Devil takes Zeitblom's position that Adrian has to overcome this individualism and its specific values of doubt and conscience, but the reason he must do this is in order to belong to him: "Du, mein Lieber, hast wohl gewußt, was dir fehlte, und bist recht in der Art geblieben, als du deine Reise tatest und dir, salva venia, die lieben Franzosen holtest" (*DF*, 305).

Die lieben Franzosen that Adrian picked up are French "enlightenment" ideas, in that he began to tinker with politics, and this occurred when he went to Leipzig. The trip referred to was then not to Graz, but to Leipzig. The beginning of the problem is equated with his decision to study music. The Devil says this adoption of "enlightenment" is progress on Adrian's part, as well as abandoning plural courtesy forms and addressing others as *Du*, as is appropriate when they are in a contract: "Siehe da, das ist ein Fortschritt auf deiner Seite. Du wirst warm. Endlich einmal lässest du die pluralische Höflichkeit fallen und sagst mir Du, wie es sich ziemt zwischen Leuten, die im Vertrage sind" (*DF*, 305). In this short passage the Devil has summed up the political situation. The monarchy has been abolished and everyone is equal, as Adrian had wanted. With the word *Vertrag*, he implies that the prevailing democracy is Rousseau's Social Contract. By using the archaic meaning of *Höflichkeit* the Devil is jumping from one extreme to the other, from the medieval to the modern. In the Devil's view, the period between the Reformation and the present is irrelevant, since it was secular and had nothing, politically, to do with him. Mann feared that it would be thought, after Germany's defeat, that only one kind of democracy is possible:

> Und doch scheint mir die nationale Gefahr eben darin zu liegen, daß der "Volksstaat" bei seiner inneren und äußeren Verwirklichung mit der Demokratie im westlichen Sinn und Verstande verwechselt werde, — vielmehr, daß es sich als unmöglich erweisen könnte, ihn anders als in den geistigen und politischen Formen des Westens zu verwirklichen. (*BeU*, 272)

The Devil is propagating this argument. In *Die Betrachtungen eines Unpolitischen* Mann describes the belief in progress — the belief that mankind can be improved by governmental imposition — as the philosophical basis of this kind of democracy. Mann rejects this belief:

> Er [der Zivilisationsliterat] fördert mit Peitsche und Sporn einen Fortschritt, — der mir, nicht selten wenigstens, als unaufhaltsam und schicksalsergeben erscheint und den an meinem bescheidenen Teile zu fördern mein eigenes Schicksal ist; dem ich aber trotzdem aus dunklen Gründen eine gewisse konservative Opposition bereite. (*BeU*, 67)

The Devil is reminding Adrian of his opposition to progress in relationship to democracy and laying the ground for his interpretation of Adrian's opposition to this as obscurantism. By his very nature the Devil sees only black or white. To him, as to Zeitblom (*DF*, 63–64), Protestant relativism is nihilism.

"The document" begins by discussing how Adrian's pure German Protestant approach to life has been contaminated by *Illumination* and the potential of this combination. Adrian's decisive act was committed four years ago, and now everything is going well from the Devil's point of view. The job is already half done (*DF*, 308). If this is compared with what happened in Mann's own life, we find that it is, in 1922, four years since *Die Betrachtungen eines Unpolitischen* appeared, and he has meanwhile become aware that it is being put to political use in a movement to sabotage the new democracy. The fascist movement is crystallizing around these very ideas expressed by Mann. The Devil's work is only half done, because it is not yet specifically National Socialism that is being discussed, but, more generally, fascism. The movement lacks intellectual cohesion, but Zeitblom is providing this through his adaptation of Adrian's *Apocalipsis cum figuris*. That this is the situation in the novel is established in the three chapters 34, from Zeitblom's point of view. What the Devil says is that, because of Adrian's contamination by "enlightenment," or preoccupation with combining "the word" with "the music," or combining polyphony with harmony, or combining the German Protestant character with politics, he has committed an irresponsible, enthusiastic act, and now he is suffering terrible pangs of conscience.

The Devil compares the present day with the fanatical enthusiasm of pre-Lutheran times (*DF*, 308–9). This, in the light of Mann's view that German culture is Protestant, implies for him the tendency to return to Catholicism or to totalitarianism, the secularized version of the medieval Church. It is a fair description of the political violence in the streets in 1922, but cannot be said to describe 1911.

The Devil then says that Spengler has also been contaminated with "enlightenment," that is, with the same thing as Adrian, *Illumination*, and there is a lengthy direct attack by the Devil on Spengler's abilities and achievements (*DF*, 309–10). That, says the Devil, is why Ines called Spengler a secret hypocrite (*Schleicher*). This is a strange association if the contamination is syphilis. It is because Spengler has this *Illumination*, says the Devil, that he likes reading Goncourt and Abbé Galiani — that is, French and Catholic literature. This sickness leads to a critical opposition to traditional society. This is the critical opposition to traditional society that Zeitblom expounds in chapter 34 (*Fortsetzung*). The Devil describes this opposition, as does Zeitblom, as a tendency to laugh at what the *Spießbürger* takes seriously (*DF*, 314). That Spengler never achieved full *Illumination* does not contradict this. Adrian has not achieved it either. What the Devil is offering Adrian is the full development of this contamination. By the very nature of syphilis, this alternative does not exist.

This Spengler undoubtedly refers indeed to Oswald Spengler, represented in the novel as Baptist (the prophet) Spengler. This reflects Mann's own view of Spengler as intellectually dishonest and irresponsibly immoral, as he said in "Von Deutscher Republik." After taking a brief initial delight in Spengler's *Der Untergang des Abendlandes*, Mann became very hostile to it. His hostility was largely due to the persuasive writing style, a *Zivilisationsliterat* skill, used to defend what Mann thought was an unacceptable, because inhuman, view of society. Spengler's work is academic and powerful, Mann says. He describes it as fiction, an intellectual novel that is very entertaining, but his position is false, comfortable, and inhuman. Mann thought, at first, that Spengler had meant it to be ironical, to serve as a warning, but no, he had meant it to be taken positively. He wanted to persuade young people not to waste their passions on culture, art, and education, but to spend their energy on mechanisms, technology, economics, and politics. These are the only things of the future and, therefore, according to Spengler, it is imperative to want them (*VDR*, 841). In "the document," this criticism of Spengler is described as just then entering Adrian's mind and in connection with the Devil. The Devil suggests that Adrian is jealous of Spengler. Significantly, volume 1 of *Der Untergang des Abendlandes* appeared roughly simultaneously with *Die Betrachtungen eines Unpolitischen*, and volume 2 appeared in 1922. Mann's changing view of Spengler's work is apparent in his diaries of the period. This has nothing to do with 1911. Spengler's views are reflected in the discussions of the Kridwiß *Kreis*. The criticism of Spengler in *Doktor Faustus* is rather stronger than it appears at first sight: it is tantamount to accusing Spengler of wanting to accept the role the Devil is offering to Adrian. In real life Spengler, like Adrian, suffered from crippling migraines.[12] The reason that the Devil does not choose Spengler for his evil purposes is that he is sick and will die soon — that is, he will not last out the twenty-four years: "Er kröpelt so dahin an Leber, Niere, Magen, Herz und Darm, wird eines Tages . . ., nach einigen Jahren ruhmlos ab[kratzen] — was weiter?" (*DF*, 310). Oswald Spengler died in 1936, twenty-five years after 1911. There is, however, another reason Spengler is not suitable. His infection did not penetrate the ultimate layer of the brain, the metaphysical level.

Next comes a criticism of Adrian's academic approach, once again showing startling similarity to Mann's approach in *Die Betrachtungen eines Unpolitischen*. The Devil discusses his own narrow specialization in the brain in studying medicine, and accuses Adrian of studying theology in too narrow a context: "Willst du leugnen, daß du die beste der Künste und Wissenschaften auch nur als Spezialist und Liebhaber studiert hast? Dein Interesse galt — mir" (*DF*, 311). The brain is, of course, what the Devil corrupts. It is important for him to know how it works. Adrian, or Mann, has been studying the effect of the influence of the Devil on social organization, but he has not been studying the means by which the Devil insinuates himself. The initiative comes from the brain, from the receptivity of the subject to surrounding ideas, not from the ideas themselves (*DF*, 311), that is, it requires a predisposition. It is a fact that Mann did not think that fascism could find an intellectual foothold in Germany because he ignored the Catholic element.

Adrian has drawn the attention of the Devil to himself because he is attracted to and invites the infection, that is, he is interested in politics. The Devil says this predisposition is the important thing. Adrian still refuses to accept that his work has anything to do with the Devil: "Verleumder, ich habe keine Kundschaft mit dir. Ich habe dich nicht geladen" (*DF*, 311). Mann, like Adrian, denied that he was interested in politics until he was forced to participate to counter the reception given to *Die Betrachtungen eines Unpolitischen*.

The Devil says that the reactionary tendency of Adrian's interest in politics slowed down the process of "enlightenment," leaving Adrian decades of irresponsible time, but now the real "enlightenment" is about to begin:

> Der Rückgang der Allgemeindurchdringung war sich selbst zu überlassen, damit die Progredienz dort oben hübsch langsam vonstatten ging, damit dir Jahre, Jahrzehnte schöner, nigromantischer Zeit salviert wären, ein ganzes Stundglas voll genialer Teufelszeit. Eng und klein und fein umschrieben ist heute, vier Jahre nachdem du dirs geholt, das Plätzchen da oben bei dir — aber es ist vorhanden —, der Herd, das Arbeitsstübchen der Kleinen, die auf dem Liquorwege, dem Wasserwege sozusagen, dorthin gelangt, die Stelle der inzipienten Illuminierung. (*DF*, 312)

Mann confesses to have been infected from the beginning with a tendency to think in a literary or "enlightened" fashion and claims that this is endemic to novel writing, even in Germany. He draws a line however, at its appearance in demagogical political form. This is not German (*BeU*, 28).

Die Betrachtungen eines Unpolitischen was not intended to be a political book, but in fact it is and was used as such. Mann thought of it largely as a lament for the passing of the nineteenth-century bourgeois tradition, something of an apocalypse. This is the point in time that the Devil is talking about: the point when Mann, in 1922, had to admit he was involved in politics and to begin openly talking about politics. Adrian is in this same position of having to decide to participate in the developing political battle. The Devil is pushing him to join the National Socialist movement, as representative of German nationalism, and, at the same time, revealing that supporting German nationalism, which Adrian instinctively inclines to emotionally, is the side of the Devil. Adrian is placed in a moral conundrum. The reality of the Devil has to do with Adrian's incipient interest in politics. It is dangerous.

The continuation of this process of "enlightenment," says the Devil, will free Adrian of all scruples and doubts and lead him to inspired Devil's time. This is the great inhibition that Adrian has to overcome: his Protestant conscience and sense of responsibility. The Protestant conscience is based on scruples and doubt. At the beginning of "the document" Adrian says that it is because of the existence of this inhibition that he cannot keep quiet about what the Devil says. Adrian's inhibitions are moral, not psychological. Zeitblom, who has sex on the brain, implies that Adrian's inhibitions have to do with sex, but the Devil is not talking about sex. Sex does not come into the Devil's argument directly. The only direct reference to it is his offer to bring the little mermaid to Adrian's bed (*DF*, 308). However, when his description of the venereal contamination of the brain is interpreted as referring to the insinuation of the erotic to replace rationality, it makes sense.

This process, says the Devil, can be compared with the osmotic growths in his brain. The chemical term, osmotic growths, can, in philosophical terms, be understood as synthesis or fusion. The application of a chemical term to describe a social phenomenon was used, and thereby legitimized, by Goethe in *Die Wahlverwandtschaften*. It is a social phenomenon that the Devil is talking about, the rise of National Socialism. Adrian will be able to develop a synthesis of his two opposing tendencies, that is, in specifically political terms, fuse his desire to maintain the German idiosyncrasy with demagogical politics and totalitarianism. This synthesis is, of course, revolutionary reaction, or reactionary revolution, or National Socialism. The synthesis is the decisive factor: "Es kommt alles von der Osmose, mein Freund, an deren neckischen Erzeugnissen du dich so früh ergötztest" (*DF*, 313). Of course, Adrian has been working from the beginning on the development of such a synthesis, with the difference that Adrian's synthesis is not revolutionary. In *Die Betrachtungen eines Unpolitischen* Mann is talking about a synthesis of French and German thinking, of an adaptation of German Protestant thinking to adjust to the need for universal suffrage. However, the Devil is interpreting this from the Catholic point of view and turning it into the opposite of what Mann meant. The fusion of German culture with the potentially totalitarian, Roman Catholic, French "enlightenment" will lead to hell in the Devil's version of this fusion. To accomplish this, he will eliminate its modifier: Protestant individualism. The Devil is offering a realization of Zeitblom's idea of the necessary breakthrough, the overcoming of this modifier. Adrian's final breakthrough is to achieve a piece of music with no solo parts, the opposite of totalitarianism (*DF*, 646). In music this is not an achievement at all, but it is verging on the impossible in politics. These osmotic growths will come to their peak with the falling away of all scruples, or Protestant inhibitions, in ten or twelve years, says the Devil (*DF*, 313). This can only refer to the electoral victory of National Socialism in 1933, eleven years after 1922. This is yet another confirmation of the correct date of "the document."

The reference to osmotic growths is a reminder of the experiment with osmotic pressure at the end of chapter 3 (*DF*, 30–32). This experiment, incidentally, also needed the help of ingredients from Zeitblom's father's pharmacy. Adrian laughs at his father's compassionate tears at causing death, which the Devil interprets as his agreement that the death of individuals is justified if the whole thrives. "Was heißt denn 'tot,' wenn die Flora doch so bunt und vielgestaltig wuchert und sprießet, und wenn sie sogar heliotropisch ist?" (*DF*, 314). This is a repetition of Mann's argument that war can be justified, which he puts forward quite vehemently in *Die Betrachtungen eines Unpolitischen*, talking about the First World War, and, of course, in his *Friedrich der Große*. This justification of war is one of the arguments taken from *Die Betrachtungen eines Unpolitischen* by those who ultimately supported National Socialism.[13] Mann was referring specifically to defensive war, not to aggressive war, to the survival, not to the thriving of the whole. The Devil, however, is talking about the elimination of dissenters, or self-sacrifice, about the supremacy of the community over the individual. The Devil is attributing the arguments to Adrian, but he is, in fact, twisting Mann's arguments in *Die Betrachtungen eines Unpolitischen* about external policy to apply them to internal policy.

The Devil talks of irresponsible enthusiasm, of doing evil so God can have the opportunity to turn it to good. This is, of course, the standard justification of all excesses in any revolution, although not usually expressed in theological terms. Mann is, at the same time, also talking about the opposite, of producing something with good intentions that is used by the Devil for evil, which is what is happening here: "Vom Gegenteil einer Sache zu sprechen ist auch eine Art, von der Sache selbst zu sprechen, — sogar eine Art, mit welcher der sachlichen Verständigung vortrefflich gedient ist" (*BeU*, 375). This irresponsible enthusiasm is a kind of craziness that the respectable man does not realize is serious, because he thinks it is just poetic license, says the Devil (*DF*, 314). Zeitblom says this of himself, for instance in chapter 34, and again in chapter 47, talking about the militarism preached by Daniel zur Höhe. The Devil at this point makes reference to how easy it is to fool the people, as has often been done in the past. What is normally seen as bad can be made to be seen as good, says the Devil. Zeitblom himself, in chapter 34, is persuaded that the arguments of the Kridwiß *Kreis*, which he has always disagreed with, are right and necessary, just as Heinz Klöpfgeißel in Schleppfuß's story in chapter 13 is convinced that the girl he has always thought a gift of God is the tool of the Devil. It is also the point about Zeitblom's attitude towards sex, which he transfers from the realm of the Devil to the realm of God. This point is exhaustively explored in chapter 13. *Der Erwählte* is a very funny illustration of this medieval view.

The Devil tells Adrian that it is all very well to make flippant and outrageous statements, but it is not so easy to determine at what point they begin to be taken seriously. He asks whether it is legitimate or irresponsible behavior to make such statements. At first, the ordinary man ignores such statements, dismissing them, because everyone knows that artists are a bit mad, but if then someone starts advocating war, just to stir things up so all hell breaks loose, then the question arises: does he really mean it or is it just a bit of Dürer-type melancholy? (*DF*, 314–15). The Devil is describing the danger of the demagogic use of Adrian's ideas. If there had been no serious opposition to the Weimar Republic, *Die Betrachtungen eines Unpolitischen* would undoubtedly have been largely ignored. "Was auf dem Todes-, dem Krankheitswege entstanden, danach hat das Leben schon manches Mal mit Freuden gegriffen und sich davon weiter und höher führen lassen" (*DF*, 314). This is what is happening to Adrian's *Apocalipsis cum figuris*. What came into existence just before the collapse of Imperial Germany has been taken up and carried further. This has to be taken as a reference to the misuse of Mann's/Adrian's arguments for fascist ends. It can also be taken as referring to Nietzsche, as it usually is. However, the Devil is arguing specifically with Adrian about something Adrian has done and he is applying it to a specific situation.

Then comes Mann's great self-criticism, applied to Adrian. What Adrian wrote was irresponsible holier-than-thou madness, says the Devil, and he cannot claim that he was not aware of the mad criminality of what he was doing: "Meinst du, daß je ein irgend belustigendes Werk zustande gekommen, ohne daß sein Macher sich dabei auf das Dasein des Verbrechers und des Tollen verstehen lernte?" (*DF*, 315). He sums up the situation that Adrian is in. The Devil does not invent anything; he just takes it out of context and sets it free, removing all scruples and doubt from it. What is the good of regretting the deed the next day, when you cannot do anything about it, and then asking for mercy? Can you expect that to be understood? Is it the literal truth or just a bit of Dürer melancholy? What

Adrian did was criminal and mad. It was entirely irresponsible not to think of the historical development of things. He has released existing ideas and published them without taking responsibility for them, and that will have to be paid for in the end. What Adrian had to offer was the classical — that is, Bach's reconciliation of polyphony with harmony — but the Devil offers something better: primitive enthusiasm without the control of reason. The result of this is holy ecstasy (*DF*, 315–16). This is the unambiguous statement that Adrian's *Apocalipsis cum figuris* is to be turned into a cult of its opposite. The Devil does not pretend to represent Adrian's views. It is not what Adrian did, not the synthesis he in fact offered, but how the Devil is going to elaborate the idea of this fusion, which is different from Adrian's suggestion. Adrian's irresponsibility is being defined as his responsibility. It is difficult to see how this could be interpreted as syphilis.

This is the most important divergence of the Devil from Adrian's (and Mann's) views. The whole argument of chapter 22, of Adrian's *Apocalipsis cum figuris*, and Mann's *Die Betrachtungen eines Unpolitischen*, is the importance of preserving the Protestant character of Germany in the face of the onslaught of French, secularized Roman Catholic ideas. Mann's/Adrian's argument could be expressed as a rejection of the French Revolution in favor of a continuation of development based on the ideas of the Reformation. However, the Devil is not only taking back the French Revolution; he is taking back the Reformation as well. Everybody in the novel is talking about the old in the new, but they are not referring to the same old and new.

So the Devil has preempted Adrian's work, because it suits his purpose, and, whether he likes it or not, Adrian is now in league with the Devil. This is a statement of fact. It is certainly a statement of what happened to Mann with his *Betrachtungen eines Unpolitischen*. Zeitblom argues that you have to accept fact and go along with it, whether you like it or not. The Devil says the same thing: he says that Adrian's criticism of this fact is unacceptably subversive, a clear threat. He accuses Adrian of being secretly attracted to what he is saying (*DF*, 316). This was the charge against Mann and the cause of the hostility towards him. The Devil is pointing out that Adrian does not support fascism. The whole argument is based on Adrian's irresponsibility, which is a recognition of his not supporting fascism. The Devil is suggesting that, because of this initial irresponsibility, it is now Adrian's responsibility to continue the irresponsibility.

* * *

The Devil uses an example from music to illustrate his point (*DF*, 316–17), which he has not done so far. Up to now the incidental allusions have been to sickness. The Devil was not talking about sickness in the medical sense but about Adrian's irresponsibility at producing a work that combines the particular German values of individualism and subjectivity with "enlightenment," or "democratic" political ideas. Now he is not talking about music; he is telling Adrian what he is going to do with this work. He does this by showing him how the academic interprets his work. This discussion is introduced by the traditional Devil's final remark that what we generally call inspirations are not that at all. There is no such thing as a new idea. What we admire is the elaboration and the ornamentation, not the idea itself. A really enthusiastic elaboration has nothing to do with God but is the work of the Devil. This is the enthusiasm that Mann associates with totalitarian politics, and he says specifically that it is no part of his idea of democracy. The Devil is correcting this lack. As Litzmann said, Mann had misinterpreted his revelation, or, as Zeitblom says, when Adrian produces his musical political solution, his *strenger Satz*, it is naïve as it stands, but it is a starting point. He predicts that the application of higher and purer intellect will develop it. There follows a prolonged musical metaphor discussing Adrian's work. Mann consistently described his own works as essentially musical, including *Die Betrachtungen eines Unpolitischen*, so reference to "the musical work" does not necessarily refer to a piece of music. In fact, since Adrian's work is music, it is totally redundant to call it musical. The "musical" is a reference to Adrian's democracy and its particularly German character. The "new music" is to be understood as the new truly German political order, which is based on a new understanding of music, and which is beginning to sound like fascism. There has been a shift from discussing the fact of the work to a discussion of its theory. This argument is presented, not by the Devil, but by a *Zivilisationsliterat*. The *Zivilisationsliterat* is a theoretician.

This *Zivilisationsliterat* is ostensibly arguing about the state of art at the present time. Mann says in *Die Entstehung* that he called on Adorno's assistance to help him get the argument right (31). This should alert the scholar to the fact that it is meant primarily to be not a discussion of the theory of art, but a discussion of a particular theory of art, a theory that is to some extent compatible with Schoenberg's atonal system. Mann has chosen this theory for the very reason that it is susceptible to use as a metaphor for the politics the Devil is describing in musical terms. Further, this discussion in "the document" does not reflect any concern about art on Mann's part that can be found in his other writings. The argument is a reworking of Hanns Eisler's communist theory of music and parallel to the discussion of art by the Kridwiß *Kreis*.

The roles have switched in the internal dialectic of "the document," and Adrian is now defending his work against its corruption by these new ideas. He says the *Zivilisationsliterat* is moralizing and is insulting and damaging his work (*DF*, 321). This is the standard charge against the *Zivilisationsliterat* in *Die Betrachtungen eines Unpolitischen*, where Mann says that the *Zivilisationsliterat* uses arguments based on abstract concepts to justify measures that tend to the destruction of individual freedom, and does it in the name of morality.

The *Zivilisationsliterat* is discussing the concept of the ornamentation and elaboration of basic ideas by taking Adrian's basic idea and developing it. He says that musical composition is in a very precarious situation and that Adrian is not the only person who is being confounded by the Devil. He tells Adrian not to be so self-centered and to look around at what the other participants in the inauguration of the new music are doing. He is referring to those who take it seriously and consider the consequences of what they are doing, not the folklorists and the neo-classical isolationists, whose modernity consists in that they reject the outbreak of the new and adopt the style of pre-individualistic times (*DF*, 318). In political terms this is a reference to the many nationalist movements that wanted a return to the monarchy and a rejection of democracy. The general situation is of helplessness, but, the *Zivilisationsliterat* says, both he and Adrian prefer the helplessness of those who refuse to hide the general sickness behind a masquerade. This statement refers to those who are trying to find a new solution to replace the democracy. The *Zivilisationsliterat* is assuming that Adrian agrees with him.

He says that Adrian is wrong to blame the situation on the state of society, on a lack of interest and a dependence on the whim of benefactors (*DF*, 318–19). This is a reference to the disastrous economic situation and the lack of food, the difficulty of interesting the general public in participation in the new democracy, and the disruptive Entente interference in Germany in the years after the First World War. It is a pocket description of the economic and social causes of fascism. These factors exist, but they are not sufficient, says the Devil. In 1936 Mann said that Marx was right to say that people's thoughts and attitudes are largely dependent on their economic circumstances. Need destroys character. However, that the response is nationalism, racism, and heroic hatred of other peoples, rather than addressing the economic problems, is vulgar nonsense.[14] It is a major criticism of *Doktor Faustus* that Mann ignores the economic and social causes of National Socialism. However, the novel is not about the economic and social causes but the philosophical backing. It is Mann's argument in *Die Betrachtungen eines Unpolitischen* that no revolution can occur without an underlying philosophical basis. That is what the Devil means when he says that these economic and social factors exist but are not sufficient. In *Doktor Faustus* Mann is explaining this underlying philosophical basis, or why it was specifically National Socialism that was accepted as the solution to the economic and social problems afflicting Germany during the 1920s. The situation is such, continues this Devil, that a self-contained masterpiece, as in traditional art, is denied by the emancipated art. In other words, the monarchy cannot be restored.

Then he adds, however, that it is no longer legitimate to use all the traditional tone combinations. There follows a list of musical definitions of combinations of notes, the means of harmony, that is, of the traditional music, and the statement that they are no longer to be used, that they are forbidden by the set of rules that the better persons understand (*DF*, 319). The system has lost its relationship to reality, says the *Zivilisationsliterat*, as the result of a historical process that cannot be reversed. The argument is that the bourgeois era has been superseded. It is a question of today's technical level, and each question requires the technical resolution of the problem of the moment. This is no longer a danger, but a fact (*DF*, 320). This statement is in contradiction to Adrian's statement in chapter 31 that the breakthrough is to escape the intellectual coldness of today's technical intellectuality and find a world of new emotion. The Devil's arguments are variations on the arguments of the Kridwiß *Kreis*, that traditional values can no longer be applied. They are in direct contradiction to Adrian's position.

Adrian, however, defends the Weimar Republic, arguing, as he did in chapter 22, and as Mann did in "Von Deutscher Republik" in 1922, that one cannot preclude the possibility of spontaneous harmony (*DF*, 320). He argues that the new conditions do not preclude the development of his system. The *Zivilisationsliterat* agrees that this is theoretically possible but criticizes Adrian's method of explaining it. In other words, he is giving a new interpretation to Adrian's system. There is no time to develop Adrian's system, which is evolutionary by nature.

> Die historische Bewegung des musikalischen Materials hat sich gegen das geschlossene Werk gekehrt. Es schrumpft in der Zeit, es verschmäht die Ausdehnung in der Zeit, die der Raum des musikalischen Werkes ist, und läßt ihn leer stehen. Nicht aus Ohnmacht, nicht aus Unfähigkeit zur Formbildung. Sondern ein unerbittlicher Imperativ der Dichtigkeit, der das Überflüssige verpönt, die Phrase negiert, das Ornament zerschlägt, richtet sich gegen die zeitliche Ausbreitung, die Lebensform des Werkes. (*DF*, 320–21)

This whole argument, if it is placed in the context of a discussion of musical theory, is obscure. Understood as a discussion about politics, it is quite straightforward. It is the argument that Adrian must abandon the ideas he expressed as impractical and inapplicable to the present situation, in the form in which he presented them. The *Zivilisationsliterat* is elaborating Adrian's fundamental idea that Rousseau's democracy is not suited to the German character in the opposite direction from that proposed by Adrian. This is exactly the problem that Mann faced in the 1920s.

Adrian does not like the turn this conversation is taking. The *Zivilisationsliterat* begins his argument sounding like the humanist moralist that Mann objects to in *Die Betrachtungen eines Unpolitischen*, but he is taking too much interest in Adrian's *Apocalipsis cum figuris*.

Ich (sehr ironisch): "Rührend, rührend. Der Teufel wird pathetisch. Der leidige Teufel moralisiert. Das Menschenleid liegt ihm am Herzen. Zu seinen Ehren hofiert er in die Kunst hinein. Ihr hättet besser getan, Euerer Antipathie gegen die Werke nicht zu gedenken, wenn Ihr nicht wolltet, daß ich in Eueren Deduktionen eitel Teufelsfürze zu Schimpf und Schaden des Werks erkenne." (*DF*, 321)

He has been talking about the identity of Adrian's ideas with traditional society and their association with the Reformation and Protestantism. Adrian sees that it is this development, the development of nineteenth-century values and forms of expression, that the Devil is determined to undo. This *Zivilisationsliterat* does not see the development of the bourgeoisie and the reflection of this in its music as an inevitable and progressive step forward in the class struggle, now to be overcome, as does Hanns Eisler. He sees it as a temporary deviation from a constant and eternal static truth, an irresponsible frivolity that is now to be repressed. Zeitblom makes this same observation when he explains away the evidence of barbarism in Adrian's *Apocalipsis cum figuris* in chapter 34 (*Schluß*). The *Zivilisationsliterat* says that Adrian is confusing the conventional lawfulness that underlies that system with the appearance that it is a continuation of the previous system, but the criticism of ornamentation, convention, and abstract generality is one and the same. Certain things are no longer possible and cannot be maintained simply for sentimental reasons. Self-sufficiency — read individualism — is no longer possible. This was maintained through precedent and the formally oppressed elements were thought to be necessary in this particular case. For 400 years it was pretended that this was maintained without a break and its intention was confused with the conventional underlying rules. Traditional society is criticized because it is essentially artificial, because it sees individual expression as an expression of the general. It has equally participated in the general madness through identifying its intentions with the mastery of the conventions. It is no longer possible to think that the general can be expressed by the specific, says the *Zivilisationsliterat*. The conventions that guaranteed freedom have been shattered. It would be possible to continue playing with these forms that one knows are dead and parody them, but this would be gloomy aristocratic nihilism and not give much pleasure (*DF*, 321–22). The Devil is methodically pointing out that all the points Mann made in *Die Betrachtungen eines Unpolitischen* must be understood in reverse. This is the rejection of traditional society, of individualism, and of the Reformation, as discussed by Zeitblom in his account of the discussions of the Kridwiß *Kreis* and in his theological reflections in chapters 11 and 13. Nineteenth-century society was wrong to think that it was a continuation of Christianity, precisely because it was based on individualism. Starting from the position of the *Zivilisationsliterat*, or of Eisler's arguments for communism, he is now adopting Adrian's views, but adapting them to apply to the State, rather than to the individual. By rejecting individualism and retaining the psychological function of *Innerlichkeit*, he is advocating a totally subjective State based on arbitrariness, irrationality, and emotion. In this passage the Devil is specifically taking back the Reformation.

He justifies this with Kierkegaard's view that music, on which Adrian's system is based, belongs to the realm of the Devil (*DF*, 322–23). At the beginning of this discussion Adrian is reading Kierkegaard's essay on Mozart's Don Juan, where he defines music as exclusively emotion. Kierkegaard's position on music is traditional Catholic humanism, with the difference that Catholic humanism rejects music as belonging to the Devil because it is pure emotion, whereas Kierkegaard is in favor of it. Adrian has identified music with the nineteenth-century tradition. It is a classic fascist position that German Protestant society belongs to the Devil. The Devil has come up with a new synthesis of "the word" and "the music." Music, as pure emotion, is divorced from intellect. Therefore, a truly German government will be based on emotion rather than intellect. Rather than expressing "the word," it turns "the word" into "the music," into emotion, or irrationality.

In the conversation of the Winfried group in chapter 14, the group discusses Kierkegaard's questioning of the need for the existence of the church for the continuation of Christianity. The argument is that Christianity, the truth, should be entirely subjective. The Christianity referred to is Lutheranism, and in Mann's view Lutheranism is equivalent to nineteenth-century German society. Adrian disagrees with the other theology students, who support Kierkegaard's view, and says that such complete subjectivity and lack of objective control would lead to social chaos, the argument he puts forward in defense of his *strenger Satz*:

> Aber ich kann euren Radikalismus, der übrigens bestimmt nicht lange vorhalten wird, der eine Studentenlizenz ist, — ich kann euere Kierkegaard'sche Trennung von Kirche und Christentum nicht mitmachen. Ich sehe in der Kirche auch noch, wie sie heute ist, säkularisiert und verbürgerlicht, eine Burg der Ordnung, eine Anstalt zur objektiven Disziplinierung, Kanalisierung, Eindämmung des religiösen Lebens, das ohne sie der subjektivistischen Verwilderung, dem numinosen Chaos verfiele, zu einer Welt phantastischer Unheimlichkeit, einem Meer von Dämonie würde. Kirche und Religion zu trennen, heißt darauf verzichten, das Religiöse vom Wahnsinn zu trennen. (*DF*, 160–61)

The Devil has just argued that it is an illusion that nineteenth-century society was a continuation of the idea of the Church, because it was based on individualism. It is time to give up this pretense and abandon the nineteenth-century idea of the church, because it is a brake on enthusiasm. He describes Adrian's position as madness and nihilism. This rejection by the Devil of the bourgeois idea of the church is equivalent to the rejection of the Weimar Republic and of traditional society by the members of the Kridwiß *Kreis*. It is an invitation to total subjectivity, which will lead to madness and chaos. However, it is to be done on the collective, not the individual level. The true idea of the Church is to be restored. The Devil is the one who identifies Adrian as mad.

* * *

The Devil, having shown Adrian the nature of the political use the *Zivilisationsliterat* is making of his music, reappears in his previous, old-fashioned German form, which represents irresponsibility. The fusion has occurred: Adrian's incipient "enlightenment" has been turned into obscurantism based on eroticism. The *Zivilisationsliterat* has reconciled the revolutionary with the conservative. The Devil's great "temptation" of Adrian is, in fact, not a temptation at all; it is an instruction, a threat. Adrian has been chosen by the Devil on the strength of a work that the Devil finds very useful for his purposes, but Adrian is not doing his part to further it. The Devil tells Adrian that he has to overcome his desire for objectivity and his suspicion of subjectivity and pure experience, because it is bourgeois (*DF*, 323). This is, of course, the breakthrough that Zeitblom argues is necessary in chapter 30. Adrian is to break through these inhibitions and, rising above himself, commit holy horrors and let things go to his head. The Devil argues that truth is experience and feeling, even if it is a lie from the point of view of virtue; enthusiastic sickness is preferable to health; life knows nothing of morality (*DF*, 323–24). These are the same values attributed to the Protestant artist in *Die Betrachtungen eines Unpolitischen*. The Devil has taken them out of context, which is precisely what he says he does. This is his means of inspired elaboration. The context, in *Die Betrachtungen eines Unpolitischen*, is that values are determined by one's conscience in the face of a specific situation and not by dogma. The great inhibition that Adrian has to overcome in order to cooperate with the Devil is precisely this: being guided by his conscience, his Protestant sense of personal responsibility. He has already committed an irresponsible act, so why should he not carry it through? Adrian is no more impressed by this suggestion than by the suggestion that he is going to develop osmotic growths. The Devil has made these traditional Protestant values into an expression of the anti-intellectual argument that one should be guided by one's feelings, not by one's brain. In Catholic thought, in Mann's view, subjectivity is synonymous with emotion, not with conscience and personal responsibility. This secularized version of Catholicism is a contemporary tendency that Mann finds particularly insidious and immoral and is related to the corruption of Nietzsche's glorification of life and the misuse of psychology. It is Zeitblom's guiding principle. In chapter 24 Zeitblom is very puzzled that Adrian does not think this way. As a musician, he should, he says. He says the same thing about Rudi Schwerdtfeger when he disagrees with him about Ludwig of Bavaria. There is no point in the novel where Adrian is guided by his feelings instead of by his intellect. Zeitblom is disturbed about this from beginning to end. He thinks that there is something fundamentally wrong with Adrian and implies that this has to do with the Devil. However, it has nothing to do with this Devil and is in opposition to his argument. The argument in chapter 25 is Adrian's account, not Zeitblom's.

The Devil is now no longer the playful German Protestant Devil. He is showing Adrian how to become a leader, how to break through the difficulties of the times and the culture. The Catholic conception of the individualist as leader is that he appeals to the collective base emotional values of the group and channels them into a compulsion to attack dissenters: he is the leader of the gang. This will be barbarism, says the Devil, particularly since it follows the period of nineteenth-century humanism. It is religion in its real form, not the secularized bourgeois version. After 500 years, says the Devil, everyone is fed up with bourgeois apostasy. Only he, the Devil, has preserved religion, and nobody can live a theological existence without the Devil (*DF*, 324–25). This is Zeitblom's view, as expressed in chapters 11 and 13. It is a return to the medieval values of Catholicism, but in secular form. It is the argument of the Kridwiß *Kreis* in chapter 34 (*Fortsetzung*), which Zeitblom presents as positive. "The document" is a clear statement of Mann's view that the National Socialist takeover in Germany was inspired by the values of the Devil, and he very clearly associates these with Catholic humanism and the medieval Church. Throughout the novel it is described as eroticism.

Hell cannot be described, says the Devil, because it is beyond language. It is the complete lack of humanity, beyond anything that can be described, and all descriptions are just symbols, not the real thing. But it does exist. This is what Zeitblom is talking about in chapter 34 (*Fortsetzung*) with his reference to Swift. The *Zivilisationsliterat* depends on language for promoting his political views, but Zeitblom advocates abandoning the use of language and symbols and just pointing to the real thing. This means, for instance, that to learn the meaning of justice, it is not necessary to consider it as an abstract concept, but simply to point at what the courts are doing. There follows a very eloquent description of hell, which Mann himself defined as a Gestapo cellar in *Die Entstehung* (217). It is hell on earth. It is this lack of humanity that Mann identifies as the fundamental defect of the utopian approach to politics of the *Zivilisationsliterat* in *Die Betrachtungen eines Unpolitischen*. It leads to hell on earth. Hell may be beyond language, but Adrian has described it with music in his *Apocalipsis cum figuris*. He illustrates it as the intolerance of dissent.

* * *

In *Die Betrachtungen eines Unpolitischen* the only reference to the idea of a terrible sin, an idea that is central to "the document," is Mann's remark that the only sin that will not be forgiven is self-righteousness. This is a sin of the *Zivilisationsliterat* and applies to Zeitblom rather than to Adrian in *Doktor Faustus*. Self-righteousness is certainly central to Zeitblom's portrayal of himself. There is, however, some considerable discussion of guilt in *Die Betrachtungen eines Unpolitischen*, where Mann compares the Protestant sense of guilt and responsibility with that of the Roman Catholic, which, Mann says, does not really exist. Mann, in *Die Betrachtungen eines Unpolitischen*, establishes his view that guilt depends on personal responsibility in distinguishing good from evil in a concrete situation. The *Zivilisationsliterat* is responsible only to dogma, in disregard of the truth or validity of the dogma, which is based on abstract principles with no reference to reality.

> Woran es dem politischen Ästhetizismus, dem bellezza- und belles-lettres-Politiker auf generöse Art gebricht, das möchte Verantwortlichkeitsgefühl, möchte Gewissen sein. Aber woher sollte denn dieses auch kommen, da niemand, auch er selbst nicht, Verantwortlichkeit ernsthaft bei ihm voraussetzt, noch seine Äußerungen in ihrem Geiste wertet? (*BeU*, 545)

Mann has Zeitblom specifically express this kind of irresponsibility in chapter 34 (*Fortsetzung*), where he admits that he adopted the views of the Kridwiß *Kreis*, fully aware that they were based on lies.

> Viel besser tat ich, im Verein mit der angeregten Tafelrunde dieses Neue zu betrachten und zu erkunden und, statt eine unfruchtbare, recht eigentlich langweilige Opposition dagegen zu machen, meine Vorstellungen dem Gange der Diskussion einzuschmiegen und mir in ihrem Rahmen ein Bild der kommenden, unterderhand schon in der Entstehung begriffenen Welt zu machen. (*DF*, 489)

This point about responsibility is the argument that the Devil, in his Protestant form, uses against Adrian. He says specifically that Adrian's deed was criminal irresponsibility. Zeitblom's statement is in direct opposition to Adrian's introductory statement to "the document" that he cannot keep quiet about the violation of the truth.

The Devil recognizes that Adrian is looking for an easy way out of his predicament, but this does not exist. Roman Catholic absolution of sin, with a few *meae culpae*, is no longer possible. Adrian has to actually mean that he repents in the Protestant sense: "Die Attritionslehre ist wissenschaftlich überholt. Als notwendig erwiesen ist die contritio, die eigentliche und wahre protestantische Zerknirschung über die Sünde, die nicht bloß Angstbuße nach der Kirchenordnung, sondern innere, religiöse Umkehr bedeutet" (*DF*, 328).

It means doing a philosophical about-face, denying his *Apocalipsis cum figuris*, Mann's position vis à vis *Die Betrachtungen eines Unpolitischen* (*DF*, 328). This will mean a tremendous humiliation for Adrian, and the longer he waits the more difficult it will be. Not repenting will mean an exciting life, but a life with terrible conflicts of conscience with no relief. Adrian rejects the Devil's offer: "Unterdessen möchte ich Euch davor warnen, Euch meiner allzu sicher zu fühlen. Eine gewisse Seichtheit Eurer Theologie könnte Euch dazu verführen" (*DF*, 329). He suggests that there is a third alternative, a proud contrition: that which recognizes the enormity of the sin and refuses to believe that he can be pardoned for it. Recognizing the true enormity of the sin is the only road to holiness. Adrian's guilt, I contend, is having written his *Apocalipsis cum figuris*, a work that like *Die Betrachtungen eines Unpolitischen* could be used to further the cause of fascism. As Mann says in his 1922 speech, "Von Deutscher Republik":

> Wenn sentimentaler Obskurantismus sich zum Terror organisiert und das Land durch ekelhafte und hirnverbrannte Mordtaten schändet, dann ist der Eintritt solchen Notfalles nicht länger zu leugnen, und die Stille, die sich, wie ich feststelle, bei dieser Anspielung im Saale verbreitet, ich weiß, junge Leute, was ich —, der fürchten muß, aus geistigem Freiheitsbedürfnis dem Obskurantentum Waffen geliefert zu haben —, was, sage ich, gerade ich dieser jetzt herrschenden Stille schuldig bin. (*VDR*, 818–19)

Adrian is suffering under the Devil's accusation in "the document"; he feels a terrible sense of guilt and responsibility.

Adrian defies the Devil, who, being an enthusiast and a vestige of Catholicism, does not really understand the strength and integrity of the Protestant conscience. The Devil uses psychology to try to persuade Adrian that he might as well go along with him and enjoy the fruits of his sin, since denying his work is more than his pride and arrogance will allow. The crux of the Devil's argument is not that Adrian committed his sin out of arrogance but that it is his arrogance that will make it impossible for him to recant his sin. Arrogance, in this context, as throughout Zeitblom's account, means insistence on individualism. It is his refusal to go along with the crowd against his better judgment, or Protestant conscience. The sin itself is not arrogance, but having made irresponsible statements that are susceptible of misuse by unscrupulous persons. This is what is comparable with Nietzsche's sin, not syphilis. However, Adrian disagrees with this theological argument. He does not recant his work — that is, his insistence on individualism — because it is not a sin, but he recognizes the enormity of his error in making these ideas public. The Devil has no answer to this. He cannot have an answer, because Adrian's response is theologically correct. The Devil is talking about Adrian's personal salvation in this world through subscribing to demonology. He simply repeats his original argument that

Adrian is bound to him. However, he adds the prohibition to love. This will indeed be Adrian's fate if he opposes the Devil, which he does, in that he opposes National Socialism and supports the Weimar Republic. In the end he will be defeated, because the damage has been done. The situation is out of his hands and in the Devil's. Adrian has not accepted the offer of twenty-four years. The Devil has corrupted Adrian's intellect — his argument — but he has no weapon against his Protestant morality (*DF*, 130–31).

It is a fundamental corruption of Mann's whole life and work to consider that in *Doktor Faustus* he describes the true German Protestant artist as willing author of National Socialism. In the novel he describes the true German artist as the unwitting contributor to National Socialism, in that his work is maliciously taken out of context, distorted, and abused by National Socialism. Then the artist himself is destroyed by National Socialism. The overall message of the novel depends on this understanding of the parallel of Adrian's *Apocalipsis cum figuris* with *Die Betrachtungen eines Unpolitischen*.

The crux is that Adrian does not take up this proposal. He sticks to his Protestant values and does participate in society. He dedicates his life and his art to opposition to fascism. The consequence is that he is destroyed in 1930, not in 1945. The Devil tells him this will happen if he does not accept his offer:

> Do, re, mi! Sei versichert, daß deine psychologischen Finten bei mir nicht besser verfangen als die theologischen! Psychologie — daß Gott erbarm, hältst du's noch mit der? Das ist ja schlechtes, bürgerliches, neunzehntes Jahrhundert! Die Epoche ist ihrer jämmerlich satt, bald wird sie das rote Tuch für sie sein, und der wird einfach eins über den Schädel bekommen, der das Leben stört durch Psychologie. Wir leben in Zeiten hinein, mein Lieber, die nicht chikaniert sein wollen von Psychologie. (*DF*, 332)

Adrian suffers isolation and hostility and eventual defeat as a result of his political activity, as did Mann. The *Zivilisationsliterat* can defend reaction and take over society by committing atrocities, all in the name of valuing feelings over rationality. Adrian already has a large following. Those who have accepted Adrian's work as political gospel were nurtured by Zeitblom's tradition, which is Catholicism and humanism. There is no humanity for Adrian if he insists on his integrity. This is a statement of Mann's isolation during the 1920s, when he refused to join the intellectual fascist movements that led to National Socialism.

* * *

Scattered through "the document" are comments, but really remarkably few, and only at the beginning, that could be taken to refer to syphilis. The specific reference the Devil makes to syphilis is in a catalogue of characteristics of the social upheaval that led to the Reformation and the beginning of Protestant bourgeois society. What Adrian has done is "seen the light," politically defined as "enlightenment," expressed by the Devil as *Illumination*. He then devised a democratic scheme based on subjective freedom and expressed it in music, in a form understood by the Devil as pure emotion. The Devil has defined this as eroticism poisoning the intellect. The argument that the discussion is about music, or art, is even more difficult to defend, because it does not make much sense — not in itself, not in the context of Mann's ideas about art, and not in the context of the novel. The discussion is made to parallel the Spieß version of Faust's conversation with the Devil, but none of this interferes with the thrust of the main argument. The parallel with the Spieß argument is for the purpose of demonstrating the parallel with the Renaissance version of Faust rather than with Goethe's denial of this version.

This interpretation of Adrian's conversation with the Devil is consistent with the text and makes sense in the context of Mann's life and works. It is an account of Mann's dilemma on finding that ideas expressed in *Die Betrachtungen eines Unpolitischen* were being used for reactionary purposes. Mann thought this trend was dangerous and that the purposes for which the ideas were being used would lead to hell on earth. He thought this in the early 1920s and said so publicly in 1922 in "Von Deutscher Republik." It is not surprising, given that his predictions all came true, that, when he planned *Doktor Faustus*, he planned it around his own sense of guilt. Mann, in writing a book that is a diatribe against utopian systems, helped lay the basis for the development of a Utopia that, even in 1922, he thought would be much worse than communism, which he was originally writing against. His error, like Adrian's, had been in thinking he was too clever. On the other hand, maybe he underestimated the stupidity of the others.

In "Von Deutscher Republik" Mann says that he is a conservative and that conservatives do not want to prevent change but just try to slow it down and prevent it from being extreme and abrupt. That is what he claims he was trying to do in *Die Betrachtungen eines Unpolitischen*. His book was meant to serve the future, not the past, a summing up of the fixed in an attempt to keep the essence on which the new is to be built in order to set the mold for the future. It is this that the Devil says is impossible under the circumstances. In *Die Betrachtungen eines Unpolitischen*, says Mann, he shows that revolutions are feverish and an end in themselves. This is how the Devil is presenting his offer to Adrian. There are essentially two political forces, says Mann, following Novalis, conservatism and obedience and freedom and equality, and neither can afford to destroy the other. Mann says that in *Die Betrachtungen eines Unpolitischen* he argued, as does Adrian, with reference to Kierkegaard, that a third force is necessary, the idea of the church. Today the idea of the church is replaced with the idea of humanity, he says (*VDR*, 829–31). It is humanity that will be denied to Adrian whether or not he follows the advice of the Devil.

However, Adrian does not accept the Devil's offer to lead his movement. He rejects it. Therefore, the Devil has no pact with Adrian. The pact is with those who accept the Devil's elaboration of Adrian's original idea. Adrian is "taken" in 1930; it is Germany that is "taken" twenty-four years later. Adrian is "taken" for opposing the intentions of the Devil. He does not have years of power and glory in between his conversation with the Devil and his final defeat. On the contrary, the Devil, in the form of National Socialism, methodically takes from him everybody he loves, as he threatened to do.

Ultimately, syphilis cannot have anything to do with Adrian's argument with the Devil. It makes no sense at all. The syphilis is part of Zeitblom's story and has to do with a different interpretation of the nature of the Devil. Adrian has been contaminated with *Illumination*, with "enlightenment," or with democracy. The Devil, as soon as his work appeared, stepped in and diverted it to obscurantism, by allowing its qualifications and reservations to be interpreted as a negation of "enlightenment," or of democracy. He has done this by removing the criterion for these qualifications and reservations, the Protestant sense of personal responsibility. This makes them arbitrary and divorced from all rationality. Where there is no rational criterion, there can be no argument but force.

"The document" presents the crux of the argument between Zeitblom and Adrian and between Mann and the Munich intellectuals. The argument in "the document" is largely a rephrasing of arguments that occur between Adrian and Zeitblom throughout the novel. The Devil, like Zeitblom, gives Adrian little opportunity to express his point of view and, like Zeitblom, interprets Adrian's arguments as the opposite of what they are. The Devil's assessment of the situation is the same as Zeitblom's assessment throughout the novel. The fascist remarks are parallel to remarks that Zeitblom makes elsewhere. "The document" is full of cross-references to *Die Betrachtungen eines Unpolitischen* and positions that Mann opposed in "Von Deutscher Republik." The Devil is quite unambiguous about the fact that Adrian is opposed to fascism.

It is my contention that the origin of "the document" lies in Mann's own wrestling with his conscience in 1921, between the receipt of the honorary doctorate for *Die Betrachtungen eines Unpolitischen* and the writing of "Von Deutscher Republik," where he pointed out that the book was being misunderstood and spoke out publicly in favor of supporting the Weimar Republic, pointing out the dangers of the growing reactionary political movement that ultimately ended in National Socialism. Mann foresaw this development and felt a moral obligation to contribute to the effort to prevent its happening. "The document" is a dramatization of Adrian's decision to support the Weimar Republic.

Notes

[1] Hanns Eisler, "The Builders of a New Music Culture," 36–58.

[2] Thomas Mann, "Carlyle's *Friedrich*," in *GW*, 10:567–73; here, 571.

[3] Heinrich Böll, *Briefe aus dem Krieg 1939–1945*, vol. 1 (Cologne: Kiepenheuer & Witsch, 2001), 276.

[4] Daniel Jonah Goldhagen, *Hitler's Willing Executioners: Ordinary Germans and the Holocaust* (New York: Knopf, 1996), 134.

[5] Thomas Mann, "Briefe an Karl Kerényi," in *GW*, 11:629–53; here, 642.

[6] Helmut Wiegand, *Thomas Manns* Doktor Faustus *als zeitgeschichtlicher Roman: Eine Studie über die historischen Dimensionen in Thomas Manns Spätwerk* (Frankfurt am Main: Fischer, 1982), 148.

[7] Thomas Mann, "Leiden an Deutschland," in *GW*, 12:684–766; here, 698.

[8] Robert Craft, "The 'Doktor Faustus' Case," *The New York Review of Books*, 7 August, 1975, 18–21.

[9] Thomas Mann, "Die Entstehung des Doktor Faustus," *GW*, 11:145–301; here, 186. Further references to this work are cited in the text using the page number alone.

[10] Joachim Fest, *Das Gesicht des Dritten Reiches* (1963; rpt., Munich: Piper, 1993), 340.

[11] This remark does not take into account comments made by students of Mann's political thought, many of whom are perfectly aware that *Doktor Faustus* is about Mann's political experience. Except for Gert Sautermeister, whose article on *Doktor Faustus* is discussed in chapter 7, I have seen no more than passing mention of the novel in their writings. These mentions, however, support the thesis being presented here.

[12] Keith Stimely, "Oswald Spengler: An Introduction to his Life and Ideas," *The Journal for Historical Review* (March/April 1998), 2.

[13] Paul Egon Hübinger, *Thomas Mann, die Universität Bonn und die Zeitgeschichte* (Munich: Oldenbourg, 1974), 46.

[14] Thomas Mann, "Hoffnungen und Befürchtungen für das Jahr 1936," in *GW*, 10:917–18; here, 917.

13: The Story of Marie

THE SITUATION IN THE NOVEL has now completely changed. The historical period of the rest of the novel is the 1920s in Munich, a time and place where the rapid increase in fascist support and political polarization and intolerance was particularly pronounced. Fascist intolerance of dissent was leading to a complete breakdown of social order and justice, and violence on the streets was routine. Adrian's *Apocalipsis cum figuris* has been preempted as an argument for fascism by the Catholic intellectual community in Munich, and Adrian, who understands the demonic implications of this distortion of his ideas, is now working, as did Mann, to support the Weimar Republic and to dissociate himself from this fascist movement. The events of the rest of the novel must be read in the light of this new situation. Otherwise they make no sense at all.

Adrian's anti-fascist activities lead eventually to his absolute rejection by the Munich intellectual community:

> . . . denn der Grund für das Verhalten der Leute war ja die Atmosphäre unbeschreiblicher Fremdheit und Einsamkeit, die ihn in wachsendem Maß — in diesen Jahren immer fühlbarer und distanzierender — umgab, und die einem wohl das Gefühl geben konnte, als käme er aus einem Lande, wo sonst niemand lebt. (*DF*, 545)

As Mann's son Michael says:

> Thomas Mann sah sich in den dreißiger und vierziger Jahren bei aller redlichen Bemühung um Kontaktaufnahme mit den westlichen Demokratien zurückgeworfen auf das Einsamkeitspathos seines Künstlertums — es ist das Einsamkeitspathos Adrian Leverkühns.[1]

Zeitblom explains the reason for the rejection of Adrian by the fashionable fascist crowd that he himself moves in. The facts of the novel show that this repeated charge of solitude and isolation is not true, in any ordinary sense of the words. Adrian is always surrounded by friends and treated with respect, as shown in chapter 38, at the dinner party at Bullinger's apartment. The scene illustrates the developing tension with the interchange between Adrian and Dr. Kranich. The basis of this dispute is once again the separation of emotion from intellect in music (*DF*, 549–50).

In the story of Marie, Zeitblom refuses to accept that Adrian now opposes what, in his view, are the opinions he expressed in his *Apocalipsis cum figuris* and attributes this apostasy on Adrian's part to arrogance and contrariness and eventually, to sadism, inhumanity, and demonic influence.

It is clear that Adrian and Zeitblom are now moving in completely separate circles and that Adrian's time is largely absorbed in work with international cultural interchange programs. He does this in cooperation with Rudi Schwerdtfeger, until their mission is aborted by the latter's death. Zeitblom shows considerable irritation at Adrian's expecting him to participate in these activities that are associated with support for the Weimar Republic.

After the First World War a distinct contradiction in Zeitblom's portrayal of Rudi is apparent. The evidence shows that he is not the irresponsible socialite, as Zeitblom describes him, who relies simply on his natural talent and considerable charm to drift through life. He has been giving solo concerts and recitals with notable success and has been appointed concertmaster in spite of his youth (*DF*, 462–63). It is this artistic seriousness that is the basis of his closer association with Adrian, as well as his sharing Adrian's political views and objectives, as shown in chapter 31 (*DF*, 430) and confirmed in the story of Marie.

Zeitblom's account of Adrian's professional activities is rather sketchy, which somewhat obscures events. He tells us in chapter 30 that Adrian is becoming well known and, before the outbreak of the First World War, is better received abroad than in Germany, particularly in France. This contact is aborted by the outbreak of the war (*DF*, 407–8), but, as early as 1922, the International Society for New Music promotes Adrian's work (*DF*, 516). The first performance of the violin concerto Adrian writes for Rudi is in Vienna in spring 1924 (*DF*, 524) and the repetition of this concert in Bern and Zurich takes place at the end of 1924 (*DF*, 553). The dramatic events in the story of Marie take place in late January and in February 1925. In the real world, outside the novel, Hitler was in jail in 1924. In February 1925, the National Socialist Party was refounded and Hitler proclaimed its undisputed leader.[2]

* * *

In 1922 in "Das Problem der Freiheit" Mann said that morality is each individual overcoming his egotistical isolation and working in cooperation with the community.[3] Giving up his egotistical isolation and working in cooperation with the community is a fair description of Mann's activities as a cultural ambassador during the 1920s. It also describes Adrian's similar activities in the chapters of *Doktor Faustus* portraying this period. Adrian does not like doing such things, as he himself says in his letter to Kretzschmar on the occasion of his decision to study music. Zeitblom suggests that Adrian was persuaded by Schwerdtfeger to go on tour, but the persuasion, together with the arguments for doing so, can be found in chapter 37, in the mouth of Fitelberg, who expresses Mann's arguments when he visits Adrian in 1923 (*DF*, 526).

Fitelberg is an impresario organizing the international avant-garde music scene in Paris, and he invites Adrian to participate. Zeitblom presents Fitelberg's proposal as the great temptation of the Devil and implies that Adrian rejects his seduction. This "Mephistopheles" comes in the form of a Jew. Zeitblom describes Fitelberg as aesthetically objectionable, as he does all his Jews: he specifically mentions ugliness in each case where he is talking about a Jew. Zeitblom further stresses that, in his view, not only is Fitelberg ugly, but he is also diabolically clever: "Daß er nichts weniger als ein Dummkopf war, darüber wird das, was ich aus noch heute frischer Erinnerung von seinen Reden mitteilen will, keinen Zweifel erlauben" (*DF*, 529–30). He dissociates himself absolutely from Fitelberg and his ideas, not just at the time he is talking about, but also at the time of writing. This is a confirmation of his insistence in chapter 1 that he has never had anything to do with the Devil (*DF*, 10). Fitelberg, like Adrian's supposed syphilis, comes from the east and, like the Devil, he adapts his appearance to circumstances with ease.

Fitelberg's account of his own intellectual development parallels Adrian's. He came from a small town, which he left behind him. He studied philosophy at the Sorbonne and found that philosophy is too abstract: he thinks that it would have been better to study metaphysics in Germany, just as Adrian gave up studying theology to study music. This is yet another veiled comparison of the Catholic approach with the Protestant approach. It is a rejection of "enlightenment." He then talks about the need for art to reach a wider public, as does Adrian in chapter 31 (*DF*, 531). He admires the German character of Adrian's work, which he describes as comparable to Bach, who, like Adrian, reconciled polyphony with harmony. Fitelberg argues that German nationalism, arrogance, hatred of joining in and equality, and refusal to participate in international society will lead to the Germans suffering the same fate as the Jews — being confined to the ghetto (*DF*, 541), an argument against the rejection of the Weimar Republic. Zeitblom, in this chapter, identifies opposition to National Socialism with Jews and the Jews with the Devil. Jewish influence was the explanation given for Mann's rejection of National Socialism.

As events show, Zeitblom's implication that Adrian found Fitelberg's ideas distasteful and did not listen to them is an outright and deliberate lie. It is Zeitblom, and not Adrian, who opposes Fitelberg's views on German nationalism, whereas Adrian obviously agrees with Fitelberg, who expresses Mann's own views. Otherwise, he would not act as he does. Chapter 37 is noteworthy for the absence of any inclusion of commentary from Adrian; Zeitblom presents exclusively his own view. After Fitelberg's visit Adrian does in fact participate in international cultural exchange programs, and the story of Marie flatly contradicts Zeitblom's implied rejection by Adrian of his proposal. The story of Marie is the story of Adrian's and Rudi's cooperation in cultural exchange programs in support of the

Weimar Republic. The events of the novel show that Adrian must have signed a contract with Fitelberg.

Fitelberg arrives on Saturday afternoon, and Zeitblom points out that he himself will be absent on the Sunday (*DF*, 526). Zeitblom has no scruples about telling the reader what happens when he is not there when it suits his argument, such as in his account of Adrian's trip to Graz. On the occasion of Fitelberg's visit, he refrains from telling the reader what he must have known, even though he was not there, because it does not suit his purpose. Zeitblom seems to be trying to conceal from the reader that Adrian is persuaded by Fitelberg. However, what he is pointing out is that he, in his capacity as guardian angel, was unable to be present to prevent Adrian from committing these two critical determining acts. He is exonerating himself from blame, while pointing out Adrian's irresponsibility and unreliability when left to his own devices.

*   *   *

The first step in untangling the story of Marie is trying to get at the facts, divested of Zeitblom's surmises and conjectures. It is clear that Zeitblom is not telling the truth about this story. The whole account of Adrian's intention to marry Marie and the farce of sending Rudi to woo her for him, together with the grimmer suggestion that Adrian deliberately sent Rudi to his death in this way, is clearly Zeitblom's invention. Except for the broader implications of the account for the novel, Zeitblom's account is very funny. It is a composite of nonsense and references to Shakespeare's comedies. We have seen that Zeitblom has his own peculiar way of interpreting Shakespeare. The story spreads over four chapters, well towards the end of the novel, and includes a remarkable amount of action, given the overall nature of the work. Interspersed with Zeitblom's erotic farce are significant scenes for the overall understanding of the underlying story of the novel, but, before considering these scenes and their implications, it is necessary to separate the fact from the fiction in Zeitblom's account. Curiously, this episode with Marie is rarely discussed in the literature, and its significance seems hardly to have been considered, which is to dismiss some forty pages of the novel with no comment.

Lieselotte Voss points out in her study of Mann's working notes, *Die Entstehung von Thomas Manns Roman* Doktor Faustus: *Dargestellt anhand von unveröffentlichten Vorarbeiten*, that the notes on Frank Harris do not appear until he has reached the Marie episode.[4] This confirms the intimate relationship of Zeitblom's comments in chapter 24 with his account of the Marie episode. Zeitblom's comment about writers seeking revenge through their works is a deliberate extraction by Mann from Harris's commentary. The way you can tell that writers have done this, according to Harris, is that their characters suddenly fall out of their roles, which is precisely what happens in the invented parts of Zeitblom's account. By invented parts, I refer to passages where Zeitblom oversteps his role of first-person narrator. These are, first, passages in direct speech, reporting conversations at which Zeitblom was not present and, second, passages where Zeitblom speculates as to what Adrian's intentions are, which he cannot know unless he has been specifically told. Indeed, Zeitblom often reports that Adrian said something quite different about his intentions from those he attributes to him and says that he simply does not believe him. The bulk of the account of Adrian's connection with Marie is told in such passages and speculations. Not only do Rudi and Adrian fall completely out of character in these invented passages, but the evidence of the rest of the account openly contradicts what is said in these passages. Marie does not fall out of character for the simple reason that there is no characterization of Marie in the novel, except that she is a pretty and witty girl. This is what Zeitblom says about Rosaline in *Love's Labour's Lost*. As Ilse Metzler says, Marie Godeau is just a quotation from Shakespeare.[5]

Zeitblom's story is that Adrian meets Marie while he and Rudi are on tour with Adrian's violin concerto. Marie is quite extraordinarily beautiful and has black eyes, just like Rosaline in *Love's Labour's Lost*. Adrian decides to marry her. Instead of proposing himself, he sends Rudi to do it for him. Rudi betrays Adrian's trust and becomes engaged himself to Marie. This, argues Zeitblom, was deliberately set up by Adrian so that Ines would kill Rudi. This story is shown in the novel itself to be a fabrication. The few critics who question Zeitblom's account, Campbell, Assmann, and Orlowski, all reject this story and question Zeitblom's motives, but I have seen no study that tries to identify what is really going on. Other studies simply ignore Zeitblom's obvious fabrication and say that Adrian killed Rudi — that is, sent him to his death — taking Zeitblom's word for it and swallowing his improbable explanation. How Adrian causes Ines's supposed killing of Rudi is not discussed in the literature. Zeitblom is, in this case as well, providing a sexual motivation for everyone's behavior. He is writing an erotic farce, which, in the novel, is Adrian's view of fascism. As in all other cases in the novel, it can be shown that accepting Zeitblom's sexual explanation of events is unwarranted. The result of simply accepting Zeitblom's improbable story is that the account of what is really going on is ignored. I shall discuss this whole episode in detail, to point out the discrepancies.

The first encounter of Rudi and Adrian with Marie occurs in chapter 39, at a dinner party in Zurich. This is a formal entertainment celebrating the success of Rudi's performance of Adrian's violin concerto and also of the concerto itself. Adrian is conversing with Marie about her work in Paris and about the Paris music scene. The conversation is strictly professional. Jeannette Scheurl is also present at this formal dinner (*DF*, 555–58). She enters the story as a good friend of Rudi's and of Adrian's in the early Munich days but is not part of Zeitblom's circle (*DF*, 346). Jeannette, who is half French, was very distressed at the outbreak of the First World War (*DF*, 404). She specializes in eighteenth-century music (*DF*, 347). During the 1920s her presence in Adrian's inner circle becomes much more pronounced and it is clear that Adrian and Jeanette are very close friends (*DF*, 601). Her role is not specifically explained in this episode, but she is clearly involved in the organization of the international cultural exchange program in which Adrian and Rudi are participating. She visits Zurich every year for a couple of weeks (*DF*, 555).

The visit to Zurich occurs at the end of 1924, at a time when Hitler was in jail and the Weimar Republic was showing signs of succeeding. At that time, Mann was actively engaged in efforts to build cultural links between Germany and the rest of Europe and to break down the distrust of Germany, particularly on the part of France. It was as part of this program that Mann made his important trip to Paris as a cultural diplomat, recounted in "Pariser Rechenschaft," published in 1926.[6] It is a similar program that Saul Fitelberg invites Adrian to participate in, in chapter 37, and that Zeitblom implies Adrian turned down, which he clearly did not. Adrian specifically asks Marie if she knows Fitelberg (*DF*, 557).

On his return from his concert trip to Switzerland, Adrian mentions Marie to Zeitblom, among other things that Zeitblom does not record. However, Adrian shows no enthusiasm for her as a person: "Gewiß war es kein enthusiastisches Portrait, das er mir lieferte, im Gegenteil waren seine Worte still und beiläufig, seine Miene unbewegt dabei und abseits in den Raum blickend" (*DF*, 559). Then Adrian announces to Zeitblom that he is planning to make some changes in his life (*DF*, 559). The reader assumes that this must in some way be related to his professional life, since that is what Zeitblom has started telling us about. Surprisingly, he immediately tells the reader that this means that Adrian is planning to get married and, since the remark seems to be related to his trip to Zurich, to Marie. This logical jump is comical. Zeitblom has just told us that Adrian shows no particular interest in Marie, beyond remembering her name. The absurdity of his response cannot escape the reader. Adrian cautions him about jumping to conclusions and tells him to keep his enthusiasm in check. He speaks of his intentions as though their becoming reality depended entirely on his own decision, a strange position if it is marriage he is contemplating, as Zeitblom points out. This, however, he attributes to Adrian's supposed arrogance rather than questioning his assumption about marriage plans (*DF*, 560). Surely the reader must be expecting some kind of farce at this point. It is a very classic Shakespearean situation. In a Shakespearean comedy, after a lot of grief, it would be Zeitblom who was called to account for jumping to unwarranted conclusions, but here it is he who is pulling the strings. Zeitblom is decidedly deficient when it comes to comedy, which should make the reader suspicious. Mann maintains this comic situation into the next episode.

Strangely enough, it does not seem to bother Zeitblom that he finds out about Marie's presence in Munich from the newspaper, given that previously he has always expressed hurt when Adrian did not confide in him about personal matters. He is, however, invited to the formal reception for her. He says that the only reason Adrian attends the reception is to see Marie: — "wie wäre er sonst überhaupt gekommen?" (*DF*, 1947, 646). However, Adrian hardly speaks to her at all (*DF*, 562–63). Rudi converses at length with Marie, not about personal matters, but about artistic happenings in Paris and Munich and about French-German relationships and the European political situation. Adrian only speaks to her briefly on leaving. That Adrian does have an interest in the gathering is clear: he spends most of the time at the reception speaking with Jeanette Scheurl and the Social-Democratic parliamentarian who is interested in music — an expert in Bach, an image long-since established as referring to a German Protestant democratic society. This is Weimar Republic politics, German cosmopolitanism, the accommodation of traditional German culture to democratic values. It is this that Adrian is showing an interest in and participating in, not wooing Marie. Incidentally, he is not conversing with Zeitblom, either. Chapter 39 ends with Zeitblom still stubbornly trying to convince the reader that Adrian is planning to marry Marie and the reader wonders where all this is going. Mann has laid it all on with a heavy hand, both Zeitblom's gratuitous assumption of marriage plans and Adrian's obvious lack of personal interest in Marie.

Zeitblom makes reference to Marie as representative of the wider world, the artistic and musical world outside Germany. It can indeed be inferred that this was Adrian's interest, given the historical time, the context, and Mann's own interests during the 1920s and, of course, the evidence of what the text itself says about Adrian's activities and associates. Zeitblom's conclusion that he expected to consummate his interest in the international artistic world by sexual means is quite gratuitous and startlingly out of place in what purports to be a serious account. The evidence of the text contradicts it. In chapter 37, Zeitblom says that he found his contact to the outside world through Frau von Tolna and deliberately kept her at a distance (*DF*, 519). In fact, the contact with Frau von Tolna is again in association with Adrian's inclusion in the international music community (*DF*, 516–17). She is traveling through Europe in close association with these cultural activities. After the success of their concert in Vienna in 1924, Adrian and Rudi visit Hungary at her invitation. The only comment Adrian makes on this visit, that Zeitblom reports, is political, about the unacceptable social and economic conditions in rural Hungary and the wide discrepancies in income. Once again, Zeitblom diverts attention from Adrian's political activity by dismissing the idea that Frau von Tolna is involved in trying to do anything to improve this situation (*DF*, 525–26). In 1928 Mann wrote a letter in defense of a Hungarian writer who was accused of treason for cooperating with the Hungarian emigrant press in their efforts to draw the attention of the outside world to the appalling social conditions in Hungary.[7] The context of this episode is thus shown to be anti-fascist activity on the part of Adrian and Schwerdtfeger. István Varga makes it clear that this is indeed the case. Mann's description of the Hungarian situation is very accurate and results from his close political connections with Hungarian intellectuals and their efforts to combat fascism.[8] In any event, these tours and international activities are particularly intense in 1924. It seems that Adrian is living a very active public life and not simply living as a recluse in Pfeiffering, as Zeitblom continues to imply he is. These activities do, however, alienate him from the intellectual crowd in Munich.

Then, in chapter 40, Zeitblom provides his eyewitness evidence for Adrian's interest in Marie. Adrian asks him to arrange an outing for Marie and her aunt. He says it is Rudi's idea, but he wants Zeitblom to imply that the invitation is from him. Zeitblom considers such an outing an improbable choice for Adrian. However, he "suppresses" the thought that Rudi may in fact have an interest in the plan, although this is what Adrian said. In the train, Marie speaks of the concert in Zurich and Adrian praises Rudi emphatically. Rudi is both embarrassed and pleased (*DF*, 567). During the lunchtime party at the hostel, Rudi gives a magnificent impromptu performance, making his virtuoso ability the center of attention. Rudi and Schildknapp dance with Marie and Helene. On the way home, Adrian chats with Helene. It is Schildknapp who converses with Marie. Zeitblom is arguing with Rudi about politics. All the centering of attention on Rudi is on his musical ability, until Zeitblom introduces this question of his political stand.

Up to this point, from the actual information given, there is no evidence whatsoever that Adrian's relationship with Marie is, even potentially, anything other than professional and formal, and there is evidence that this professional interest exists, although Zeitblom gives it little importance. There have been broad hints that Rudi's interest is more personal, but once again, the actual evidence given is that it is professional, and, in any case, Zeitblom's obsession with Rudi's sexual attractiveness has become a leitmotif. The evidence here centers on his virtuoso ability, not his person. The previous two chapters have established beyond doubt that Zeitblom is misleading the reader, that Adrian is not contemplating marriage with Marie. The question of what Adrian is planning has been bypassed, but it has been clearly suggested that he is planning something, and Zeitblom has recorded his actual activities: they are cultural and diplomatic, in support of the Weimar Republic and reconciliation with France. Zeitblom continues with his obsession about marriage into the next chapter.

What follows in Zeitblom's account is simply not true. It is his literary revenge on Adrian: in chapter 41 Zeitblom's characters fall completely out of their roles. The improbability of this private conversation between Adrian and Rudi at Pfeiffering, which is outrageous when viewed rationally, and the deliberate clumsiness of the reporting, leave no doubt that Mann means the reader to see through it. Zeitblom is establishing a sexual motivation to justify his claim that Adrian was responsible for Rudi's death. Mann is illustrating another characteristic of the *Zivilisationsliterat*: Zeitblom's story is intellectual dishonesty, a lie, but put forward with the complete assurance of the morally self-justified: "Aber heute ist seelische Tatsache, daß ich dabei gewesen bin, denn wer eine Geschichte erlebt und wieder durchlebt hat, wie ich diese hier, den macht seine furchtbare Intimität mit ihr zum Augen- und Ohrenzeugen auch ihrer verborgenen Phasen" (*DF*, 576). This chapter, reporting a supposed private conversation between Adrian and Rudi, is based not on an actual conversation, but on what Zeitblom surmises must have happened. The events are such that there is no corroboration possible in the world of the novel, since the principals are dead. At the end of chapter 36, where Zeitblom is reporting on Adrian's trip to Hungary with Rudi, he says this:

> Im übrigen bin ich nicht der Mann, von dieser leicht exzentrischen Episode in meines Freundes strengem Leben ein mehr als skizzenhaftes Bild zu geben. Nicht ich war ihm dabei zur Seite und hätt' es nicht sein können, selbst wenn er mich dazu aufgefordert hätte. Schwerdtfeger war es, er könnte berichten. Aber er ist tot. (*DF*, 526)

The corroboration must lie in the circumstantial evidence of the probability that the characters that the reader has come to know in the course of the novel so far could behave in the way Zeitblom reports them to have behaved and the philosophical positions they represent. The historical environment in which all this takes place must also be taken into account. Zeitblom gives almost exact dates. He claims that Adrian summons Rudi to his presence and Rudi comes running. He emphasizes Adrian's peremptory manner and Rudi's obsequiousness. Contradictorily, in Zeitblom's earlier account it is Rudi whom he describes as the protagonist, dominating and controlling Adrian: Rudi is supposed to have seduced Adrian. The account also ignores the very close professional association that has developed between them. Then, says Zeitblom, Adrian coerces Rudi into wooing Marie on his behalf, knowing that Rudi is himself interested in her. Adrian demands that Rudi deliberately sacrifice himself in his interest and Rudi agrees to do this. The reader knows that Adrian is not interested in Marie. He also knows that Adrian does not behave in this way.

The conversation Zeitblom presumes to have taken place is a discussion of Adrian's inhumanity. He has Adrian repeat his remark about getting old and not wanting to miss out and say that it — the marriage is still implicit — will help give human content to his future work. Rudi agrees, as though it were a matter of fact that Adrian, his good friend and collaborator,

is inhuman, as is his work that Rudi so much admires. Rudi is also presumed to agree that the solution to this problem is marriage. Apart from
the fact that humanity has been stressed as characteristic of Adrian and his
work — except by Zeitblom — this is an improbable remark to attribute
to Schwerdtfeger, whose principal characteristic, as Zeitblom has told us
time and again, is to ingratiate himself with people for his own ends, or, to
put it another way, who is kind and gentlemanly. Zeitblom's fictitious
account continues, becoming more preposterous with each remark: Adrian
objects to this charge of inhumanity and says it is horrible to be told that
he is inhuman, particularly by the first person to awaken human warmth in
him; Rudi's dreadful remark shows ingratitude for the concerto he wrote
for him; Adrian says that Rudi freed the human in him and taught him to
be happy. This is Zeitblom's doubtful thesis, put into Adrian's mouth.
Zeitblom is identifying the human with sex. Furthermore, it has been long
established that Schildknapp plays the role of Adrian's human companion.
That relationship, however, is based on chastity.

Then, says Zeitblom, Adrian says he got an inspiration, as in composing; like all inspirations it is not entirely new, but in this place and context
and highlighting will be quite unique. The inspiration is that Rudi will propose to Marie for him; he will be more effective than his usual messenger,
Zeitblom. This philosophical diversion about the nature of inspiration is
hardly appropriate unless it refers to Zeitblom's inspiration to invent this
plan, not at all new, but copied from Shakespeare's *Much Ado about
Nothing*. The Devil in chapter 25 took someone else's — Adrian's — plan
and gave it a new context and highlighting, which is what Zeitblom is
doing here, although he is attributing this inspiration to Adrian. Zeitblom,
in this invention, has Adrian call him Serenus, which, he has told us bit-
terly, he never does. Rudi then tells Adrian he has been wooing Marie for
himself and that the outing was his idea. In the previous chapter Zeitblom
has just said that he does not believe this. Now he is saying it is fact, by
putting it into Rudi's mouth. Adrian says that Rudi is to woo Marie for
him as a sacrifice and that he will be recognized as a victim, in the spirit of
the role he has played in his life. It will be a fulfillment of the merit he has
earned for giving Adrian humanity. This remarkable hypothetical conversation, containing gross accusations and extreme hostility, is portrayed as
having been carried out in conditions of amiability and absolute normality.

Zeitblom claims that he was also "there" during the ensuing conversation between Marie and Rudi, but it is unnecessary to tell us what was
said, he says, because the reader knows the result. He then proceeds to tell
us anyway. Zeitblom's account is good theatrical farce, but it is, as he says,
superfluous.

And that is the end of the story of Marie. Rudi is about to leave his
post in Munich to join a new orchestra that is being formed in Paris. If one
ignores the nonsense business of this whole story, what is revealed is that

Adrian has been arranging to go to Paris and that Rudi is to go instead of him. It requires a high suspension of disbelief to accept that this plan to go to Paris was the result of a decision to marry Marie, taken only twenty-four hours previously (*DF*, 591–92). Marie disappears from sight, which shows her complete irrelevance to the story.

This conversation between Adrian and Rudi can be seen more plausibly as Zeitblom's transference to Rudi of his own relationship with Adrian: underlying the later chapters of the novel are clear signs of Zeitblom's increased alienation from Adrian and of his resentment. Zeitblom says that Rudi was jealously annoyed by Adrian's change of opinion and felt he was just being used as a tool (*DF*, 587). This, which is a good description of Zeitblom's status with Adrian, as he himself has carefully made clear, would justify Rudi in betraying Adrian's trust, in Zeitblom's view. Mann has had Zeitblom set up a situation and, in commenting on it, betray his own motive for taking revenge on Adrian. Zeitblom feels that he is being used as a tool to promote Adrian's anti-fascist activities that he does not agree with and that he thinks represent a change of mind on Adrian's part. This can be read as Zeitblom's justification of his betrayal of Adrian.

Shakespeare's *Much Ado about Nothing* is a comedy, full of wit, but then so is *Love's Labour's Lost*, and Zeitblom did not see much humor in that play, either. Mann makes fun of Zeitblom in chapter 24 for misinterpreting humor. In chapter 41 Zeitblom, in parodying Shakespearean comedy, has written a tragedy. Mann's use of Shakespeare for this episode explains the deliberate parallel with chapter 24, where its significance was not apparent. Anticipation is not as obvious as repetition. The chapters complement one another, in that they deal with the same subject: Adrian's chastity and Zeitblom's suggestion that the lack of chastity is something shameful. Zeitblom says he feels humiliated by his own lack of chastity in chapter 24, which, as the reader knows, is not a true statement. His argument in chapter 41 is that Adrian is too proud to accept humiliation, meaning the loss of his chastity, and will take revenge, and he puts this argument in Adrian's mouth. Zeitblom implies, as he has hinted all along, without offering any concrete evidence, that the relationship between Adrian and Rudi is sexual. In fact, the association between Adrian and Rudi is professional: specifically, cooperation in the promotion of cultural ties between Germany and the rest of Europe in the service of the Weimar Republic. It is this political content that Zeitblom is trying to conceal. He attributes Rudi's participation in these activities to cold self-interest: the advancement of his career, and Adrian's participation to sexual seduction. This is nonsense.

Zeitblom's purpose in telling this story is to lay an erotic basis for his claim that Adrian was deliberately responsible for Rudi's death, and in so doing he is turning serious activity into an erotic farce. Adrian did not kill Rudi; Adrian was not there when Rudi was killed. The reader knows this, because Zeitblom describes the event as an eyewitness. Zeitblom's story about Adrian sending Rudi to his death in this way is so preposterous and unreal that it does not succeed in convincing the reader — or should not. Like Berowne in *Love's Labour's Lost*, Adrian falls completely out of his role in this chapter. So does Rudi. What is Mann's purpose? Of course, he is showing how far the *Zivilisationsliterat* will go in forcing the evidence to fit his theory, and Zeitblom has to find concrete evidence that Adrian is inhuman to support his claim that his behavior resulted from his association with the Devil. Adrian was clearly not intending to marry Marie and, therefore, could not conceivably have sent Rudi to woo her for him. Adrian is not inhuman and the idea that he killed Rudi out of revenge for cracking his shell of invulnerability, as Zeitblom claims, is nonsense. In Mann's view, Zeitblom, as a Catholic humanist, cannot understand either real humanity or the inward nature of personal responsibility. He has to find his explanation in the crude application of vulgar psychology. Of course, it will be sexual.

At the beginning of chapter 42 Adrian refers to something stupid that he has done, using an image from *Much Ado about Nothing* that refers specifically to a plan in the play to woo a girl through a third party:

> Eines Benehmens . . . so albern, daß es mich lebhaft an das eines Schuljungen erinnert, der vor lauter Freude über ein gefundenes Vogelnest es einem andren zeigt, — und der geht hin und stiehlt's ihm weg. (*DF*, 585)
> The flat transgression of a schoolboy, who, being overjoyed with finding a bird's nest, shows it to his companion, and he steals it. (Much Ado about Nothing, act 2, scene 1)

He has received a letter and says it is from an untrue friend, but he refuses to discuss it with Zeitblom. Zeitblom assumes it is from Rudi announcing his marriage to Marie. The reader does not know from the novel what friend and betrayal Adrian is referring to.[9] However, he probably has very serious doubts that it is about Rudi's marriage to Marie, because he is unlikely to have accepted Zeitblom's idea that Adrian intended to marry Marie in the first place and is probably rather doubtful about Zeitblom's speculations about Rudi's plans as well. The reader should not forget that in chapter 39 Zeitblom introduced this episode with Adrian's announcement that he had plans to change his way of life, but he does not tell the reader what Adrian had to say about these plans. It is three chapters later and Adrian has still not said anything. The entire episode of Marie is based on Zeitblom's conjecture, and Adrian's plans have been totally concealed from the reader.

The background of this story has to be looked at more carefully if we are to see through the filter Mann has created by having Zeitblom narrate nonsense, and discover something of what was actually going on. The context is that of Mann's primary interest at the time, the renewal and improvement of interchange between France and Germany at the intellectual level. Like Mann, Adrian does not feel comfortable in this environment, but participates out of a sense of duty, out of a desire to incorporate Germany as a full member into the European community. Adrian's and Rudi's activities as cultural diplomats are clearly there in the text. It is also clear in the text that Zeitblom is becoming antagonistic towards Adrian. It was such activities by Mann that so infuriated the intellectual circle in Munich, represented in the novel by the Kridwiß *Kreis*. Zeitblom is sympathetic with this group and is finding his friendship with Adrian trying. This irritation with Adrian is apparent throughout the Marie episode. He grumbles frequently at the way Adrian treats him and generally paints Adrian as being thoroughly self-centered and arrogant. He does not believe a word Adrian says, he misrepresents him, attributing base motives to him, as shown above, and then this is all explained as political in origin by the superficially irrelevant, but actually central, episode of the dispute about Ludwig of Bavaria.

The most important scene in this story of Marie is Zeitblom's defense of Ludwig of Bavaria, the mad king, and his long argument with Rudi about his position (*DF*, 570–74). His defense is an elaborate political speech, based on a typically Zeitblom reading of *Die Betrachtungen eines Unpolitischen*. There Mann quoted Schopenhauer as saying that constitutional monarchs have a license to live like gods, without a care in the world: ". . . die konstitutionellen Könige besäßen eine unleugbare Ähnlichkeit mit den Göttern des Epikur, als welche 'ohne sich in die menschlichen Angelegenheiten zu mischen, in ungestörter Seligkeit und Gemütsruhe, da oben in ihrem Himmel sitzen' " (*BeU*, 126). Both Mann and Schopenhauer are arguing against constitutional monarchy, on the grounds that it is irresponsible. Zeitblom, however, argues fervently in favor, precisely on these grounds. He gets it backwards. Ludwig's withdrawal from the world was the expression of a desire to glorify his majesty, he says. He claims that dethroning Ludwig and declaring him mad was completely unjustifiable, a dirty political move, brutal Philistine behavior. Rudi disagrees. Rudi, says Zeitblom, takes the bourgeois, official attitude that committing Ludwig to a madhouse was necessary for the good of the country, since he was completely mad (*DF*, 571). He says, as the Devil says in chapter 25, that the *Spießbürger* is not competent to judge madness. Kings are above criticism and responsibility and, if Ludwig saw fit to build himself beautiful palaces as monuments to his avoidance of society, it was his royal prerogative to do so. Unsociability is not ordinarily considered madness. Of course, we know that Zeitblom considers unsociability very suspect in Adrian's case, but then Adrian's unsociability is better described as expressing a dissenting opinion. Ludwig's unsociability was, excusably, sexual. His castle Linderhof is beautiful, like a castle in a fairytale, and it has a huge bed instead of a throne. Zeitblom argues further that the common people did not think about whether he was mad; all they saw in him was a king and that is what they wanted. At Rudi's objection that the king was not exercising his responsibilities as king, Zeitblom counters that the country could easily have been ruled by the ministers and, as for his wasting money, he provided employment and left a heritage that has proved very profitable as a tourist attraction. Zeitblom, believing that he is expressing Adrian's views, is amazed that Rudi, particularly since he is an artist, does not agree with him (*DF*, 570–74): "Und was, noch einmal, finge mit seiner [that of the *Zivilisationsliterat*] 'Lehre' ein Musiker an?" (*BeU*, 320). Schwerdtfeger, however, does not agree with him. He, like Adrian, rejects fairytales and prefers common sense. Zeitblom's arguments are a jumble of ideas from *Die Betrachtungen eines Unpolitischen*, taken out of context and turned upside-down. In *Königliche Hoheit*, Mann specifically argues that the days are over when such a thesis as Zeitblom has just put forward about Ludwig of Bavaria could be defended.[10] Zeitblom is rejecting the consideration of social problems in favor of a fairytale. In 1937 Mann said that this is precisely what the Germans were doing and that in the area of politics the fairytale is a lie.[11] Mann said, in "Von Deutscher Republik," that the traditional powers decayed into theatrical banality and when they did not rule well, we ignored the fact. There was a separation of national and State life and this could not last (*VDR*, 821).

Zeitblom insists that the arguments he has just put forward reflect Adrian's real views. He feels that it is not appropriate for him to be expressing such views in his presence, because Adrian should have expressed them himself, since they are his ideas. However, he worries that Adrian is so contrary as to be capable of declaring Rudi to be in the right. Therefore, it is necessary for him to express Adrian's real opinions for him. This is a specifically political question, with Zeitblom treating Adrian as the authority. Zeitblom is using arguments from *Die Betrachtungen eines Unpolitischen*, turning them around and misinterpreting them, just in the way the National Socialist supporters were doing at the time. He is identifying Adrian with his own distorted version of these ideas and Adrian is not pleased. Zeitblom does not get the impression that Adrian supports him as his representative. This, he thinks, is Adrian being contrary and unkind (*DF*, 574). In the whole Marie episode Adrian and Schwerdtfeger represent Mann's political activities and opinions. The coincidence is far too close for it to be overlooked.

Zeitblom has now been identified as supporting National Socialism. Up to this point in the novel, it is possible to argue that he was simply one of many who had fascist, but not National Socialist, views. His denials and reservations about his position are not really such and reflect rather his disillusion at the failure of National Socialism at the time of writing, when the war was being lost. It is not only Mann, but also Zeitblom, who waits for this sign of the end of the threat of not being published. His comment about those present at the reception for Marie does not imply a rejection of National Socialism, but the reverse:

> ... unter denen sich immerhin noch Leute von Familie, wie ein von Grund aus jovialer und zu allem bereiter Herr von Stengel, befanden, — aber auch schon gewisse, der "liberalistischen" Republik tatkräftig abholde Elemente, denen das Vorhaben, die deutsche Schmach zu rächen, und das Bewußtsein, eine kommende Welt zu repräsentieren, in dreisten Zeichen an der Stirn geschrieben stand. (*DF*, 562)

Mann is ironical; Zeitblom is not. The liberal character of the Republic is put in quotation marks; Herr von Stengel is an opportunist, jumping on any bandwagon; the budding National Socialists are energetic and audacious; Germany's humiliation is a fact and should be avenged.

Zeitblom expresses, in the argument about Ludwig, a view that was widespread among those who, although not necessarily National Socialists themselves, voted for Hitler. It does not matter that he is mad. He represents the glory of Germany in the eyes of the people, and the ministers will run the country. His grandiose schemes are economically beneficial to the country. It is this point that Zeitblom argues about with Rudi for several hours. Rudi does not share this view and, not long after this exchange, he is shot. It is to be stressed that, instead of a throne, Ludwig has an enormous bed. Once again National Socialism is described as an erotic farce.

Speaking of the refounding of the National Socialist party in February 1925, the time of these events in the novel, Kershaw says:

> The theme of personality and leadership, little emphasized before 1923, was a central thread of Hitler's speeches and writings in the mid- and later 1920s. The people, he said, formed a pyramid. At its apex was "the genius, the great man." Following the chaos in the *völkisch* movement during the "leaderless time," it was scarcely surprising that there was heavy emphasis in 1925 and 1926 on the leader as the focus of unity. In his refoundation speech on 27 February 1925, Hitler had stressed his task as leader as "bringing together again those who are going different ways." The art of being leader lay in assembling the "stones of the mosaic." The leader was the "central point" or "preserver" of the "idea." This demanded, Hitler repeatedly underlined, blind obedience and loyalty from the followers. The cult of the leader was thus built up as the integrating mechanism of the movement.[12]

This is Zeitblom's argument in February 1925. Mann has very carefully fixed the date precisely.

The entire story of Marie is introduced by Zeitblom's denial of Adrian's willingness to consider Fitelberg's Jewish advocacy of international cooperation, which is a deliberate lie. The story is twisted by Zeitblom's insistence throughout the novel that Rudi is a flirt and deliberately trying to seduce Adrian sexually. From the first mention of Rudi's interest in Adrian, it is the professional interest, the cooperation through the concerto Adrian wrote for Rudi, that describes the relationship, as Adrian says (*DF*, 272). Through the supposed sexual seduction of Adrian by Rudi, Zeitblom is trying to provide an erotic rather than a rational motivation for Adrian's participation in these international activities. The friction between Adrian and Zeitblom, as well as between Rudi and Zeitblom, is finally shown in the Ludwig episode to be openly political. Zeitblom is defending the erotic farce of National Socialism against Adrian's and Rudi's rejection of it. Zeitblom is demonstrating his impatience with Adrian and resentment at being used for activities he clearly opposes. He stubbornly insists that Adrian's real views are fascist.

Zeitblom actually says that the whole wooing episode seems farfetched, contrived and inexcusable. It is a puzzling absurdity (*DF*, 586). It certainly seems that way to the reader, since everything Zeitblom reports of what Adrian says contradicts the story he tells. Zeitblom, however, turns nasty. He says that he suspects that Adrian concocted the wooing scheme, not out of being stupidly trustworthy, as Adrian claims in the quote from *Much Ado about Nothing*, but deliberately and fully aware of the consequences. Zeitblom finds the episode so out of character for Adrian that it could only have happened with the help of the Devil, although he does not say this, but only implies it. It is to be remembered that in chapter 25 Adrian's Devil is advocating National Socialism and, further, that Zeitblom refuses to identify this Devil as the Devil. Zeitblom identifies the Devil with Fitelberg, with Judaism and internationalism, which is to say that he identifies Adrian's and Rudi's activities in these chapters as collaboration with the Devil. This casts quite a different light on the episode. Adrian was quite aware of what he was doing when he persuaded Rudi to participate in such activities, according to Zeitblom, and must, therefore, have had malicious intentions against Rudi. Adrian must have known that Rudi's decision to go to Paris would be seen as apostasy and not accepted. What makes Adrian's betrayal of Rudi so dreadfully unacceptable, in Zeitblom's view, is that, according to Zeitblom's perception of the situation, Adrian does not even believe in the Weimar Republic. When Adrian persists publicly in his perverse support of the Weimar Republic in chapter 74, precipitating his own destruction, Zeitblom describes it as madness. Zeitblom means literally that Adrian caused Rudi's death by encouraging his move to Paris. He is so convinced of Adrian's deliberate guilt that he does not inform him of Rudi's death. His not calling Pfeiffering is a clear illustration of the extreme antagonism that has developed between Adrian and himself.

By now, it is perfectly clear that Zeitblom is obsessed by sex. He is using psychology to prove his points. Nowhere in the novel does Zeitblom's "psychological" approach to understanding people and their motivations come as clearly to the fore as in the story of Marie. In chapter 25 the Devil refers to Adrian's rejection of psychology as a contradiction, since Adrian had once defended psychology: "Geh, dir ist es nicht recht zu machen. Sogar gegen meine Psychologie bist du grob, — wo du doch selbst einmal auf dem heimischen Zionsberg die Psychologie einen netten, neutralen Mittelstand und die Psychologen die wahrheitsliebenden Leute genannt hast" (*DF*, 306). Speaking of Schleppfuß's lectures about the religious psychology of the Inquisition, Zeitblom is sympathetic to the idea that the Devil reaches and influences man through the sexual:

> Gewiß hätte er nicht Theolog sein dürfen, um sich nicht zu dieser Psychologie bis zum Einklange sympathisch zu verhalten. Der Grund aber, weshalb ich mich wunderte, daß nicht mehr junge Leute von seiner Vorlesung angezogen wurden, war der, daß, wann nur immer von der Macht der Dämonen über das Menschenleben darin die Rede war, das Geschlechtliche eine hervorstechende Rolle spielte. Wie hätte es auch anders sein können? Der dämonische Charakter dieser Sphäre war ein Hauptzubehör der "klassischen Psychologie"; für sie bildete dieses Gebiet den Vorzugstummelplatz der Dämonen, den gegebenen Ansatzpunkt für Gottes Gegenspieler, den Feind und Verderber. (*DF*, 140)

However, it is clearly established in chapter 22 that Zeitblom no longer thinks that sex has to do with the Devil. Nevertheless, he is very clear that he thinks sex is the prime motivation to human action.

Unless one accepts Zeitblom's sexual explanation — and his sexual explanations can always be shown to cover up a more probable explanation of events — there is no possible explanation of why Ines should kill Rudi. It is completely out of character. She is married to a fascist, but is not a fascist herself, although this is not stated in the novel. However, it is implicit in her background and values as described by Zeitblom in the early years in Munich. She is a northern conservative and does not feel at home in southern Germany (*DF*, 262). Zeitblom describes the difference between Ines and Institoris as the personification of the contemporary opposition of morality and aesthetics, of the opposition of glorifying life and honoring suffering. Her values are strictly traditional Protestant values, whereas Institoris is presumably Roman Catholic, a Renaissance man. Ines defends Schwerdtfeger's position against Institoris's position, using the values Mann defends in *Die Betrachtungen eines Unpolitischen* (*DF*, 384–86). Zeitblom describes their home atmosphere as oppressively threatening (*DF*, 598). Ines's supposed serious addiction to drugs begins when her economic security is threatened by the post-war inflation, says Zeitblom (*DF*, 511), but, at this same time, Institoris is involving himself in fascism, a fact that would be more disruptive of the marriage than the economic situation. Institoris is the name of the medieval Inquisitor who wrote the basic manual on identifying, hunting, and persecuting witches. He was the world's foremost authority on demonology.[13]

There is little evidence that Adrian has much contact with Ines after he moves to Pfeiffering. She is never mentioned as present at any of the functions Adrian attends in the latter part of the novel and even in 1914, at the Carnival festivities, he does not join her group. On the other hand, the whole relationship of Zeitblom with Ines is suspect. He states in chapter 29 that he manipulated her into marrying Institoris, when he thought she loved Rudi, for a specific reason, which he does not state:

> . . . denn gleich verantwortungsvoll schien es mir, das Mädchen in ihren Zweifeln zu bestärken und ihr das Obdach zu verleiden, nach dem es sie verlangte, wie sie zu überreden, daß sie sich, diesen Zweifeln entgegen, darunter begäbe; ja, dann und wann wollte mir, aus einem besonderen Grunde, das Zureden noch verantwortungsvoller scheinen als das Abraten. (*DF*, 389)

He remains, throughout the novel, in close contact with her and with Institoris.

Zeitblom's remark on Ines's murder of Rudi tends to be overlooked by the critics. He is proud of her! Like all such remarks, he weakens it by casting doubt on her ability to have done it: "Aber so sehr auch mir vor der Untat schauderte, so war ich doch, aus alter Freundschaft, fast stolz, nein, entschieden stolz darauf, daß sie in ihrer Gesunkenheit die Kraft und wilde Energie zu der Handlung gefunden hatte" (*DF*, 514).

A careful reading of Zeitblom's account of Ines's affair with Rudi, in chapter 32, leaves some considerable doubt that Ines is talking about an affair at all. She is talking about suffering and the right to enjoy life and decadence, about the human value of the emotions, and other such philosophical, nineteenth-century Protestant attitudes, but there is not a word from Ines that necessarily refers to an affair. Before Zeitblom makes his statement that Ines had an affair with Schwerdtfeger for several years — and he makes it as a supposition, not a fact — he makes his standard protest, when he is about to invent his account, that he is not an all-knowing author who can see into things that are hidden from the world (*DF*, 439). He then says that, although, of course, everybody knew about the affair, he never heard anyone mention it (*DF*, 440–41). This suspicious remark is followed by a long general discussion of the psychology of how people behave in such situations (*DF*, 441). It is not a discussion of Ines, but an exposition of his understanding of sexual motivation in the abstract. Furthermore, he has preceded this discussion with a long discussion of his all-knowing and quite unwarranted certainty that Institoris is sexually inadequate, something that he cannot know. Thus, the entire basis of Zeitblom's interpretation of the discussion disappears. The conversation can be read as Ines's contradiction of this interpretation. Zeitblom belittles the object of her passion as physically defective. It is true that he has reported that Rudi is missing a kidney, but he has just now been belittling Institoris as physically defective. In fact, Zeitblom dwells on Institoris's feeble, clumsy physique (*DF*, 382–84). There is no justification for assuming it is Rudi and not Institoris that she is referring to. She expresses jealousy of some previous concern about Rollwagen's daughters (*DF*, 445), friends out of Institoris's circle, and does not believe that the man she loves is faithful to her. Ines's statement at the end of the conversation that "he" will abandon her, in that case, and much more consequentially, refers to Institoris and not to Rudi at all (*DF*, 445). As Voss says, what Ines loves about her man is "das liebe Leben," and this is Institoris' philosophy.[14] There is no reason to suppose that the conversation has anything to do with Rudi, except seduction by Zeitblom's demagogic power of persuasion. The only other reference to this supposed affair in the novel comes up in the private conversation Zeitblom has invented between Adrian and Rudi in chapter 33, where he is trying to establish a sexual explanation for the professional association between them. Zeitblom has laid the ground for Ines's affair with Rudi in chapter 29, where he tries to make the case that Ines is really in love with Rudi and only marries Institoris because she wants the security of his wealth (*DF*, 381). Rudi is not courting Ines in this chapter. The only evidence Zeitblom provides for their affair is his simple statement that they were having an affair. The implication provides a sexual motivation for Ines to murder Rudi and evidence of Zeitblom's understanding of sexual motivation. However, there is no evidence that the intense unhappiness that Ines is expressing in this discussion has anything whatsoever to do with Rudi. It appears to have to do with Institoris.

While this conversation is taking place, Institoris is at his club "Allotria" (*DF*, 445). The allotria is a moth, a night-time, or obscurantist, butterfly, the counterpart for Zeitblom to Adrian's transparent Haetera Esmeralda.

The reason Rudi is killed is because he is leaving Munich to go to France. There are several allusions to this surrounding the episode. Rudi has difficulty severing his contract with the orchestra in Munich and this goes slowly, because they do not want him to leave (*DF*, 592). Curiously, applying for the position in France, waiting for it to be confirmed and severing his contract in Munich, which, Zeitblom says, went slowly, all took place in Zeitblom's account in the time between the supposed conversation with Adrian and the very next concert (*DF*, 592). Rudi's wooing of Marie, the reason Zeitblom offers for Rudi's decision to go to Paris, is squeezed in between these two events. This sequence is highly improbable. Zeitblom's account of events does not hold up.

Further, the program of Rudi's final concert is Berlioz and Wagner, a mixture of French and German music, ending with the overture to *Die Meistersinger* (*DF*, 592). *Die Meistersinger* has clearly political connotations: it is a declaration of German democracy, the reconciliation of the French with the German. The political connotation of combining French music with German music is particularly commented on and condemned by Holzschuher, the Dürer expert from the Kridwiß *Kreis*. He is not talking about the quality of the music, but about the leadership of the orchestra. Designing such a program conceals a tendency to pacifism and reconciliation with France. He describes the conductor as a Republican and politically unreliable. Rudi is also a declared Republican and has a commitment with France. He is also part of the direction of the orchestra — he is concertmaster. Holzschuher has been thinking this over all evening and has decided that in order to restore intellectual purity it is necessary to have men at the top of great orchestras who are unquestionably on the German side. Zeitblom points out that mixing politics with music is party policy, not a question for academic discussion, and deflects the conversation away from politics (*DF*, 593). The party in question is no longer some vague nationalism or sentimental fascist utopianism, but National Socialism.

On the tram Rudi avoids looking at Zeitblom (*DF*, 594–95). Zeitblom says that this is because he is, in Rudi's eyes, really Adrian's alter ego (*DF*, 595). Adrian's alter ego is, in Zeitblom's view, the real Adrian, the one who wrote the *Apocalipsis cum figuris*, the bible for fascism. This is the Adrian that Zeitblom represents and that Rudi feels uncomfortable with. Rudi's discomfort is caused by their recent political argument. His decision to go to Paris is a public declaration of his political disagreement with Zeitblom and with National Socialism. Presumably the delay in Rudi's breaking his contract with the orchestra, because they did not want him to leave, refers to what Zeitblom views as a humanistic attempt to persuade Rudi to repent of his error before he is damned.

There are simply no grounds for Ines's wanting to kill Rudi. It is completely out of character for her to be involved in fascism and the only possible motive for Rudi's death is his opposition to fascism. He is killed because he is betraying the fascist cause. What Rudi's death achieves is the removal of two persons opposed to fascism, Ines and Rudi, and a suspension of Rudi's and Adrian's activities in opposition to National Socialism. Rudi cannot give evidence — he is dead. Ines cannot give evidence — she has been declared mad. Zeitblom is not going to tell the reader — his morality is defending the cause. It seems necessary to question yet another of Zeitblom's accounts, his eyewitness account of Rudi's death (*DF*, 595–96).

Rudi is shot on a crowded streetcar. The car is delayed, which Zeitblom attributes to a possible traffic jam. A traffic jam at that time of night on this wide avenue in 1925 is a highly improbable explanation. The much more probable explanation for a delay, given the date and place of the incident, is that there was political rioting in the street. In his 1918–21 diaries, every time Mann reports trouble on the street he comments on the trams being stopped. The two events go together. Holzschuher has just given an explanation for the rioting. The passengers are primarily concertgoers leaving this politically controversial concert. Among them are Rudi, Ines, and Zeitblom, as well as many others, some of whom are mentioned by name. Zeitblom reports that there were shots, but he does not say that he saw the shooting. At the time the shots occur, the ticket collector has just moved in front of him and is collecting his ticket, thus blocking his view and distracting his attention. Then Zeitblom looks at Rudi and describes carefully how he falls. While he is looking at Rudi, there is panic and scramble on the streetcar as many passengers get off and others get on. It is not until all this has happened that Zeitblom looks up and grabs Ines, who is standing in the aisle in a state of shock. She is not holding the gun; it is on the floor some distance away from her. Zeitblom says she did it, but he has provided no evidence that she did. He did not see her do it. It is Zeitblom himself who personally accuses Ines and takes charge of having her arrested and accused. There is no evidence in the novel that Ines shot Rudi. It could have been, and was more probably, given the violent political atmosphere in Munich at the time, someone in the crowd. For instance, it could have been Dr. Kranich, who is a member of the Kridwiß *Kreis* and the person who declares Adrian mad in chapter 47. He is sitting next to the back door of the streetcar at the beginning of the account, but appears suddenly at Rudi's side after he has been shot. Ines — and names do help to identify the role of characters in Mann's works — is the Spanish form of Agnes, the sacrificial lamb.

Zeitblom is clear that he thinks that Adrian was responsible for Rudi's death, that he acted quite deliberately and calculatedly, and that his inspiration to jeopardize his own marriage plans by doing this came from the Devil. This implies that it was Adrian who "seduced" Rudi to active defense of the Weimar Republic. Since Zeitblom refuses to accept that Adrian actually holds the views he expresses, his taking this political stand must have resulted from the work of the Devil, and the Devil is represented by Fitelberg. Zeitblom is furious with Adrian and does not inform him of Rudi's death. Zeitblom's interpretation of Adrian's motivation for causing Rudi's death has logically nothing to do with Ines, except insofar as Ines, also opposed to National Socialism, is therefore also a tool of Zeitblom's Devil.

Although the surface story Zeitblom recounts is clearly nonsense and must be rejected, it cannot be simply dismissed. It is expressed in yet another complicated metaphor and is really talking about Adrian's work towards German and French reconciliation and not about marriage. The discussion about Adrian's search for humanity carries undertones suggesting that it reflects a discussion that Zeitblom has heard and "misunderstood." In chapter 22, when Adrian and Zeitblom are discussing marriage, Adrian makes oblique references to Martin Buber's *Ich und Du*. One of the leitmotifs describing Adrian's social problems is his hesitancy to use the familiar form "du" and it is his using this form to address Rudi that so exasperates Zeitblom. In chapter 22, Adrian, like Buber, was talking about the difficulty of finding a social order that is based on mutual confidence and respect for and trust in the other, in other words, a social order where "du" is the appropriate form of address, as the Devil points out in chapter 25. In chapter 22 Adrian was talking about a political problem, although the context of the discussion was marriage. Zeitblom thought that the views Adrian expressed about marriage showed that he belonged to the Devil and were an expression of his inhumanity. Buber was a Jew and his political arguments were based on Jewish theology. Zeitblom's "human" view was that marriage, and by implication social order, was all about sex and the glorification of procreation. It follows that Zeitblom would give a sexualinterpretation to a conversation about finding a social order that would make music, or traditional society, human.

The image of reconciliation with France is concealed behind each discussion of marriage. Clarissa's effort to establish a stable social environment for herself by marrying a Frenchman is thwarted by sexual abuse. Her marriage is presented as an effort on the personal level to find a reconciliation with France and it was prevented by sex, the tool of the Devil — that is, by fascism. Why else is her intended husband French? Zeitblom defines the difficulty in Ines's marriage with Institoris as sexual, whereas it more probably reflects their conflicting views on politics. The names, Institoris and Ines, imply underlying ulterior motives for the accusation of Ines. The dominant political question in the microscopic world of the novel is Adrian's desire to achieve reconciliation with France and the opposition of the Kridwiß *Kreis* to this reconciliation, the basic cause of Mann's conflict with Munich academic circles. In the story of Marie, the marriage image is reversed. The context is not marriage but reconciliation with France, and Zeitblom presents it as marriage. In his final speech, Adrian refers to reconciliation with France in terms of marriage. Adrian's future plans, which are not revealed in so many words, are revealed in his sending Rudi to make the arrangements for these plans, which resulted in Rudi's being the one to assume the mission instead of Adrian. The mind behind all this was undoubtedly Fitelberg's. Zeitblom describes Adrian's sending Rudi on this mission instead of going himself as based on an inspiration. This, he says, is the great inspiration that Adrian got from the Devil, the inspiration to send Rudi instead of himself. He turned down the inspiration offered by the Devil in chapter 25. When Zeitblom's story of Adrian's plans to marry Marie is read as a sustained metaphor for Adrian's efforts to achieve reconciliation with France as an agent under contract to Fitelberg, the contradictions, impossibilities, improbabilities, and ambiguities of the story disappear. Zeitblom is describing these activities as an erotic farce.

Adrian feels responsible for Rudi's death. The nature of this guilt, however, has nothing to do with Zeitblom's interpretation of these events.

The real sense of guilt that Adrian feels is not guilt at having persuaded Rudi to participate in the programs of the Weimar Republic to reintegrate Germany in European cultural life, as Zeitblom implies. As Adrian says in chapter 47, his guilt is having written his *Apocalipsis cum figuris*, his having unwittingly contributed to intellectual support for the development of National Socialism. It is National Socialism that is responsible for Rudi's death. It is Adrian's view that the Devil is the medieval Catholic Devil of chapter 25 and that the modern agent of this Devil is National Socialism. He is working against this Devil and this Devil does not tolerate subversion. Adrian has drawn Rudi into this political activity and is, therefore, from his own point of view, indirectly responsible for Rudi's death, again, not because he involved Rudi in fighting fascism, but because he had contributed to the development of fascism. Just as Adrian is destroyed in 1930, simultaneously with the confirmation of National Socialism in power, Rudi is killed simultaneously with the refounding of the National Socialist party in February 1925 and the confirmation of Hitler as its leader.[15]

Zeitblom's account, taken literally, is a fabrication from beginning to end. He is reducing Adrian's and Rudi's activities to selfish individualism and the pursuit of individual gain. He sees these activities as antisocial, as contrary to the interests of the community. Mann's international activities were described in Munich circles as motivated by purely selfish ambition. Zeitblom's accusations are largely the search for psychological explanations that provide ulterior motives to his political opponents and that justify the actions of fascism by concealing the evidence of political violence. He is, of course, concealing this violence from himself. The only way that intellectual fascists like Zeitblom can support a bunch of thugs like the National Socialists is by convincing themselves that they are not thugs. It is for this reason that Zeitblom feels compelled to find a rational, bourgeois explanation of Rudi's death and to deflect attention away from the political scene. Mann has provided sufficient evidence in Zeitblom's account of what is in fact going on for the reader to see through Zeitblom's interpretation of these events. In 1928, in his "Neujahrswunsch an die Menschheit," Mann specifically attacked this kind of political stupidity:

> Nie nun, so will uns scheinen, war der Abstand zwischen Materie und Geist, die Spannung zwischen dem, was im Wirklichen noch für möglich gehalten wird, und dem "eigentlichen" geistigen Erkenntnisstande der Menschheit so skandalös, gefährlich, krankhaft, verhängnisgeladen wie heute — und zwar ohne daß die große Masse der Menschheit sich dessen im entferntesten bewußt wäre. Sie glaubt sich von peinlichen Zwischenfällen zu erholen und zu "restaurieren," von denen sie offenbar rein akzidentiellerweise betroffen worden, und ergeht sich in Dummheiten, die einen intelligenten Hund zum Heulen bringen könnten, ohne sich von den Katastrophen auch nur träumen zu lassen, die ihr

gewiß sind, wenn sie nicht, statt abgestandene Allotria zu treiben, allen
Ernst und alle Eile daransetzt, den Geist einzuholen und die Zustände
ihrer Wirklichkeit seinen Erkenntnissen und Forderungen leidlich anzu-
passen. Dies ist es, was "Klugheit," was Geistwilligkeit aus erhaltendem
Sinn genannt wurde. Vorbauende, auf Anpassung und rechtzeitiges
Zugeständnis bedachte Geistfreundlichkeit ist das einzige, was die
Zivilisation vor dem Untergang zu retten vermag, und jeder konservativ
Gestimmte, das heißt jeder, der nicht die Katastrophe will, sondern
Vernunft, Folge und Fortschritt, muß heute — weit entfernt, die
Renitenz der Dummheit zu ermutigen — ein gut Teil revolutionären
Willens in sich aufnehmen, muß weitgehend das noch Bestehende, aber
Überholte verneinen und lieber den Vorwurf des Radikalismus tragen, als
den unheilschwangeren Zwiespalt zwischen Wirklichkeit und Geist ver-
tiefen helfen.[16]

The underlying story of Marie refutes any claim that Zeitblom does not
ultimately support National Socialism, not only theoretically, but also in
practice. It also refutes the generally accepted idea that Adrian represents
National Socialism in the novel. He does not.

Notes

[1] Michael Mann, "Adrian Leverkühn: Repräsentant oder Antipode?" *Neue Rundschau* (1965): 202–6; here, 205.

[2] Ian Kershaw, *Hitler, 1889–1936: Hubris* (London: Penguin 1998), 257.

[3] Thomas Mann, "Das Problem der Freiheit," in *GW*, 11:952–72; here, 958.

[4] Lieselotte Voss, *Die Entstehung von Thomas Manns Roman* Doktor Faustus: *Dargestellt anhand von unveröffentlichten Vorarbeiten* (Tübingen: Niemeyer, 1975), 223.

[5] Ilse Metzler, *Dämonie und Humanismus: Funktion und Bedeutung der Zeitblomgestalt in Thomas Manns Doktor Faustus* (Essen: Rhoden, 1960), 86.

[6] Thomas Mann, "Pariser Rechenschaft," in *GW*, 11:9–97.

[7] Thomas Mann, "Brief an den Verteidiger L. Hatvany's," in *GW*, 11:773–75.

[8] István Varga, "Das ungarische Dorf im *Doktor Faustus*," *Arbeiten zur deutschen Philologie* 6 (1972): 115–22.

[9] As an arbitrary suggestion, it could be from Schildknapp. Mann admitted that he was modelled on Hans Reisiger, who refused to leave Germany with the advent of National Socialism, when he could quite easily have done so. Mann saw this as a betrayal ("Hans Reisiger," in *GW*, 10:539–43; here, 542). In the novel this is portrayed as his refusal to go with the others in the sleigh at the end of the outing. Instead, he drags along behind on skis.

[10] Thomas Mann, *Königliche Hoheit*, GW, 7: 9–363.

[11] Thomas Mann, "Richard Wagner und der 'Ring des Niebelungen,'" in *GW*, 9:302–527; here, 526.

[12] Ian Kershaw, *Hitler*, 289.

[13] Rossel Hope Robbins, *The Encyclopedia of Witchcraft and Demonology* (New York: Crown, 1965), 337–40.

[14] Voss, *Die Entstehung von Thomas Manns Roman* Doktor Faustus, 102.

[15] Kershaw, *Hitler*, 257.

[16] Thomas Mann, "Neujahrswunsch an die Menschheit," in *GW*, 10:896–98; here, 897–98.

14: Adrian's Last Speech and Final Defeat

IN CHAPTER 47, THE LAST OF THE FEW opportunities in the novel for Adrian to present his point of view, he is presenting his new work, his *Dr. Fausti Weheklag*. During his presentation his physical appearance is, symbolically, that of the German artist, head to one side (*BeU*, 113), and his speech is clumsy. Zeitblom objects that his language is Reformation German, which he finds barbaric because it is not as tightly controlled by rules as modern speech (*DF*, 656–57) — in other words, it represents Protestantism, which is not subject to dogma. Adrian's new work does not make much sense in isolation, but its meaning is quite clear when it is recognized that the images are those that have been clearly defined in the course of the novel. The work is the summing up and continuation of his account in chapter 25 of his association with the Devil, slightly modified to make it into a Faust story.

Zeitblom makes several remarks that show that he is aware of the impending disaster, pointing out that most of the guests are opposed to Adrian's views and activities (*DF*, 652–53). Right from the beginning he shows that he is very upset about Adrian's talk, presumably because he is afraid that Adrian is going to expose his perverse view that National Socialism is evil. This, in Zeitblom's opinion, is quite mad and dangerous. He is aware that National Socialism does not tolerate dissent, and he understands this as necessary, something to be expected and madness to oppose. He explains the guests' negative reaction to the work as just human nature: ". . . denn Mitmenschen sind nicht gemeint und gemacht, solcher Wahrheit anders zu begegnen als mit kaltem Grauen und mit der Entscheidung, die sie sehr bald, als es nicht mehr anging, sie als Poesie zu betrachten, einhellig darüber aussprachen" (*DF*, 661). Zeitblom is tempted to dissociate himself from the event (653), which he does, in that, although he tries to give the impression that he takes over its organization, nothing is in fact prepared. He has quite literally abandoned Adrian to his fate.

Zeitblom describes Adrian's presence on the scene with a reminder of Fitelberg (*DF*, 655). Fitelberg represents Adrian's association with the Devil in Zeitblom's eyes: it is the contract with Fitelberg that he thinks has prompted Adrian to actively oppose National Socialism. The audience initially takes Adrian's story as poetry and likes it, but what Adrian is saying is deadly serious, comments Zeitblom, nothing to do with Zur Höhe's joking talk of obedience, force, and plundering the world (660–61). It is clear from this remark that he is still, in 1930, closing his eyes to the violent nature of National Socialism, as illustrated in the story of Marie. He is also pointing out that Adrian is not advocating National Socialism.

Adrian begins to tell his Faust story in the first person. However, his *Dr. Fausti Weheklag* is meant to be a work of fiction. It is, of course, auto-biographically based, since no artist writes about anyone but himself, but it remains a work of fiction, a giving of form to the ambiguities of reality. His story is based on the same premise as the "document": that Faust is unwittingly in league with the Devil because of his work, but Adrian's account is not quite the same as the Devil's account. Adrian's Faust "married" the Devil when he was twenty-one years old because he wanted to be famous. So all his work over the last twenty-four years has been the Devil's work, the result of the influx of the "angel of poison" (*DF*, 658–59). This poisoning was achieved through deliberately flirting with a butterfly, because he liked its transparent nakedness (660). Adrian's story identifies choosing the Devil instead of God with his Faust's obeying his destiny and giving up theology to study music. Thus, as in chapter 25, what leads to the pact is the combination of "enlightenment," or transparency, with music: "Was aber zum Teufel will, das läßt sich nicht aufhalten noch Ihm wehren, und war nur ein kleiner Schritt von der Gottesfakultät hinüber gen Leipzig und zu der Musik" (661).

It was not Faust's intention to work with the Devil, but his good intentions went wrong. The reference here is clearly to his *Apocalipsis cum figuris*, the work that was written with "höllisch Feuer unter dem Kessel." Like the Devil, he is talking about a work that only became great because of the help of the Devil:

> Item, mein verzweifelt Herz hat mir's verscherzt. Hatte wohl einen guten geschwinden Kopf und Gaben, mir von oben her gnädig mitgeteilt, die ich in Ehrsamkeit und bescheidentlich hätte nutzen können, fühlte aber nur allzu wohl: Es ist die Zeit, wo auf fromme, nüchterne Weis, mit rechten Dingen, kein Werk mehr zu tun und die Kunst unmöglich geworden ist ohne Teufelshilf und höllisch Feuer unter dem Kessel . . . Ja und ja, liebe Gesellen, daß die Kunst stockt und zu schwer worden ist und sich selbsten verhöhnt, daß alles zu schwer worden ist und Gottes armer Mensch nicht mehr aus und ein weiß in seiner Not, das ist wohl Schuld der Zeit. (*DF*, 662)

Adrian's Faust, however, takes full responsibility for the work: "Lädt aber einer den Teufel zu Gast, um darüber hinweg und zum Durchbruch zu kommen, der zieht seine Seel und nimmt die Schuld der Zeit auf den eigenen Hals, daß er verdammt ist" (*DF*, 662). This shift in the date of the beginning of Adrian's Faust's association with the Devil changes the story of the Devil in chapter 25 into a Faust story (which, in chapter 25, it is not), at least with respect to Adrian. Adrian has given artistic form to the ambiguities of reality.

In the light of the novel as a whole, Faust's central statement can only be interpreted as a political warning that National Socialism is the work of the Devil. It is the basic argument of *Die Betrachtungen eines Unpolitischen*, the argument that Zeitblom misinterprets in chapter 24 in his analysis of Shakespeare's version of the story in *Love's Labour's Lost*:

> Denn es heißt: Seid nüchtern und wachet! Das aber ist manches Sache nicht, sondern, statt klug zu sorgen, was vonnöten auf Erden, damit es dort besser werde, und besonnen dazu zu tun, daß unter den Menschen solche Ordnung sich herstelle, die dem schönen Werk wieder Lebensgrund und ein redlich Hineinpassen bereiten, läuft wohl der Mensch hinter die Schul und bricht aus in höllische Trunkenheit: so gibt er sein Seel daran und kommt auf den Schindwasen. (*DF*, 662)

Adrian is arguing that his audience is being irresponsible in not cooperating with the development of the Weimar Republic to establish an honorable adjustment of Germany to the European community and a solid basis for developing German culture. This is what he himself was trying to do. Adrian is directly associating National Socialism with the Devil. It is 1930, the year of the breakthrough of National Socialism, and National Socialism has become respectable.[1] At the 1930 elections Mann campaigned for the Social Democrats. It was during this election campaign that Mann made his great plea to his audience to reject fascism and support socialism, the general message of which Adrian has just summed up in these words.[2] This speech, which is directly political, has been substituted in the novel for Mann's own fatal speech, in that the crowd Adrian is addressing represents the Munich audience to whom Mann addressed his Wagner speech in 1933, many of whom turned on him after at first praising his speech, as happens here.

His Faust then compares the pains he suffers with those of the little blue-eyed mermaid in H. C. Andersen's story, who is trying to marry the dark-eyed Prince so that she can achieve a soul, by cutting her tail into legs and taking on human form. The reader is now familiar with this image as representing Adrian's effort to find a true German democracy through reconciliation with France. It is used each time to refer to adapting the German culture to accept democracy. In chapter 25 her pains are compared with the alternating periods of melancholy and enthusiasm that Adrian can expect to suffer. In chapter 33 Adrian himself describes his efforts to write his *Apocalipsis cum figuris* in the same way, according to Zeitblom. It is parallel to the intellectual difficulties and pain suffered by Mann during the process of writing *Die Betrachtungen eines Unpolitischen* and then, finally, in his struggle to counter the rise of National Socialism. Adrian's Faust says he preferred the mermaid with legs, that is, he preferred her in human form (*DF*, 663), meaning that he preferred democracy.

The result of this union between the mermaid and Faust, or between her ambition and traditional German society, is Echo, the child who represents the promise of a new generation of German democrats. The Devil took this child, because Faust loved him, or because he represented democracy, through the use of his own evil eye. His eye is evil, because the glance of all those promoting evil is poisonous. Adrian's Faust is saying here that the child was taken by National Socialism, but, as throughout this speech, assuming the guilt himself. Faust's evil eye, the tool of the Devil, represents Adrian's own *Apocalipsis cum figuris*, used by the Devil against him. It is a reference to its prototype, *Die Betrachtungen eines Unpolitischen*: *Betrachtungen* means observations. In the practical sense, Echo's death is caused by the absence of competent doctors, another result of rising National Socialism, since so many of the doctors were Jews. His fatal illness is a totally unnecessary sequel to measles, a complication that had been prevented for the previous 70 years by advances in medical science. Echo's death is the culmination of the "dead tooth" motif, of the consequences of ignoring the achievements of our ancestors.

When Zeitblom visits, as Echo is dying, Adrian virtually accuses Zeitblom of responsibility for his death. First he refers to his Catholicism, with reference specifically to the superstitious belief in the efficacy of the symbol of the cross as sufficient protection against evil. A variant of the cross is, of course, also the symbol of National Socialism. He insults Zeitblom's humanism, which Adrian has consistently criticized. Then Adrian addresses Zeitblom specifically, as though he were addressing the Devil, and accuses him directly of having caused Echo's death. This passage is read and dismissed as though Adrian were talking nonsense, or talking literally to the Devil, which means that it is simply not read. Zeitblom clearly recognizes it as being addressed to him: " 'Nimm ihn, Scheusal!' rief er mit einer Stimme, die mir ins Mark schnitt. 'Nimm ihn, Hundsfott, aber beeil dich nach Kräften, wenn du denn, Schubiak, auch dies nicht dulden wolltest!' " (*DF*, 632).

The Devil also obliged Faust to send his friend to his death because they had become intimate friends and Faust is not allowed to have friends. As the reader knows, just before his death Rudi rejected National Socialism in his argument with Zeitblom, declaring himself for the Weimar Republic. His decision to go to Paris resulted from his international cultural cooperation activities, which were also opposition to National Socialism. Adrian is identifying the murderer of Rudi as National Socialism and the reason for the murder as his association with himself in these reconciliation activities.

There is a virtually unnoticed comment in Adrian's story about this depriving him of a friend:

Denn der magisterulus hatte gemerkt, daß ich mich ehelich zu verheiraten gedachte, und war voller Wut, weil Er im Ehestande den Abfall ersah von Ihm und einen Schlich zur Versöhnung. Also zwang Er mich, gerade dies Vorhaben zu brauchen, daß ich kalt den Zutraulichen mordete. (*DF*, 664)

The "magisterulus" must refer to Zeitblom, since all such references in the novel do refer to Zeitblom. He is the only schoolmaster in the novel. He is the character in the novel who thinks that Adrian is going to marry and is angry about it, because this would mean a distancing of Adrian from himself. This literal interpretation of events is stressed in the novel, leaving no doubt that Adrian is implicating Zeitblom in Rudi's death, however the novel is interpreted. Adrian, however, is using the image of marriage to refer to his attempts to reconcile Germany with France, as does Zeitblom in the story of Marie. These activities were stopped by Rudi's death. *Er* with the capital E is usually taken to refer to the Devil, as it does in chapter 25, the other passage written by Adrian and not by Zeitblom. In a Faust story this *Er*, who has the same view as Zeitblom, can only be understood as the Devil. Adrian is speaking, so the capital E would result as simply a stress and therefore reinforce the logical reference to Zeitblom in the ears of the audience. Once again Adrian is speaking of Zeitblom as though he were the Devil, or, alternatively, speaking of the Devil as though he were Zeitblom. Zeitblom, as he himself makes clear throughout the book, considers himself to be the liaison between Adrian and Munich society and has proudly claimed to be the link between Adrian's *Apocalipsis cum figuris* and the Kridwiß *Kreis*. On every occasion, except his conversation with Ines, when he tells the reader about his activities that do not include Adrian, he is associating with those persons who are shown in the novel to support the rising National Socialist movement. While he is at work, he is in an environment that supported National Socialism, at the Catholic University. What the Devil says in chapter 25 is largely repeated elsewhere in the novel by Zeitblom. In this passage, Adrian is accusing him of being behind Rudi's death. Thus Zeitblom is revealed as having betrayed Rudi to National Socialism.

Adrian's Faust is a work of fiction within the novel, as is the story of Marie. Zeitblom has written a fiction accusing Adrian of being behind Rudi's death, although he does not present it as fiction, but as fact, and Adrian has written a fiction accusing Zeitblom of being behind it. Both stories imply that his death was caused by the Devil. It is strange that most critics are so ready to accept Zeitblom's patently obviously ridiculous story of Marie and ignore Adrian's story implicating Zeitblom in National Socialism and Rudi's death. The use of marriage as a metaphor for reconciliation with France makes the attack on Adrian parallel with the fatal attacks on Rudi and Clarissa. In each case the victim is contemplating marriage with France. It is only in the case of Clarissa that this image can be taken literally to mean marriage, but why to a Frenchman? In each case Zeitblom has provided a sexual explanation of the aggression.

Zeitblom says *Dr. Fausti Weheklag* is Adrian's confession, but it is not. It is not a confession but a lament and an accusation, both of himself and of his audience, but more specifically of Zeitblom. He is pointing out that National Socialism is the work of the Devil and is destroying Germany. The losses of Echo and of Rudi are only superficially the loss of these individuals. They represent the loss of Adrian's ideal modern version of the traditional German. They are children of God, not of the Devil. Adrian's Faust, being a true German Protestant and a Christ figure, is assuming all the guilt for these agents of the Devil and is hoping for God's mercy, because of his industry in working to counteract the influence of the Devil on them (*DF*, 664). His purpose with this opposition to National Socialism is to try to turn his original evil deed into good (*DF*, 666). This is another variant on the story in chapter 25, where the Devil offers him salvation in this world. It is difficult to understand how Adrian's work against the Devil can be understood as turning syphilis into good: the work he was doing was international cultural liaison in collaboration with the Weimar Republic. However, there is no doubt that Zeitblom is implying a causal relationship and relating the syphilis, the madness, and the contract with Fitelberg with this activity. When Adrian collapses, Frau Schweigestill says the others have no human understanding, Mann's charge against the *Zivilisationsliterat*. Adrian's collapse represents the violent destruction of music, the symbol of German culture. It is the defeat of the Protestant German and of German art.

Adrian assumes the ultimate guilt for the acts of National Socialism, because he himself contributed to making it possible. Therefore, in his view, he is guilty of the deaths of Rudi and Echo. According to Zeitblom's version he is guilty only of Rudi's death. Echo's death, as is Adrian's defeat, is the result of the pursuit of Germany's destiny: it is necessary to root out dissent and weakness to prepare for the coming glory. Zeitblom sees Adrian's international activities as corrupt and immoral, as treason and irresponsibility. His self-accusation of responsibility for Echo's death is, in Zeitblom's view, evidence of his madness. The real responsibility for all the deaths lies in the now corrupt values of the society and the complete disappearance of any sense of personal responsibility, except in the person of Adrian. There is no humanity left. By presenting Adrian's collapse into Frau Schweigestill's arms as a tableau of a Pietà, Mann suggests the parallel with the crucifixion of Christ by the Jewish people in preference to the real criminal. The roles have been reversed and it is National Socialism that has taken on this role of the Jew. As Fitelberg says, the Germans, with National Socialism, become the Jews.

Dr. Kranich, who was also first on the scene when Rudi was shot, says that it has been evident for some time that Adrian is mad. However, he cancels this comment with the ambiguous remark that there is nobody in their circle who understands what madness is: "Dieser Mann ist wahnsinnig. Daran kann längst kein Zweifel bestehen, und es ist sehr zu bedauern, daß in unserem Kreise die irrenärztliche Wissenschaft nicht vertreten ist" (*DF*, 666–67). We have been told by Zeitblom and by the Devil that the *Spießbürger* is not reliable in determining madness. There is no evidence of madness in this scene, by usual standards, unless it is Adrian's opposition to National Socialism or, as Zeitblom suggests, his expression of this opposition. It is highly probable that Adrian's collapse and the accusation of madness requiring psychiatric treatment means Adrian's arrest and delivery to a concentration camp. After all, Dr. Kranich has just told us that they have no psychiatric doctors.

Adrian's story is not the same story as the Devil tells him, however, because the Devil in chapter 25 makes it quite clear that the pact begins with a specific work that is the exposition of the idea of a synthesis. Both Adrian's decision to leave theology for music and his flirtation with "enlightenment" are illustrations of his predisposition in the Devil's account, not the definition of the pact (*DF*, 330–31). Adrian's Faust story ascribes the writing of the work to the Devil, whereas the Devil does not claim this. The original idea of a synthesis of the true German character with democracy is entirely Adrian's work in chapter 25. The Devil was not involved in the original idea but only comes into the picture *ex post facto*. It is the inspired elaboration of this idea that the Devil is planning to develop. Chapter 25 shows very clearly that Adrian's intellectual product was not corrupt in itself but only susceptible to corruption. Participating in this corruption requires Adrian to get rid of his inhibitions, that is his Protestant morality, which Adrian refuses to do. The inspired elaboration of Adrian's work is the work of the Catholic intellectuals who do not share this inhibition and are therefore subject to corruption by the Devil. It was specifically Zeitblom who introduced the work to this circle. Adrian's Faust blames the contamination with "enlightenment" from the first, from the conception of the whole idea of combining "the word" with "the music," attributing not only the elaboration but also the inspiration to the Devil. Adrian has made this change to turn his story into a Faust story. In the Devil's version in chapter 25, he is not shown as Faust.

Adrian's story of twenty-four-years begins with his beginning to work on the synthesis of "the word" with "the music" in 1906 and ends with the breakthrough to National Socialism in 1930. The Devil's story begins with the fascist adoption of Adrian's idea of synthesis in 1919 and ends with Germany's military reversal in 1943. This difference in time span shows what is, in any event, perfectly clear in the novel, that although Adrian represents Germany, this representation is not the same in the two periods. The first period, 1906 to 1930, is Adrian as the German Protestant artist who is destroyed by National Socialism. The second period, 1919 to 1943, is Adrian's alter ego, as represented by Zeitblom, the Catholic interpreter of the German character of the Protestant artist. It is this second Adrian, his alter ego, who is identified with the German catastrophe. It is this period that the Devil claims for himself.

There is a further parallel. Adrian's twenty-four-year time period coincides with Mann's association with the Bonn Literary Society, which explains very nicely Adrian's explanation in chapter 47 of why he let himself be tempted by the Devil: he wanted to be famous. The date of the original infection in Adrian's account coincides with the date when the Society began to take an interest in Mann's work, specifically in *Buddenbrooks*, which provides the hazy background to chapter 25, in that the setting of Adrian's conversation with the Devil is Palestrina, where the book was written. The title of the novel is *Doktor Faustus*, yet, as Zeitblom tells us, Adrian did not finish even his first degree (*DF*, 183). However, Zeitblom introduces this last speech, referring to him as "Dr. Leverkühn," a reference to Mann's honorary doctorate (*DF*, 656).

This has nothing to do with Zeitblom's coincidental time span, 1906 to 1930. He does not make this connection. His calculation of the beginning of the contamination is calculated backwards from 1930 in order to fix the presumed date. This is his criterion for dating "the document" and the explanation of why he has misplaced it in his biography. Both the Devil's argument and Adrian's Faust story are quite different from Zeitblom's story. Zeitblom's explanation of what leads to Adrian's madness at rejecting National Socialism is the syphilitic infection. This is confirmed as a pact with the Devil when Adrian signs the contract with Fitelberg. This has nothing to do with Adrian's and the Devil's story. The two accounts remain separate to the end of the novel. They are alternative arguments from opposing sets of values.

Zeitblom's definition of Adrian's talk as a confession is based on Adrian's criticism of the followers of National Socialism, understood in reverse:

> Denn es heißt: Seid nüchtern und wachet! Das aber ist manches Sache nicht, sondern, statt klug zu sorgen, was vonnöten auf Erden, damit es dort besser werde, und besonnen dazu zu tun, daß unter den Menschen solche Ordnung sich herstelle, die dem schönen Werk wieder Lebensgrund und ein redlich Hineinpassen bereiten, läuft wohl der Mensch hinter die Schul und bricht aus in höllische Trunkenheit: so gibt er sein Seel daran und kommt auf den Schindwasen. (*DF*, 662)

As Zeitblom has shown us in his story of Marie, instead of cooperating in establishing a proper order in Germany under National Socialism, Adrian was gallivanting around Europe engaged in an egotistical erotic farce with the cavalier, Schwerdtfeger.

* * *

The *Nachschrift* is separated from the novel in that it is not given a chapter number. This is because it is not autobiographical, as is the rest of the novel. It would be something of an anticlimax if the novel ended with Adrian, like Mann, escaping because he was fortuitously out of the country when he was attacked. The story of Adrian now parallels the story of Carl Ossietzsky, a journalist who spoke out very strongly against National Socialism in the summer of 1930, just as Adrian spoke out an unequivocal warning against fascism in the summer of 1930. Ossietzky was arrested and tortured for opposition to National Socialism. He was later let free, but effectively silenced, since his health was destroyed in the prison camp and he died, a weak and broken man, in 1938. His death was accelerated by the revenge taken against him, and Mann thought it was possible that in time his struggle for humanity would become legendary. With *Doktor Faustus* Mann is fixing this legend.

Zeitblom says that Adrian was drugged and taken to hospital where he was diagnosed as mentally ill. The three months in the hospital were a kind of treatment with tranquillizers (*DF*, 670). This hospital is clearly a concentration camp for political dissidents. In 1941 Mann recounted the story of Pastor Niemöller, who was arrested for opposing National Socialism out of moral duty and in full awareness of the consequences. His fate also resembles Adrian's fate:

> Es ist schrecklich, in die Hände der Menschen zu fallen; aber in die Hände der Nazis zu fallen, das ist denn doch noch etwas ganz anderes. Niemand weiß, ob Martin Niemöller heute noch lebt, ich meine: ob das, was von ihm übrig ist, noch irgendwelche Ähnlichkeit hat mit seinem früheren Selbst. Vielleicht ist er nur noch eine menschliche Ruine, mit zitterndem Kopf, zitternden Händen, den Rücken voller Prügelnarben, ein von verblödenden Drogen, die man ihm in die Suppe schüttete, zum speichelnden Idioten gemachtes Gespenst seiner selbst, das nichts mehr weiß und nichts mehr versteht. Ich kann es nicht sagen; aber so lieben die Nazis ihre Feinde zu sehen, und darum ist es wahrscheinlich.[3]

As Mann says in this article, National Socialists used drugs to destroy the brains of their opponents.[4] This is the ultimate dismissal of the syphilis thesis. In his analysis of the verisimilitude of the account of Adrian's syphilis, Alfred Kaufmann points out that the symptoms described in the novel are Nietzsche's symptoms. However, there is serious doubt that Nietzsche died of syphilis, something that could not have been diagnosed in his lifetime. He refers to an article on Nietzsche that appeared in 1931[5] and that was, therefore, very likely known to Mann. This article claims that it is much more likely that Nietzsche's paralysis was due to the extremely high doses of hashish that he consumed than to syphilis. Kaufmann's argument is that these symptoms are very unusual in the case of syphilis.[6]

There is no syphilis in Zeitblom's account. What he is talking about is "Versyphilisierung." This is Hitler's term, meaning "trafficking with the Devil."[7] When Hitler talks about the "Devil" he is talking about the "Jew."

"Versyphilisierung" is synonymous with "Verjudung."[8] In Zeitblom's biography Adrian's great sin is not against God, it is against the race: "Die Sünde wider Blut und Rasse ist die Erbsünde dieser Welt und das Ende einer sich ihr ergebenden Menschheit."[9] As Egon Schwarz points out, the Jewish stereotypes are exaggerated in *Doktor Faustus*.[10] The prostitute is very specifically identified as a Jewess with "ihre chamäleonartige Anpassung an die Umwelt" (94), her almond-shaped eyes (95), and her name, all of which are basic characteristics of the stock Jew. All of these characteristics are also attributed to Fitelberg. Schwarz claims that in Mann's work the identifying symbol of the Jewess is her vulgar jewelry, a great sparkly stone (87). The Esmeralda motif refers quite specifically to Judaism.

Adrian was released to Pfeiffering but kept under guard. When Zeitblom visits him he is hostile (*DF*, 671–72). When he deteriorates, his mother comes to take him home. Adrian, however, is not immediately entirely destroyed, but escapes. Zeitblom says he tries to drown himself, but Adrian denies this, saying it is difficult to drown yourself in water you used to swim in, water that he had once associated with freedom (*DF*, 672–73). Adrian is being treated as though he is dangerous, but there is no evidence that he has lost his reason. Adrian attacks his mother on the trip home and has to be kept under guard (*DF*, 673–74). Both of these episodes are evidence that Adrian is still attempting to fight back. Then he gives up. He is once again "*unter dem Lindenbaum*" in the nineteenth century with memories of Hanne's canons (*DF*, 674). His entire artistic achievement has been wiped out. In fact, the whole of German music since Bach has been wiped out. When Zeitblom visits him in 1935, Adrian takes no interest in him (*DF*, 674–75). Zeitblom visits him again in 1939, after the siege of Poland. Adrian gives him a threatening look (*DF*, 675). Adrian has been totally destroyed, but he has not lost his sense of values. Nor is there evidence that he has lost his mind. The evidence Zeitblom gives for thinking he is mad is all evidence of his complete rejection of Zeitblom and of National Socialism. Zeitblom's refusal to recognize the underlying implication of the concentration camp and attempts at brainwashing is his refusal, as on the occasion of Rudi's death, to recognize the negative aspects of National Socialism. He has told us that he believes that before eliminating dissenters it is only humane to make efforts to persuade them to see the light; Adrian did not.

Sending Adrian back to his mother is further depriving Adrian of human contact and love, of the environment in which he had built his life. Not only his art but his individuality as a person is eliminated. Zeitblom tells us that Adrian's mother thought his life had been sinful, incomprehensible error and was pleased that he was now helpless (*DF*, 670–71). He presents this as though the reader would, of course, think that it is perfectly natural that Adrian's mother would reject her son in this way.

Zeitblom has been sympathetic with Adrian's mother throughout the novel, whereas Adrian has consistently opposed her. She has been portrayed as rejecting music, right from the beginning. She also has, inexplicably, brown eyes, but is definitely German. Sending Adrian to his mother is his final humiliation.

Zeitblom learned of Adrian's death on August 25, 1940. Historically, this date marks the beginning of British night bombing in Germany and heralds the failure of the Battle of Britain. Mann mentions this in his diary on August 24, 1940. Adrian's death represents the moment when the lights went out in Germany. Hitler had been expecting to conquer and control Britain, as he had France, which required leaving open the possibility of collaboration. He was quite aware that the British would not collaborate in this program. The historical significance of the failure of the Battle of Britain is that it removed this last obstacle to the wholesale initiation of Hitler's policy to exterminate the Jews, the beginning of the holocaust. August 25, 1940 is, then, the day Germany began its trip to hell. Adrian, the traditional German Protestant, is no longer even latently or silently there. All traces of traditional Protestant German culture have ceased to exist.[11]

Notes

[1] Ian Kershaw, *Hitler, 1889–1936: Hubris* (London: Penguin, 1998), 333 and 336.

[2] Thomas Mann, "Kultur und Sozialismus," in *GW*, 12:639–49.

[3] Thomas Mann, "Niemöller," in *GW*, 12:910–18; here, 917.

[4] Thomas Mann, "Niemöller," 916.

[5] Kaufmann refers to this article, but does not further identify it: Paul Cohn, "Um Nietzsches Untergang: Beiträge zum Verständnis des Genies" (Hannover: n.p., 1931).

[6] Alfred Kaufmann, "Gedanken zu Thomas Manns Roman *Doktor Faustus* aus medizinischer Perspektive," in *Thomas Mann zum Gedenken*, ed. Georg Wenzel (Potsdam: VEB, 1949), 149–64; here, 162–63.

[7] Joachim Fest, *Hitler* (London: Penguin, 1974), 102.

[8] Adolf Hitler, *Mein Kampf* (n.p.: n.p., n.d.), 270.

[9] Hitler, *Mein Kampf*, 272.

[10] Egon Schwarz, "Die jüdischen Gestalten in *Doktor Faustus.*" *Thomas Mann Jahrbuch* 2 (1989), 79–101.

[11] Ritchie Robertson lists more historical dates that correspond to events of the novel, all of them confirming the thesis presented here and contradicting the thesis he himself presents. He dismisses them as external and uninformative. The dates

are: the correspondence of the completion of the *Apocalipsis cum figuris* and Adrian's new birth of creativity with the approval of the constitution of the Weimar Republic; the correspondence of Adrian's supposed plans to marry Marie with the 1925 Locarno conference, with plans for closer ties between Germany and France. See Ritchie Robertson, "Accounting for History: Thomas Mann, *Doktor Faustus*," in *The German Novel in the Twentieth Century: Beyond Realism*, ed. David Midgley (Edinburgh: Edinburgh UP, 1993), 128–48; here, 143.

Conclusion

15: *Doktor Faustus*: A New Perspective

Der intellektuelle Gedanke im Kunstwerk wird nicht verstanden, wenn man
ihn als Zweck seiner selbst versteht; er ist nicht literarisch zu werten, —
was selbst raffinierte Kritiker zuweilen vergessen oder nicht wissen; er ist
zweckhaft in Hinsicht auf die Komposition, er will und bejaht sich selbst
nur in Hinsicht auf diese, er kann banal sein, absolut und literarisch
genommen, aber geistreich innerhalb der Komposition. (*BeU*, 229)

*D*OKTOR *FAUSTUS* IS NOT A PHILOSOPHICAL TRACT; it is a novel. It is an
unusual novel in that the action is largely in the dialogue, but action
it is, nevertheless. The fundamental underlying argument, that Catholic
humanism is a secularization of the medieval approach to social control
and nineteenth-century humanism is a secularization of the values of the
Reformation, is illustrated over and over again in a multiplicity of practical
applications. All of these episodes are simply variations on this one basic
theme. They each show how opinion about whatever is being talked about
depends on the position of the speaker with respect to this fundamental
opposition. The theme itself is an opposition and, by its very nature,
requires, in each instance, two views that are at variance with each other.

The culmination of the novel is the rise of National Socialism. The novel
is, therefore, meant to be an illustration of intellectual acceptance or rejection of National Socialism as a function of the attitudes and predispositions
prevalent in the intellectual environment of the time, rather than as a specifically political decision taken by any of the characters. Although *Doktor
Faustus* is almost entirely a novel of ideas, with hardly any action whatsoever,
the fundamental point is that, in the end, the ideas determine the action.
The sudden eruption of violence at the end of the novel in the story of Marie
has been gradually prepared for and explained from the beginning.

This study has shown that the first part of the text of *Doktor Faustus*
is based on parallels from Mann's other writings, particularly from *Die
Betrachtungen eines Unpolitischen*. The basic argument of the novel is
expounded and illustrated through the exposition of the differences
between the representatives of what Mann saw as these two opposing systems of values. The second part of the text is based, in general terms, on
Mann's controversy with the Munich academic community during the
1920s over the interpretation of the arguments he presented in *Die
Betrachtungen eines Unpolitischen* in favor of traditional German values.

This approach of understanding the basic theme as dialogue rather
than monologue reveals an underlying story line that is very much at odds

with the traditional interpretation of the content of the novel. The story is told simultaneously from the two opposing points of view, from the point of view of what I understand to be Mann's position, the perspective of the hero, and from the point of view of the Munich academic community, represented by the narrator. The actual events recounted are the same from both points of view, but the two interpretations of these events are presented from radically opposed systems of values. This opposition is stated very clearly at the outset of the novel.

The present analysis leans heavily towards acceptance of the idea that Mann meant the narrator to be discredited, which may be unfair since it is, after all, his story. However, this seems to be necessary, because the narrator's version of the events is the only version that is normally taken into account in the literature. If the narrator is questioned, then the novel is the story of the narrator's interpretation of the events, and this can be made clear only through insistence on stressing what it is that he is passing judgment on and questioning these judgments. For this reason, it has been important to constantly refer to the ideas expressed by the protagonists. However, there has been no serious attempt in this study to analyze these closely. The ideas reach far beyond the novel and there is little specific evidence in the novel of what lies behind these ideas. One can read in, but one cannot with confidence read out. By this I mean that there is no doubt in my mind that in the various episodes recounted in the novel there is a wealth of cross-references to the multiplicity of intellectual movements of the time. Identifying, positing, and illustrating these influences is the stuff of literary criticism and the way in which Mann has used these arguments to develop his variations on his basic theme is fundamental to an appreciation of his artistry.

The validity of the reading that has been offered here does not depend on the specific detail of each point, but on the identification of the central points of conflict and of their general nature. In other words, the object of this study is to establish that the novel is built on the basic dual theme of the conflict between Catholic humanism and German Protestant humanism and that the various episodes are variations of it. A variation without a theme is not a variation, but simply an episode, and a novel that is simply a series of episodes with no connecting theme is of no artistic interest. My position provides a more probable and precise suggestion of what the basic theme is than traditional readings and resolves the contradictions in the text itself to these readings. The basic point of reference is the correspondence between the positions of the characters in the novel with the positions of the characters in *Die Betrachtungen eines Unpolitischen*. These are the Catholic humanist and the Protestant humanist, the absolutist and the individualist.

This study questions virtually all political interpretations of Thomas Mann's *Doktor Faustus* on the grounds that they are simply not supported by the text. It is not possible to determine why something happens in a text without first finding out what happens, and this has not yet been established in the literature in any intelligible way. Unlike ideas, what happens *can* be read out of the novel with a much greater degree of certainty, whereas in the case of *Doktor Faustus* it is usually read in. Mann has not meant this to be easy, because that would be an indication that *Doktor Faustus* is not a profound German work of art. As he commented on a Novelle by Joseph Ponten: "[It is] sehr deutsch und dichterisch, fern von Literatur, nichts, was an der Oberfläche schwimmt."[1] The narrator does not simply announce his position on the basic theme, that he supports fascism and that his hero does not. He, instead, makes innumerable pronouncements of his opinions and of his hero's opinions on the variations of this theme. The statement of the resolution of the problem is illustrated by what happens at the end of the novel: he supports National Socialism and his hero does not.

This study shows that it is not necessary to read as contradictions the observations on the text that point out aspects of the novel that contradict the generally accepted view of Mann's intentions. It is possible to construct a coherent account of the plot of the novel simply by suspending previous critics' presumptions about Mann's intentions. As a reminder, these comments are: the syphilis and the pact are redundant to the story, but the syphilis has a causal relationship in Zeitblom's account, and is therefore necessary to his account, yet at the same time it is questionable whether Adrian has syphilis; Adrian advocates democracy and Zeitblom supports fascism, yet Zeitblom worships Adrian; Zeitblom's view of what constitutes the Devil is not represented by the Devil in chapter 25; Adrian has solved his central problem around which the novel is constructed (how to integrate "French" democracy and the German Protestant tradition of individualism) near the beginning of the novel, in chapter 22, making the rest of it redundant. It has been shown that Zeitblom clearly misrepresents Adrian's character, unjustifiably describing it as negative. He is not telling the truth and he has a reason for this, therefore Mann is not telling the story that everybody thinks he is. This new reading, based on a close analysis of the text in the light of *Die Betrachtungen eines Unpolitischen* and the events resulting from its publication subsumes these so-called contradictions into the account, showing them to be integral parts of the argument. What happens in the novel is that the Catholic humanist becomes a National Socialist and destroys the Protestant humanist. The process, as described in the novel, is relatively complex, but the end is clear, simple, and straightforward.

* * *

The predominant story is Zeitblom's account of the life of Adrian, his intimate childhood friend whom he loved. Zeitblom's Adrian is the genius who is going to be Germany's savior, as he anticipates in chapter 22, in connection with the discussion of Adrian's *strenger Satz*. This is the statement of Adrian's political solution for Germany, based on musical organization, with individual freedom as the determining factor. Zeitblom misinterprets Adrian's presiding constitution as dictatorial rather than regulatory, a standard misunderstanding by the *Zivilisationsliterat*. Adrian is successful in coming up with a formula for Germany's salvation, in Zeitblom's eyes, when, in Germany's time of need, her defeat in the First World War and the abusive occupation by the Entente powers, Adrian releases his *Apocalipsis cum figuris*. Zeitblom finds that the superficially somewhat dubious arguments of the Kridwiß *Kreis* for fascism, a kind of medieval Catholic humanism, can be given a sound academic justification through his own interpretation of this work, specifically by disregarding the Protestant individualism and morality on which it is based. In chapter 34 (*Schluß*) he develops Adrian's musical arguments into the idea of a national "cult of music" and introduces this idea to the Kridwiß *Kreis*. This results in the adulation of Adrian as a hero. However, this adoration is very short-lived, because Adrian does not act in the way Zeitblom, as representative of this group, expects him to in the new political situation. He signs a contract with the Devil, in the person of the Jew, Fitelberg. Signing this contract leads Adrian to oppose fascism, by working towards a cultural reconciliation, or "marriage," with France. As a result of this activity, Adrian is increasingly isolated from Munich society until (with the success of Hitler) he is declared mad and destroyed, as a result of his talk about his new work, *Dr. Fausti Weheklag*. This work is a plea to abandon National Socialism in favor of the Welfare State. Zeitblom muddles this story for the purpose of blaming Adrian for the atrocities of National Socialism. In his view, the cause of Adrian's downfall is his perverse refusal to go along with the forces of destiny. In the course of his story, Zeitblom highlights the characteristics of Adrian that predisposed him to this dangerous and fatal course: his stubborn individualism, his sense of humor, and his rejection of the erotic in favor of love. In other words, his Lutheran tradition predisposed him to reject fascism. The Devil in Zeitblom's account, with whom Adrian signed a dreadful contract, is International Judaism. Zeitblom posits syphilis, or "Versyphilisierung," as the probable cause of Adrian's apostasy and mental deterioration.

This is a fictionalization of the account Hübinger gives of Mann's own life.[2] Mann was revered as a genius and, on the publication of his *Die Betrachtungen eines Unpolitischen*, was awarded the highest academic honor, an honorary doctorate. The book was interpreted as a kind of Bible for proto-fascism. However, Mann did not act as was expected in the new political situation. He rejected the nationalistic opposition to the Weimar Republic, which he actively supported, even advocating socialism, and became a cultural diplomat. As a result, he was increasingly isolated from

Munich society until, when Hitler came to power, he escaped Adrian's fate only by not returning to Germany. Poisoning by Judaism was the explanation given in Germany for Mann's rejection of National Socialism.

The Devil's account in chapter 25 of these events, as reported by Adrian, not by Zeitblom, is virtually the same. The Devil says he has taken Adrian's original idea of a synthesis of "the word" and "the music" and made another synthesis. By taking advantage of the communist, or totalitarian, interpretation of "the music" as a tool of "the word" he has turned "the music" into an ideal, rather than a system. He has deliberately encouraged the misinterpretation of Adrian's *Apocalipsis cum figuris*, and turned it into a cult of the culture that provides an intellectual basis for a nationalistic fascism. The reason it was possible for him to do this, he says, is that Adrian had irresponsibly adopted some "enlightenment" approaches, that is, advocated democracy, but at the same time preserved the German character. Furthermore, he is perfectly justified in doing this, since music, in the "enlightenment," or secularized Catholic, view, belongs in the realm of the Devil, and Adrian had proposed a government based on a musical system as an alternative to standard "enlightenment" politics, based on "the word."

The misinterpretation of Adrian's *Apocalipsis cum figuris* is now a *fait accompli*, and there is nothing Adrian can do about it. Opposing the Devil's inspired elaboration of this misinterpretation into National Socialism will only ostracize Adrian completely from society and lead to his destruction. Adrian does oppose it and this opposition does lead to his isolation and ultimate destruction. There is no syphilis and no madness in the Devil's account. The relevant points are Catholicism and Protestantism and the catalyst is "enlightenment." The Devil is using Catholic humanism to promote this misunderstanding, and Adrian is using his Protestant sense of responsibility and conscience to oppose it.

This account is also a reflection of what happened with the reception of *Die Betrachtungen eines Unpolitischen*, but this time told from Adrian's, or Mann's, point of view. The Devil's account of what has happened is essentially the same as Zeitblom's story. Where it differs radically is in the identification of the Devil. In the Devil's account it is not Adrian who has sold his soul to him, but those who misinterpreted the meaning of the *Apocalipsis cum figuris*. Adrian's own fictionalization of the events in chapter 47 is the same as the Devil's, except that his Faust takes all the blame on himself. He does not blame the Devil, or the others, but himself, for having written the work in the first place, or more accurately — although only the reader who is familiar with the underlying historical facts will recognize it — for ever having had anything to do with the Bonn Literary Society. Adrian adopts this shift in ultimate responsibility to turn his story into a Faust story. The Devil's account in chapter 25 does not show Adrian as Faust. This subtext, given by Adrian, the opponent of

National Socialism and the truly representative German Protestant artist, underlies Zeitblom's story.

Zeitblom's adulation of Adrian culminates in his reverence for the *Apocalipsis cum figuris*. However, throughout the novel, and not just in the case of his analysis of this work, Zeitblom either misunderstands or rejects Adrian's arguments and distorts them. The reader has been well prepared to expect that he will do this again. He turns Adrian's *Apocalipsis cum figuris* into a philosophical argument for fascism and the rejection of the Weimar Republic, whereas all of Adrian's musical arguments are clearly in support of democracy. Adrian recognizes his ultimate responsibility for this negative version of his *Apocalipsis cum figuris* in his conversation with the Devil. Mann presents him as a martyr to the cause of humanity. Zeitblom presents him as a tragic figure, the victim of fate.

Actually, on the more mundane level, the story of Adrian is that he is plagued by a childhood friend who never leaves him a moment to himself. Although Zeitblom reveres Adrian as a genius, he is in fact self-righteous and superior, taking it upon himself to know better than Adrian in every instance. His role in Adrian's life is to put him in a false position — with the best of intentions, of course — and ultimately, as a result of this, to be the cause of Adrian's destruction and death. He, however, is saving Adrian's works for some future, more auspicious occasion, when they will not be understood, because they will have become irrelevant.

The traditional interpretation of the novel, that Adrian sells his soul to the Devil of chapter 25 through deliberately contracting syphilis in return for inspiration does not appear anywhere in the text of the novel. The Devil in Zeitblom's account represents International Judaism and the syphilis belongs in this context. Adrian's purpose with this contract is not inspiration, in Zeitblom's view, but an erotic and irrational compulsion to assist Schwerdtfeger's self-seeking personal aggrandizement. The Devil that Adrian is talking with and about is the medieval Catholic Devil who, in the eyes of the Church, is responsible for music. The inspiration Adrian's Devil offers to provide is for purposes of developing and leading a political application of the misinterpretation of his *Apocalipsis cum figuris*, not for composing it. It is *ex post facto*, and Adrian rejects this offer. It is Zeitblom who carries out the political application of the work. Adrian's inspiration in Zeitblom's account is what produced the *Apocalipsis cum figuris* in the first place, and Zeitblom does not attribute this to the Devil. The inspiration from the Devil in Zeitblom's account is Adrian's scheme to send Rudi to France instead of himself. His story is the story of a saint who went wrong when he was corrupted by International Jewry. Adrian's contract with Zeitblom's Devil, that is, with Fitelberg, is, in his eyes, the cause of his rejection of the political interpretation of the *Apocalipsis cum figuris*. Adrian does not sell his soul to the Devil in return for inspiration, no matter how you look at it. The closest version to this interpretation is Adrian's fiction in chapter 47, where he says his Faust's association with the Devil was the result of an attempt to become famous that went wrong. This is a direct reference to Mann's acceptance of the honorary doctorate. This Devil, however, is not the Devil associated with syphilis and Jewish influence but the Devil associated with Roman Catholic humanism.

The extent to which Zeitblom collaborates in the death of Rudi and the arrest of Adrian is not clear in the novel. After all, the account is Zeitblom's and the *Zivilisationsliterat* is self-righteous and never accepts responsibility for anything. His humanism and pursuit of higher goals justifies inhumanity in the name of "the cause." It is certainly clear that Zeitblom expects these things to happen, and even that he knows they will happen. He portrays himself as sitting in the audience watching these dramatic events happen, as Adrian predicted he would do. However, there seems to be little doubt that Zeitblom was instrumental in Ines's arrest. He accuses Adrian of having deliberately brought these tragedies about out of arrogance and inhumanity, by thinking he knew better than his contemporaries. It is Zeitblom's view that the cause of these disasters was not fascism but Adrian's opposition to fascism.

Zeitblom thinks he knows better than Adrian. He excuses himself of all blame by painting himself as a kind of guardian angel, trying to protect Adrian from his propensity to fall into evil and to keep him on the right path. The great determining evils that he does not succeed in protecting Adrian from, in his account, are the trip to Graz, signing the contract with Fitelberg, and giving his last speech. In point of fact, he plays the role of Mephistopheles, putting forward the arguments expressed by the Devil in chapter 25.

* * *

The subject of the novel is undoubtedly Zeitblom and not Adrian. The novel begins and ends with Zeitblom. It is Zeitblom who rambles on, propounding his own views on everything under the sun. In spite of the fact that the first failure of the critical literature lies in ignoring what Adrian says in favor of accepting Zeitblom's assessments of him, Zeitblom himself has been remarkably little subjected to analysis. He is virtually always studied only in relationship to what he says about Adrian, not for his own sake. As Orlowski has pointed out, Mann gives Zeitblom various tricks of narration that put the validity of his statements and observations in doubt:[3] he feels, he senses, he assumes, and sometimes he makes categorical statements about things he cannot know. These passages are instrumental in revealing his own character, but they say nothing about Adrian. Why does he make the assumptions he does? Mann shows Zeitblom as fundamentally irrational, misidentifying causal relationships, using emotional criteria for making decisions, and refusing to objectively observe reality out of wishful thinking. This is represented in the novel primarily through the erotic. In *Die Betrachtungen eines Unpolitischen* Mann sums up the philosophy of the *Zivilisationsliterat* as consisting in rhetoric, psychology, and eroticism (*BeU*, 303).

Mann's use of these techniques in his characterization of Zeitblom has received very little attention. Surely, the characterization of Zeitblom is Mann's major artistic achievement in the writing of *Doktor Faustus*, a veritable tour de force. The illustration in the story of Marie of Zeitblom's use of the combination of all three — rhetoric, psychology, and eroticism — for purposes of misleading the reader is an indication of the potential of this approach to the novel. Zeitblom is a remarkably interesting character.

Doktor Faustus is very much time- and place-specific. Through the imposition of his own personal experience of having been misunderstood, Mann has created an immense complication in the untangling of the story. It allows the narrator to represent Adrian as instrumental in the development of fascism simultaneously with his description of all the characteristics that led him to reject fascism. Mann's rhetorical skill in persuading the reader to jump to the wrong conclusions, which are in open contradiction to the clear evidence provided in the novel itself, demands further study, if justice is to be done to his artistic achievement.

* * *

The starting point — Catholic humanist *Literat* versus Protestant musician — is illustrated by two fundamental oppositions throughout the novel: Adrian's insistence on his individualism contrasted with Zeitblom's view that individualism is immoral, and Adrian's intellectualism contrasted with Zeitblom's reliance on instinct and emotion, or eroticism. Zeitblom describes Adrian's individualism and intellectualism in derogatory terms. He describes his own eroticism as natural and normal and presents it as though the reader will, of course, share his view that Adrian's apparent lack of eroticism is in some way demonic.

The political philosophy, as distinct from the political events, is usually presented metaphorically. Adrian describes Protestant German society through a discussion of the development of music. Zeitblom describes fascist social philosophy through the metaphor of marriage, leaning on Bachofen. Thus, Zeitblom's comments on music and Adrian's comments on marriage are also political comments. These metaphors waver between obvious and not so obvious, which blurs the image. Underlying the whole is the opposition of "the word" and "the music," which, because of the specific combination of the events portrayed in the novel, keeps turning back on itself. The crucial moments in the novel include Adrian's decision to study music, the development of his *strenger Satz*, the composition of his *Apocalipsis cum figuris* and its adaptation by Zeitblom to Catholic humanism, the story of Marie, Adrian's last speech and his defeat and, of course, Adrian's conversation with the Devil. The story told in chapter 25 is not part of Zeitblom's story about syphilis and Jewish influence. It is Adrian's story of Catholic influence in Germany and of the corruption by Catholic humanism of his work. The two accounts are entirely separate and opposed to each other. Confusing them leads to a muddle.

* * *

Literary critics demonstrate quite a remarkable tendency to close their minds to an understanding of the period of the novel. This is bound to hamper understanding of the arguments. Heinrich Böll wrote: "Ich glaube, das ist eines der wichtigsten Prinzipien bei der Beurteilung von Literatur, daß man in die Zeit, in der sie geschrieben ist, zurückgehen muß, und zwar ganz. Sich auch vorstellen muß, wie war das damals, was passierte damals, als das geschrieben worden ist."[4] An explanation of why critics are generally unwilling to question the stand of the narrator, or even to read it correctly, seems to have much to do with the general unwillingness to look the problem of the rise of National Socialism squarely in the face. Critics feel sympathetic towards Zeitblom and therefore quite illogically reject what seems to me the indisputable evidence in the novel that it is he, and not Adrian, who finally supports National Socialism. At the time and in the environment portrayed, a large number of German intellectuals, like Zeitblom, rejected the Weimar Republic and supported various versions of *Volk* and national parties. A rejection of Protestant individualism and its accompanying values in favor of a return to the medieval idea of a social order based on authority and obedience was widely seen as a viable and desirable solution to the problems of modern society. This was particularly the case in Zeitblom's environment. As Joachim Fest points out:

> Bereits im Jahre 1931 verfügte die Partei an den Hochschulen mit 50% bis 60% der Stimmen über eine nahezu doppelt so hohe Anhängerschaft wie im Reichsdurchschnitt. Der dominierende Einfluß rechtsgerichteter Stimmungen bekundete sich ebenso im Lehrkörper wie in der weithin vom NSDStB bestimmten studentischen Selbstverwaltung.[5] (Fest 342–43)

Mann has quite deliberately made Zeitblom sympathetic, largely by letting him speak for himself. It is my impression that it was Mann's intention to point out that intellectual support for fascism, and ultimately for Hitler, was not at all the result of evil intention but of wishful thinking and self-delusion. In *Doktor Faustus* he is pointing out that the problem is not simple and straightforward, to be explained in terms of good and bad, although that is precisely how he appears to portray it. It is the narrator and not Mann who passes judgment. Mann is simply portraying. Personally, I think he is portraying the whole thing ironically and as gross parody. There is no doubt that Mann disliked and distrusted Catholic humanism intensely.

* * *

Mann was convinced that underlying any revolution there is an intellectual argument that supports it and provides the basis of its demagogy. The Devil says this specifically in chapter 25. In the case of fascism these arguments are based on the kind of Catholic humanism that opposed Luther and later opposed Rousseau. As Schleppfuß points out, the Inquisition was based on this same Catholic humanism. The argument is not that Catholicism leads to National Socialism. It is that the application to politics of metaphysics leads to totalitarianism, and the relevant instance of this is Catholic humanism. In his *Glasperlenspiel*, Hermann Hesse attributes specifically this idea to Mann in his portrayal of Thomas von der Trave, who is generally assumed to be based on Mann:

> Philosophieren soll man nur mit den legitimen Mitteln, denen der Philosophie. Unser Spiel aber ist weder Philosophie, noch ist es Religion, es ist eine eigene Disziplin und im Charakter am meisten der Kunst verwandt, es ist eine Kunst sui generis. Man kommt weiter, wenn man sich daran hält, als wenn man es erst nach hundert Mißerfolgen einsieht. Der Philosoph Kant — man kennt ihn wenig mehr, aber er war ein Kopf von Rang — hat vom theologischen Philosophieren gesagt, es sei "eine Zauberlaterne von Hirngespinsten." Dazu dürfen wir unser Glasperlenspiel nicht machen.[6]

In *Das Glasperlenspiel*, Thomas von der Trave inexplicably disappears and dies not long after having made this remark.

The religious origin of this basic difference in approach to politics is largely forgotten today. Indeed, large sections of the population have forgotten about the existence of religion altogether. However, the basic argument between a social order based on reliance on the individual and a social order based on a belief in the need for government control to achieve uniformity is still the single most important prevailing difference in political approaches. It is this difference that Mann is illustrating with the Protestantism-Catholicism parallel.

The argument that Mann's point in *Doktor Faustus* has nothing to do with reality is not shared by all historians, many of whom support his argument:

> Seine [fascism's] Vernunftfeindschaft war intellektuell, wie er denn selbst ganz wesentlich eine Bewegung gescheiterter, an der Vernunft verzweifelter

Intellektueller war. Sie vor allem ermöglichten ihm jene geistige Maskerade, ohne die in einer wissenschaftgläubigen Zeit die kleinbürgerlichen Massen nicht zu gewinnen sind.[7]

The various fascist movements began to crystallize into support for Hitler at the exact historical moment that Zeitblom makes his passionate argument in support of Ludwig of Bavaria in the novel. Mann makes the point in the novel that, although Zeitblom supports National Socialism, he misunderstands, or disregards, the implications of doing so and later regrets his support for Hitler. However, he also makes the point that Zeitblom does not abandon his fundamentally nationalistic and fascist views but limits his criticism to Hitler's policy towards the Jews. However, he does not recognize, and this is Mann's most important point, that in the name of an ideal, or a cause, our gentle, likeable humanist has become so inhuman as to sacrifice his childhood friend in the name of a cause and feel no remorse.

I have not seen any defense of the argument that Zeitblom does not support National Socialism that is based on the text of the novel; critics have simply rejected the idea that Zeitblom could possibly support National Socialism and assumed that Adrian does, in some way, without justifying their claim. It is not the task of this study to explain this. Mann thought that introducing Zeitblom would illustrate the humor behind an otherwise serious matter. He was depressed about the fact that critics did not see the humor in his works. In 1953, in "Humor und Ironie" he said that the whole idea of presenting Adrian through Zeitblom is funny.[8] In "Dieser Friede" (1938), Mann says it is in the nature of art to make fun of victorious nonsense, but always in relationship with the best.[9] In "Bruder Hitler" (1939), he says that hatred is a violent emotion and very uncomfortable to maintain. It is much healthier to turn it into irony.[10] It really does seem redundant to talk about irony in the context of *Doktor Faustus*. The whole novel is a tour de force of sustained irony. From beginning to end the novel is a tongue-in-cheek portrayal of the opposite of Mann's views. In 1926, in his preface to Joseph Conrad's "The Secret Agent," Mann said that modern art is fusing the tragic with the comic. This leads to the grotesque.[11] Many would agree that *Doktor Faustus* is grotesque, but nobody seems to see the reason: it is that Mann is telling a tragic story with a comic technique. Schleppfuß's stories about the Inquisition strike us today as humorous, but they were not humorous when they were happening. Mann is putting fascism into this same kind of historical perspective, but it seems that the world is not yet ready for this. The novel exposes Zeitblom's irrationality, his misidentification of causal relationships, his emotional criteria for making decisions, and his refusal to observe reality, based on wishful thinking. When *Doktor Faustus* is read in this spirit it is extremely funny, verging on slapstick. Zeitblom takes himself so very seriously.

He is so very melodramatic. He describes his quiet, unassuming friend as though he were dancing around on a cleft foot in a bright red suit with a garden fork in his hand. Sitting in the midst of fascist rioting in the streets and the violent death of his friend, Rudi Schwerdtfeger, he sees nothing more than an unfortunate family situation to be discreetly tidied away.

It is my impression that Mann fully expected his novel to be misinterpreted, because he knew that the general view of what fascism actually is, what the real danger confronting society is, continues to be fully misunderstood. *Die Betrachtungen eines Unpolitischen* was understood as its opposite and *Doktor Faustus*, which is based on *Die Betrachtungen eines Unpolitischen*, is misunderstood in the same way.

* * *

The overall anti-Semitism underlying Zeitblom's account and his conclusions about Adrian's contamination by syphilis and International Jewry are as *ex post facto* as Adrian's association with National Socialism. His extreme anti-Semitism was caused by National Socialism; his thesis, or explanation of why Adrian behaved the way he did, does not represent his views at the time he is writing about, but at the time of his actual writing. He is seeking an explanation of why Adrian acted as he did, why he rejected the natural, healthy, and erotic aspirations of his own people. He has come to think that International Judaism was ultimately responsible for Adrian's death, a fact that would confirm the "fact," established by National Socialism, that the Jew is the source of all evil. This is the ultimate illustration of Zeitblom's irrationality and unquestioning acceptance of the current popular view. *Doktor Faustus* is an extremely anti-Semitic novel. It is not Mann who is anti-Semitic, but Zeitblom, the character he is portraying.

Adrian's destruction, in Zeitblom's view, is parallel to Germany's defeat in the Second World War, in that both were destroyed by International Judaism. He implies that Germany is defeated by the God of Wrath and Vengeance, the Jewish God, destroyed, like Sodom and Gomorrah, for turning life into an erotic farce. What the novel says is that both were destroyed by fascism. To identify Adrian with the German catastrophe in 1945, as is so generally assumed, is to agree with Zeitblom that Adrian was destroyed by International Jewry, like Germany in his understanding of events. In point of fact, Zeitblom's specific identification of Adrian with Germany occurs in chapter 34 (*Schluß*), where he identifies him with his peculiar misunderstanding of the *Apocalipsis cum figuris* as representing Germany's breakthrough out of the fetters of inhibiting Protestant morality. The novel is not about anti-Semitism. It is about the return of the concept of heresy. It is about the persecution and destruction of Adrian, an unquestionable and representative member of the society in good standing, for the simple reason that he opposed the official dogma.

* * *

Zeitblom's biography reflects his revenge on Adrian for his betrayal of the National Socialist cause. The novel itself, however, is meant to be an exposé of fascist intellectuals. It is quite pointedly directed against the Bonn Literary Society, as represented by Zeitblom. In "Das Ende" Mann states quite clearly that this exposé is what most pleases him at Germany's defeat:

> Genugtuung. Gewiß, wir fühlen sie. Das Zuschandenwerden einer Schandphilosophie, die uns quälte und verjagte; die Bloßstellung der Intellektuellen mit den schwachen, unterworfenen Gehirnen, die die schmutzigste Travestie des Deutschtums mit diesem selbst verwechselten und in einem eklen Popanz, einem hysterischen Schwindler, den "Retter" den "charismatischen Führer" sahen; die rückgratlos alles mitmachen, jede Gemeinheit, und dabei von "geistiger Strukturveränderung" schwatzten, für welche "die alten Maßstäbe nicht mehr gälten" (ich höre es noch); das Versinken des Nationalsozialismus, dieses schamlosen Volksbetruges, dorthin, wohin er immer gehörte, in den Untergrund, die Unterwelt — denn Unterwelt, Hefe, Abhub war er von je, das Unterste war mit ihm nach oben gekommen, — wie sollte das nicht mit Genugtuung erfüllen![12]

* * *

For those who find it useful to discover a real-life model for the characters of the novel, I suggest they consider Ernst Bertram as a model for Zeitblom. Just as Zeitblom stresses his collaboration with Adrian in his earlier works, Bertram and Mann were very close during the writing of Mann's *Die Betrachtungen eines Unpolitischen* and of Bertram's *Nietzsche*. However, their political differences in the 1920s cooled relations, just as a clear distancing from Adrian is apparent in Zeitblom's account of the 1920s. Bertram was an enthusiastic supporter of National Socialism.[13] He was the prime enthusiastic interpreter of *Die Betrachtungen eines Unpolitischen* in the Bonn Literary Society, where the fascist interpretation of Mann's argument originated. His interpretation was the basis of his convincing the university to grant Mann his honorary doctorate. The role of Zeitblom in *Doktor Faustus* appears to be the same, explaining away, as he does, the Protestant, individualist aspects of the *Apocalipsis cum figuris* that do not conform with such a political application and drawing it to the attention of the Kridwiß *Kreis*. Bertram was active in the National Socialist program for rewriting all German literary criticism in such a way as to show that the whole of German culture led naturally and inevitably to fascism, just as Zeitblom reinterprets Adrian's works, in direct contradiction to the evidence he provides. Manfred Frank says that the idea of the association of music with the uniqueness of the German character is taken from Bertram's *Nietzsche*.[14] However, as used by Adrian, the idea is clearly taken from *Die Betrachtungen eines Unpolitischen*, where Mann associates music with the development of Protestant middle-class culture and democracy. Bertram's interpretation of Mann's book, like Zeitblom's interpretation of Adrian's *strenger Satz* and his *Apocalipsis cum figuris*, shows specifically this same difference, the replacement of a specific form of social organization by a mystical national character. It is, perhaps, Zeitblom whose understanding of the relationship of Germany to music is taken from Bertram. Further, Hans Hilgers suggests that Zeitblom's procedure and philosophy of history is the same as Bertram's, as outlined in his preface to *Nietzsche: Versuch einer Mythologie*.[15]

Bertram was a great expert on Nietzsche. It was Mann's basic definition of fascism that it is an application of Nietzsche to politics. It is always assumed that Adrian represents Nietzsche, and Zeitblom is specifically applying Adrian's ideas to politics. Does not Zeitblom equally represent Nietzsche, but a Nietzsche in what Mann considered a corrupted interpretation? As for Zeitblom's preoccupation with sex, in his diary Mann commented about Bertram: "Er ist stark sexualistisch orientiert, erklärt Schopenhauer und Nietzsche für päderastisch."[16] As Karl Otto Conrady points out in his study of the fascist literary movement, *Völkisch-nationale Germanistik in Köln: Eine unfestliche Erinnerung*, one of Bertram's early themes was the solitude and isolation of the modern artist.[17] This is one of Zeitblom's central arguments, which Mann shows in the novel to be nonsense.

The specific role of Bertram in Mann's life is paralleled by the specific role of Zeitblom in Adrian's life. In the novel, as in real life, it is the academic circle that supports and advocates fascism. Zeitblom is the member of this circle who is always at Adrian's house, as in real life Bertram was the academic who considered himself to have a special, almost family, relationship with Mann. However, there is further evidence. On 10 May 1919, Mann complained in his diary that Bertram was childishly dependent on him (233), which is a characteristic of Zeitblom's relationship with Adrian. Ultimately, it was Bertram who deliberately removed Mann's works from the list of books to be burned in the great symbolic National Socialist book-burning festivities. Bertram deliberately saved Mann's works on grounds of personal friendship.[18] Mann's exclusion from this list is otherwise quite inexplicable. Zeitblom, in turn, jealously protects Adrian's works. The reference to book-burning in chapter 6, the chapter on Kaisersaschern, is quite arbitrary in the context (*DF*, 52). The main reason Mann did not immediately write *Doktor Faustus*, his book to take revenge for the way he was treated, was to prevent the banning of his books in Germany, another indication of the possibility that Zeitblom is based on Bertram. Bertram, if he is indeed portrayed in Zeitblom, would have no trouble in seeing this.

In a letter to Bertram, dated 30 July 1934, Mann says quite clearly that, had he followed Bertram's advice — as Adrian follows Zeitblom's — he would be dead:

> Es geschieht gewiß nicht mit übertriebener Feierlichkeit, daß ich Sie darauf aufmerksam mache: hätte ich Ihrem freundschaftlich gemeinten Anraten und Insistieren Folge geleistet, so wäre ich heute mit soviel Wahrscheinlichkeit, daß man ebenso gut von Gewißheit sprechen kann, nicht mehr am Leben. Was verschlüge es, werden Sie sagen, gegen die im Gange befindliche "Geschichtsschöpfung"! Gewiß nichts. Und doch denke ich manchmal, daß diese Gewißheit, einfach ihrer Natur nach, vermögend sein sollte, Ihr gläubig dienendes Verhältnis zu den Mächten, vor deren Zugriff ein gnädiges Geschick mich bewahrt hat, leise zu modifizieren.
>
> "Wir werden sehen," schrieb ich Ihnen vor Jahr und Tag, und Sie antworteten trotzig: "Gewiß, das werden wir." Haben Sie angefangen zu sehen? Nein, denn mit blutigen Händen hält man Ihnen die Augen zu, und nur zu gern lassen Sie sich den "Schutz" gefallen. Die deutschen Intellektuellen — verzeihen Sie das rein sachlich gemeinte Wort — werden sogar die allerletzten sein, die zu sehen anfangen, denn zu tief, zu schändlich haben sie sich eingelassen und bloßgestellt.[19]

There are, therefore, very good grounds for considering that Bertram is the model for Zeitblom.

Notes

[1] Thomas Mann, *Tagebücher, 1918–21* (Frankfurt am Main: Fischer, 1977), 300, entry for 10 Sept. 1919.

[2] Paul Egon Hübinger, *Thomas Mann, die Universität Bonn und die Zeitgeschichte* (Munich: Oldenbourg, 1974).

[3] Hubert Orlowski, "Prädestination des Dämonischen: Zur Frage des bürgerlichen Humanismus in Thomas Manns *Doktor Faustus*" (diss., U of Posen, 1969).

[4] Heinrich Böll, *Weil die Stadt so fremd geworden ist* . . . (Bornheim-Merten: Lamuv, 1985), 112.

[5] Joachim Fest, *Das Gesicht des Dritten Reiches* (1963; rpt., Munich: Piper, 1993), 342–43.

[6] Hermann Hesse, *Das Glasperlenspiel* (Frankfurt am Main: Suhrkamp, 2002), 140.

[7] Fest, *Das Gesicht des Dritten Reiches*, 340.

[8] Thomas Mann, "Humor und Ironie," in *GW*, 11:801–5.

[9] Thomas Mann, "Dieser Friede," in *GW*, 12:829–45; here, 845.

[10] Thomas Mann, "Bruder Hitler," in *GW*, 12:845–52; here, 846.

[11] Thomas Mann, "Vorwort zu Joseph Conrads Roman 'Der Geheimagent,'" in *GW*, 10:643–56; here, 651.

[12] Thomas Mann, "Das Ende," in *GW*, 12:944–50; here, 949–50.

[13] Fest, *Das Gesicht des Dritten Reiches*, 338.

[14] Manfred Frank, "Die alte und die neue Mythologie in Thomas Manns *Doktor Faustus*," in *Invaliden des Apoll: Motive und Mythen des Dichterleids*, ed. Herbert Anton (Munich: Fink, 1982), 78–94; here, 85.

[15] Hans Hilgers, *Serenus Zeitblom: Der Erzähler als Romanfigur in Thomas Manns Doktor Faustus* (Frankfurt am Main: Peter Lang, 1995), 128–29.

[16] Thomas Mann, *Tagebücher 1918–21* (Frankfurt am Main: Fischer, 1977), 302–3, entry for 16 Sept. 1919.

[17] Karl Otto Conrady, *Völkisch-nationale Germanistik in Köln: Eine unfestliche Erinnerung* (Schernfeld: SH-Verlag, 1990), 19.

[18] Fest, *Das Gesicht des Dritten Reiches*, 351.

[19] Thomas Mann, *Briefe, 1889–1936* (Berlin: Fischer, 1961), 367.

Bibliography

Adolphs, Dieter W. " *'Wenn der gegenwärtig tobende Krieg, so oder so, sein Ende gefunden hat . . .* ': Die Bedeutung der Kriegsthematik in Thomas Manns *Doktor Faustus.*" In *Der Zweite Weltkrieg und die Exilanten: Eine literarische Antwort,* edited by Helmut F. Pfanner, 229–37. Bonn: Bouvier, 1991.

Albrecht, Ján. "Leverkühn oder die Musik als Schicksal." *Deutsche Vierteljahrsschrift für Literaturwissenschaft und Geistesgeschichte* 45 (1971): 375–88.

Allen, Marguerite De Huszar. "Montage and the Faust Theme: The Influence of the 1587 *Faustbuch* on Thomas Mann's Montage Technique in *Doktor Faustus.*" *Journal of European Studies* 13:1–2 (1983): 109–21.

Apter, T. E. "Thomas Mann's *Doktor Faustus*: Nihilism or Humanism?" *Forum for Modern Language Studies* 11 (1975): 59–73.

Assmann, Dietrich. " 'Herzpochendes Mitteilungsbedürfnis und tiefe Scheu vor dem Unzukömmlichen': Thomas Manns Erzähler im *Doktor Faustus.*" *Hefte der Thomas Mann Gesellschaft* 6–7 (1987): 87–97.

———. "Thomas Manns Faustus-Roman und das Volksbuch von 1587." *Neuphilologische Mitteilungen* 68 (1967–68): 130–39.

Bahr, Ehrhard. "Art Desires Non-Art: The Dialectics of Art in Thomas Mann's *Doctor Faustus* in the Light of Theodor W. Adorno's *Aesthetic Theory.*" In *Thomas Mann's Doctor Faustus: A Novel at the Margin of Modernism,* edited by Herbert Lehnert and Peter Pfeiffer, 145–66. Columbia, SC: Camden House, 1991.

Becher, Hubert S. J. "Thomas Mann und sein Faustbuch." *Stimmen der Zeit* 3 (1948): 213–22.

Berendsohn, Walter A. *Thomas Mann: Künstler und Kämpfer in bewegter Zeit.* Lübeck: Schmidt-Römhild, 1965.

———. "Thomas Manns Goethe-fernstes Werk: *Doktor Faustus.*" *Moderna Sprak* 61, 5 (1967): 1–16.

Bergsten, Gunilla. " *Doctor Faustus* as a 'Historical' Novel." In *Thomas Mann,* edited by Harold Bloom. New York: Chelsea, 1986.

———. *Thomas Manns* Doktor Faustus: *Untersuchungen zu den Quellen und zur Struktur des Romans.* Stockholm: Bonnier, 1963.

Bertram, Ernst. *Dichtung als Zeugnis.* Bonn: Bouvier, 1967.

Beyerle, Dieter. "Thomas Mann und der Teufel." In *Literarhistorische Begegnungen: Festschrift zum sechzigsten Geburtstag von Bernard König,* edited by Andreas Kablitz and Ulrich Schultz-Buschhaus, 1–16. Tübingen: Narr, 1993.

Bloom, Harold. *Shakespeare: The Invention of the Human*. London: Fourth Estate, 1998.

Boeninger, Helmut R. "Zeitblom, Spiritual Descendent of Goethe's Wagner and Wagner's Beckmesser." *German Life and Letters* 13 (1959): 28–43.

Bohm, Arnd. "Who was Serenus Zeitblom?" *Carleton Germanic Papers* 22 (1994): 25–38.

Böll, Heinrich. *Briefe aus dem Krieg, 1939–1945*. Vol. 1. Cologne: Kiepenheuer & Witsch, 2001.

———. *Weil die Stadt so fremd geworden ist. . . .* Bornheim-Merten: Lamuv, 1985.

Bonyhai, Gábor. "Handlungssystem und Wertsystem: Semiotische Randbemerkungen zur Struktur des *Doktor Faustus*." *Neohelicon* 2 (1974): 227–54.

Borcherdt, Hans Heinrich. "Das Faust-Problem bei Thomas Mann." *Jahrbuch des Wiener Goethe-Vereins* 65 (1961): 5–12.

Bridges, George. "Sublimation in Thomas Mann's *Doktor Faustus*: Love's Labor Lost." *Monatshefte* (1999): 28–44.

Buber, Martin. *Ich und Du*. Leipzig: Insel-Verlag, 1923.

Campbell, James. "Thomas Mann's *Doctor Faustus*: Weighing the Testimony of Serenus Zeitblom." In *Doctor Faustus: Archetypal Subtext at the Millennium*, edited by Armand E. Singer and Jürgen Schlunk, 25–42. Morgantown, WV: West Virginia UP, 1999.

Carnegy, Patrick. *Faust as Musician: A Study of Thomas Mann's Novel* Doctor Faustus. London: Chatto & Windus, 1973.

Cerf, Steven. "Love in Thomas Mann's *Doktor Faustus* as an Imitatio Shakespeari." *Comparative Literature Studies* 18 (1981): 475–86.

———. "The Shakespearean Element in Thomas Mann's *Doktor Faustus*-Montage." *Revue de Littérature Comparée* 4, 1985, 427–41.

Cobley, Evelyn. "Political Ambiguities in *Under Western Eyes* and *Doktor Faustus*." *Canadian Review of Comparative Literature* (Sept. 1983): 377–88.

Conrady, Karl Otto. *Völkisch-nationale Germanistik in Köln: Eine unfestliche Erinnerung*. Schernfeld: SH-Verlag, 1990.

Craft, Robert. "The *Doctor Faustus* Case." Review of *Doktor Faustus*, by Thomas Mann. *New York Review of Books*, 7 August 1975, 18–21.

Del Caro, Adrian. "The Political Apprentice: Thomas Mann's Reception of Nietzsche." *Studies in the Humanities* 12:1 (June 1985): 21–28.

Durrani, Osman. "Echo's Reverberations: Notes on a Painful Incident in Thomas Mann's *Doktor Faustus*." *German Life and Letters* 37 (1984): 125–34.

———. "The Tearful Teacher: The Role of Serenus Zeitblom in Thomas Mann's *Doktor Faustus*." *Modern Language Review* 80 (1985): 652–58.

Dvoretzky, Edward. "Thomas Manns *Doktor Faustus*: Ein Rückblick auf die frühe deutsche Kritik." *Blätter der Thomas Mann Gesellschaft* 17 (1979): 9–24.

Eisler, Hanns. "The Builders of a New Music Culture." In Eisler, *A Rebel in Music*, 36–58.

———. *A Rebel in Music*. New York: International, 1978.

Elema, Hans J. "Thomas Mann, Dürer und *Doktor Faustus*." *Euphorion* 59 (1965): 97–117.

Ezergailis, Inta. *Male and Female: An Approach to Thomas Mann's Dialectic*. The Hague: Nijhoff, 1975.

Faesi, Robert. *Thomas Mann: Ein Meister der Erzählkunst*. Zurich: Atlantis, 1955.

Fest, Joachim. *Das Gesicht des Dritten Reiches*. 1963; rpt., Munich: Piper, 1993.

———. *Hitler*. London: Penguin, 1974.

Fetzer, John F. *Changing Perceptions of Thomas Mann's* Doctor Faustus: *Criticism 1947–1992*. Columbia, SC: Camden House, 1996.

Fischer, Ernst. *Dichtung und Deutung*. Vienna: Globus, 1953.

Frank, Manfred. "Die alte und die neue Mythologie in Thomas Manns *Doktor Faustus*." In *Invaliden des Apoll: Motive und Mythen des Dichterleids*, edited by Herbert Anton, 78–94. Munich: Fink, 1982.

Frey, Erich. "Response to Egon Schwarz." In *Thomas Mann's* Doctor Faustus: *A Novel at the Margin of Modernism*, edited by Herbert Lehnert and Peter Pfeiffer. Columbia, SC: Camden House, 1991, 141–43.

Fullenwider, Henry F. "Adrian Leverkühn's Corrupt Diction in Thomas Mann's *Doktor Faustus*." *Neophilologus* 75 (1991): 581–90.

Gockel, Heinz. "Faust im Faustus." *Thomas Mann Jahrbuch* 1 (1988): 133–48.

Goldhagen, Daniel Jonah. *Hitler's Willing Executioners: Ordinary Germans and the Holocaust*. New York: Knopf, 1996.

Grenzmann, Wilhelm. *Dichtung und Glaube: Probleme und Gestalten der deutschen Gegenwartsliteratur*. Bonn: Athenäum, 1950.

Hage, Volker. "Vom Einsatz und Rückzug des fiktiven Ich-Erzählers: *Doktor Faustus* — ein moderner Roman?" In *Text und Kritik: Sonderaufgabe Thomas Mann*, edited by Heinz Ludwig Arnold (1976): 88–98.

Hagen, Joshua. "The Most German of Towns: Creating an Ideal Nazi Community in Rothenburg ob der Tauber." Annals of the Association of American Geographers 94:1 (2004): 207–27.

Hannum, Hildegarde Drexel. "Self-sacrifice in *Doktor Faustus*: Thomas Mann's Contribution to the Faust Legend." *Modern Language Quarterly* 35 (1974): 289–301.

Harris, Frank. *The Man Shakespeare and His Tragic Life-story*. New York: Frank Harris, 1921.

Hasselbach, Karlheinz. *Thomas Mann*: Doktor Faustus; *Interpretation*. Munich: Oldenbourg, 1978.

Heftrich, Eckhard. "Radikale Autobiographie und Allegorie der Epoche: *Doktor Faustus*." In *Vom Verfall zur Apokalypse*, vol. 2 of *Über Thomas Mann*, edited by Eckhard Heftrich, 2:173–288. Frankfurt am Main: Klostermann, 1982.

Henning, Margrit. *Die Ich-Form und ihre Funktion in Thomas Manns* Doktor Faustus *und in der deutschen Literatur der Gegenwart*. Tübingen: Niemeyer, 1966.

Hesse, Hermann. *Das Glasperlenspiel*. Frankfurt am Main: Suhrkamp, 2002.

Hilgers, Hans. *Serenus Zeitblom: Der Erzähler als Romanfigur in Thomas Manns* Doktor Faustus. Frankfurt am Main: Peter Lang, 1995.

Hitler, Adolf. *Mein Kampf*. n.p.: n.p., n.d.

Hoelzel, Alfred. *The Paradoxical Quest: A Study of Faustian Vicissitudes*. New York: Lang, 1988.

Hofe, Gerhard vom. "Das unbehagliche Bewußtsein des modernen Musikers." In *Geist und Zeichen: Festschrift für Arthur Henkel zu seinem sechzigsten Geburtstag dargebracht von Freunden und Schülern*, edited by Herbert Anton, Bernard Gajek, and Peter Pfaff, 144–56. Heidelberg: Winter, 1977.

Hofstaetter, Ulla. "'Dämonische Dichter': die literarischen Vorlagen für Adrian Leverkühns Kompositionen im Roman *Doktor Faustus*." In *"Die Beleuchtung, die auf mich fällt, hat . . . oft gewechselt": Neue Studien zum Werk Thomas Manns*, edited by Hans Wißkirchen, 146–88. Würzburg: Königshausen & Neumann, 1991.

Holthusen, Hans Egon. "Die Welt ohne Transzendenz: Eine Studie zu Manns *Doktor Faustus* und seinen Nebenschriften." *Merkur* 3 (1949): 38–58, 161–80.

Honsa, William. "Parody and Narrator in Thomas Mann's *Doctor Faustus*." In *Thomas Mann*, edited by Harold Bloom, 219–26. New York: Chelsea House, 1985.

Hübinger, Paul Egon. *Thomas Mann, die Universität Bonn und die Zeitgeschichte*. Munich: Oldenbourg, 1974.

Jendreiek, Helmut. *Thomas Mann: Der demokratische Roman*. Düsseldorf: Bagel, 1977.

Johnson, E. Bond. "Self-Conscious Use of Narrative Point of View: Controlling Intelligence and Narrating Consciousness in *The Good Soldier* and *Doctor Faustus*." In *Literary Criticism and Psychology*, edited by Joseph Strelka, 137–49. University Park: Pennsylvania State UP, 1976.

Kahler, Erich. *The Orbit of Thomas Mann*. Princeton: Princeton UP, 1969.

Kaiser, Gerhard. *". . . und sogar eine alberne Ordnung ist immer noch besser als gar keine." Erzählstratagien in Thomas Manns* Doktor Faustus. Stuttgart: Metzler, 2001.

Kann, Irene. *Schuld und Zeit: Literarische Handlung in theologischer Sicht; Thomas Mann — Robert Musil — Peter Handke.* Paderborn: Schöningh., 1992.

Kaufmann, Alfred. "Gedanken zu Thomas Manns Roman *Doktor Faustus* aus medizinischer Perspektive." In *Thomas Mann zum Gedenken*, edited by Georg Wenzel, 149–64. Potsdam: VEB, 1949.

Kershaw, Ian. *Hitler, 1889–1936: Hubris.* London: Penguin, 1998.

Klemperer, Viktor. *Ich will Zeugnis ablegen bis zum Letzten.* Berlin: Aufbau, 1995.

Kluge, Gerhard. "Luther in Thomas Manns *Doktor Faustus*." In *Lutherbilder im 20. Jahrhundert: Symposium an der Freien Universität Amsterdam*, edited by Ferdinand van Ingen and Gerd Labroisse, 91–117. Amsterdam: Rodopi, 1984.

Koopmann, Helmut. "Doktor Faustus und sein Biograph." In *Thomas Manns Doktor Faustus und die Wirkung*, edited by Rudolph Wolff. Bonn: 1983.

———. " 'Mit Goethes *Faust* hat mein Roman nichts gemein': Thomas Mann und sein *Doktor Faustus*." In *Vierhundert Jahre Faust: Rückblick und Analyse*, edited by Peter Boemer and Sydney Johnson, 213–28. Tübingen: Niemeyer, 1989.

———. *Der schwierige Deutsche: Studien zum Werk Thomas Manns.* Tübingen: Niemeyer, 1988.

———, ed. *Thomas-Mann-Handbuch.* Stuttgart: Kröner, 1995.

Krieck, Ernst. "Agonie: Schlußwort zu Thomas Mann." *Volk im Werden*, March 1937: 121–25.

Kurzke, Hermann. *Thomas Mann: Das Leben als Kunstwerk.* Munich: Beck, 1999.

———. *Thomas Mann: Epoche — Werk — Wirkung.* Munich: Beck, 1991.

Lehnert, Herbert. "Die Dialektik der Kultur: Mythos, Katastrophe und die Kontinuität der deutschen Literatur in Thomas Manns *Doktor Faustus*." In *Schreiben im Exil: Zur Ästhetik der deutschen Exilliteratur, 1933–1945*, edited by Alexander Stephan and Hans Wagener, 95–108. Bonn: Bouvier, 1985.

———. "The Luther-Erasmus Constellation in Thomas Mann's *Doktor Faustus*." *Michigan Germanic Studies* 10 (1984): 142–58.

———. "Der Taugenichts, der Geist und die Macht: Thomas Mann in der Krise des Bildungsbürgertums." In *Thomas Mann, 1875–1975: Vorträge in München — Zürich — Lübeck*, edited by Beatrix Bludau, Eckhard Heftrich, and Helmut Koopmann, 75–93. Frankfurt: Fischer, 1977.

———. "Thomas Manns Lutherbild." In *Betrachtungen und Überblicke: Zum Werk Thomas Manns*, edited by Georg Wenzel. Berlin: Aufbau, 1966.

———. "Zur Theologie in Thomas Manns *Doktor Faustus*." *Deutsche Vierteljahrsschrift für Literaturwissenschaft und Geistesgeschichte* 40 (1966): 248–56.

Lem, Stanislaw. "Über das Modellieren der Wirklichkeit im Werk Thomas Manns." *Sinn und Form: Sonderheft Thomas Mann*, 1965.

Lukács, Georg. "Auf der Suche nach dem Bürger: Die Tragödie der modernen Kunst." *Aufbau* 5, 1 (1949): 59–79, 154–69.

Mádl, Antal. "Zwei donauländische Kapitel in Thomas Manns *Doktor Faustus*." *Lenau-Forum* 3, 3/4 (1971): 32–46.

Mahlendorf, Ursulla. "Aesthetics, Psychology and Politics in Thomas Mann's *Doctor Faustus*." *Mosaic* 11, 4 (1978): 1–18.

Mann, Michael. "Adrian Leverkühn — Repräsentant oder Antipode?" *Neue Rundschau*, 1965: 202–6.

Mann, Thomas. "Adolf von Hatzfeld." In *Gesammelte Werke in zwölf Bänden*, 10:631–32.

———. "An das Nobel-Friedenpreis-Comité, Oslo." In *Gesammelte Werke in zwölf Bände*, 12:779–83.

———. "Ansprache in Lübeck." In *Gesammelte Werke in zwölf Bänden*, 11:533–36.

———. "Die Bäume im Garten." In *Gesammelte Werke in zwölf Bänden*, 11:861–69.

———. "Bekenntnis zum Sozialismus," In *Gesammelte Werke in zwölf Bänden*, 12:678–84.

———. "Brief an den Verteidiger L. Hatvany's." In *Gesammelte Werke in zwölf Bänden*, 11:773–75.

———. *Briefe, 1889–1936*. Berlin: Fischer, 1961.

———. "Briefe an Karl Kerényi." In *Gesammelte Werke in zwölf Bänden*, 11:629–53.

———. "Bruder Hitler." In *Gesammelte Werke in zwölf Bänden*, 12:845–52.

———. "Carlyle's *Friedrich*." In *Gesammelte Werke in zwölf Bänden*, 10:567–73.

———. "Dieser Friede." In *Gesammelte Werke in zwölf Bänden*, 12:829–45.

———. *Doktor Faustus*. Stockholm: Bermann-Fischer, 1947.

———. "Das Ende." In *Gesammelte Werke in zwölf Bänden*, 12:944–50.

———. *Die Entstehung des Doktor Faustus*. In *Gesammelte Werke in zwölf Bänden*, 11:145–301.

———. "Erwiderung," In *Gesammelte Werke in zwölf Bänden*, 11:785–87.

———. "Gegen die *Berliner Nachtausgabe*." In *Gesammelte Werke in zwölf Bänden*, 11:766–73.

———. "Geist und Wesen der deutschen Republik." In *Gesammelte Werke in zwölf Bänden*, 11:853–60.

———. *Gesammelte Werke in zwölf Bänden*. Frankfurt am Main: Fischer, 1960.

———. "Hans Reisiger." In *Gesammelte Werke in zwölf Bänden*, 10:539–43.

———. "Hans Reisigers Whitman-Werk." In *Gesammelte Werke in zwölf Bänden*, 10:626–27.

———. "Hoffnungen und Befürchtungen für das Jahr 1936." In *Gesammelte Werke in zwölf Bänden*, 10:917–18.

———. "Humor und Ironie." In *Gesammelte Werke in zwölf Bänden*, 11:801–5.

———. *Königliche Hoheit*. In *Gesammelte Werke in zwölf Bänden*, 7:9–363.

———. "Kultur und Sozialismus." In *Gesammelte Werke in zwölf Bänden*, 12:639–49.

———. "Leiden an Deutschland." In *Gesammelte Werke in zwölf Bänden*, 12:684–766.

———. "Leiden und Größe Richard Wagners." In *Gesammelte Werke in zwölf Bänden*, 9:363–428.

———. "Maß und Wert." In *Gesammelte Werke in zwölf Bänden*, 12:798–820; here, 819.

———. "Neujahrswunsch an die Menschheit." In *Gesammelte Werke in zwölf Bänden*, 10:896–98.

———. "Niemöller." In *Gesammelte Werke in zwölf Bänden*, 12:910–18.

———. "Pariser Rechenschaft." In *Gesammelte Werke in zwölf Bänden*, 11:9–97.

———. "Das Problem der Deutsch-Französischen Beziehungen." In *Gesammelte Werke in zwölf Bänden*, 12:604–24.

———. "Das Problem der Freiheit." In *Gesammelte Werke in zwölf Bänden*, 11:952–72.

———. "Rede über Lessing." In *Gesammelte Werke in zwölf Bänden*, 9:229–45.

———. "Richard Wagner und der 'Ring der Niebelungen.'" In *Gesammelte Werke in zwölf Bänden*, 9:502–527.

———. "*Romane der Welt*: Geleitwort." In *Gesammelte Werke in zwölf Bänden*, 10:673–77.

———. "Schicksal und Aufgabe." In *Gesammelte Werke in zwölf Bänden*, 12:918–39.

———. *Tagebücher, 1918–21*. Frankfurt am Main: Fischer, 1977.

———. *Tagebücher, 1940–1943*. Frankfurt am Main: Fischer, 1982.

———. *Tagebücher, 1944–1946*. Frankfurt am Main: Fischer, 1986.

———. "Über die Ehe." In *Gesammelte Werke in zwölf Bänden*, 10:191–207.

———. "Über die Lehre Spenglers." In *Gesammelte Werke in zwölf Bänden*, 10:172–80.

———. "Vom kommenden Sieg der Demokratie." In *Gesammelte Werke in zwölf Bänden*, 11:910–41.

———. "Von Deutscher Republik." In *Gesammelte Werke in zwölf Bänden*, 11:809–52.

Mann, Thomas. "Vorwort zu Joseph Conrads Roman 'Der Geheimagent.'" In *Gesammelte Werke in zwölf Bänden*, 10:643–56.

―――. "Die Wiedergeburt der Anständigkeit." In *Gesammelte Werke in zwölf Bänden*, 12:649–77.

―――. "*Zehn Millionen Kinder.*" In *Gesammelte Werke in zwölf Bänden*, 12:825–29.

―――. "Zum Tode Carl von Ossietzkys." In *Gesammelte Werke in zwölf Bänden*, 12:825.

―――. "Zum Urteil des Reichsgerichts, Leipzig, im 'Weltbühnen'-Prozess gegen Carl von Ossietzky." In *Gesammelte Werke in zwölf Bänden*, 12:677–78.

Masini, Ferruccio. "*Doktor Faustus* im nihilistischen Spiegelbild Nietzsches oder die Enthumanisierung der Kunst." In *Thomas-Mann-Symposium Bochum 1975: Vorträge und Diskussionsberichte*, edited by Paul G. Klussmann and Jörg-Ulrich Fechner,. Kastellaun: Henn, 1978.

Mayer, Hans. *Thomas Mann: Werk und Entwicklung.* Berlin: Volk & Welt, 1950.

Mayer, Ute. "Th. Manns *Dr. Faustus* als Zwölfton Komposition." *Utah Foreign Language Review* (1992–93): 126–30.

Mendelssohn, Peter de. "Doktor Faustus." In Nachbemerkungen zu *Thomas Mann*, 1:109–95. Frankfurt am Main: Fischer, 1982.

―――. *Von deutscher Repräsentanz.* Munich: Prestel, 1972.

―――. *Der Zauberer: Drei Briefe über Thomas Manns* Doktor Faustus *an einen Freund in der Schweiz.* Berlin: Ullstein-Kindler, 1948.

Metzler, Ilse. *Dämonie und Humanismus: Funktion und Bedeutung der Zeitblomgestalt in Thomas Manns* Doktor Faustus. Essen: Rhoden, 1960.

Meyers, Jeffrey. "Dürer and Mann's *Doctor Faustus.*" *Art International* 17 (1973): 56–60, 63–64.

―――. "Shakespeare and Mann's *Doctor Faustus.*" *Modern Fiction Studies* 19 (1973–74): 541–45.

Michelsen, Peter. "Faust und die Deutschen (mit besonderem Hinblick auf Thomas Manns *Doktor Faustus*)." In *Faust through Four Centuries*, edited by Peter Boerner and Sidney Johnson, 229–47. Tübingen: Niemeyer, 1989.

Molinelli-Stein, Barbara. *Das Werk als Selbstinszenierung eines problematischen Ichs.* Tübingen: Stauffenburg, 1999.

Montesi, Gotthard. "Thomas Mann, der Teufel und die Deutschen." *Wort und Wahrheit* 3 (July 1948): 495–510.

Müller, Joachim. "Faustus und Faust: Thomas Manns Roman und Goethes Tragödie." *Universitas* 16 (1961): 731–43.

―――. "Thomas Manns *Doktor Faustus*: Grundthematik und Motivgefüge." In *Ansichten zu Faust: Karl Theens zum 70. Geburtstag*, edited by Günter Mahal, 199–218. Stuttgart: Kohlhammer, 1973.

Müller-Seidel, Walter. "Sprache und Humanität in Thomas Manns *Doktor Faustus.*" *Acta Germanica: Jahrbuch des sudafrikanischen Germanistenverbandes* 3 (1968): 241–56.

Neuberger, Helmut. *Winkelmaß und Hakenkreuz: Die Freimaurer und das Dritte Reich.* Munich: Herbig, 2001.

Nixen, Liana De Bona. "The Concept of Barbarism in Thomas Mann's *Doctor Faustus.*" *Midwest Quarterly* 16 (1974–75): 438–52.

Noble, C. A. M. *Krankheit, Verbrechen und künstlerisches Schaffen bei Thomas Mann.* Bern: Lang, 1970.

Nolte, Ernst. *Three Faces of Fascism: Action Française — Italian fascism — National Socialism.* New York: Mentor, 1969.

Oates, Joyce Carol. " 'Art at the Edge of Impossibility': Mann's *Dr. Faustus.*" *The Southern Review* 5 (1969): 375–97.

Orlowski, Hubert. "Prädestination des Dämonischen: Zur Frage des bürgerlichen Humanismus in Thomas Manns *Doktor Faustus.*" Diss., U of Posen, 1969.

Oslo, Allan. *Die Freimaurer.* Düsseldorf: Albatross, 2002.

Oswald, Victor A. "Full Fathom Five: Notes on Some Devices in Thomas Mann's *Doktor Faustus.*" *Germanic Review* 24 (1949): 274–78.

———. "Thomas Mann and the Mermaid: A Note on Constructivistic Music." *Modern Language Notes* 65 (1950): 171–75.

Pache, Walter. "Ein Ibsen-Gedicht im *Doktor Faustus.*" *Comparative Literature* 25 (1973): 212–20.

Palmer, John. *Comic Characters of Shakespeare.* London: Macmillan, 1949.

Parkes-Perret, Ford B. "Thomas Mann's Silvery Voice of Self-Parody in *Doktor Faustus.*" *The Germanic Review* 64:1 (Winter 1989): 20–30.

Pattison, George. "Music, Madness and Mephistopheles: Art and Nihilism in Thomas Mann's *Doctor Faustus.*" In *European Literature and Theology in the Twentieth Century: Ends of Time,.* Basingstoke: Macmillan, 1990, 1–14.

Petersen, Jürgen H. "Gegen-Lesen: Widerstände gegen die Rezeptionslenkung durch Erzähler, Hauptfigur und Autor bei der Lektüre von Thomas Manns Roman *Doktor Faustus.*" In *Erzähler — Erzählen — Erzähltes: Festschrift für Rudolf Freudenberg*, edited by Wolfgang Brandt, 1–12. Stuttgart: Franz Steiner, 1996.

Prutti, Brigitte. "Women Characters in *Doctor Faustus.*" In *Thomas Mann's Doctor Faustus: A Novel at the Margin of Modernism*, edited by Herbert Lehnert and Peter Pfeiffer, 99–118. Columbia, SC: Camden House, 1991.

Puknat, Siegfried, and E. M. Puknat. "Mann's *Doktor Faustus* and Shakespeare." *Research Studies* 35 (1967): 148–54.

Puschmann, Rosemarie. *Magisches Quadrat und Melancholie in Thomas Manns* Doktor Faustus: *Von der musikalischen Struktur zum semantischen Beziehungsnetz.* Bielefeld: AMPAL, 1983.

Rehm, Walter. "Thomas Mann und Dürer." In *Die Wissenschaft von deutscher Sprache und Dichtung: Festschrift für Friedrich Maurer zum 65. Geburtstag am 5. Januar 1963*, edited by Siegfried Gutenbrunner, Hugo Moser, Walter Rehm, and Heinz Rupp, 478–97. Stuttgart: Klett, 1963.

Reinhardt, George W. "Thomas Mann's *Doctor Faustus*: A Wagnerian Novel." In *Music and Literature*, edited by W. John Rempel and Ursula M. Rempel, 109–23. Winnipeg: U of Manitoba, 1985.

Remys, Edmund. *Hermann Hesse's* Das Glasperlenspiel: A *Concealed Defense of the Mother World*. New York: Lang, 1983.

Renner, Rolf Günter. *Lebens-Werk: Zum inneren Zusammenhang der Texte von Thomas Mann*. Munich: Fink, 1985.

Robbins, Rossel Hope. *The Encyclopedia of Witchcraft and Demonology*. New York: Crown, 1965.

Robertson, Ritchie. "Accounting for History: Thomas Mann, *Doktor Faustus*." In *The German Novel in the Twentieth Century: Beyond Realism*, edited by David Midgley, 128–48. Edinburgh: Edinburgh UP, 1993.

Roth, Joseph. *Briefe, 1911–1939*. Berlin: Kiepenheuer & Witsch, 1970.

Ruprecht, Erich. "Thomas Manns *Doktor Faustus*: Ein Dokument der Krise des Romans." *Jahrbuch der Raabe Gesellschaft* (1967): 7–30.

Ryan, Judith. *The Uncompleted Past: Postwar German Novels and the Third Reich*. Detroit, MI: Wayne State UP, 1983.

Sagave, Pierre-Paul. *Réalité sociale et idéologie religieuse dans les romans de Thomas Mann*. Paris: Belles Lettres, 1954.

———. "Zum Bild des Luthertums in Thomas Manns *Doktor Faustus*." *Sinn und Form: Sonderheft Thomas Mann* (1965): 347–56.

Sautermeister, Gert. "Zwischen Aufklärung und Mystifizierung: Der unbewältigte Widerspruch in Thomas Manns *Doktor Faustus*." In *Antifaschistische Literatur*, edited by Lutz Winkler, 77–125. Königstein: Scriptor, 1979.

Schäfermeyer, Michael. *Thomas Mann: Die Biographie des Adrian Leverkühn und der Roman* Doktor Faustus. Frankfurt am Main: Lang, 1983.

Schaper, Eva. "A Modern Faust: The Novel in the Ironical Key." In *Thomas Mann* edited by Harold Bloom. New York: Chelsea, 1986, 103–22.

Scheiffele, Eberhard. "Das Theologische, Mythologische, Religiöse als strukturbestimmendes Moment im *Doktor Faustus*." In *Doitsu bungaku kenkyu* 30 (1985): 30–63.

Schlee, Agnes. *Wandlungen musikalischer Strukturen im Werke Thomas Manns: Vom Leitmotiv zur Zwölftonreihe*. Frankfurt am Main: Lang, 1981.

Schoeps, Hans-Joachim. "Bemerkungen zu einer Quelle des Romans *Doktor Faustus* von Thomas Mann." *Zeitschrift für Religions- und Geistesgeschichte* 22 (1970): 324–55.

Schubert, Bernhard. "Das Ende der bürgerlichen Vernunft? Zu Thomas Manns *Doktor Faustus*." *Zeitschrift für deutsche Philologie* 105:4 (1986): 568–92.

Schwarz, Egon. "Die jüdischen Gestalten in *Doktor Faustus*." *Thomas Mann Jahrbuch* 2 (1989): 79–101.

Schwerte, Hans. *Faust und das Faustische: Ein Kapitel deutscher Ideologie.* Stuttgart: Klett, 1962.

Seidlin, Oskar. "*Doctor Faustus:* The Hungarian Connection." *German Quarterly* 56 (1983): 594–607.

———. "Doktor Faustus reist nach Ungarn: Notiz zu Thomas Manns Altersroman." *Heinrich-Mann-Jahrbuch* 1 (1983): 187–204.

———. "The Open Wound: Notes on Thomas Mann's *Doktor Faustus.*" *Michigan Germanic Studies* (1975): 301–15.

Sender, Ramón. "Faustian Germany and Thomas Mann." *New Mexico Quarterly Review* 19 (1949): 193–206.

Shakespeare, William. *The Complete Works of William Shakespeare.* Edited by W. J. Craig. London: Oxford, 1965.

Sontheimer, Kurt. *Thomas Mann und die Deutschen.* Munich: Nymphenburger, 1961.

Sötér, István. "Tagebuch eines Lesers: Zur Struktur des Romans *Doktor Faustus.*" In *Thomas Mann und Ungarn: Essays, Dokumente, Bibliographie,* edited by Antal Mádl and Judit Györi, 141–54. Cologne: Böhlen, 1977.

Spengler, Oswald. *Untergang des Abendlandes.* Munich: Beck, 1920.

Sprengel, Peter. "Teufels-Kunstler." In *Exilliteratur, 1933–1945,* edited by Wulf Koepke and Michael Winkler, 424–50. Darmstadt: Wissenschaftliche Buchgesellschaft, 1989.

Steiner, George. "A Little Night Music." *Times Literary Supplement,* October 11, 2002.

Stern, Joseph P. *History and Allegory in Thomas Mann's* Doktor Faustus. London: Lewis, 1975.

Stimely, Keith. "Oswald Spengler: An Introduction to His Life and Ideas." *The Journal for Historical Review* (March/April 1998): 2.

Straus, Nina Pelikan. "'Why Must Everything Seem Like Its Own Parody?' Thomas Mann's Parody of Siegmund Freud in *Doctor Faustus.*" *Literature and Psychology* 33, 3–4 (1987): 59–75.

Swales, Martin. "In Defence of Weimar: Thomas Mann and the Politics of Republicanism." In *Thomas Mann,* edited by Michael Minden, 70–84. New York: Longman, 1995.

Tenckhoff, Jörg. "Prinzip der Verantwortlichkeit in Thomas Manns *Doktor Faustus:* Festschrift für Helmut Koopman." In *In Spuren gehen . . . ,* edited by Andrea Bartl, Jürgen Eder, Harry Frohlich, Klaus Dieter Post, and Ursula Regener, 339–55. Tübingen: Niemeyer, 1998.

Timm, Eitel. *Ketzer und Dichter: Lessing, Goethe, Thomas Mann und die Postmoderne in der Tradition des Häresiegedankens.* Heidelberg: Winter, 1989.

Tollinchi, Esteban. "El *Doctor Faustus* de Thomas Mann." *Asomante* 25:2 (1969): 7–38.

Vaget, Hans Rudolf. "Amazing Grace: Thomas Mann, Adorno, and the Faust Myth." In *Our "Faust"? Roots and Ramifications of a Modern German Myth*, edited by Reinhold Grimm and Jost Hermand, 168–89. Madison: U of Wisconsin P, 1987.

———. "Kaisersaschern als geistige Lebensform: Zur Konzeption der deutschen Geschichte in Thomas Manns *Doktor Faustus.*" In *Der deutsche Roman und seine historischen und politischen Bedingungen*, edited by Wolfgang Paulsen, 200–235. Berne: Francke, 1977.

———. "Mann, Joyce, Wagner: The Question of Modernism in *Doctor Faustus.*" In *Thomas Mann's Doctor Faustus: A Novel at the Margin of Modernism*, edited by Herbert Lehnert and Peter Pfeiffer,. Columbia, SC: Camden House, 1991, 167–191.

Varga, István. "Das ungarische Dorf im *Doktor Faustus.*" *Arbeiten zur deutschen Philologie* 6 (1972): 115–22.

Vogel, Harald. "Die Zeit in Thomas Manns Roman *Doktor Faustus*. Eine Untersuchung zur polyphonen Zeitstruktur des Romans." In *Zeitgestaltung in der Erzählkunst*, edited by Alexander Ritter, 337–67. Darmstadt: Wissenschaftliche Buchgesellschaft, 1973.

Voss, Lieselotte. *Die Entstehung von Thomas Manns Roman* Doktor Faustus: *Dargestellt anhand von unveröffentlichten Vorarbeiten.* Tübingen: Niemeyer, 1975.

Wagner, Richard. *Die Meistersinger von Nürnberg.* Reinbek bei Hamburg: Rowohlt, 1981.

Wald, H. "Strukturprobleme der Romane F. M. Dostoevskijs und Thomas Manns: Das Paradigma der Musik in *Doktor Faustus* unter komparatistischem Aspekt." *Zeitschrift für Slawistik* 28 (1983): 693–703.

Wehrmann, Harald. " 'Der Roman praktiziert die Musik, von der er handelt': Über den Versuch Thomas Manns, seinem Roman *Doktor Faustus* eine dodekaphonische Struktur zu geben." *Die Musikforschung* 46 (1993): 5–16.

———. *Thomas Manns* Doktor Faustus: *Von den fiktiven Werken Adrian Leverkühns zur musikalischen Struktur des Romans.* Frankfurt am Main: Lang, 1988.

Weigand, Hermann J. "Zu Thomas Manns Anteil an Serenus Zeitbloms Biographie von Adrian Leverkühn." *Deutsche Vierteljahrsschrift für Literaturwissenschaft und Geistesgeschichte* 51 (1977): 477–501.

Wiegand, Helmut. *Thomas Manns* Doktor Faustus *als zeitgeschichtlicher Roman: Eine Studie über die historischen Dimensionen in Thomas Manns Spätwerk.* Frankfurt am Main: Fischer, 1982.

Wolff, H. M. *Thomas Mann: Werk und Bekenntnis.* Bern: n.p., 1957.

Wysling, Hans, and Marianne Eich-Fischer, eds. *Thomas Mann: Selbstkommentare,* Doktor Faustus *und* Die Entstehung des *Doktor Faustus.* Frankfurt am Main: Fischer, 1992.

Žmegač, Viktor. *Die Musik im Schaffen Thomas Manns.* Zagreb: Philosophische Fakultät der Universität, 1959.

Index